Aesthetics of Music

Volume 2

Books by David Whitwell

Philosophic Foundations of Education
Foundations of Music Education
Music Education of the Future
The Sousa Oral History Project
The Art of Musical Conducting
The Longy Club: 1900–1917
A Concise History of the Wind Band
Wagner on Bands
Aesthetics of Music in Ancient Civilizations

The History and Literature of the Wind Band and Wind Ensemble Series

Volume 1 The Wind Band and Wind Ensemble Before 1500
Volume 2 The Renaissance Wind Band and Wind Ensemble
Volume 3 The Baroque Wind Band and Wind Ensemble
Volume 4 The Classic Period Wind Band and Wind Ensemble
Volume 5 The Nineteenth-Century Wind Band and Wind Ensemble
Volume 6 A Catalog of Multi-Part Repertoire for Wind Instruments or for Undesignated Instrumentation before 1600
Volume 7 Baroque Wind Band and Wind Ensemble Repertoire
Volume 8 Classic Period Wind Band and Wind Ensemble Repertoire
Volume 9 Nineteenth-Century Wind Band and Wind Ensemble Repertoire
Volume 10 A Supplementary Catalog of Wind Band and Wind Ensemble Repertoire
Volume 11 A Catalog of Wind Repertoire before the Twentieth Century for One to Five Players
Volume 12 A Second Supplementary Catalog of Early Wind Band and Wind Ensemble Repertoire
Volume 13 Name Index, Volumes 1–12, The History and Literature of the Wind Band and Wind Ensemble

www.whitwellbooks.com

David Whitwell

Aesthetics of Music

VOLUME 2
AESTHETICS OF MUSIC IN THE MIDDLE AGES

Edited by Craig Dabelstein

Whitwell Books • Austin, Texas, USA

Whitwell Publishing, Austin 78701
www.whitwellbooks.com

© 1995, 2012 by David Whitwell
All rights reserved. First edition 1995.
Second edition 2012

Printed in the United States of America

Paperback ISBN-13: 978-1-936512-27-0
Paperback ISBN-10: 1936512270

Composed in Minion Pro

CONTENTS

PART 1: THE CONTEST BETWEEN GOOD AND EVIL;
    THE CHRISTIANS AND PAGANS IN THE FIRST THREE CENTURIES

  1 *On the State of Musical Performance in the First Three Centuries*   3

  2 *Philosophers of the First Three Centuries*   11

  3 *Poets of the First Three Centuries*   39

  4 *Church Philosophers of the First Three Centuries*   45

  5 *The New Testament*   81

PART 2: THE TRIUMPH OF THE CHURCH;
    THE FOURTH AND FIFTH CENTURIES

  6 *On the State of Musical Performance in the Fourth and Fifth Centuries*   87

  7 *Poets of the Fourth and Fifth Centuries*   99

  8 *Philosophers of the Fourth and Fifth Centuries*   107

  9 *Church Philosophers of the Fourth and Fifth Centuries*   115

  10 *Saint Augustine*   135

PART 3: THE DARK AGES;
    THE SIXTH THROUGH THE EIGHTH CENTURIES

  11 *On the State of Music and the Liberal Arts in the Sixth Through Eighth Centuries*   175

  12 *Poets of the Sixth Through Eighth Centuries*   197

  13 *Church Music of the Sixth Through Eighth Centuries*   209

  14 *Comments on Aesthetics in the Music Treatises of the Sixth Through Eighth Centuries*   213

Part 4: The First Dawnings of the Restoration; The Ninth Through Eleventh Centuries

15 *The State of Music and Aesthetics in Society in the Ninth Through Eleventh Centuries* — 229

16 *Aesthetics of Music in the Literature of the Ninth Through Eleventh Centuries* — 241

17 *Comments on Aesthetics in the Music Treatises of the Ninth Through Eleventh Centuries* — 247

Part 5: The Glory of the Late Middle Ages

18 *The State of Music in Society in the Twelfth and Thirteenth Centuries* — 271

19 *Aesthetics of Music in the Writings of the Scholastic Philosophers of the Thirteenth Century* — 287

20 *Aesthetics of Music in the Writings of the Church Philosophers of the Twelfth and Thirteenth Centuries* — 311

21 *Saint Thomas Aquinas* — 333

22 *Aesthetics of Music in the French Romances and Chansons de Geste of the Twelfth and Thirteenth Centuries* — 355

23 *Aesthetics of Music in the Songs of the Troubadours and Trouvères of the Twelfth and Thirteenth Centuries* — 369

24 *Aesthetics of Music in Italian Literature of the Twelfth and Thirteenth Centuries* — 395

25 *Aesthetics of Music in the Minnesinger Songs and German Romances of the Twelfth and Thirteenth Centuries* — 409

26 *Aesthetics of Music in the Poetry of the Goliards of the Twelfth and Thirteenth Centuries* — 427

27 *Aesthetics in the Music Treatises of the Twelfth and Thirteenth Centuries* — 433

Epilogue — 443
Bibliography — 445
Index — 457
About the Author — 463

FOREWORD

We define Music to be that form of music performed live before listeners. We define Aesthetics in Music to be a study of the nature of the perception of music by the listener.

We believe the performance of music in actual practice falls naturally into four classes. These are: Art Music, Educational Music, Functional Music and Entertainment Music.

I. Art Music

Art Music we believe is defined by four conditions, *all* of which *must always be present*. These are:

1. *Art music is inspired.* Art music is music in which it seems evident that the composer has made an honest attempt to communicate genuine feelings. Feelings, which may range from lofty and noble to superficial and vulgar, must be presumed to be generally recognizable in music, as they are in any other art form, including painting, sculpture, dance, and architecture. In Art Music, lofty and noble feelings are paramount.

    Due to the common genetically understood nature of emotions, it must also be understood that in music emotions or feelings can not be 'faked.' They will always be recognized as such by any contemplative listener.

2. *Art Music has no purpose other than the communication of its own aesthetic content.* Art Music is free of any purpose or function, save the spiritual communication of pure beauty.

3. *Art Music is that which enjoys a performance faithful to the intent of the composer.*

4. *Art Music must have a listener capable of contemplation.*

If any of these conditions are missing, the performance must result in a lesser aesthetic experience. For example, the *Ninth Symphony* of Beethoven played in a stadium, during the half-time of a professional football game, would fail for the lack of the presence of Condition Number Four. The same Symphony heard in a concert hall, but in a poor performance, not faithful to the intent of the composer, would fail for the lack of the presence of Condition Number Three.

II. Educational Music

Educational Music may or may not have the same conditions as Art Music, excepting Condition Number Two; it may or may not occur within an educational institution. Educational Music is didactic music, music which has the specific and *additional* aim to educate. In the strictest sense, if the *primary purpose* of Music is to educate, it cannot be Art Music—for Art Music has no purpose.

III. Functional Music

Functional Music is music put at the service of something else. We include here, for example, all kinds of religious music, music for weddings, music for the military, and occupational music. Functional Music may share the same conditions as Art Music, excepting Condition Number Two.

One may ask, How can a Mozart Mass be called Functional Music, and not Art Music? If the observer were not contemplatively listening to the music, but were rather contemplating religious thoughts, then the Mozart Mass becomes merely a very high level of Functional Music. If, on the other hand, the observer is a contemplative listener of music, forgetting about religion, then the Mozart Mass is Art Music, but has failed in its purpose as church music.

Military and wedding music are examples of music in which the contemplative listener is missing entirely. How about airport, supermarket and elevator music where there is no listener at all? According to the definition we have given above, recorded music without listeners is not to be considered music at all.

IV. Entertainment Music

Entertainment Music is music with no object other than to please. It will always be missing Condition Four, the contemplative listener. For this reason, Entertainment Music may be inspired music, but the composer is unlikely to be inspired by lofty and noble emotions, knowing there will be no contemplative listener. Entertainment Music and Art Music can never be the same thing because of Condition Number Two: Art Music has no purpose other than the communication of its own aesthetic content. It is inconsistent with the nature of great art to have any extrinsic purpose, including the purpose to entertain.

The first philosopher to address the impact which Art has on an observer was Aristotle, in his *Poetics*, as part of a discussion of Tragedy, which like Music has both a material, written, form and a live performance form. In this treatise, Aristotle first considers the nature and contribution of each of the specific components of the written form of the Tragedy in his typically methodical style. His great contribution, however, comes when he has completed this discussion, for he then goes beyond the material form of the play itself to discuss the observer. He makes it clear that not only is the end purpose of the elements of the play to produce a specific experience in the observer, but that the nature of this experience is what distinguishes Tragedy from other dramatic forms, such as Spectacle. It was in this moment that he created a new branch of Philosophy which we call 'Aesthetics.'

Our purpose is to provide a source book of representative descriptions of actual performances, observations by philosophers, poets and other commentators which contribute insights to our understanding of what Music meant to listeners during the Middle Ages.

We are also interested in contemporary views on the physiology of knowing, especially with regard to the relationship of the senses and Reason, and related psychological ideas, such as Pleasure and Pain and the Emotions, which might offer a frame of reference for their perspective on the perception of Music. Philosophers of the first several centuries of the Christian era who were in the tradition of the ancient Greek and Roman philosophers have been included in volume 1, whereas the Church philosophers of the same period appear in this volume.

Our principal interest in the musical practice of the Middle Ages is limited to aesthetics as expressed in actual performance. We should therefore note that it is for this reason that we do not delve into the technical descriptions of early instruments or the theoretical practices of tuning systems, descriptions of scales, etc., which are the primary subjects most books on medieval music discuss in detail.

This is the second volume in a series of eight, ranging from the music of the ancient civilizations through the Baroque Period.

David Whitwell
Austin, Texas

ACKNOWLEDGMENTS

This new edition would not have been possible without the encouragement and help of Craig Dabelstein of Brisbane, Australia. His experience as a musician and educator himself has contributed greatly to his expertise as editor of this volume.

                      David Whitwell
                      Austin, 2011

PART 1

The Contest Between Good and Evil; The Christians and Pagans in the First Three Centuries

1 ON THE STATE OF MUSICAL PERFORMANCE IN THE FIRST THREE CENTURIES

IN THE DISCUSSION OF ROMAN MUSIC in the first volume of this series we have presented many accounts of various emperors who were practicing musicians, foremost among whom was Nero. After Nero, extant accounts of actual performances of music become much more rare. This is explained in large part by the contemporary writers who turned their attention to the details of what we know as the Fall of Rome, the military defeats which were beginning to happen for the first time, in addition to the consequences of general economic decline.

Nevertheless, from the list of rapidly changing emperors[1] we still find some who were practicing musicians. Among these were Elagabalus (219–222 AD), who sang and performed on several instruments, including the organ. His successor, Severus Alexander (222–235 AD), frequently attended the theater, composed poetry, and also performed on several instruments.

> He could play the lyre, the aulos, and the organ, and he could even blow the trumpet, but this he never did openly while emperor.[2]

1 In one thirty-five year period in the third century there were no fewer than thirty-seven emperors!

2 *The Scriptores Historiae Augustae*, trans. David Magie (London: Heinemann, 1924), II, 231, 269. 'Clarinet' is given for aulos here. Regarding his interest in poetry, he once called Virgil, 'the Plato of poets,' and kept a portrait of him.

ART MUSIC

While first-hand accounts of the solo art singer are rare from the early centuries of the Christian era, there is an occasional clue which suggests this form of music may have still been widely practiced. In one first-century poem, for example, we read of such a poet–singer who, upon his death, left a library of twenty-five cases of music!

> Eutychides the lyric poet is dead. Fly, ye people who dwell under earth; Eutychides is coming with odes, and he ordered them to burn with him twelve lyres and twenty-five cases of music. Now indeed

Charon has got hold of you. Where can one depart to in the future, since Eutychides is established in Hades too?[3]

3 Lucilius, quoted in *The Greek Anthology*, trans. W. R. Paton (Cambridge: Harvard University Press, 1939), IV, 133.

Some of the extant first-century poems offer insights into the musical practice of these solo art singers. An anonymous poem of the first century, found on the statue of a famous lyre player, Eunomus, is particularly interesting for its reference to the performance of 'an elaborate piece' on the lyre. This poem relates a charming story of a cricket which plays a role in the poet's performance.

> Thou knowest, Apollo, how I, Eunomus the Locrian, conquered Spartis, but I tell it for those who ask me. I was playing on the lyre an elaborate piece, and in the middle of it my plectron loosened one chord, and when the time came to strike the note I was ready to play, it did not convey the correct sound to the ear. Then of its own accord a cicada perched on the bridge of the lyre and supplied the deficiency of the harmony. I had struck six chords, and when I required the seventh I borrowed this cicada's voice; for the midday songster of the hillside adapted to my performance that pastoral air of his, and when he shrilled he combined with the lifeless chords to change the value of the phrase. Therefore I owe a debt of thanks to my partner in the duet, and wrought in bronze he sits on my lyre.[4]

4 Ibid., IX, 584. A poem from the first century BC, also associates the cricket with the lyre. Noisy cicada, drunk with dew drops, thou singest thy rustic ditty that fills the wilderness with voice, and seated on the edge of the leaves, striking with saw-like legs thy sunburnt skin thou shrillest music like the lyre's. But sing, dear, some new tune to gladden the woodland nymphs, strike up some strain responsive to Pan's pipe, that I may escape from Love and snatch a little midday sleep. [Ibid., IV, 196]

One poet of the first century, Honestus, moans for the loss of the old art music associated with the lyre. The modern aulos music, more associated with entertainment, he seems to suggest lacks an emphasis on beautiful harmony.

> I, Thebes, rose at the sound of the lyre and sunk in ruins at that of the aulos.[5] Alas for the Muse that was adverse to harmony! They now lie deaf, the remains of my towers, once charmed by the lyre, the stones that took their places of their own accord in the muse-built walls, a gift that cost thee, Amphion, no labor; for with thy seven-stringed lyre thou didst build thy seven-gated city.[6]

5 The original here is 'flute,' a frequent mistranslation for the aulos.

6 Ibid., IX, 250.

We know that the Roman water organ became well-known during the early centuries of the Christian era. An enthusiastic description of the instrument in the writings of the second-century Church philosopher, Tertullian, invites the thought that there may have been solo organ recitals by this time.

> Look at that very wonderful piece of organ mechanism by Archimedes,—I mean his hydraulic organ, with its many limbs, parts,

bands, passages for the notes, outlets for their sounds, combinations for their harmony, and the array of its pipes; but yet the whole of these details constitute only one instrument. In like manner the wind, which breathes throughout this organ at the impulse of the hydraulic engine, is not divided into separate portions from the fact of its dispersion through the instrument to make it play: it is whole and entire in its substance, although divided in its operation.[7]

References in this early literature suggest that solo artists were in great demand for performance in the homes of the wealthy. Occasionally we read of these artists being given expensive gifts, for example 'gold and silver and garments of silk.' The gift of clothes, a tradition which also kept the minstrels of the later Middle Ages warm, seems to have been a common reward.

Indeed, the name of Messalla's wife is still embroidered on the violet mantle of an aulos player, who exults in it as the spoils of a noble house.[8]

A second-century poem clearly implies that during the performance of art music the audience was still expected, as in earlier centuries, to listen in silence. Here a poet–singer complains,

Why did you make a disturbance and stop my song? A rider has learnt how to ride, and a singer how to sing. But if one who has learnt riding wants to sing, he is a failure in both riding and singing.[9]

There are three first-century poems which are not complimentary to specific solo performers, but perhaps these poets simply did not appreciate music.

Hegelochus, my Lord Caesar, once emptied a Greek city by appearing to sing the part of Nauplius [a famous naval figure]. Nauplius is ever an evil to the Greeks, either sending a great wave on their ships or having a lyre-singer to play his part.

...

The night raven's song bodes death, but when Demophilus sings the night raven itself dies.

...

Simylus the lyre-player killed all his neighbors by playing the whole night, except only Origenes, whom Nature had made deaf, and therefore gave him longer life in the place of hearing.[10]

---

7 Tertullianus, *De Anima*, trans. Alexander Roberts and James Donalson (Edinburgh: T. & T. Clark, 1884), XV, 439. Tertullian is using the organ as an analogy for the soul being one, despite its parts.

8 *Scriptores Historiae Augustae*, 449.

9 Nestor of Nicaea, in *The Greek Anthology*, IX, 537

10 Lucilius, 185; Nicarchus, 186; and Leonidas of Alexandria, 187, in ibid., IV.

In the third-century poetry of Callimachus, we find the suggestion that the tradition of accompanying choral music with instruments was still being practiced.

'Apollo is in the choir; I hear the lyre.'[11]

In another work by this poet there is a reference to the style of this choral repertoire, where we read of a chorus singing 'a sweet ode.'[12] It would also appear that the ancient tradition of the choral-dance was still in evidence at this time, or so a passing reference to those who are 'unmusical at dances,' by Clement of Alexandria would suggest.[13]

FUNCTIONAL MUSIC

It is clear from references in the literature of the first three centuries that many celebrations of the various religious-cults were still being observed. These 'pagan rituals,' as we shall see below, were particular objects of denouncement by the early Church philosophers. The historian, Gibbon, writing from the perspective of sympathy with the Church, describes the music heard in a ceremony worshiping the sun.

> The richest wines, the most extraordinary victims, and the rarest aromatics, were profusely consumed on his altar. Around the altar a chorus of Syrian damsels performed their lascivious dances to the sound of barbarian music.[14]

A curious poem of the second-century poet, Dioscorides, describes the celebration of Cybele, with the sound of a great drum which we may presume was used in these ceremonies.

> Chaste Atys, the gelded servant of Cybele, in frenzy giving his wild hair to the wind, wished to reach Sardis from Phrygian Pessinus; but when the dark of evening fell upon him in his course, the fierce fervor of his bitter ecstasy was cooled and he took shelter in a descending cavern, turning aside a little from the road. But a lion came swiftly on his track, a terror to brave men and to him an inexpressible woe. He stood speechless from fear and by some divine inspiration put his hand to his sounding tambor. At its deep roar the most courageous of beasts ran off quicker than a deer, unable to bear the deep

11 *Callimachus*, trans. C. A. Trypanis (Cambridge: Harvard University Press, 1975), 163.

12 Ibid., 239. A very intriguing fragment by this poet reads, in entirety, '... who ... invented the Italian scale.'

13 Clement of Alexandria, 'The Miscellanies,' trans. Alexander Roberts, in *Ante-Nicene Christian Library* (Edinburgh: T. & T. Clark, 1869), XII, bk. V, iv.

14 Edward Gibbon, *The History of the Decline and Fall of the Roman Empire* (Philadelphia: Coates, n.d.), I, 199ff.

note in its ears, and he cried out, 'Great Mother, by the banks of the Sangarias I dedicate to thee, in thanks for my life, my holy *thalame* and this noisy instrument that caused the lion to flee.'[15]

15 Dioscorides, in *The Greek Anthology*, VI, 220. The *thalame* were receptacles in which the organs of these castrated priests were deposited.

One type of functional music which is mentioned in all ancient literature is wedding music. A popular theme of poets was the tragic situation where either the bride or bridegroom dies just before the ceremony, representing the irony of death occurring at the moment which should be the happiest in one's life. In the following second-century example by Philippus, we read of the usual wedding hymns, but also a reference to 'sweet' aulos music.

But now the sweet aulos was echoing in the bridal chamber of Nikippis, and the house rejoiced in the clapping of hands at her wedding. But the voice of wailing burst in upon the bridal hymn, and we saw her dead, the poor child, not yet quite a wife. O tearful Hades, why didst thou divorce the bridegroom and bride, thou who thyself takest delight in ravishment?[16]

16 Ibid., VII, 186.

In all early literature the trumpet was associated with war and thus its very sound was usually associated with terror in the heart of the listener. Given this image, one can understand that this instrument is rarely the subject of humor, such as we find by the first-century poet, Lucilius.

Lean Marcus sounding a trumpet just blew into it and went straight headforemost down it.[17]

17 *The Greek Anthology*, IV, 94.

A second-century poem contains a rare reference to the use of the aulos as a war instrument in Italy.

Miccus of Pellene hung in the temple of Ilian Athene this deep-toned aulos of Ares, the Tyrrhenian instrument by which he formerly uttered many a loud message of peace and war.[18]

18 Tymnus, in ibid., VI, 151. The aulos had been a common military instrument among the early Greek armies.

There are numerous references in the literature of the first three centuries to various kinds of occupational music. The most familiar, as in older literature, is that of the shepherd. In the second-century poem, 'Daphnis and Chloe,' we read of the shepherd's use of the three kinds of instruments still found today, the transverse flute, the panpipe and the reed-pipe.[19] This same poet describes the construction of the panpipe.

19 Longus, *Daphnis & Chloe*, trans. Paul Turner (London: Penguin Books, 1956), I, 4.

Daphnis, after cutting some slender reeds, piercing them at the joints, and fastening them together with soft wax, would practice playing the panpipe until it was dark.[20]

We read here also of a more 'modern' panpipe construction, 'nine reeds fastened together with bronze instead of wax.'[21]

This same poem also mentions the singing of seamen[22] and the agricultural songs of reapers, of a 'rustic nature.'[23]

A poem of Callimachus, mentions the music of the laborers who draw water from wells.

> … many a drawer of water is singing the Song of the Well … [24]

[20] Ibid., I, 10.
[21] Ibid., I, 15.
[22] Ibid., III, 21.
[23] Ibid., IV, 38.
[24] *Callimachus*, 197.

ENTERTAINMENT MUSIC

During the reign of the emperors, Carus, Carinus and Numerian, large-scale public entertainments were instituted in Rome. An account of one of these shows includes hundreds of musicians!

> For there was exhibited a rope-walker, who in his buskins seemed to be walking on the winds, also a wall-climber, who, eluding a bear, ran up a wall, also some bears which acted a farce, and, besides, one hundred trumpeters who blew one single blast together, one hundred horn-blowers, one hundred aulos players, also one hundred aulos players who accompanied songs, one thousand pantomimists and gymnasts, moreover, a mechanical scaffold, which, however, burst into flames and burned up the stage.[25]

Gibbon describes an entertainment of a similar scale, namely a nine-hour long procession throughout Rome, during the reign of Aurelian.[26]

The most frequently described form of entertainment music in early literature was that heard at private and public banquets. In the case of a solo performer, he was often invited to join the guests in a round of drinking before the music began. One such performer sent his host a song as a thank-you note for his generosity.

> A little dew is enough to make the cicadas tipsy, but when they have drunk they sing louder than swans. So can the singer who has received hospitality repay his benefactors with song for their little

[25] *Scriptores Historiae Augustae*, 447. Gibbon, *The History of the Decline and Fall of the Roman Empire*, I, 249, refers to a similar celebration in 248 AD.

[26] Gibbon, *The History of the Decline and Fall of the Roman Empire*, I, 374. An unusually enthusiastic warrior, Aurelian, according to an ancient writer, in one battle killed 48 of the enemy by his own hand [Gibbon, ibid., 354, fn. 17].

gifts. Therefore first I send thee these lines of thanks, and if the Fates consent thou shalt be often written in my pages.[27]

Two extant poems by the first-century poet, Lucilius, suggest that banquet music ranged from solo lyre singers to choral-dance ensembles. In his case, he was not favorably disposed to either.

> You know the rule of my little banquets. Today, Aulus, I invite you under new convivial laws. No lyric poet shall sit there and recite, and you yourself shall neither trouble us nor be troubled with literary discussions.
>
> ...
>
> I never knew, Epicrates, that you were a tragedian or a choral flute-player or any other sort of person whose business it is to have a chorus with them. But I invited you alone; you, however, came bringing with you from home a chorus of dancing slaves, to whom you hand all the dishes over your shoulder as a gift. If this is to be so, make the slaves sit down at the table and we will come and stand at their feet to serve.[28]

Finally, we might quote a description, by the famous second-century medical philosopher, Galen, of music used by children at play. Interestingly enough, one can still see this very same activity in Spain today.

> Children take the bladders of pigs, fill them with air, and then rub them on ashes near the fire, so as to warm, but not to injure them. This is a common game in the district of Iona, and among not a few other nations. As they rub, they sing songs, to a certain measure, time, and rhythm, and all their words are an exhortation to the bladder to increase in size.[29]

---

[27] Antipater of Thessalonica, in *The Greek Anthology*, IX, 92.

[28] Ibid., IV, 10, 11.

[29] Galen, *On the Natural Faculties*, trans. Arthur John Brock (Cambridge: Harvard University Press, 1979), I, vii.

2 PHILOSOPHERS OF THE FIRST THREE CENTURIES

ALL THE LITERATURE OF THE EARLY CHURCH FATHERS focuses on the struggle against the 'Pagan.' It is important to remind the modern reader that among the 'pagans' were Socrates, Plato, Aristotle, and the entire library of Greek and Roman philosophy of the ancient world. With the final victory of the Church, philosophy, as it had been previously known, comes to an end. Before that happened, however, there were in the early centuries a few philosophers in the older tradition whose works have been preserved.

ON THE PHILOSOPHY OF AESTHETICS

From the first century of the modern era we have an extraordinary treatise on aesthetics, called 'On the Sublime,' by a writer named Longinus, of whom nothing else is known. His treatise was well-known through the Renaissance and deeply influenced such writers as Dryden and Pope. This work concerns itself with the sublimity of expression in language, but the author also relates his ideas to the other arts, in particular music—which, of course, is also a language of expression.

Longinus begins by defining sublimity as 'a certain distinction and excellence in expression.'[1] But, by 'excellence in expression' he does not have in mind merely technical skill in writing. Longinus is clearly thinking of some other quality when he describes, 'Sublimity flashing forth at the right moment scatters everything before it like a thunderbolt.'[2] It is obvious that Longinus could not separate a sublime, lofty, style from its emotion tone.

> I would affirm with confidence that there is no tone so lofty as that of genuine passion, in its right place, when it bursts out in a wild gust of mad enthusiasm and as it were fills the speaker's words with frenzy.[3]

[1] Longinus, *On the Sublime*, trans. W. Rhys Roberts, (Cambridge: University Press, 1935), I, 3.

[2] I, 4.

[3] X, 4.

It follows that the effective communication of sublimity to the observer is not so much an appeal to his reason as to his emotions and this was the goal of oratory. As Longinus put it,

> The effect of elevated language upon an audience is not persuasion but transport.[4]

[4] I, 4.

In considering further the emotional impact of the sublime on the observer, Longinus enumerates a number of very significant aesthetic ideas. First, he appears to have in mind something very much like Aristotle's concept of catharsis—something which reaches us personally, lifts us, improves us, and stays with us in our memory. In addition, sublimity is characterized by quality and universality. We find it particularly interesting that he emphasizes that it is quality which creates the desire for repeated hearings.

> For, as if instinctively, our soul is uplifted by the true sublime; it takes a proud flight, and is filled with joy and vaunting, as though it had itself produced what it has heard. When, therefore, a thing is heard repeatedly by a man of intelligence, who is well versed in literature, and its effect is not to dispose the soul to high thoughts, and it does not leave the mind more food for reflection than the words seem to convey, but falls, if examined carefully through and through, into disesteem, it cannot rank as true sublimity because it does not survive a first hearing. For that is really great which bears a repeated examination, and which it is difficult or rather impossible to withstand, and the memory of which is strong and hard to efface. In general, consider those examples of sublimity to be fine and genuine which please all and always.[5]

[5] VII, 2.

Before leaving the subject of positive emotions Longinus reminds us that humor is also an emotion, an emotion based on pleasure.[6]

[6] XXXVIII, 5.

Longinus provides three examples of what he calls false emotions in expression, which we find also have a similar application to music. The first is exaggeration, or tumidity, which he discusses after quoting some lines by Aeschylus.

> They are turbid in expression and confused in imagery rather than the product of intensity, and each one of them, if examined in the light of day, sinks little by little from the terrible into the contemptible. But since even in tragedy, which is in its very nature stately and prone to bombast, tasteless tumidity is unpardonable … Altogether,

tumidity seems particularly hard to avoid. The explanation is that all who aim at elevation are so anxious to escape the reproach of being weak and dry that they are carried, as by some strange law of nature, into the opposite extreme. They put their trust in the maxim that 'failure in a great attempt is at least a noble error.'[7]

[7] III, 1ff.

The second type of false emotion in expression Longinus calls puerility, that which is silly or childish.

> While tumidity desires to transcend the limits of the sublime, the defect which is termed puerility is the direct antithesis of elevation, for it is utterly low and mean and in real truth the most ignoble vice of style. What, then, is this puerility? Clearly, a pedant's thoughts, which begin in learned trifling and end in frigidity. Men slip into this kind of error because, while they aim at the uncommon and elaborate and most of all at the attractive, they drift unawares into the tawdry and affected.

The third example of false emotion he calls 'parenthyrsus,' by which he means inappropriate or empty emotion, where no emotion is required.

> For men are often carried away, as if by intoxication, into displays of emotion which are not caused by the nature of the subject, but are purely personal and wearisome.

This third type, in particular, he says, fails to achieve empathy in the observer.

Longinus concludes this general discussion of the emotions in expression with an observation that some emotions are, in and of themselves, not sublime.

> Some passions are found which are far removed from sublimity and are of a low order, such as pity, grief and fear.

As Longinus begins to define the components of sublimity of expression in language, he speaks of a number of principles which again have a similar applicability with respect to the sublimity of expression in music.

First he presents what he calls the 'five principal sources of elevated language.'[8] First, one must have the power of forming great

[8] VIII, 1ff.

conceptions. With respect to music, we would say one must have the ability of creating music of substance.

Second, Longinus recognizes there is usually, in the performer, a combination of 'talent' and a learned craft, which he calls here, 'art.' It is clear that he believes that natural ability is the most effective, when he says there must be,

> vehement and inspired passion. These two components of the sublime are for the most part innate. Those which remain are partly the product of art.

The third component refers to the creation of figures of speech. These, Longinus says, are of two sources, some of thought and some of expression. This seems to us very close to the way modern psychologists describe the production of speech in our twin brain hemispheres. The left hemisphere produces the language (thought) and the right hemisphere the emotional tone of the language (expression).

The final two characteristics of sublimity of expression in language, noble diction and dignified and elevated composition, seem to us also characteristic of the highest expression in music.

Longinus also recognizes here that 'passion' and 'elevation' are not always appropriate in the same type of speech.

> Among the orators, too, eulogies and ceremonial and occasional addresses contain on every side examples of dignity and elevation, but are for the most part void of passion. This is the reason why passionate speakers are the worst eulogists, and why, on the other hand, those who are apt in encomium are the least passionate.

9 X, 1ff.

In another place,[9] Longinus offers two additional characteristics which he calls contributors to sublimity of style. The first we would call today, unity, 'the systematic selection of the most important elements, and the power of forming, by their mutual combination, what may be called one body.' The second he calls, amplification.

> Now the definition given by the writers on rhetoric does not satisfy me. Amplification is, say they, discourse which invests the subject with grandeur. This definition, however would surely apply in equal measure to sublimity and passion and figurative language, since they too invest the discourse with a certain degree of grandeur. The point of distinction between them seems to me to be that sublim-

ity consists in elevation, while amplification embraces a multitude of details. Consequently, sublimity is often comprised in a single thought, while amplification is universally associated with a certain magnitude and abundance.

Turning now to the specific methods[10] for producing sublimity of expression, Longinus begins a lengthy discussion by observing that one must learn to be one's own best critic. How would I hear this if I were in the audience, or, more formidable still, what would Homer think, if he were in the audience? To imagine 'great heroes, acting as judges,' does, he admits, make the 'ordeal' of speaking a 'severe one.' But now he adds 'greater incentive' by proposing the question,

[10] XV, 1ff.

> 'In what spirit will each succeeding age listen to me who have written thus?' But if one shrinks from the very thought of uttering aught that may transcend the term of his own life and time, the conceptions of his mind must necessarily be incomplete, blind, and as it were untimely born, since they are by no means brought to the perfection needed to ensure a futurity of fame.

The first of the specific methods for producing sublimity of expression is imagery, or as some call it, according to Longinus, 'mental representations.' Here he offers a very interesting observation.

> You will be aware of the fact that an image has one purpose with the orators and another with the poets, and that the design of the poetical image is enthrallment, of the rhetorical—vivid description. Both, however, seek to stir the passions and the emotions.

He also points out that poets use imagery for exaggeration, but the orator must present reality and truth. Thus, if an orator uses the poetical style it lends a 'strange and alien air.'

Longinus next begins a detailed discussion of figures of speech, relative to their role in producing sublimity of expression. We shall only mention a few of these which have reference to art in general.

In discussing metaphors, Longinus again returns to the emotions.

> The proper time for using metaphors is when the passions roll like a torrent and sweep a multitude of them down their resistless flood.[11]

[11] XXXII, 1.

He quotes Aristotle as observing that one can soften the impact of a metaphor by the use of qualifying words, such as 'as if.' But why, Longinus wonders, would anyone want to do this?

> For it is the nature of the passions, in their vehement rush, to sweep and thrust everything before them …[12]

12 XXXII, 4.

In arguing for the effectiveness of Periphrasis,[13] Longinus uses a musical analogy. This comment provides us with a more interesting description of multi-part music at this time than do most music treatises, which to the present day tells students that the music of this time consisted of single melodies and no harmony whatsoever.

13 XXVIII, 1. Meaning the use of longer phrasing in place of a possible shorter form of expression.

> For just as in music the so-called accompaniments bring out the charm of the melody, so also periphrasis often harmonizes with the normal expression and adds greatly to its beauty, especially if it has a quality which is not inflated and dissonant but pleasantly tempered.

Regarding the crucial element of the choice of words, Longinus points out that while beautiful words are usually envied, sometimes elegant language is not appropriate.

> The choice of proper and striking words wonderfully attracts and enthralls the hearer, and such a choice is the leading ambition of all orators and writers, since it is the direct agency which ensures the presence in writing … of the perfection of grandeur, beauty, mellowness, dignity, force, power, and any other high qualities there may be, and breathes into dead things a kind of living voice. All this it is, I say, needless to mention, for beautiful words are in very truth the peculiar light of thought. It may, however, be pointed out that stately language is not to be used everywhere, since to invest petty affairs with great and high-sounding names would seem just like putting a full-sized tragic mask upon an infant boy.[14]

14 XXX.

He is aware that great writers sometimes use rather common language, citing Theopompus who referred to a person as having had a genius for 'stomaching' things. The use of such phrases, says Longinus, 'graze at the very edge of vulgarity, but they are saved by their expressiveness.'[15]

15 XXXI, 2.

Further, Longinus points out that great talents sometimes have flaws—but that one should not permit this to cloud one's vision of that which is really important. There are thoughts here worthy of contemplation by all persons who judge music contests!

> Is it not worth while … to raise the general question whether we ought to give the preference, in poems and prose writings, to grandeur with some attendant faults, or to success which is moderate but altogether sound and free from error? Yes, and further, whether a greater number of excellences, or excellences higher in quality, would in literature rightly bear away the palm? For these are inquiries appropriate to a treatise on the sublime, and they imperatively demand a settlement.
>
> For my part, I am well aware that lofty genius is far removed from flawlessness; for invariable accuracy incurs the risk of pettiness, and in the sublime, as in great fortunes, there must be something which is overlooked. It may be necessarily the case that low and average natures remain as a rule free from failing and in greater safety because they never run the risk or seek to scale the heights, while great endowments prove insecure because of their very greatness.
>
> In the second place, I am not ignorant that it naturally happens that the worse side of human character is always the more easily recognized, and that the memory of errors remains indelible, while that of excellences quickly dies away.
>
> I have myself noted not a few errors on the part of Homer and other writers of the greatest distinction, and the slips they have made afford me anything but pleasure. Still I do not term them willful errors, but rather oversights of a random and casual kind, due to neglect and introduced with all the heedlessness of genius. Consequently I do not waver in my view that excellences higher in quality, even if not sustained throughout, should always on a comparison be voted the first place, because of their sheer elevation of spirit if for no other reason …
>
> It is true that Bacchylides and Ion are faultless and entirely elegant writers of the polished school, while Pindar and Sophocles, although at times they burn everything before them as it were in their swift career, are often extinguished unaccountably and fail most lamentably. But would anyone in his senses regard all the compositions of Ion put together as an equivalent for the single play of the *Oedipus*?[16]

16 XXXII.

After this discussion of the choice of language, Longinus now turns to the arrangement of the language, to word order. The significance of this can be seen, he suggests, if you take any sentence of Euripides and shape it in a different way. This will prove that

Euripides was a poet more in virtue of his composition than his invention.[17] Longinus gives further evidence that the arrangement of the language 'is not only a natural source of persuasion and pleasure among men but also a wonderful instrument of lofty utterance and of passion' through an analogy with music. This passage is particularly interesting in his reference to the universal understanding of music and his observation that it is not the physical materials of music which move the listener. Even more astonishing is his insight into the genetic aspects of music and language, the non-conceptual nature of this genetic heritage and his brilliant analysis of how music and language communicate to the listener.

17 XL, 3.

> For does not the aulos instill certain emotions into its hearers and as it were make them beside themselves and full of frenzy, and supplying a rhythmical movement constrain the listener to move rhythmically in accordance therewith and to conform himself to the melody, although he may be utterly ignorant of music? Yes, and the tones of the harp, although in themselves they signify nothing at all, often cast a wonderful spell … over an audience by means of the variations of sounds, by their pulsation against one another, and by their mingling in concert.
>
> And yet these are mere semblances and spurious copies of persuasion, not genuine activities of human nature. Are we not, then, to hold that composition (being a harmony of that language which is implanted by nature in man and which appeals not to the hearing only but to the soul itself), since it calls forth manifold shapes of words, thoughts, deeds, beauty, melody, all of them born at our birth and growing with our growth, and since by means of the blending and variation of its own tones it seeks to introduce into the minds of those who are present the emotion which affects the speaker and since it always brings the audience to share in it and by the building of phrase upon phrase raises a sublime and harmonious structure: are we not, I say, to hold that harmony by these selfsame means allures us and invariably disposes us to stateliness and dignity and elevation and every emotion which it contains within itself, gaining absolute mastery over our minds? But it is folly to dispute concerning matters which are generally admitted, since experience is proof sufficient.[18]

18 XXXIX, 2.

Finally, in discussing the rhythm of language, Longinus, as might be anticipated, again turns to music for illustration. Here again our writer demonstrates a remarkable insight into the nature of the aesthetic understanding of the listener.

There is nothing in the sphere of the sublime, that is so lowering as broken and agitated movement of language, such as is characteristic of pyrrhics and trochees and dichorees, which fall altogether to the level of dance music. For all over-rhythmical writing is at once felt to be affected and finical and wholly lacking in passion owing to the monotony of its superficial polish.

And the worst of it all is that, just as petty lays [songs] draw their hearer away from the point and compel his attention to themselves, so also over-rhythmical style does not communicate the feeling of the words but simply the feeling of the rhythm.[19]

19 XLI, 1.

Longinus also engages a topic which had been much discussed among the ancient philosophers, and indeed is often still discussed today. Is one born with artistic ability, or is it susceptible of being learned? His views appear to us to be somewhat ambiguous on this question. Here he seems to suggest that the highest gifts of the performer can indeed be learned.

First of all, we must raise the question whether there is such a thing as an art [craft] of the sublime or lofty. Some hold that those are entirely in error who would bring such matters under the precepts of art. A lofty tone, says one, is innate, and does not come by teaching; nature is the only art that can compass it. Works of nature are, they think, made worse and altogether feebler when wizened by the rules of art.

But I maintain that this will be found to be otherwise if it be observed that, while nature as a rule is free and independent in matters of passion and elevation, yet is she wont not to act at random and utterly without system ... Moreover, the expression of the sublime is more exposed to danger when it goes its own way without the guidance of knowledge,—when it is suffered to be unstable and unballasted,—when it is left at the mercy of mere momentum and ignorant audacity. It is true that it often needs the spur, but it is also true that it often needs the curb.[20]

20 II, 1

However, in another place, where he is comparing the relative merits of two speakers, Hyperides and Demosthenes, in casting his vote for the latter he seems to suggest that the difference is not learning, but a God-given ability.

But Demosthenes draws—as from a store—excellences allied to the highest sublimity and perfected to the utmost, the tone of lofty speech, living passions, copiousness, readiness, speed (where it is legitimate), and that power and vehemence of his which forbid approach. Having, I say, absorbed bodily within himself these mighty gifts which we may deem heaven-sent (for it would not be right to term them *human*), he thus with the noble qualities which are his own routs all comers even where the qualities he does not possess are concerned, and overpowers with thunder and with lightening the orators of every age. One could sooner face with unflinching eyes a descending thunderbolt than meet with steady gaze his bursts of passion in their swift succession.

In the end Longinus retreats from having to make a choice between a studied craft, which he calls 'art,' and that talent which is a gift of nature. The highest achievement, he concludes, requires both.

> Since freedom from failings is for the most part the successful result of art, and excellence (though it may be unevenly sustained) the result of sublimity, the employment of art is in every way a fitting aid to nature; for it is the conjunction of the two which tends to ensure perfection.[21]

21 XXXVI, 3.

In conclusion, we must credit Longinus for a powerful and moving description of the end of art (as we use the word) and how the listener profits from the exposure to great art. It is the universality of great art which allows the observer to draw from it, to absorb it and to improve himself. Here is a way, says Longinus, which leads to the sublime.

> It is the imitation and emulation of previous great poets and writers. And let this, my dear friend, be an aim to which we steadfastly apply ourselves. For many men are carried away by the spirit of others as if inspired, just as it is related of the Pythian priestess when she approaches the tripod, where there is a rift in the ground which exhales divine vapor. By heavenly power thus communicated she is impregnated and straightaway delivers oracles in virtue of the afflatus. Similarly from the great natures of men of old there are borne in upon the souls of those who emulate them (as from sacred caves) what we may describe as *effluences*, so that even those who seem little likely to be possessed are thereby inspired and succumb to the spell of the others' greatness.
>
> Was Herodotus alone a devoted imitator of Homer? No, Stesichorus even before his time, and Archilochus, and above all Plato, who from the great Homeric source drew to himself innumerable tributary streams …

> The proceeding is not plagiarism; it is like taking an impression from beautiful forms or figures or other works of art.[22]

[22] XIII, 2.

Nature herself, says Longinus, prepares us genetically to do this.

> Nature has appointed us men to be no base or ignoble animals; but when she ushers us into life and into the vast universe as into some great assembly, to be as it were spectators of the mighty whole and the keenest aspirants for honor, forthwith she implants in our souls the unconquerable love of whatever is elevated and more divine than we.[23]

[23] XXXV, 2.

But the listener's role is not merely a passive one. If he is to profit from his innate susceptibility to the sublime, he must rid himself of the ignoble.

> Sublimity is the echo of a great soul. Hence also a bare idea, by itself and without a spoken word, sometimes excites admiration just because of the greatness of soul implied. Thus the silence of Ajax in the Underworld is great and more sublime than words.
> First, then, it is absolutely necessary to indicate the source of this elevation, namely, that the truly eloquent must be free from low and ignoble thoughts. For it is not possible that men with mean and servile ideas and aims prevailing throughout their lives should produce anything that is admirable and worthy of immortality.[24]

[24] IX, 2.

Another second-century philosopher, Sextus Empiricus, takes the opposite view, raising the question whether anyone at all is capable of judging art. First, following the line of reasoning of Anacharsis the Scythian, he asks, should the expert or non-expert be the judge? Rejecting the idea of having non-experts judge as absurd, he next asks, can an expert in one art judge work in another art? No, for this judge would also be a non-expert in that art. The remaining possibility is for an expert to judge work in the same art in which he is an expert. But this too, he questions.

> Who is he that judges those who stand on the same level inasmuch as they are engaged in the same art? And besides, if this fellow-craftsman judges that one, the same thing will be both judging and judged, both trusted and distrusted; for in so far as the other man is a fellow-craftsman of the man who is being judged, he himself also will be subject to judgment and distrusted, whereas, in so far as he is giving judgment, he will be trusted. But it is not possible for the

same thing to be both judging and judged, trusted and distrusted. Therefore there is none who judges by rules of art.[25]

Empiricus gives another reason why art cannot be judged, this time quoting the views of Protagoras of Abdera, who asserts that,

> all sense-impressions and opinions are true and that truth is a relative thing inasmuch as everything that has appeared to someone or been opined by someone is at once real in relation to him.[26]

This is the essential problem with contests in music and why it is a universal experience that whoever participates in a music contest will always reject the conclusions and comments of the adjudicators.

Finally, the second-century physician–philosopher, Galen, makes one contribution to a much discussed topic in art, the imitation of nature. He offers a definition, but unfortunately does not elaborate on it.

> Nature is a constructive artist and the substance of things is always tending towards unity and also towards alteration because its own parts act upon and are acted upon by one another.[27]

ON THE PHYSIOLOGY OF AESTHETICS

Lacking our modern understanding of the brain, and especially the roles of the twin hemispheres, the one dealing with reason and conceptual input and the other with sensory and experiential input, it was extremely difficult for the ancient philosophers to deal with the broad question of our faculties, how they work and how they are related. Their viewpoint on this general subject greatly colored their opinion with respect to the perception of art.

We begin with the second-century philosopher, Sextus Empiricus, who stated:

> Man, you know, is said to be compounded of two things, soul and body, and in both these we differ one from another.[28]

It is interesting that, even today, when we speak of something absorbing us completely, we use the expression, 'body and soul.' But for Empiricus, this phrase represented the current sum of the

25 Sextus Empiricus, *Against the Logicians*, trans. R.G. Bury (London: Heinemann, 1935), 31. Voltaire once wrote a charming discussion based on this twisted logic in which he says the blind should be the judges of pictures.

26 Ibid.

27 Galen, *On the Natural Faculties*, trans. Arthur John Brock (Cambridge: Harvard University Press, 1979), 73.

28 Sextus Empiricus, *Outlines of Pyrrhonism*, trans. R.G. Bury (London: Heinemann, 1933), I, 79.

understanding of what man represented. The real problems came when anyone tried to define 'soul.' Empiricus gives a summary of a number of branches of philosophy which tried to define the soul and concludes that since the problem cannot be solved by Reason, one must conclude that man, himself, cannot be understood.

> Thus, neither by the intellect will the dispute about the soul be decided; therefore there is no means to decide it. And this being so, it is non-apprehensible; and, in consequence, Man, too will not be apprehended.[29]

29 Ibid., II, 31ff.

Empiricus even concludes that what we call intellect, itself, cannot be yet understood.

> But let it be granted that the intellect has been apprehended, and let us agree, by way of assumption, that it really exists; I still affirm that it cannot judge objects. For if it does not even discern itself accurately but contradicts itself about its own existence and the mode of its origin and the position in which it is placed, how can it be able to apprehend anything else accurately? And even if it be granted that the intellect is capable of judging objects, we shall not discover how to judge according to it.[30]

30 Ibid., II, 58.

Empiricus further believed that the senses could not be relied on for judgment. First, because the information from the various senses differs one with the other, as in the case of a painting where the eyes may report three dimensions, but the touch does not, or in the case of rain-water, which is beneficial to the eyes but roughens the wind-pipe and lungs.[31] Consequently, he says, it is impossible to say what is the real nature of these things, only what they appear to be at the moment.

31 Ibid., I, 92.

Second, all senses 'are relative to those who have the sensation.'[32] Thus,

32 Ibid., I, 175.

> The sense of taste declares the same food to be unpleasant in the case of those full-fed, but pleasant in the case of those who are hungry; and the sense of hearing likewise perceives the same sound as loud at night but as faint by day; and the sense of smell regards the same objects as malodorous in the case of most people, but not so in the case of tanners.[33]

33 Ibid., II, 55.

Regarding the sense of hearing, he also asks,

> And as for the sense of hearing, how could we say that its perceptions are alike in animals with a very narrow auditory passage and those with a very wide one, or in animals with hairy ears and those with smooth ears? For, as regards this sense, even we ourselves find our hearing affected in one way when we have our ears plugged and in another way when we use them just as they are.[34]

Returning to his original question, then, if one cannot judge things by the intellect or the senses alone, can we then judge by the intellect in combination with the senses? No, says Empiricus, because it is clear that when it comes to the senses, no one agrees.

> The only remaining alternative is judgment by means of both senses and intellect. But this again is impossible; for not only do the senses not guide the intellect to apprehension, but they even oppose it. For it is certain, at any rate, that from the fact that honey appears bitter to some and sweet to others, Democritus declared that it is neither sweet nor bitter, while Heraclitus said that it is both.[35]

In his book, *Against the Logicians*, Empiricus examines the nature of the senses in more detail. First, it is interesting that, although he was unaware of the correct reason, the dissimilar hemispheres of the brain, Empiricus correctly observes that whatever one understands by the senses, it is something which cannot be put into words and therefore communicated to another person.

> For the means by which we communicate is speech, and speech is not the real and existent things; therefore we do not indicate to our neighbors the existent things but speech, which is [something] other than the existing realities. Thus, just as the visible thing will not become audible, and *vice versa*, so too, since the existent subsists externally, it will not become our speech; and not being speech it will not be made clear to another person.[36]

Empiricus next attempts to explain the relationship of the senses and Reason, again something we understand easily today through our knowledge of the roles of the twin hemispheres of the brain. He begins by quoting a musical analogy by the philosopher Speusippus, which demonstrates that the senses and the intellect are capable of working toward the same end.

---

34 Ibid., I, 50.

35 Ibid., II, 63.

36 Sextus Empiricus, *Against the Logicians*, I, 84.

> But Speusippus declared that, since some things are sensible, other intelligible, the cognitive reason is the criterion of things intelligible and the cognitive sense of things sensible. And cognitive sense he conceived as being that which shares in rational truth. For just as the fingers of the flute player or harpist possess an artistic activity, which, however, is not primarily brought to perfection by the fingers themselves but is fully developed as a result of joint practice under the guidance of reasoning,—and just as the sense of the musician possesses an activity capable of grasping the harmonious and the non-harmonious, this activity, however, not being self-produced but an acquisition due to reasoning,—so also the cognitive sense naturally derives from the reason the cognitive experience in which it shares, and which leads to unerring discrimination of subsisting objects.[37]

[37] Ibid., I, 145.

While Empiricus seems to accept this argument, he has much more difficulty in understanding that one can perceive sensory and intellectual information in an independent and equal manner.

> Man is nothing more than his substance and senses and intellect, so that, if he is to apprehend himself with one of his parts, either he will perceive his senses and intellect with his body, or conversely he will apprehend his body with his senses and intellect.[38]

[38] Ibid., I, 287ff.

The most important point he makes here is that once anything sensory, such as hearing, is thought of in a rational way it is no longer of the realm of the senses but of the intellect. It is a fundamental mistake made today in music education.

> [The senses] are solely passive and are stamped like wax, and not a single thing else do they know, since, to be sure, if we ascribe to them a seeking for anything they will become no longer irrational but rational and endowed with the nature of intellect.[39]

[39] Ibid., I, 293.

In another place, he makes the same argument.

> Wherefore the intellect also, if it receives the affection of each sense, is sensitively moved, and being sensitively moved it is sense, and being sense it is irrational, and having become irrational it will cease from being any longer thought, and not being thought it will not receive as thought the affection of sense.[40]

[40] Ibid., I, 356.

Because Empiricus could not have known that the experiential–sensory information is *real* in the right hemisphere of the brain, yet of a nature incapable of being understood in the rational, conceptual left hemisphere, he makes an understandable error by concluding that the 'senses do not perceive either the body or themselves or one another.'[41] The underlying problem here, and it exists among some thinkers today, is that while the right hemisphere of the brain is indeed *non-rational* it is wrong and denigrating to call it *irrational*. The fact is that the right hemisphere and all it represents do not need to be 'explained' by the left hemisphere. Each side has its own valid form of Truth. Empiricus' basic argument, and error, here is that once one begins to 'think' of the irrational, it makes thinking irrational. For this reason, also, he cannot connect intelligence and experience.

41 Ibid., I, 302ff.

> For the young are believed to fall short in intelligence because of the great experience of the old, though the opposite is the fact; for while the aged are more experienced, they are not more intelligent than the young.[42]

42 Ibid., I, 323.

Failing to arrive at a satisfactory explanation of the relationship of the senses and the intellect, this philosopher arrives at a rather pessimistic conclusion.

> [Since man] cannot discover the truth by employing either the senses only or the intellect by itself or both the senses and the intellect conjointly; therefore Man is not capable of discovering the truth.[43]

43 Ibid., I, 343.

The one early philosopher who might have contributed the most interesting insights into brain–body functions was the second-century physician, Galen, but unfortunately, he wrote little which illuminates this subject. Nevertheless, we find particularly interesting two lists of disciplines which he describes. The first, he says, are those which 'sharpen the soul': geometry, arithmetic, computation, architecture and astronomy.[44] A similar list he describes as 'skills which depend on reason, those skilled in numbers and calculations,' which includes 'the geometricians, the astronomers, the architects, the lawyers, the orators, the grammarians, and the musicians.'[45]

44 Galen, *On the Passions and Errors of the Soul*, trans. Paul W. Harkins (Columbus: Ohio State University Press), 78.

45 Ibid., 107.

To the modern reader it seems odd to associate music with numbers, rather than soul. For many early philosophers, however, music was numbers and many found a close association with grammar. Sextus Empiricus, for example, provides an interesting quotation from Asclepiades, who, in discussing 'expertness' and 'expertness for the most part' with respect to grammar, observed,

> For this is a feature of arts which are conjectural and subject to accidents such as navigation and medicine; but Grammar is not a conjectural art but akin to Music and Philosophy.[46]

On the other hand, Empiricus quotes Dionysius as setting grammar apart from 'the alien disciplines of Music and Mathematics, on the ground that they have no connection with it.'[47]

46 Sextus Empiricus, *Against the Professors*, trans. R. G. Bury (Cambridge: Harvard University Press, 1949), I, 72.

47 Ibid., I, 80.

ON THE PSYCHOLOGY OF AESTHETICS

It is curious that none of the non-Church philosophers of the first three centuries discuss in detail their ideas on Beauty as an aesthetic principle.[48] And of these philosophers, only the second-century philosopher, Sextus Empiricus, discusses Pleasure. He, however, who expressed doubt on the existence of almost everything, also doubts whether the subject of Pleasure is susceptible of understanding. He observes first that Pleasure and Displeasure have primarily to do with man's choice and avoidance of things, and second, that Pleasure and Displeasure have to do with the senses. However, he observes that some choose the very things avoided by others and those things chosen by all affect different men differently. Since, in both cases, we must attribute this to the differences in men, he concludes that no general understanding of the subject is possible.[49]

48 In volume 1 of this series we have discussed some philosophers of this period who discuss this concept with respect to *earlier* Greek and Roman ideas.

49 Sextus Empiricus, *Outlines of Pyrrhonism*, 53.

Empiricus also attacks the Epicurean idea that Pleasure is the chief Good, quoting their observation that animals, upon birth, instinctively seek after pleasure and avoid pain. But Empiricus points out the contradiction found in the fact that every pleasure has an associated pain, and pain, according to the Epicureans, is a natural evil. Therefore he once again rejects any meaningful definition for these concepts.

> Thus, for example, the drunkard feels pleasure when filling himself with wine, and the glutton with food, and the lecher in immoderate sexual intercourse, yet these things are productive of both poverty and sickness, which, as they say, are painful and evil. Pleasure, therefore, is not a natural good. Similarly, too, what is productive of good

is not naturally evil, and pains bring about pleasures; it is, in fact, by toil that we acquire knowledge, and it is thus also that a man becomes possessed both of wealth and of his lady-love, and pains preserve health. Toil, then, is not naturally evil. Indeed if pleasure were naturally good, and toil bad, all men, as we said, would have been similarly disposed towards them, whereas we see many of the philosophers choosing toil and hardship and despising pleasure.[50]

50 Ibid., 459.

Regarding emotions, the second-century physician–philosopher, Galen, wrote that things like growth and nutrition are the effects of nature, while feeling and voluntary motion are the effects of the soul.[51] Today we understand that emotions, at least in a general sense, are indeed part of nature and come to us genetically.

51 Galen, *On the Natural Faculties*, 3.

One often reads that music has the virtue of 'calming the passions.' One passage in Galen perhaps reflects on the real significance of this phrase to the ancients. If his descriptions here of a passionate man were typical, descriptions which would seem quite extraordinary in our times, then perhaps this virtue attributed to music would have been thought very important indeed. That is to say, perhaps the word, 'passion,' had an entirely different meaning at this time.

> In the whole of life and in the individual arts, it is usual for any man to recognize outstanding superiority and differences in things, but only those who are prudent men and skilled craftsmen can recognize slight superiority and differences. The same holds good in the matter of errors and passions. Whenever a man becomes violently angry over little things and bites and kicks his servants, you are sure that this man is in a state of passion.
>
> …
>
> I watched a man eagerly trying to open a door. When things did not work out as he would have them, I saw him bite the key, kick the door, blaspheme, glare wildly like a madman, and all but foam at the mouth like a wild boar.[52]

52 Galen, *On the Passions and Errors of the Soul*, 29, 38.

The second-century philosopher, Empiricus, seems to take the position that whereas the emotions are engaged through the senses,[53] and the emotions are individually understood, then for the individual it is the emotions which are *real* and not the objects which caused them. He says that some assert, 'there exists no criterion common to mankind, but common names given to objects,' however,

53 Empiricus, *Pyrrhonism*, 483.

for all in common use the terms 'white' or 'sweet,' but they do not possess in common anything white or sweet. For each man perceives his own particular emotion, but as to whether this emotion is produced by a white object both in himself and his neighbor, neither the man himself can affirm without experiencing his neighbor's emotion, nor can the neighbor without experiencing that of the man. But since there is no emotion which is common to us all, it is rash to assert that the thing which appears of this kind to me appears to be of this kind to the man next to me as well.[54]

54 Empiricus, *Against the Logicians*, 107.

Today we understand him to be incorrect as the emotions are both general and personal, that is, a word like, 'pain,' is understood generally *and* individually by everyone.

ON THE AESTHETICS OF MUSIC

At the beginning of the Christian era we find some books dealing with the aesthetics of music which are entirely negative in attitude. They are shocking for us to read, thinking as we do that everyone loves music, or that 'music is the international language.'

We will expect the early Church Fathers, in their battle against the 'pagan,' to find much to fault in music. But how does one explain the extraordinary lack in faith in and hostility toward music which is voiced among these philosophers? Since we must assume their views were based on their own experience, perhaps these views reflect the significant decline in the quality of musical performance which is mentioned by many writers from about the third century BC. This seems to be suggested by Philodemus' comments that 'music was first approved and then rejected' and that 'possibly others had found music a profitless pursuit even before.'[55] Sextus Empiricus is more specific in his condemnation of contemporary music.

55 Quoted in Warren D. Anderson, *Ethos and Education in Greek Music* (Cambridge: Harvard University Press, 1966), 153.

> Nor ... ought we to run down the ancient music because the present-day music is hackneyed and effeminate, when the Athenians, who devote great care to temperance, appreciating the dignity of music have handed it down to their descendants as a most necessary branch of learning. A witness to this is the poet of the Old Comedy, who says,
>
> > I will now relate from the start the life which I have provided for mortals.

> The first rule was that none should hear from an urchin the sound of a mutter,
> Next, they must walk in order good on their way to their master of music.
>
> Hence, even if music now weakens the mind by its effeminate tunes and womanish rhythms, this is no argument against the ancient and virile music.[56]

The discovery in Herculaneum of fragments of a first century book, *On Music*, by the Epicurean philosopher, Philodemus of Gadara, has provided us with the first of these unusually negative assessments of music. We know of no other early philosopher who maintains, for example, that music lacks even the power to arouse or soothe emotions![57]

Among Philodemus' list of indictments against music are musicians who 'produce pieces which are devoid of significance [such as] instrumental music and trilling'[58] and the fact that music naturally 'equates with disorderliness and lack of restraint.'[59]

Music, he says, has no serious value, 'on the contrary, most of it ends up at dinner parties.'[60] Its function, he continues, must therefore be to give pleasure. But it is only a very simple and low level of pleasure,

> a direct titillation of the ear in which the mind has no share, analogous to the taste of pleasant food and drink.[61]

If there is any value in such a primitive level of pleasure, it would be one appropriate only to the common masses. Here, as well as in the following quotation, the reader can see an example of the evidence which can be found that suggests real aesthetic concerts continued into the Middle Ages, a fact almost impossible to discover in modern texts.

> The conclusion that music is profitable does not obtain. If it actually does profit any group, that group is the common people. And the common people are not profited by every kind of music; nor is this true of the quantity of very elaborate music that is heard … and not by all but some Greeks, and under certain circumstances, and … now through hired performers.[62]

Certainly a man of the upper class should not spend his time going to hear concerts—they last too long, wasting valuable time,

---

56 Sextus Empiricus, 'Against the Musicians,' in *Against the Professors*, VI, 14.

57 Quoted in L. P. Wilkinson, 'Philodemus on Ethos in Music,' *Classical Quarterly* 32 (1938), 174. An extant poem by Philodemus demonstrates that the philosopher was not immune to love. Here he seems to give testimony to the power of romantic music, although he notes he does not understand how it works!

> Xanthippe's touch on the lyre, and her talk, and her speaking eyes, and her singing, and the fire is just alight, will burn thee, my heart, but from what beginning or when or how I know not. Thou, unhappy heart, shalt know when thou are smoldering. [*Greek Anthology*, V, 131.]

58 Wilkinson, 'Philodemus on Ethos in Music,' 175.

59 Anderson, *Ethos and Education in Greek Music*, 163.

60 Ibid., 167.

61 Wilkinson, 'Philodemus on Ethos in Music,' 179.

62 Anderson, *Ethos and Education in Greek Music*, 166.

and they are exhausting and cause our attention to wander. And, in addition, there is no point in actually learning to perform music when there are already so many concerts available.

> It is a sign that men are poor-spirited and have nothing worth while with which to occupy themselves—for why should I say, 'make themselves happy?'—if they labor to learn music for the sake of providing pleasure for themselves in the future, and do not realize what a wealth of recitals is provided publicly, and the chance that we have of sharing in them continually in the city, if we wish; and if they fail to consider that when it goes on for long it exhausts our powers and begins to pall, so that often when performances are long drawn out our attention wanders. Not to mention the fact that the pleasure is not necessary, and that the process of learning and practice that our enjoyment involves is laborious, and cuts out the things most important to our well-being; nor the impropriety of singing like any boy or actively playing the lyre.[63]

Philodemus also sees no social value for the educated person in even acquiring an understanding of music. In his opinion, it doesn't even serve to make a good topic for conversation!

> To have something to say and start the ball rolling at parties and other gatherings is not a peculiar gift (of musical knowledge), and it is not, as we decided, a thing valued by all; perhaps it might even provoke laughter if a philosopher were to indulge in it; and the theoretical side is not understood by most people, and, if it is to be mastered, demands trouble, which is a departure from the things that make for happiness.[64]

As a philosopher, Philodemus did make two important observations regarding the universality of music. First, he seemed to have come to the correct view that there is a genetic aspect of music and he found significance for this in the fact that an infant (presumed to have no Reason) was clearly affected.

> We have an innate affinity with the Muses, one which does not have to be learned. This is clearly shown by the way infants are lulled to sleep with wordless singing.[65]

It was his next observation which led Philodemus down a wrong path. We know today that music does communicate on both a general and an individual basis. Philodemus's error was that he was

---

63 Wilkinson, 'Philodemus on Ethos in Music,' 180.

64 Ibid., 181.

65 Anderson, *Ethos and Education in Greek Music*, 173.

aware of only the latter. He had noticed that, 'not everyone will be moved in the same way by the same music.'[66] He believed that the differing reactions which listeners had to music was due not to the music itself, or anything in it, but simply to the varying moods of the listeners themselves. He failed to understand that it is the experience of the listener which affects his perception.

[66] Ibid., 172.

> Now with regard to these things it is possible for varying impressions to be received corresponding to predispositions; but with regard to the actual hearing there is no difference whatsoever, all having the same perceptions of the same melody and deriving like pleasure from it; thus both in the case of the Enharmonic and the Chromatic scale people differ, not in respect of the irrational perception, but in respect of their opinions, some, like Diogenes, saying that the Enharmonic is solemn and noble and straightforward and pure, and the Chromatic unmanly and vulgar and mean, while others call the Enharmonic severe and despotic, and the Chromatic mild and persuasive; both sides importing ideas which do not belong to either scale by nature. Whereas the more scientific [modern] thinkers bid us cull from each what pleases the ear, thinking that none of the qualities imputed belongs to either by its nature.[67]

[67] Wilkinson, 'Philodemus on Ethos in Music,' 177.

He assumed, therefore, that music must not communicate anything real or anything of substance. If it did, everyone would receive the same communication. He is wrong, of course, for music could not communicate anything, even pleasure, were it not through the actual musical materials themselves.

In any case, we can see here the perspective from which he wrote his book, which is primarily a strong attack against the long held educational idea that music can influence character. Indeed, the very pretext for writing this book seems to have been a rebuttal to a book by the Stoic philosopher, Diogenes, who had lived a century earlier, and who had contended that the correct use of music, 'will create a disposition which is harmonious and rhythmic in the highest degree.'[68] Regarding this well-known Greek association of music and character, Philodemus quotes an anecdote, for which Diogenes was apparently the source, of a painter who could only capture the correct character of his subject through listening to music as he worked. Perhaps in seeking another opportunity to denounce the ideas of Diogenes, Philodemus pretends to miss the real point.

[68] Anderson, *Ethos and Education in Greek Music*, 159.

Presumably Diogenes did not suppose that music endows men with added technical proficiency. If he did, he was simpleminded.[69]

Philodemus was, in fact, well acquainted with the Greek association of music and character, as the following demonstrates.

> (They have proposed the theory) that every mode has a Tonos which relates to the emotions assumed to be present [in it]. Melodic composition, rhythms, and the rest are dealt with similarly. Therefore, as they maintain, our inner attitudes become familiarized with the modes in a kind of rapture (literally, 'in the manner of one who is *entheos*,' who has the god within him).[70]

For Philodemus these kinds of ideas could not be supported by Reason. This entire body of Greek philosophical claims, he pronounces, is 'filled full of "divine" inspiration and varnishing over, in a way that has no reason or order.'[71] Indeed, he says, they were attempting to credit music with something which only Reason can accomplish.

> As for those who say that music makes us gentle, softening our spirit and taking away its savageness, one must consider them utter fools; for it is only the instruction of reason which accomplishes this.[72]

He is particularly enthusiastic in his denunciation of any notion that music can promote action.

> And therefore the musical specialist who seeks the kind of understanding that will enable him to discern the nature of the various kinds of sense perception is looking for precise knowledge in things which do not have it, and his teaching on this matter is empty of meaning. The fact is that no melody, as melody (that is, with an irrational nature), rouses the soul from immobility and repose and brings it toward its natural ethical disposition, any more than it soothes or sets at rest the soul that is carried away by frenzy ... Nor does melody have the power to divert the soul from one impulse to another or to cause intensification or lessening of the state in which the soul may find itself. For music is not an imitative thing, as some foolishly claim; nor does it, as Diogenes supposes, contain ethical likenesses that are non-imitative while showing in full all such ethical qualities ... as magnificence and humbleness of spirit, or manliness and its opposite, or orderliness and boldness. This is no more true of music that it would be of cooking.[73]

---

69 Ibid., 167. A first century poem by Lucilius tells of another painter who had a somewhat similar difficulty, 'Eutychus the painter was the father of twenty sons, but never got a likeness even among his children.' [*Greek Anthology*, IV, 215]

70 Ibid., 158.

71 Ibid., 171.

72 Ibid., 168.

73 Ibid., 164.

Taken as it reads, Philodemus is mostly correct, but the problem is that he is describing only secondary influences and values which music might have. The real value of music is none of those he discusses, its value lies in its ability to promote and facilitate self-awareness and personal Truth through contemplation.

In another reference to this same idea, Philodemus curiously refuses to believe that even the human face is a reflection of inner emotions. Today, of course, all psychologists are aware that the face not only expresses emotions in man, prenatal man, and even animals, but that the expressions together with their associated emotions are *universal*. Philodemus writes,

> Inducing to action means impulse and choice; but melody does not, like reason, impel us rationally or implant a choice. [It is absurd to say that music] somehow affects the disposition not only of the body but of the mind as well. How can it even be claimed that the body is affected? A singer's altered facial expression does not prove this.[74]

In the view of Philodemus, if music could be said to have any effect on man whatsoever, it was not the music itself but the words which the music accompanied, particularly in the case of the use of music by the Greeks to inculcate religious attitudes in the young.[75]

Philodemus attacks even Diogenes' suggestion that in erotic poetry music has the power to stimulate. It was not the melodies of Ibycus, Anacreon and others who corrupted the young, says, Philodemus, but their words.[76]

Thus one can understand how Philodemus could find no independent place in education for music. He would have us believe that his view was widely shared.

> Many say that those who lack natural capacity are not made one whit better by music.[77]

Regarding music's place in education, he proposes that while music itself cannot educate, it can serve as a vehicle to aid rational processes.

> It is not the theoretical knowledge of good and bad or suitable and unsuitable melodies that educates, but philosophy working through literary and musical training.[78]

---

74 Ibid., 165, the final two sentences being paraphrases by Anderson.

75 A reference to the young Roman Christian Church.

76 Ibid., 170.

77 Ibid., 174.

78 Ibid., 175.

As we shall see below, this is an early expression of a line of thought which, however indirect, would be responsible for preserving the great writings of the liberal arts during the Dark Ages.

The second treatise which we have mentioned which is thoroughly negative toward music, is the 'Against the Musicians,' by the second-century philosopher, Sextus Empiricus.

Empiricus begins by noting that at his time the term 'Music' was used in three meanings. First, as a science 'dealing with melodies and notes and rhythm-making and similar things.' Second, to connote instrumental skill, 'as when we describe those who use auloi and harps as musicians.'

> It is with these significations that the term 'Music' is properly and generally used.

And, finally, as an adjective referring to the other arts. 'Thus we speak of a work as 'musical,' even though it be a piece of painting.'[79]

The plan of this treatise is to first list the characteristics which most people praise in music, the views, he admits, the majority of people hold. He will then set out to prove that each of these views is false. We will summarize the positive characteristics[80] he mentions and then devote more attention to his refutation of them.

First, like philosophy, most people believe that music helps in 'regulating human life and repressing the passions of the soul.' Here he quotes the often related story that Pythagoras once calmed some youths, who 'were in a state of Bacchic frenzy' from drinking, by having an aulos player perform a 'spondean' melody, whereupon they suddenly became sober.

Second, that 'Music gives sober sense to those lacking in sense and incites the cowards to courage,' as in the use of music in the military. He recalls that ancient literature often mentions that it was for this reason that the heroes, when leaving on a long voyage, left the musicians as the most trusty guardians of their wives.

Third is the role of music in education, in forming character. Here he quotes the anecdote of Socrates who began the study of music as an old man. When someone made fun of him, he responded, 'that it was better to be accused of being late-learned than unlearned.'

The fourth concerns the role of music in poetry. We quote his remarks here to remind the reader that most poetry was still sung.

79 Empiricus, 'Against the Musicians,' VI, 1.

80 Ibid., VI, 7ff.

> If poetry is useful for life, and music appears to adorn it by its melodies and by making it fit for singing, then music will be beneficial. And, of course, the poets are called 'tune-makers,' and of old the verses of Homer were sung to the lyre. So likewise were the songs and choral odes of the tragic poets.

The fifth, is concerning the use of music in religious ceremonies, to 'incite the mind to emulate the good.'

The sixth, and last, regards the use of music as 'a consolation to those in grief; and for this reason those who are trying to lighten the grief of mourners sing for them to the aulos.'

Now Empiricus begins his refutation of all these attributions,[81] beginning with the notion that music helps in 'regulating human life and repressing the passions of the soul.' Here he says he does not concede that any melody has, in itself, any particular quality, 'that some tunes are in their nature stimulating, others repressive.'

> In the case of musical tunes it is not by nature that some are of this kind and others of that kind, but it is we ourselves who suppose them to be such. Thus the same tune serves to excite horses, but not at all to excite men who hear it in a theater.

And, he says, it may not actually excite the horses, only distract them. This becomes his principle refutation, that music only distracts. Thus the drunken youths, in the Pythagoras story, only experienced a momentarily moderating influence of the music, soon thereafter to return to their original state.

> As to Pythagoras, in the first place he was foolish in desiring to render drunkards sober at the wrong moment, instead of quitting the place; and secondly, by trying to reform them in this way he confesses that flute players have more influence than philosophers for the reforming of morals.

He also mentions, in this regard, that this is the reason why men who engage in 'toilsome work' often sing, 'to divert their minds from the distress caused by their work.'

This is the same reason why he rejects any notion that music can supply courage in the soldier, rather, he says, it merely diverts his attention from the realities of battle. Regarding the stories of the heroes leaving their wives with musicians, as 'sober-minded guardians,' this is, he says, 'the fictions of story-tellers.'

[81] Ibid., VI, 19ff.

With regard to the role of music and poetry, anyone who sees utility in music in this regard is 'simple-minded.' For Empiricus, the fact that poetry has words gives it a substance which cannot be proven in music.

> One can argue that poetry is useless, and prove equally well that while music, being concerned with melody only, naturally serves to give pleasure, poetry which is concerned with thought as well, is able to be of benefit and teach prudence.

Empiricus at this point seems to lose interest and breaks off with his refutation of the above listed positive characteristics presumed of music. Instead, he turns his attention to the question: Does the performer benefit more from music than the non-performer who only listens to music? His real concern here is with regard to the reputed ability of music to improve the character, because if this is true, then the performer has a distinct advantage over the non-trained listener. This, again, makes no sense to Empiricus.

> Firstly, the pleasure felt by ordinary people is not inevitable as are those caused by food, drink and warmth after hunger, thirst and cold; and secondly, even if they are inevitable we can enjoy them without musical skill.

He provides here the example of the infant who is 'lulled to sleep by listening to a tuneful cradle song,' yet obviously has no skill in music.

> And for this reason it may be that, just as we enjoy tasting food or wine though without the art of cooking food or that of wine-tasting, so also, though without the art of music, we take pleasure in hearing a delightful melody; for though the expert musician understands that it is artistically performed better than the ordinary man, he gets from it no greater feeling of pleasure.

From this observation, Empiricus concludes that there is no evidence that music leads one either to wisdom or virtue. Indeed, he believes, music often has the effect of 'making young people easily led into incontinence and debauchery.'

Finally, Empiricus indulges in a bit of circuitous nonsense, the kind of philosophizing which the Christian writers complain about—philosophy which proves nothing. His intent is to prove that music does not exist.

First he surveys the elements of music, notes, intervals, and 'Ethos.'

> Just as every interval in music consists of notes, so also does every 'Ethos' (or 'character'); and it is a certain 'Genus' of melody. For just as of human characters some are gloomy and stubborn, such as those of the ancients are reported to have been, while others yield easily to lusts and debauchery and lamentations and groanings, so a certain kind of melody produces in the soul stately and refined motions, another kind motions that are base and ignoble. Melody of this sort is called, in general, by the Musicians 'Ethos' from the fact that it is productive of 'character'.[82]

If music exists, says Empiricus, everything must be based on the individual note. He then offers the following reasoning illustrating that notes do not exist. The Cyrenaic philosophers say only feelings exist, nothing else. Democritus says sense-objects do not exist, hence neither sound. If sound exists, it must be either incorporeal or corporeal and the Stoics prove it is not the former and the Peripatetics demonstrate it is not the latter. He continues in this vein and finally concludes,

> Now, then, as sound does not exist, neither does the note ... and when the note does not exist, neither does the musical interval exist, nor symphony, nor melody, nor the Genera formed by these. Therefore, Music does not exist either.[83]

But our faithless philosopher is not satisfied by stopping there. Next he offers a series of arguments intended to demonstrate that rhythm and time do not exist. Here is his conclusion to the first of these arguments.

> If time is anything, it is either limited or unlimited. But it is not limited, since, if so, we shall be saying that there was once a time when time did not exist, and that there will sometime be a time when time will not exist. Nor is it unlimited; for a part of it is past, a part future, and if each of these does not exist time is limited, and if each does exist, then both the past and the future will exist in the present, which is absurd. Therefore time does not exist.[84]

---

82 Ibid., VI 48.

83 Ibid., VI, 58.

84 Ibid., VI, 62. In this writer's book, 'Outlines of Pyrrhonism,' III, 239–273, he 'proves,' in a similar fashion that nothing can be taught and that neither teacher nor student exists.

3 POETS OF THE FIRST THREE CENTURIES

Relatively little Greek poetry is extant from the early Christian era, much of it being merely epigrams or material collected from tombstones. Among this fragmentary repertoire we can still find poems commemorating the lyric poets, the great poet-musicians of the seventh and sixth centuries BC. This tribute to Alcman, by Antipater of Thessalonica, is interesting for its suggestion that such material was internationally known by an early date.

> Do not judge the man by the stone. Simple is the tomb to look on, but holds the bones of a great man. Thou shalt know Alcman the supreme striker of the Laconian lyre, possessed by the nine Muses. Here resteth he, a cause of dispute to two continents, if he be a Lydian or a Spartan. Minstrels have many mothers.[1]

Another tribute to the same lyric poet is somewhat more humorous.

> Alcman the graceful, the swan-singer of wedding hymns, who made music worth of the Muses, lieth in this tomb, a great ornament to Sparta, or perhaps at the end he threw off his burden and went to Hell.[2]

These final Greek poets shared with the older lyric poets the tales of the Muses as themes for their work. Here, the first-century poet Tullius Sabinus tells a story of a mouse killed by the lyre of Apollo (also known as Phoebus) who was a God of both the bow and the lyre.

> A mouse once, lickerish of every kind of food and not even shy of the mouse trap, but one who won booty even from death, gnawed through Phoebus' melodious lyre string. The strained chord springing up to the bridge of the lyre, throttled the mouse. We wonder at the bow's good aim; but Phoebus uses his lyre, too, as a weapon wherewith to aim well at his enemies.[3]

1 *Greek Anthology*, VII, 18.

2 Leonidas of Alexandria, in ibid., VII, 19. A half-starved Grammarian sent a little poem to the Emperor Hadrian reading, 'The half of me is dead, and starvation is subduing the other half. Save, Sire, a musical semitone of me.' The emperor told him, in the metaphors of the Greeks, to go to Hell, 'Thou does wrong both Pluto and the Sun by looking still on the latter and failing to go to the former.' Ibid., IX, 137.

3 Ibid., IX, 410.

A few poems from first-century tombs have preserved for us the names of performers, as in the case of this aulos player.

> Orpheus won the highest prize among mortals by his harp, Nestor by the skill of his sweet-phrased tongue, divine Homer, the learned in lore, by the art of his verse, but Telephanes, whose tomb this is, by the aulos.[4]

4 Nicarchus, ibid., VII, 159.

One poem honors a first-century lyre player named, Plato, who seems to have been a specialist in the performance of earlier music.

> When Orpheus departed, perchance some Muse survived, but at thy death, Plato, the lyre ceased to sound. For in thy mind and in thy fingers there yet survived some little fragment at least of ancient music.[5]

5 Leontius Scholasticus, ibid., VII, 571.

We have a tragic poem of the second century which refers to the suicide of a musician, but also provides interesting detail of the several musical instruments he played during his career.

> Clytosthenes, his feet that raced in fury now enfeebled by age, dedicates to thee, Rhea of the lion-car, his tambourines beaten by the hand, his shrill hollow-rimmed cymbals, his aulos that calls through its horn, on which he once made shrieking music, twisting his neck about, and the two-edged knife with which he opened his veins.[6]

6 Philippus of Thessalonica, in ibid., VI, 94. The reference to the aulos 'with horn' describes a bell of animal horn which had begun to be used in Rome after the first century AD.

The most important poem which is extant from the first three centuries is the 'Daphnis and Chloe' by Longus. This is a poem entirely in the spirit of the ancient poems of Greece and it is therefore no surprise to find the principal musical instrument is the rural panpipe. We read here, once again, the myth of the invention of this instrument.

> This panpipe of ours was originally not a musical instrument but a beautiful girl who had a lovely voice. She used to graze goats and play with the Nymphs and sing—just as she does now. While she was grazing and playing and singing, Pan came up to her and tried to talk her into doing what he wanted by promising to make all her she-goats have twins. But she laughed at his love and said she didn't want a lover who was neither one thing nor the other—neither a goat nor a man. So Pan started chasing her with the intention of offering her violence. She started running away, and when she was tired of running away from Pan and his violence she hid among some reeds and disappeared into a marsh. Pan angrily cut the reeds—but he didn't find the girl. So profiting by this experience he fastened some

of the reeds together with wax—using reeds of unequal length since even Love had proved unequal to them—and thus invented the musical instrument.[7]

We learn here of a shepherd who broke his panpipes, because 'they charmed my cows,' but didn't have an effect on the girl.[8] And in another passage we find an erotic employment of the panpipe.

> And he used to give her lessons in playing the panpipe, and the moment she had begun to blow into it he would snatch it away and run his own lips over the reeds. This was supposed to show her where she had gone wrong, but actually it was a good excuse to kiss Chloe *via* the pipe.[9]

We read of the shepherd's goats being charmed by the panpipes[10] and, indeed, during a description of a 'concert' for fifty-two goats, it would appear that the animals had been trained to respond to a number of specific goat tunes.

> Daphnis made [the goats] sit down like the audience at a theater, and standing under the oak he produced his panpipe from his knapsack and began by blowing on it softly—and the goats raised their heads and stood still. Then he blew the grazing tune—and the goats put their heads down and started to graze. He played another tune, very sweet and clear—and they all lay down. He also piped a shrill sort of tune—and they ran away into the wood as though a wolf was approaching.[11] A little later he sounded a recall—and they came running out of the wood and collected round his feet. You would not have found even human slaves being so obedient to their master's orders.[12]

One of the most familiar themes in earlier Greek rural poems was the music contest. While a god was often the adjudicator of these mythical contests, here the cows are the judges.

> Once upon a time there was a beautiful girl who used to graze a great many cows in a wood. Now she was also very musical, and in her day cows enjoyed music. So she was able to control them without either hitting them with a staff or pricking them with a goad. She would simply sit down under a pine, and after crowning herself with pine-twigs would sing the story of Pan and the Pine, and the cows would stay close enough to hear her voice. A boy who grazed cows not far away, and who was also good-looking and musical, chal-

---

[7] Longus, *Daphnis and Chloe*, II, 34.

[8] Ibid., II, 7.

[9] Ibid., I, 24.

[10] Ibid., I, 22.

[11] In another place, II, 26, Longus mentions that the panpipe could be as frightening as a trumpet.

[12] Ibid., IV, 15. In bk I, 29, we also read of cows being trained to respond to the panpipe.

lenged her to a singing contest. Because of his sex, he was able to produce more volume than she could, and yet because he was only a boy, his voice had a very sweet tone. So he charmed away her eight best cows and enticed them into his own herd. The girl was annoyed at the damage done to her herd, and at being beaten at singing, and she prayed to the gods to turn her into a bird before she arrived home. The gods granted her prayer and turned her into this mountain bird, which is as musical as she was. And even now she still goes on singing, telling her sad story, and saying that she's looking for her missing cows.[13]

A final story told in this poem is a very lovely myth concerning the origin of the echo.

There are several kinds of Nymphs. There are the Nymphs of the Ash, the Nymphs of the Oak, and the Nymphs of the Meadow. All of them are beautiful and all are musical. Well, one of these Nymphs had a daughter called Echo, who was mortal because her father was mortal, but beautiful because her mother was beautiful. She was brought up by the Nymphs and taught by the Muses to play the pipe and the flute, to perform upon the lute and the lyre, and to sing songs of every kind. So when she grew up and reached the flower of girlhood, she used to dance with the Nymphs and sing with the Muses. But she avoided all males, whether human or divine, for she loved virginity. Pan grew angry with the girl, partly because he envied her gift for music, and partly because he had failed to enjoy her beauty. So he sent the shepherds and goatherds mad, and they like dogs or wolves tore her to pieces and scattered her limbs about the whole earth—or rather scattered her hymns, for she still went on singing. As a favor to the Nymphs, the Earth concealed these singing limbs and preserved their music; and they, by order of the Muses, are still able to sing and imitate sounds of every kind, just as the girl did once—sounds made by gods, by men, by musical instruments, and by wild beasts. They even imitate Pan when he plays his pipe, and he, when he hears them, jumps up and goes rushing over the mountains in pursuit. But the only love that he pursues is Knowledge—he would love to know who his invisible imitator is.[14]

---

13 Ibid., I, 37. In bk I, 9, we read of birds teaching Nymphs to sing.

14 Ibid., III, 23.

ON THE AESTHETICS OF MUSIC

One of the most frequently cited purposes of music in all early literature is to soothe the feelings of those who are sad. The first-century poet, Cyrus, wished for skill in music for this purpose.

> Would that my father had taught me to shepherd fleecy flocks, so that, sitting under the elms or piping under a rock, I might cheer my sorrows with music.[15]

15 *The Greek Anthology*, IX, 136.

In the second-century poem, 'Daphnis and Chloe,' there is a description of a rural pan-pipe player which seems to carry, in its appreciation for his musicianship, rather than mere virtuosity, an unusual insight into the aesthetic value of performance from the perspective of this listener.

> So Philetas roused himself, and got up and sat on a chair. First of all he tested the reeds to see if they were in proper condition for playing. Then, having made sure that the air could pass freely through them, he began to play with a loud and powerful tone. You would have thought you were listening to several flutes playing in unison, so great a volume of sound did he produce. Then with a gradual *diminuendo* he changed to a sweeter tune, and showing his skill in every form of pastoral melody he played music that would be suitable for a herd of cattle, music that would be appropriate for goats, and music that would appeal to a flock of sheep. The tune for sheep was sweet, the tune for cattle was loud, and the tune for goats was shrill. In short, with that one pipe he imitated all the pipes in the world.[16]

16 Longus, *Daphnis & Chloe*, II, 35.

There are many references in ancient literature which attribute to performers of Art Music a certain 'divine connection.' We have suggested in the first volume of this series that the root of this perhaps might be found in the fact that Music, unlike the other arts, cannot be seen, although its effect on the listener is visible. In addition, we have pointed out that the similarity of these two characteristics with the mysteries of religion must have been significant to the ancients. Indeed, a third-century Church philosopher, Lactantius, confirms this association.

> His offering is innocence of soul; His sacrifice praise and a hymn. For if God is not seen, He ought therefore to be worshipped with things which are not seen.[17]

17 Lactantius, 'The Divine Institutes,' in *The Works of Lactantius*, trans., William Fletcher (Edinburgh: T. & T. Clark, 1886), I, 420.

A first-century poet, Archias, mentions this divine connection in his ode to song birds.

A blackbird, driven over the hedge together with field-sares, entered the hollow of the suspended net. The cords from which there is no escape caught and held fast the whole flock of them, but let the blackbird alone go free from the meshes. Of a truth the race of singers is holy. Even deaf traps show fond care for winged songsters.[18]

18 Ibid., IX, 343.

4 CHURCH PHILOSOPHERS OF THE FIRST THREE CENTURIES

FROM OUR DISTANT PERSPECTIVE, many people assume that the new Christian Church was founded immediately after the death of Christ and grew in a steady, uninterrupted fashion until the present day. Actually, while there was a remarkably wide spread of Christianity during the first three centuries, it was a church divided on many fronts. There was not one Christian church, but many branches, or factions, so many that one writer in the year 187 AD counted twenty different Christian Churches and a writer in 384 AD found eighty.[1]

It must have also been very difficult, at first, to maintain discipline among the early Christians, especially as the anticipated reappearance of Christ failed to occur. An anonymous poem of the early second century, 'The Shepherd of Hermas,' complains that one is beginning to see among Christians the re-emergence of pagan customs, including rouge, dyed hair, painted eyelids, drunkenness, avarice, and adultery.[2]

It was against this background, then, that the early Church leaders and philosophers struggled to create the Church as we know it. In order to facilitate the growth of the new religion, the early Church Fathers had two paramount challenges. First, they had to finally overcome a 'pagan' intellectual environment which had roots a thousand years old. Hence they immediately commenced their attack on education, philosophy, poetry, music and all forms of entertainment known to their contemporaries—in short, everything we think of as the glorious traditions of ancient Greek and Roman culture. And, in the end, the Church was successful; the Church won! Her victory we call today, 'The Dark Ages.'

Second, in order to successfully take all these things away from the people, it was necessary to re-invent the people. The new Christian would need to be a different, and more austere, kind of person. Physically, St. Basil described him thus:

[1] Will Durant, *Caesar and Christ* (New York: Simon and Schuster, 1944), 616.

[2] Quoted in ibid., 599.

> As plumpness and a healthy color betoken the athlete, so leanness of body and the pallor produced by the exercise of continency mark the Christian.[3]

It was recommended that proper deportment should preclude the Christian even laughing!

> Indulging in unrestrained and immoderate laughter is a sign of intemperance, of a want of control over one's emotions, and of failure to repress the soul's frivolity by a stern use of reason ... Moreover, Jesus appears to have experienced those emotions which are of necessity associated with the body ... but, so far as we know from the story of the Gospel, He never laughed.[4]

Needless to say, anything touching on carnal love was discouraged in the Christian. For example, the second-century Church Father, Saint Cyprian, admonishes,

> For God has indeed given man a voice, and yet he should not sing love songs and songs that are coarse.[5]

Another Church writer of this same century criticizes women for singing love songs.

> You are rejecting the law when you wish to please the world. You dance in your houses; instead of psalms, you sing love songs.[6]

Not satisfied with discouraging further interest in the old pagan philosophies, the Church urged the new Christian to let the Church do his thinking for him. Once you believe, the second-century Church Father, Tertullian says, search no further. You should accept the Church's answers and curiosity ought not to range beyond it. Such restless curiosity, the feature of heresy, is never gratified.[7] Basil is more to the point: Don't question the Church authorities!

> No one is to concern himself with the superior's method of administration or make curious inquiries about what is being done.[8]

Thus, Clement gives a new Christian interpretation of the most famous phrase of Greek antiquity, 'Know thyself.'

> And the maxim 'Know thyself' means here to know for what we are born. And we are born to obey the commandments.[9]

---

3 St. Basil, 'The Long Rules,' trans. Sister Monica Wagner, in *Saint Basil Ascetical Works* (New York: Fathers of the Church, Inc., 1950), 273.

4 Ibid., 271. Basil further cites Luke 6:25, 'Woe to you that laugh now, for you shall mourn and weep.' Clement of Alexandria, *The Instructor*, trans. William Wilson (Edinburgh: T. & T. Clark, 1884), 219ff, makes a similar injunction against laughter.

5 Saint Cyprian, *On the Dress of Virgins*, trans. Sister Angela E. Keenan (New York, Fathers of the Church, Inc., 1958), 11.

6 Commodianus, 'In Favor of Christian Discipline,' quoted in *The Writings of Tertullianus* (Edinburgh: T. & T. Clark, 1895), 464.

7 Tertullian, 'On Prescription Against Heretics,' trans. Alexander Roberts in *Ante-Nicene Christian Library* (Edinburgh: T. & T. Clark, 1884), XIff.

8 St. Basil, 'The Long Rules,' 326.

9 Clement of Alexandria, *The Miscellanies*, trans. Alexander Roberts (Edinburgh: T. & T. Clark, 1869), XII, bk. VII, p. 420.

Another perspective for understanding what the early Church leaders desired in their followers, is obtainable by looking at those elements of contemporary life which they wished to eliminate.

ART MUSIC

In the early Greek literature we read of impressive music festivals, musical contests and theater productions in which art music was an important element. In the succeeding centuries it appears that these festivals had evolved into lower and lower forms and we read of the disappointment of the later Greek philosophers and of the outrage of the Church philosophers.

The large festival was a particular target of the Church, for by the second century AD, these festivals were still popular. They were a rival of the Church in the competition for the attention of the public. Justin Martyr admonished the Greeks at this time as follows:

> I have come to detest even your public festivals. There you indulge in immoderate banquets, listen to finely polished pipes which incite you to lustful actions, and you needlessly submit to elaborate anointing with perfume, while your heads are crowned with flowers. With such an accumulation of evil practices you determine your reverence. With such practices are your minds filled, while your intemperance excites you to Bacchic frenzy, whence you indulge in your customary unholy and mad intercourse. I would like to make another observation. Why do you, who are Greeks, become angered when your son, in imitation of Jupiter, turns against you and robs you of your own wife? ... Why do you complain of your wife's infidelity, yet honor Venus with temples? If these events had been narrated by others, they could be presumed to have been false and slanderous accusations, but even now your own poets extol them in song, and your histories blatantly describe them.[10]

A similar description by Minucius Felix suggests how a 'pagan' might have responded to the Christians.

> Look: you Christians are menaced with threats, torments and tortures ... And where is that god of yours who can help those who come to life again, but cannot help those who are alive? ...
> But in the meantime, in your anxious state of expectation, you refrain from honest pleasures: you do not go to our shows, you

10 Justin Martyr, 'Discourse to the Greeks,' trans. Thomas B. Fall, in *Saint Justin Martyr* (New York: Christian Heritage, 1948), IV. Born, ca. 100 AD, St. Justin was one of the first important defenders of the Christian faith against non-Christians and enemies of the Church.

take no part in our processions, you are not present at our public banquets, you shrink in horror from our sacred games, from food ritually dedicated by our priests, from drink hallowed by libation poured upon our altars. Such is your dread of the very gods you deny.

You do not bind your head with flowers, you do not honor your body with perfumes; ointments you reserve for funerals, but even to your tombs you deny garlands; you anemic, neurotic creatures, you indeed deserve to be pitied—but by our gods. The result is, you pitiable fools, that you have no enjoyment of life while you wait for the new life which you will never have.

And so, if you do have any trace of sense or shame, stop prying into the tracks of heaven, the destinies and the mysteries of the universe. Keep your eyes fixed on where you walk—that's employment enough for utter boors and yokels, ungraced by any manners or culture. If you have not been privileged to understand the concerns of a citizen, you most surely have been denied discussion of the affairs of heaven.[11]

11 Marcus Minucius Felix, *Octavius*, trans. G. W. Clarke (New York: Newman Press, 1974), XII, 4.

The third century Church philosopher, Novatian, attacks all kinds of Greek festivals for having at their core some form of idolatry.

The celebrated Grecian contests—whether they deal with poetry, or musical instrumentation, or speech, or feats of strength—have diverse demons as their patrons. And anything else that draws the eyes and soothes the ears of the spectators has at bottom either an idol, or a demon, or some deceased person … [The devil] combined idolatry with the spectacles so that idolatry would be loved through the pleasure that the spectacles afforded.[12]

12 Novatian, 'The Spectacles,' trans. Russell J. DeSimone, in *Fathers of the Church* (Washington, DC: The Catholic University of America Press, 1947), IV, 5.

The productions of the theater, in which music also played a fundamental role, were attacked by the early Christian writers for the same reason. Tertullian provides some interesting background on this association.

When Pompey the Great, a man who was surpassed only by his theater in greatness, had erected that citadel of all vile practices, he was afraid that some day the censors would condemn his memory. He therefore built on top of it a shrine to Venus, and when he summoned the people by edict to its dedication, he termed it not a theater, but a temple of Venus, 'under which,' he said, 'we have put tiers of seats for viewing the shows.'[13]

13 Tertullian, 'Spectacles,' trans. Rudolph Arbesmann in *Disciplinary, Moral and Ascetical Works* (New York: Fathers of the Church, 1959), X, 5. Tertullian, born ca. 160, was the son of a Roman Centurion, who studied rhetoric and practiced law in Rome before being converted to Christianity in mid-life. In his old age he embraced the faction called Montanism.

He also makes an interesting passing reference to the tradition of the theater procession, in which the actors and their company would proceed through the town as a means of drawing spectators. This was a tradition that continued in Western Europe for some time.

> A procession is held to the theater from the temples and altars, with that whole wretched business of incense and blood, to the tune of auloi and trumpets, under the direction of the two most polluted masters of ceremonies at funerals and sacrifices: the undertaker and soothsayer.[14]

Tertullian summarizes the productions of the theater, together with its music, as follows:

> Those features which are peculiar to, and characteristic of, the stage, that wantonness in gesture and posture, they dedicate to Venus and Liber, deities both dissolute: the former by sex perversion, the latter by effeminate dress.
> And all else that is performed with voice and melodies, instruments and musical notation, belongs to the Apollos and the Muses, the Minervas and Mercuries.[15]

In a sarcastic vein, he wonders how any Christian who might be present can watch this and keep his mind on appropriate thoughts.

> But, while the tragic actor is ranting, our good friend will probably recall the outcries of some prophet! Amid the strains of the effeminate aulos player, he will no doubt meditate on a psalm![16]

Merely by being present, Tertullian warns, the Christian is damned—for he cannot hide!

> What will you do when you are caught in that surging tide of wicked applause? Not that you are likely to suffer anything at the hands of men … but consider how you would fare in heaven. Do you doubt that at the very moment when the Devil is raging in his assembly, all the angels look forth from heaven and note down every individual who has uttered blasphemy, who has listened to it, who has lent his tongue, who has lent his ears to the service of the Devil against God?[17]

---

[14] Ibid., X, 2. In VII, 2, Tertullian describes more extensive processions to the circus, which included civic officials and various institutions of the city, again a familiar tradition throughout the Middle Ages. He also mentions that plays were already advertised through the use of posters.

[15] Ibid., X, 8. In Greek mythology Apollo was the god of music and patron of the voice, the Muses were in charge of music and dramatic performances; Minerva made the first flute and was the guardian of musical instruments; and Mercury, having invented letters, is cited here as the god of musical notation.

[16] Ibid., XXV, 3.

[17] Ibid., XXVII, 2.

Another early Church writer, Commodianus, attacks the theater and its music in a chapter entitled, 'Worldly Things to be Absolutely Avoided.'

> With an undisciplined mind you seek what you presume to be easily lawful, both your dear actors and their musical strains; nor do you care that the offspring of such an one should babble follies. While you think that you are enjoying life, you are improvidently erring.[18]

Novatian attacks the productions of the theater at length, especially for the treatment of women and the performances by the musicians. He reveals that plays were still widely attended at this time, but forbids Christians from going.

> Permit me now to pass on to the brazen witticisms of the stage. I am ashamed to tell you what is said there. I am embarrassed even to expose what things take place—the artificial turnings of the plots, the deceits of adulterers, the immoralities of women, the scurrilous jokes, the sordid parasites, even the toga-clad heads of households, at times simply silly, at other times morally disgusting—in all instances senseless, on certain counts shameless.
>
> No man—regardless of his background or profession—is spared by the despicable tongue of these rogues. Yet everyone still frequents the theater. Indecorum, commonly encountered, evidently delights to know and to learn of vice. There is a general rush to that despicable brothel of public shame, to the teaching of obscenity …
>
> When one is accustomed to see such things, one also learns to act accordingly. As for those unfortunate women who have been debased in the service of public lewdness, they find concealment in their very location. In hiding they alleviate their shameful behavior. They who prostitute their virtue are ashamed to be seen doing so. But that public monstrosity takes place for all to see and surpasses the foulness of prostitutes. A method is sought whereby adultery may be committed with one's eyes!
>
> An evil quite worthy of it is added to this infamy: a completely broken down human being, a man soft beyond effeminacy, devoted to the art of expressing words with his hands. Because of one single I-don't-know-what, neither man nor woman, the entire city is excited so that the legendary orgies of bygone ages are carried out with frenzied dancing. So true is it that what is not permissible is eagerly sought after that what time itself has obscured is again remembered and brought to light.
>
> Since the evils of the present day do not suffice to glut the sensuality of our times, recourse has to be had in the theater where the

18 Commodianus, quoted in *The Writings of Tertullianus* (Edinburgh: T. & T. Clark, 1895), III, 462.

aberrations of a past age are again presented. It is not permissible, I repeat, for faithful Christians to be present. It is absolutely unlawful even for these whom—to charm their ears—Greece sends everywhere to all who are instructed in her vain arts.

One person tries to imitate the harsh war cry of the trumpet. A second person by blowing with his breath into pipes modulates their lugubrious sounds. A third, accompanied with dancing and a man's melodious voice, strains with his breath—laboriously drawn from the viscera to the upper parts of his body—to play upon the small openings of pipes. At times he releases and forces it into the air by means of fixed apertures. He even labors actually to speak with his fingers by breaking down the sound into definite rhythmic patterns. He is ungrateful to his Maker who gave him a tongue.

Why should I even mention the wasted efforts of comedy and those senseless ravings of the tragic voice? Why mention the din made by the vibrating strings of instruments? Even if such things were not consecrated to idols, faithful Christians should not go there and look at them. Even if they were not sinful, their distinguishing characteristic is unspeakable vanity, unbefitting the faithful.[19]

19 Novatian, 'The Spectacles,' VI.

The late third-century Church philosopher, Lactantius, catalogs the perceived evils of the theater in similar detail.

I am inclined to think that the corrupting influence of the stage is still more contaminating. For the subjects of comedies are the dishonoring of virgins, or the loves of harlots; and the more eloquent they are who have composed the accounts of these disgraceful actions, the more do they persuade by the elegance of their sentiments; and harmonious and polished verses more readily remain fixed in the memory of the hearers. In like manner, the stories of the tragedians place before the eyes the parricides and incests of wicked kings, and present tragic crimes. And what other effect do the immodest gestures of the players produce, but both teach and excite lusts? Whose enervated bodies, rendered effeminate after the gait and dress of women, imitate unchaste women by their disgraceful gestures. Why should I speak of the actors of mimes, who hold forth instruction in corrupting influences, who teach adulteries while they feign them, and by pretended actions train to those which are true? What can young men or virgins do, when they see that these things are practiced without shame, and willingly beheld by all? They are plainly admonished of what they can do, and are inflamed with lust, which is especially excited by seeing; and every one according to his sex forms himself in these representations. And they approve of these things, while they laugh at them, and with vices clinging to them, they return more corrupted to their apartments; and not boys only, who ought not to be inured to vices prematurely, but also old men, whom it does not become at their age to sin.[20]

The third-century Church philosopher, Origen, even makes a demeaning reference to the great Tragedies of Sophocles and Euripides. His purpose is to question the reputation of Socrates, with reference to a quotation by Suidas.

> For if the oracle did call Socrates the wisest of all men, it takes from the value of that eulogy by what is said in regard to Euripides and Sophocles. The words are:
>
> *Sophocles is wise, and Euripides is wiser,*
> *But wiser than all men is Socrates.*
>
> As, then, he gives the designation 'wise' to the tragic poets, it is not on account of his philosophy that he holds up Socrates to veneration, or because of his love of truth and virtue. It is poor praise of Socrates to say that he prefers him to men who for a paltry reward compete upon the stage, and who by their representations excite the spectators at one time to tears and grief, and at another to unseemly laughter.[21]

The smaller, sung poetry forms were also attacked by the Church, primarily because these works were used to glorify the 'pagan' gods. Clement of Alexandria called poetry that 'which is occupied entirely with what is false.'[22] Commodianus agreed.

> Such are the delusive fables that we learn not only on the knees of our parents who know no better; what is more serious, we take great pains to acquire knowledge of them by study and education, particularly from the works of poets—it is they who have done unrivaled harm to the truth by the weight of their authority.[23]

Tertullian, the most important of the second-century Church philosophers, also objected because the poets attributed emotions to the gods and depicted them as interesting personalities.

> The poets are fools when they depict the gods with human passions and as fabulous characters.[24]

---

20 Lactantius, 'The Divine Institutes,' trans. William Fletcher in *The Works of Lactantius* (Edinburgh: T. & T. Clark, 1886), I, bk. VI, xx.

21 Origen, 'Against Celsus,' trans. Frederick Crombie, in *The Writings of Origen* (Edinburgh: T. & T. Clark, 1871), VII, vi. Origen succeeded Clement of Alexandria as the head of the Catechetical School, which attempted to join the beliefs of Christianity with the philosophy of Greece.

22 Clement of Alexandria, *Exhortation to the Greeks*, trans. G. W. Butterworth (Cambridge: Harvard University Press, 1939) 163.

23 Commodianus, 'In Favor of Christian Discipline,' XXIII.

24 Tertullian, *The Testimony of the Soul*, trans. Rudolph Arbesmann (New York: Fathers of the Church, Inc., 1950), I.

FUNCTIONAL MUSIC

Needless to say, the ceremonies worshiping the pagan gods were treated with the greatest contempt by the early Christian philosophers. Minucius Felix mentions the drums which were a frequent participant in cult-religious celebrations.

> In a survey of Roman rituals you would find so many practices that are laughable if not pitiable. Some devotees run about naked in the depths of winter; others move in procession wearing felt caps and parading old shields; or they beat drums of hides and go begging from quarter to quarter, dragging their gods with them. Some sanctuaries they allow you to approach once a year, others it is totally anathema to visit. There is a ritual where a man may not be present, there are several rites forbidden to women, there are certain ceremonies where the mere presence of a slave constitutes an outrage that requires expiation. Some sacred objects are garlanded by a matron married once, others by one married several times. Zealous and devout search is made for a woman who has a large tally of adulteries.[25]

[25] Marcus Minucius Felix, *Octavius*, trans. G. W. Clarke (New York: Newman Press, 1974), XXV, 11.

The second-century writer, Clement of Alexandria, also mentions music in the course of his attack on the Greeks and their cult-religions. It is especially difficult for him to understand how anyone could believe these tales, much less turn them into serious works for the theater.

> How in the world is it that you have given credence to worthless legends, imagining brute beasts to be enchanted by music, while the bright face of truth seems alone to strike you as deceptive, and is regarded with unbelieving eyes? Cithaeron, and Helicon, and the mountains of Odrysians and Thracians, temples of initiation into error, are held sacred on account of the attendant mysteries, and are celebrated in hymns. For my own part, mere legend though they are, I cannot bear the thought of all the calamities that are worked up into tragedy; yet in your hands the records of these evils have become dramas, and the actors of the dramas are a sight that gladdens your heart.

In another place he provides a rare description of the role of music in the Egyptian religious service.

> We shall find another testimony in confirmation ... of certain of the tenets which pertain to each sect being culled from other Barbarians,

chiefly from the Egyptians … For the Egyptians pursue a philosophy of their own. This is principally shown by their sacred ceremonial. For first advances the Singer, bearing some one of the symbols of music. For they say that he must learn two of the books of Hermes, the one of which contains the hymns of the gods, the second the regulations for the king's life. And after the Singer advances the Astrologer, with a horologe in his hand and a palm, the symbols of astrology.[26]

In a satirical reference to music, Clement retells the story of the cricket which supplied a missing note on a lyre, this time, he claims, as part of a funeral ode for a dead snake sung by Eunomus.

> Whether his song was a hymn in praise of the snake, or a lamentation over it, I cannot say; but there was a competition, and Eunomus was playing the lyre in the heat of the day, at the time when the [crickets], warmed by the sun, were singing, you see, not to the dead serpent of Pytho, but to the all-wise God, a spontaneous natural song, better than the measured strains of Eunomus.[27]

Later he also castigates the Roman cult-religions, and those of Cyprus, several times mentioning the music associated with them.

> Yes, and let the sanctuaries of Egypt and the Tuscan oracles of the dead be delivered over to darkness. Homes of hallucination in very truth they are, these schools of sophistry for unbelieving men, these gambling-dens of sheer delusions. Partners in this business of trickery are goats, trained for divination; and ravens, taught by men to give oracular responses to men …
>
> The raving Dionysus is worshiped by Bacchants with orgies, in which they celebrate their sacred frenzy by a feast of raw flesh. Wreathed with snakes, they perform the distribution of portions of their victims, shouting the name of Eve, that Eve through whom error entered into the world; and a consecrated snake is the emblem of the Bacchic orgies …
>
> I could never be beguiled by the claims of the islander Cinyras, of Cyprus, who had the audacity to transfer the lascivious orgies of Aphrodite from night to day, in his ambition to deify a harlot of his own country. Others say that it was Melampus the son of Amythaon who brought into Greece from Egypt the festivals of Demeter, that is, the story of her grief celebrated in hymns.[28]

Clement's personal feelings are clearly evident in his unkind description of the pagan priests.

---

26 Clement of Alexandria, *The Miscellanies*, trans. Alexander Roberts (Edinburgh: T. & T. Clark, 1869), XII, bk. V, iv.

27 Clement of Alexandria, *Exhortation to the Greeks*, trans. G. W. Butterworth (Cambridge: Harvard University Press, 1939), 3ff.

28 Ibid., 29ff.

Let any of you look at those who minister in the idol temples. He will find them ruffians with filthy hair, in squalid and tattered garments, complete strangers to baths, with claws for nails like wild beasts; many are also deprived of their virility.²⁹

[29] Ibid., 201.

Let's do away with all this, says Clement, and replace it with 'a new song,' a frequently used metaphor for the new religion.

Yes, and this Eunomus of mine sings not the strain of Terpander or of Capio, nor yet in Phrygian or Lydian or Dorian mode; but the new music, with its eternal strain that bears the name of God. This is the new song, the song of Moses,

Soother of grief and wrath, that bids all ills be forgotten.

There is a sweet and genuine medicine of persuasion blended with this song.³⁰

[30] Ibid., 7.

ENTERTAINMENT MUSIC

The most frequently described Entertainment Music in ancient secular literature is that performed for the banquet. For Clement of Alexandria, it was music which inspired most of the evils he saw in banquets. Therefore, in an extraordinary attack on music entitled, 'How to Conduct Ourselves at Feasts,' he urges the Christians to have 'rational entertainment' and rid themselves of the music.

Let revelry keep away from our rational entertainments, and foolish vigils, too, that revel in intemperance. For revelry is an inebriating pipe, the chain of an amatory bridge, that is, of sorrow. And let love, and intoxication, and senseless passions, be removed from our choir. Burlesque singing is the boon companion of drunkenness. A night spent over drink invites drunkenness, rouses lust, and is audacious in deeds of shame. For if people occupy their time with pipes, and psalteries, and choirs, and dances, and Egyptian clapping of hands, and such disorderly frivolities, they become quite immodest and intractable, beat on cymbals and drums, and make a noise on the instruments of delusion; for plainly such a banquet, as seems to me, is a theater of drunkenness … Let the pipe be resigned to the shepherds, and the flute to the superstitious who are engrossed in idolatry. For, in truth, such instruments are to be banished from a temperate banquet, being more suitable to beasts than men, and the more irrational portion of mankind.[31]

It is obvious that it was the character of the banquet music which Clement objected to. One regrets that he did not go into more specific detail regarding both this music and the music which he recommended for the Christian banquet, hymns and 'temperate harmonies' and 'liquid harmonies.'

> Among the ancient Greeks, in their banquets over the brimming cups, a song was sung called a skolion, after the manner of the Hebrew psalms, all together raising the paean with the voice, and sometimes also taking turns in the song while they drank healths round; while those that were more musical than the rest sang to the lyre. But let amatory songs be banished far away, and let our songs be hymns to God … For temperate harmonies are to be admitted; but we are to banish as far as possible from our robust mind those liquid harmonies, which, through pernicious arts in the modulations of tones, train to effeminacy and scurrility. But grave and modes strains say farewell to the turbulence of drunkenness. Chromatic harmonies are therefore to be abandoned to immodest revels, and to florid and meretricious music.

Naturally, the Church leaders called for an end to the barbaric games of the colosseum. Novatian, a third-century Church philosopher, for example, objected to them as being based on idolatry, adding, 'Idolatry is the mother of all games.'

> It is not necessary that I go into further detail and describe for you the monstrous kinds of sacrifices current in the games whereby even a man, at times, becomes a sacrificial victim because of sacerdotal chicanery.[32] Blood from the jugular is still hot when it is received into the spuming libation-cup. It is then hurled, seething, into the face of a thirsting idol and given him to drink as a ruthless beast. And amid the delights of the spectators, the death of certain victims is expended so that the bloody spectacle can teach others brutality. You would think that one's own private madness were not enough and that one had to learn more in public … If I should ask [the spectator] what road he took to get to that public display, he will admit that he got there by way of brothels and the naked bodies of prostitutes, wanton licentiousness, public vice, notorious lechery, and general contempt for all things.[33]

---

31 Clement of Alexandria, *The Instructor*, trans. William Wilson (Edinburgh: T. & T. Clark, 1884), 215ff.

32 Tertullian, in 'Spectacles,' trans. Rudolph Arbesmann in *Disciplinary, Moral and Ascetical Works* (New York: Fathers of the Church, 1959), VIII, 2, reminds us that the Circus takes its name from the god Circe, in honor of the sun.

33 Novatian, 'The Spectacles,' trans. Russell J. DeSimone, in *Fathers of the Church* (Washington, DC: The Catholic University of America Press, 1947), IV, 4ff.

According to the late third-century Church philosopher, Lactantius, for one to attend these contests, which included murder, was to participate in the slaughter.

> It remains to speak of public shows, which, since they have a more powerful influence on the corruption of the mind, ought to be avoided by the wise, and to be altogether guarded against, because it is said that they were instituted in celebration of the honors of the gods ... he who takes part in these shows appears to have left the worship of God, and to have passed over to profane rites. But I prefer to speak of the matter itself rather than of its origin. What is so dreadful, what so foul, as the slaughter of man? Therefore our life is protected by the most severe laws; therefore wars are detestable. Yet custom finds how a man may commit homicide without war, and without laws; and this is a pleasure to him, that he has avenged guilt. But if to be present at homicide implies a consciousness of guilt, and the spectator is involved in the same guilt as the perpetrator, then in these slaughters of gladiators, he who is a spectator is no less sprinkled with blood than he who sheds it ... These spectacles are viewed by youths, whose dangerous age, which ought to be curbed and governed, is trained by these representations to vices and sins. The circus, in truth, is considered more innocent, but there is greater madness in this, since the minds of the spectators are transported with such great madness, that they not only break out into reveling, but often rise to strifes, and battles, and contentions. Therefore all shows are to be avoided, that we may be able to maintain a tranquil state of mind. We must renounce hurtful pleasures, lest, charmed by pestilential sweetness, we fall into the snares of death.[34]

Lactantius finds the same evils in the traditional athletic contests.

> What else does the practice of the Circensian games contain but levity, vanity, and madness? For their souls are hurried away to mad excitement with as great impetuosity as that with which the chariot races are there carried on; so that they who come for the sake of beholding the spectacle now themselves exhibit more of a spectacle, when they begin to utter exclamations, to be thrown into transports, and to leap from their seats. Therefore all spectacles ought to be avoided.[35]

Even the games of the Olympics were attacked. Clement of Alexandria called for an end to these games,[36] and Novatian called them sacrilegious and urged Christians to stay away.

34 Lactantius, 'Epitome of the Divine Institutes,' trans. William Fletcher in *The Works of Lactantius* (Edinburgh: T. & T. Clark, 1871), lxiii.

35 Lactantius, 'The Divine Institutes,' trans. William Fletcher in *The Works of Lactantius* (Edinburgh: T. & T. Clark, 1886), I, bk. VI, xx.

36 Clement of Alexandria, *Exhortation to the Greeks*, trans. G. W. Butterworth (Cambridge: Harvard University Press, 1939), 71.

How revolting are those bouts! One man clings with indecent holds and embraces to another man who lies beneath him. In such a contest there may be a question as to who the winner is—modesty is always the loser. Look at the nude man who leaps your way! At another who strains to toss a bronze ball into the air. Such is the glory of folly. In short, do away with the spectator, and the emptiness of the games is quite evident. I have repeatedly stated that faithful Christians must shun such vain, such pernicious, such sacrilegious spectacles. It is imperative that our eyes and ears be guarded from them. We soon get accustomed to what we hear and more quickly still to what we see ... You must turn the mind's attention away from such things.[37]

The second-century Church philosopher, Tertullian, writes that if one must have the diversion of contests, try those of the Church!

> Do you want contests in boxing and wrestling? Here they are—contests of no slight account, and plenty of them. Behold impurity overthrown by chastity, faithlessness slain by faith, cruelty crushed by mercy, impudence put in the shade by modesty. Such are the contests among us, and in these we win our crowns. Do you have desire for blood, too? You have the blood of Christ.[38]

ON EDUCATION

The Christian philosophers attacked with the greatest vigor most of the earlier Greek and Roman philosophy, primarily because it ostensibly supported 'pagan' values and also because it formed the basis of traditional education. Writers such as Tertullian were quick to point out a warning against philosophy which is found in the New Testament,

> *See to it that no one makes a prey of you by philosophy and empty deceit, according to human tradition ... and not according to Christ.*[39]

The Church writers particularly criticized the many branches of earlier philosophy for posing questions and then going round and round in circles without ever arriving at answers. Tertullian, who associates philosophers with 'magicians, mountebanks and astrologers,'[40] refers to this as the 'building up and tearing down' of ideas.

---

37 Novatian, 'The Spectacles,' VIII, 2.

38 Tertullian, 'Spectacles,' XXIX, 5.

39 Colossians 2:8, cited in ibid., XV, 9.

40 Tertullian, 'On Prescription Against Heretics,' trans. Alexander Roberts in *Ante-Nicene Christian Library* (Edinburgh: T. & T. Clark, 1884), XLIII.

> This intelligence has been caught up by philosophy, and, with the view of glorifying her own art, has been inflated with straining after that facility of language which is practiced in the building up and pulling down of everything, and which has a greater aptitude for persuading men by speaking than by teaching.[41]

The late third-century Church philosopher, Lactantius, was another who strongly attacked earlier Greek and Roman philosophy because they could never agree on the truth—which, of course, the Church had.

> Therefore, leaving the authors of this earthly philosophy, who bring forward nothing certain, let us approach the right path; for if I considered these to be sufficiently suitable guides to a good life, I would both follow them myself, and exhort others to follow them. But since they disagree among one another with great contention, and are for the most part at variance with themselves, it is evident that their path is by no means straightforward; since they have severally marked out distinct ways for themselves according to their own will, and have left great confusion to those who are seeking for the truth. But since the truth is revealed from heaven to us who have received the mystery of true religion ...[42]

In another treatise he describes this failure of the older philosophers to agree on anything as a virtual war among themselves.

> [Philosophy] is not uniform; but being divided into sects, and scattered into many and discordant opinions, it has no fixed state. For since they all separately attack and harass one another, and there is none of them which is not condemned of folly in the judgment of the rest, while the members are plainly at variance with one another, the whole body of philosophy is brought to destruction. Hence the Academy afterwards originated. For when the leading men of that sect saw that philosophy was altogether overthrown by philosophers mutually opposing each other, they undertook war against all, that they might destroy all the arguments of all; while they themselves assert nothing except one thing—that nothing can be known.[43]

Clement of Alexandria dismissed the Greek philosophers as 'barbarians.'

[41] Tertullian, *De Anima*, in ibid., II.

[42] Lactantius, 'The Divine Institutes,' trans. William Fletcher in *The Works of Lactantius* (Edinburgh: T. & T. Clark, 1886), I, bk. I, i.

[43] Lactantius, 'Epitome of the Divine Institutes,' trans. William Fletcher in *The Works of Lactantius* (Edinburgh: T. & T. Clark, 1871), II, xxxii.

These are the times of the oldest wise men and philosophers among the Greeks. And that the most of them were barbarians by extraction, and were trained by barbarians, what need is there to say?[44]

He used painting as an analogy to illustrate how these philosophers deceive men.

> But it gives a false description of the view, according to the rules of the art, employing the signs that result from the incidence of the lines of vision. By this means, the higher and lower points in the view, and those between, are preserved; and some objects seem to appear in the foreground, and others in the background, and others to appear in some other way, on the smooth and level surface. So also the philosophers copy the truth, after the manner of painting. And always in the case of each one of them, their self-love is the cause of all their mistakes.[45]

For Clement, useful philosophy meant philosophy which was free from the emotions and senses.

> Now the sacrifice which is acceptable to God is unswerving abstraction from the body and its passions. This is the really true piety. And is not, on this account, philosophy rightly called by Socrates the practice of Death? For he who neither employs his eyes in the exercise of thought, nor draws aught from his other senses, but with pure mind itself applies to objects, practices the true philosophy. This is, then, the import of the silence of five years prescribed by Pythagoras, which he enjoined on his disciples; that abstracting themselves from the objects of sense, they might with the mind alone contemplate the Deity.[46]

Lactantius stresses that these famous earlier philosophers should not be thought of as *wise* men, for philosophy is not wisdom but the search for wisdom. He points out that in the other arts, when one makes a study of an art he arrives at a point where he is no longer called a 'follower of the profession,' but an artist. The philosophers, on the other hand, never arrive at wisdom.

> But I am not prepared to concede even that philosophers are devoted to the pursuit of wisdom, because by that pursuit there is no attaining to wisdom. For if the power of finding the truth were connected with this pursuit, and if this pursuit were a kind of road to wisdom, it would at length be found. But since so much time and talent have

[44] Clement of Alexandria, *The Miscellanies*, trans. William Wilson (Edinburgh: T. & T. Clark, 1884), I, xv.

[45] Clement of Alexandria, *The Miscellanies*, trans. Alexander Roberts (Edinburgh: T. & T. Clark, 1869), XII, bk. VI, p. 336.

[46] Clement of Alexandria, *The Miscellanies*, trans. Alexander Roberts, in *Ante-Nicene Christian Library* (Edinburgh: T. & T. Clark, 1869), XII, bk. V, xi.

been wasted in the search for it, and it has not yet been gained, it is plain that there is no wisdom there.[47]

He believed the purpose of knowledge should be to lead to a good life, whereas the ancient philosophers were never able to make this connection. He attributes their chief fault to looking in the wrong place for knowledge.

> All the philosophers, those who have embraced either knowledge or virtue as the chief good, have kept the way of truth, but have not arrived at perfection. For these are the two things which together make up that which is sought for. Knowledge causes us to know by what means and to what end we must attain; virtue causes us to attain to it. The one without the other is of no avail; for from knowledge arises virtue, and from virtue the chief good is produced. Therefore a happy life, which philosophers have always sought, and still do seek, has no existence either in the worship of the gods or in philosophy; and on this account they were unable to find it, because they did not seek the highest good in the highest place, but in the lowest. For what is the highest but heaven, and God, from whom the soul has its origin?[48]

For Lactantius, the only hope for traditional philosophers was for them to be retrained by the Church. These commonly esteemed wise men,

> will only need to be trained by us,—that is, to be recalled from the error in which they are entangled to a better course of life.[49]

As time went on, some Church philosophers began to see a value in philosophy, to the extent that it helped the Christian understand the Scriptures. Indeed, it was this attitude, as we shall see below, which saved the liberal arts from extinction during the Dark Ages. We see an early example of this foresight even in Clement of Alexandria, who says traditional learning, including music, may be useful, so long as we pick and choose.

> I call him truly learned who brings everything to bear on the truth; so that, from geometry, and music, and grammar, and philosophy itself, culling what is useful, he guards the faith against assault.[50]

The third-century Church philosopher, Origen, was another who recognized that there is an important value to some subjects, including music, which stood apart from spiritual association. In

---

[47] Lactantius, 'The Divine Institutes,' bk. III, ii.

[48] Ibid., bk. III, xii. One of the ideas Lactantius perceives from the highest source is distinctly prejudiced.

> What need is there of the female sex, since God, who is almighty, is able to produce sons without the agency of the female? [Ibid., bk. I, viii.]

This negative attitude toward women is shared by many early Church fathers and the origin can perhaps be found in the writings of the founder of the Church, Paul, in First Corinthians 11:3ff.

[49] Ibid., bk. I, i.

[50] Clement of Alexandria, *The Miscellanies*, I, ix.

his discussion, he sarcastically used the term, 'princes of this world,' to mean the famous Greek philosophers.

> I am of the opinion ... that there is another wisdom of this world besides those ... which belong to the princes of this world, by which wisdom those things seem to be understood and comprehended which belong to the world. This wisdom, however, possesses in itself no fitness for forming any opinion either respecting divine things, or the plan of the world's government,[51] or any other subjects of importance, or regarding the training for a good or happy life; but is such as deals wholly with the art of poetry, or grammar, or rhetoric, or geometry, or music, with which also, perhaps medicine should be classed. In all these subjects we are to suppose that the wisdom of this world is included.[52]

51 A reference to Plato's *Republic*.

52 Origen, 'De Principiis,' trans. Frederick Crombie, in *The Writings of Origen* (Edinburgh: T. & T. Clark, 1871), III, iii.

ON THE PHYSIOLOGY OF AESTHETICS

THE SOUL

The ancient Greek philosophers devoted numerous treatises to the discussion of the 'soul.' Not understanding brain function, it was to the soul which they attributed one's sense of self-awareness. The subject is important with respect to the aesthetics of music, for any discussion of the soul had to include the role of the senses, which in turn leads to insights regarding how music was heard.

The Christian philosophers faced the same struggle in attempting to explain the human faculties, our mind, Reason and the senses. But they had an additional burden, necessary to their beliefs due to scriptural references, in that the soul—the most impossible thing to explain—had to have precedence. Tertullian begins his commentary on the soul by observing that the soul must be older than language. Then he qualifies this by supposing man must have always had language, or he could not have spoken about God. And besides, how would anyone have ever invented alphabet letters, if there were no language?[53]

53 Sometimes Tertullian's mind gets a bit irrational, as when he also maintains that the amount of hair a man has on his head is in proportion to the 'exuberance of the brain.' [*De Anima*, trans. Alexander Roberts in *Ante-Nicene Christian Library* (Edinburgh: T. & T. Clark, 1884), LI].

> At all events, the soul was prior to letters; speech, prior to books; ideas, prior to setting them down in writing; and man himself, prior to the philosopher and poet. Are we to believe, therefore, that before literature and its dissemination men lived without making utterances

of this sort? That no one should have spoken of God and His goodness .... Speech went abegging, I suppose, or rather could not exist at all, since those things were lacking without which it cannot exist even today, although it has become more perfect, more rich, and more refined. Indeed, it could not have existed, if those things which are today so simple, so constantly present, so obvious, and born somehow on our very lips, did not exist in the past ... And whence, I ask, did it happen that letters came to know and disseminate for the use of speech things which no mind had ever conceived, or tongue had ever expressed, or ear had ever heard?[54]

One of the questions about the soul which seems to have been most important to the early Church Fathers, was 'Is the soul corporeal or incorporeal?' Tertullian answers this by way of the perception of our senses.

> It is the soul which moves the feet in walking, the hands in touching, the eyes in seeing, and the tongue in speaking, as a sort of internal image which moves within and stirs the surface. How could an incorporeal soul have this power to move solid bodies if it were itself incorporeal?
>
> How would you say the corporeal and intellectual powers of sensation are divided in man? The Platonists tell us that physical substances such as earth and fire are perceived by the bodily senses of touch and sight, while immaterial things such as kindness or meanness are apprehended by the intellectual powers. Therefore, they conclude that the soul is incorporeal since its properties are perceived by the intellectual and not by the bodily senses.
>
> All this would be fine, except that I shall now upset the basis of their argument. For, you see, incorporeal objects *can* be perceived by the bodily senses: thus, sound by the hearing, color by the sight, odors by the sense of smell, in all of which cases the soul has contact with the body.[55]

He mentions the arts again in a reference to Stoic philosophers, who agree with his conclusion, but for the wrong reason.

> It is, moreover, a happy circumstance that the Stoics affirm that even the arts have corporeality; since at that rate the soul too must be corporeal, since it is commonly supposed to be nourished by the arts. Such, however, is the enormous preoccupation of the philosophic mind, that it is generally unable to see straight before it.[56]

---

54 Tertullian, *Testimony of the Soul*, trans. Rudolph Arbesmann (New York: Fathers of the Church, Inc., 1950), V.

55 Tertullian, *On the Soul*, trans. Edwin A. Quain (New York: Fathers of the Church, Inc., 1950), VI, 3ff.

56 Tertullian, 'On Prescription Against Heretics,' trans. Alexander Roberts in *Ante-Nicene Christian Library* (Edinburgh: T. & T. Clark, 1884), p. 423.

Tertullian concludes that the soul is corporeal and that its form is exactly the same as the body.[57]

Regarding the characteristics of the soul, Tertullian argues that soul is also a near synonym for 'spirit,' and the latter for breath. He makes a very interesting reference here to some unnamed philosophers ('heretics') who proposed a genetic basis for the spirit.

> I would not tarry a moment longer on this point, were it not for those heretics who introduce into the soul some spiritual germ which passes my comprehension: [they make it to have been] conferred upon the soul by the secret liberality of her mother Sophia (*Wisdom*), without the knowledge of the Creator.[58]

But he gives this no further thought, declaring we must take the Scripture as the authority, citing from Isaiah 57:16, 'From me proceeds the spirit, and I have made the breath of life.'

Perhaps the most interesting contention by Tertullian regarding the soul, is his statement, 'The soul, in my opinion, is sensual.'

> Nothing, therefore, pertaining to the soul is unconnected with sense, nothing pertaining to sense is unconnected with the soul. And if I may use the expression for the sake of emphasis, I would say, *Animae anima sensus est* ('Sense is the soul's very soul').[59]

On Reason

The second-century Christian philosopher, Minucius Felix, presents an interesting genetic explanation for Reason.

> All men, regardless of age, sex, and class, have been born with the capacity for reason and with the power of understanding; wisdom is not acquired by the accidents of fortune, it is implanted by nature.[60]

But we obviously have faculties which are not rational in nature, those which today we know are in the right hemisphere of the brain. The question becomes, how are they related? For Tertullian, the problem is that if we recognize the irrational we seem to be saying God is irrational, for He created man. He resolves this by saying God created the rational man and that the irrational came later, 'from the suggestion of the serpent.'

---

57 Tertullian, 'On the Soul,' IX, 7. Although in *De Anima*, ibid., XV, he says the soul is contained in the heart.

58 Tertullian, *De Anima*, XI.

59 Tertullian, 'On the Flesh of Christ,' trans. Alexander Roberts in *Ante-Nicene Christian Library* (Edinburgh: T. & T. Clark, 1884), p. 190.

60 Marcus Minucius Felix, *Octavius*, trans. G. W. Clarke (New York: Newman Press, 1974), XVI, 5.

The impulse to sin proceeds from the Devil and, since all sin is irrational, the irrational therefore proceeds from the Devil whence comes sin. Sin is alien to the nature of God, as is also anything irrational. The distinction, then, between these two elements of the soul arises from the difference of their authors.[61]

61 Tertullian, 'On the Flesh of Christ,' trans. Alexander Roberts in *Ante-Nicene Christian Library* (Edinburgh: T. & T. Clark, 1884), XVI, 2.

The Senses

Tertullian is one of the few early philosophers who enthusiastically embraces the value of the information perceived by the senses, indeed he demonstrates a remarkable understanding of the contribution of the senses. He points out that the earlier Greek philosophers believed the senses could not be trusted, citing an example in which the eyes deceive us in showing the oars under water as appearing to be bent, whereas we know them to be straight. The Epicureans, on the other hand, felt the senses report the truth, but our mind leads us astray. Tertullian's belief was much closer to fact, 'these "deceptions" are caused by natural things, which should never be construed as a lie.' These earlier philosophers, he cries, are robbing us of one of our most precious assets.

> O Academics! What impudence you are showing! Don't you see that your assertions would destroy the normal conduct of human life and the very order of nature? Are you not claiming that Divine Providence was blind? The senses of man have been given the mastery over all God's creation that by them we might understand, inhabit, dispose of, and enjoy His goodness ... Is not all life dependent upon the senses? Are not our senses the second source of knowledge with which we are endowed? Whence, do you think, come the various arts, the ingenious developments in business, politics, commerce, medicine? ... Without his senses, man's life would be deprived of all joy and satisfaction, the only rational being in creation would thus be incapable of intelligence or learning, or even of founding an Academy![62]

62 Ibid., XVII, 1ff.

In another place he considers further the relationship of the senses and the intellect and seems to have intuitively understood the twin hemisphere brain functions, which we know today to be medical fact. First, he says the mind is nothing else than an instrument of the soul,[63] reflecting, as we indicated above, that for the Christian the soul must have precedence. He not only understood

63 Tertullian, *De Anima*, p. 451.

the way the twin hemispheres contribute to our 'understanding,' but he understood the role of the senses in educating the intellect.

> For is it not true, that to employ the senses is to use the intellect? And to employ the intellect amounts to a use of the senses? What indeed can sensation be, but the understanding of that which is the object of sensation? And what can the intellect or understanding be, but the seeing of that which is the object understood? ...
>
> For how can the intellect be superior to the senses, when it is these which educate it for the discovery of various truths?[64]

He concludes that the intellect is not to be preferred above the senses, and that the intellect must not be separated from the senses.[65]

Another Church philosopher who wrote on the contribution of the senses to knowledge was Clement of Alexandria, although he makes an exception in the case of Faith!

> There are four things in which the truth resides—Sensation, Understanding, Knowledge, Opinion,—intellectual apprehension is first in the order of nature; but in our case, and in relation to ourselves, Sensation is first, and of Sensation and Understanding the essence of Knowledge is formed; and evidence is common to Understanding and Sensation. Well, Sensation is the ladder to Knowledge; while Faith, advancing over the pathway of the objects of sense, leaves Opinion behind, and speeds to things free of deception, and reposes in truth.[66]

A much more narrow appreciation of the senses is found in the third-century Church philosopher, Origen. He particularly attacks the ancient Greek lyric poets and dramatists for even suggesting that common people could understand these things.

> Thus we should justly condemn a man who put into the mouths of barbarians, slaves, or uneducated people the language of philosophy; because we know that the philosophy belonged to the author, and not to such persons, who could not know anything of philosophy ...
>
> For if those whom he represents as speaking are the unlearned, how is it possible that such persons could distinguish between 'sense' and 'reason,' between 'objects of sense' and 'objects of reason?'[67]

He admits that the senses contribute to knowledge and cites, by way of illustration, the question: 'How do we know that God exists?' His answer, taken from Romans 1:20, is by observing God's cre-

---

64 Ibid., 451, 453.

65 Ibid., 454.

66 Clement of Alexandria, 'The Miscellanies,' trans. Alexander Roberts, in *Ante-Nicene Christian Library* (Edinburgh: T. & T. Clark, 1869), XII, 8.

67 Origen, 'Against Celsus,' trans. Frederick Crombie, in *The Writings of Origen* (Edinburgh: T. & T. Clark, 1871), VII, xxxvi–xxxvii.

ations on earth. The important thing for the Christian, therefore, is not to be concerned with the senses themselves ('their knowledge must not stop short with the objects of sense'), but to use them for the purpose of going on to knowledge itself.[68] Later his prohibition of the senses for the Christian is even stronger.

> All true Christians therefore have the eye of the mind sharpened, and the eye of sense closed; so that each one, according to the degree in which his better eye is quickened, and the eye of sense darkened, sees and knows the Supreme God, and His Son, who is the Word, Wisdom, and so forth.[69]

Only the third-century philosopher, Lactantius, among these early Church writers, attempted to speculate on how the various components of mind, soul and senses were organized to work together physically. He begins his discussion[70] with the disclaimer that some things are just not intended to be understood.

> For as it must be confessed that many things are unknown, since God has willed that they should exceed the understanding of man; so, however, it must be acknowledged that there are many which may both be perceived by the senses and comprehended by the reason.

Next, he asks, 'Where is the mind?' First, he reviews briefly the beliefs of earlier philosophers, some saying that it is in the breast and others in the brain. He seems to be inclined toward not presenting a position of his own, regarding the location of the mind, but rather to consolidate these two views: the mind is in the brain, although when we engage in thinking, it seems to disappear into the breast! This is an extraordinary passage from the perspective of modern brain research, for we know that not only does the rational left hemisphere deny the very existence of the right hemisphere, but clinical subjects can often be seen looking in an upper right direction, as if the rational left hemisphere is looking somewhere it knows not, for answers it has not.

> That the nature of the mind is also incomprehensible, who can be ignorant, but he who is altogether destitute of mind, since it is not known in what place the mind is situated, or of what nature it is? ...
> For the mind, which exercises control over the body, appears to be placed in the highest part, the head, as God is in heaven; but when it is engaged in any reflection, it appears to pass to the breast, and,

68 Ibid., VII, xxxvii.

69 Ibid, VII, xxxix.

70 Lactantius, 'On the Workmanship of God,' trans. William Fletcher in *The Works of Lactantius* (Edinburgh: T. & T. Clark, 1871), II, xvff.

as it were, to withdraw to some secret recess, that it may elicit and draw forth counsel, as it were, from a hidden treasury. And therefore, when we are intent upon reflection, and when the mind, being occupied, has withdrawn itself to the inner depth, we are accustomed neither to hear the things which sound about us, nor to see the things which stand in our way. But whether this is the case, it is assuredly a matter of admiration how this takes place, since there is no passage from the brain to the breast. But if it is not so, nevertheless it is no less a matter of admiration that, by some divine plan or other, it is caused that it appears to be so.

Next, Lactantius addresses the question of the mind–body connection, but again fails to present an explanation of his own. He does, however, pause to attack one of the most familiar figures of speech in Greek philosophy—the analogy of the 'harmony' of the body with the construction of the lyre.

But take care that you never think it probable, as Aristoxenus said, that the mind has no existence, but that the power of perception exists from the constitution of the body and the construction of the organs, as harmony does in the case of the lyre. For musicians call the stretching and sounding of the strings to entire strains, without any striking of notes in agreement with them, harmony. They will have it, therefore, that the soul in man exists in a manner like that by which harmonious modulation exists on the lyre; namely, that the firm uniting of the separate parts of the body and the vigor of all the limbs agreeing together, makes that perceptible motion, and adjusts the mind, as well-stretched things produce harmonious sound. And as, in the lyre, when anything has been interrupted or relaxed, the whole method of the strain is disturbed and destroyed; so in the body, when any part of the limbs receives an injury, the whole is weakened, and all being corrupted and thrown into confusion, the power of perception is destroyed: and this is called death. But [Aristoxenus], if he had possessed any mind, would never have transferred harmony from the lyre to man. For the lyre cannot of its own accord send forth a sound, so that there can not be in this any comparison and resemblance to a living person; but the soul both reflects and is moved of its own accord. But if there were in us anything resembling harmony, it would be moved by a blow from without, as the strings of the lyre are by the hands; whereas without the handling of the artist, and the stroke of the fingers, they lie mute and motionless. Doubtless he ought to have been beaten by the hand, that he might at length observe; for his mind, badly compacted from his members, was in a state of torpor.

ON THE PSYCHOLOGY OF AESTHETICS

Unfortunately, among the early Church philosophers one does not find speculation concerning Beauty or Pleasure in an aesthetic sense. Moreover, the word Pleasure was almost a synonym for the evils of the various public entertainments which the Church found so objectionable. Nevertheless, it is important to read some of these Church attacks on 'pleasure,' because they are also attacks on the environment in which aesthetic pleasure existed.

The second-century philosopher, Tertullian, has written a treatise called 'Spectacles,' which is in actuality a Church warning on the pleasures of watching any form of large-scale public entertainment.

> For so strong is the appeal of pleasure that it can bring about a prolongation of ignorance with a resulting facility for sin, or a perversion of conscience leading to self-deception.[71]

We find it especially interesting that Tertullian quotes some of the arguments used *against* the Church, that is to say arguments which the 'pagans' offered in favor of aesthetic pleasure. The first argument which Tertullian quotes, reasons as follows. Spectacles, public entertainments, etc., are merely external pleasures of the eyes and ears, whereas religion takes place in the mind, therefore God is not offended by man's enjoying himself. Another argument used by the pagans, is that since God created everything (as the Christians themselves taught), therefore God created entertainment and it must subsequently be good. Tertullian does not immediately debate these ideas, but he does admit they are clever and then coins a truly memorable line.

> How clever in adducing proofs does human ignorance think itself, especially when it is afraid of losing some of these delights and enjoyments of the world!
> Accordingly, you will find more people turned away from our religion by the danger to their pleasures than by the danger to their lives.[72]

Regarding these entertainment spectacles, Tertullian now makes an extraordinary aesthetic definition.

> In my opinion, under the general heading of lust, there are also included pleasures; similarly, under the general idea of pleasures, spectacles are treated as a special class.[73]

---

71 Tertullian, 'Spectacles,' trans. Rudolph Arbesmann in *Disciplinary, Moral and Ascetical Works* (New York: Fathers of the Church, 1959), I, i.

72 Ibid., II, 2.

73 Ibid., XIV, 3.

He is contending here that large-scale entertainments invite lust for money, lust for high station in life, lust for gluttony, lust for sensual gratification, lust for fame, and the lust for pleasure itself.

Tertullian catalogs the characteristics of these entertainments which are opposed to God.[74] They cause frenzy, bitterness of feeling, anger, and grief. This, in turn, defiles man because what enters through the eyes and ears affects the spirit.

Finally, Tertullian returns to the definition of Pleasure given by the pagan, Greek philosophers and compares this to the experiences he observes in the new Christians.

> The philosophers at least have given the name 'pleasure' to quiet and tranquility; in it they rejoice, they find their diversion in it, they even glory in it. But you—why, I find you sighing for goal posts, the stage, dust, the arena.
> I wish you would say plainly: 'We cannot live without pleasure!'[75]

Were they to so confess, Tertullian's response is rather extraordinary.

> What greater pleasure is there than distaste of pleasure itself … ?[76]

Thus, with this obsession on pleasure as sin, one can understand Clement of Alexandria's belief that man was born innocent, but was led astray by Pleasure.

> The first man played in Paradise with childlike freedom, since he was a child of God. But when he fell a victim to pleasure (for the serpent, that creeps upon the belly, an earthy evil, reared to return to matter, is an allegory of pleasure), and was led astray by lusts, the child, coming to manhood through disobedience and refusing to listen to the Father, was ashamed to meet God.[77]

Therefore, he also criticized his fellow early Christians for following the desire for pleasure, rather than reason.

> Let me give you an illustration: you ought to doubt whether it is right for a man to get drunk; but your practice is to get drunk before considering the question. Or in the case of riotous indulgence, you do not make careful examination, but indulge yourselves with all speed.[78]

Judging by the observations of the third-century philosopher, Lactantius, the Church could now only think of Pleasure in a very narrow perspective, associated with materialistic gratification.

---

74 Ibid., XV.

75 Ibid., XXVIII, 4.

76 Ibid., XXIX, 2.

77 Clement of Alexandria, 'Exhortation to the Greeks,' trans. G. W. Butterfield (Cambridge: Harvard Unviersity Press, 1939), 237.

78 Ibid., 209.

Whatever the greatest good is, it must be an object proposed to all men. There is pleasure, which is desired by all; but this is common also to man with the beasts, and has not the force of the honorable, and brings a feeling of satiety, and when it is in excess is injurious, and it is lessened by advance of age, and does not fall to the lot of many: for they who are without resources, who constitute the greater part of men, must also be without pleasure. Therefore pleasure is not the chief good; but it is not even a good.[79]

For Lactantius it is the five senses, which in their search for pleasure, lead man to sin.

It remains that I should speak against the pleasures of the five senses ... all of which, since they are vicious and deadly, ought to be overcome and subdued by virtue.[80]

He goes on to suggest that man should follow the example of animals, who use their senses only for the preservation of life.

In another treatise, he extends this warning to the early Christians that the search for the pleasure of the senses, including music, leads inevitably to Hell!

For a too great eagerness for pleasure both produces danger and generates disgrace, and that which is especially to be avoided, leads to eternal death. Nothing is so hateful to God as an unchaste mind and an impure soul. Nor let any one think that he must abstain from this pleasure [sex] only, but also the other pleasures which arise from the rest of the senses, because they also are of themselves vicious, and it is the part of the same virtue to despise them. The pleasure of the eyes is derived from the beauty of objects, that of the ears from harmonious and pleasant sounds, that of the nostrils from pleasant odor, that of taste from sweet food,—all of which virtue ought strongly to resist, lest, ensnared by these attractions, the soul should be depressed from heavenly to earthly things, from things eternal to things temporal, from life immortal to perpetual punishment.[81]

[79] Lactantius, 'The Divine Institutes,' trans. William Fletcher in *The Works of Lactantius* (Edinburgh: T. & T. Clark, 1886), I, bk. III, xi.

[80] Ibid., bk. VI, xx.

[81] Lactantius, 'Epitome of the Divine Institutes,' trans. William Fletcher in *The Works of Lactantius* (Edinburgh: T. & T. Clark, 1871), II, lxii.

On Emotions

Another difficult subject for early philosophers was an explanation of the emotions—how do they affect our behavior so much, and where are they located? The second-century Church philosopher, Tertullian, although through reasoning unfamiliar to us today, arrives at the correct answer: the emotions are perceived in the mind. Indeed, if one substitutes right hemisphere of the brain for 'soul,' his explanation, except for the final sentence, is quite modern.

> Since it is clear that the soul is subject to those emotions which it happens to undergo, it must feel them through the mind or at least in conjunction with the mind …
>
> Aristotle makes all sensations to be passions, and in this he is right. To have sensation is to be acted upon and to be acted upon is to feel …
>
> If we postulate a complete distinction into mind and soul so that they are two different substances, then one of them must produce all emotion, sensation, and every sort of perception, action and motion, while the other is completely passive and unmovable. There is no other alternative: either the mind or the soul is completely useless …
>
> The only question remaining, then, will be as to the nature of their union: whether one is swallowed up by the other or each has a separate function. We hold that the soul is so united to the mind that they are not distinct substances, but that the mind is a faculty of the soul.[82]

In another place, where he is also thinking of the emotions and the mind, Tertullian raises the problem of what is going on in the 'mind' when one has fantastic dreams. He describes such dreams as 'ecstasy,' translating Genesis 2:21 as, 'And God sent an ecstasy upon Adam and he slept.'

> This power we call *ecstasy*, in which the sensuous soul stands out of itself, in a way which even resembles madness.[83]

With the Church's absorption with the fight against the pagan entertainments, spectacles and the theater, by the third century it appears that for some Church philosophers the emotions themselves had become associated only with negative ideas, as we can read in Lactantius.

> There are two parts of which man is made up, soul and body … the body, because it is solid, and capable of being grasped, must contend with objects which are solid and can be grasped; but the soul, on the other hand, because it is slight and subtle, and invisible, contends with those enemies who cannot be seen and touched. But what are the enemies of the soul, but lusts, vices, and sins?[84]

82 Tertullian, *On the Soul*, trans. Edwin A. Quain (New York: Fathers of the Church, Inc., 1950), XII, 3ff.

83 Tertullian, 'De Anima,' trans. Alexander Roberts in *Ante-Nicene Christian Library* (Edinburgh: T. & T. Clark, 1884), XLV.

84 Lactantius, 'Epitome of the Divine Institutes,' I, bk. III, xii.

Indeed, so narrow was the perspective of Lactantius, that when he enumerates the emotions, each is connected to vice.

> There are three passions, or, so to speak, three furies, which excite such great perturbations in the souls of men, and sometimes compel them to offend in such a manner, as to permit them to have regard neither for their reputation nor for their personal safety: these are anger, which desires vengeance; love of gain, which longs for riches; lust, which seeks for pleasures.[85]

85 Ibid., lxi.

ON THE PHILOSOPHY OF AESTHETICS

> We should not worship the work of men's hands ... for ... the creator is greater than his work.[86]

86 Justin Martyr, 'The First Apology,' trans. Thomas B. Fall, in *Saint Justin Martyr* (New York: Christian Heritage, 1948), XX.

This statement by the second-century Church philosopher, Justin Martyr, might well epitomize the core problem the early Church had with art. There was a descending level of importance—God makes man, man makes art—which could not be reversed without questioning the very basis of their beliefs.

Needless to say, the early Christian philosophers considered God to be the supreme artist.

> I am all the more convinced that men are possessed of neither reason nor any sense, not even eyesight, when they refuse to regard the whole of this beautiful universe as the finished work of a divine intelligence.[87]

87 Marcus Minucius Felix, *Octavius*, trans. G.W. Clarke (New York: Newman Press, 1974), XVII, 3.

The Church's lack of appreciation of art turned to hostility when her philosophers contemplated the art and sculpturing which resulted in the images of the pagan gods. In the view of Clement of Alexandria,

> There is no room for doubt, then, that when the common masses say prayers and render public worship to their consecrated images, their simple minds and thoughts are being deluded by the elegance of art, dazzled by the radiance of gold, and dulled by the lustre of silver and the whiteness of ivory.
>
> Picture to yourself the instruments of torture, the devices that men use in fashioning every statue, and you will become ashamed

of any dread you have for matter abused according to a craftsman's fancy in order to create a god. A god of wood—a remnant, perhaps, from a funeral pyre or a gallows tree—is hoist up, hewn, hacked, and planed.

A god of bronze or silver—frequently made from a filthy vessel, as for the king of Egypt—is cast into the melting pot, beaten with hammers, shaped on anvils. A god of stone is cut, carved, and polished by some lewd workman; the god is just as unaware of the indignities that attend his birth as he is later of the homage you pay him in your veneration.[88]

Why, wondered Clement, would a sculptor want to spend his time making an earthen image of a real man, one which would be only a temporary impression upon matter? It is madness, he says.

In my opinion, then, nothing else but madness has taken possession of life, when it spends itself with so much earnestness upon matter.[89]

Among the ancient philosophers one often encounters the suggestion that poets and musicians had a kind of 'divine connection.' St. Justin Martyr mentions this, when he recalls a comment by a poet-musician in Homer, 'God inspired me with melodies.'[90] We have suggested that, with respect to music, this concept of the 'divine connection' came, in part, from the fact that the mysteries of music, like religion, were unseen, while their effect is obvious. A third-century Church philosopher, Origen, provides a more extended explanation of the nature of this 'divine connection.'

> There are besides ... certain special energies of this world, spiritual powers, which bring about certain effects ... there being, for example, a peculiar energy and power, which is the inspirer of poetry; another, of geometry; and so a separate power, to remind us of each of the arts and professions of this kind. Many Greek writers have been of opinion that the art of poetry cannot exist without madness; whence also it is several times related in their histories, that those whom they call poets were suddenly filled with a kind of spirit of madness ... Now these effects we are to suppose are brought about in the following manner: As holy and immaculate souls, after devoting themselves to God with all affection and purity, and after preserving themselves free from all contagion of evil spirits, and after being purified by lengthened abstinence, and imbued with holy and religious training, assume by this means a portion of divinity, and earn the grace of prophecy, and other divine gifts ... And the result of this

---

88 Ibid., XXIV, 5. Clement of Alexandria, in 'The Miscellanies,' trans. William Wilson (Edinburgh: T. & T. Clark, 1884), I, xvi, nevertheless recounts all the old Greek myths regarding the invention of the various musical instruments, choral forms, etc., and in I, xxiii, recalls that Moses studied music in Egypt.

89 Clement of Alexandria, *Exhortation to the Greeks*, trans. G. W. Butterworth (Cambridge: Harvard University Press, 1939), 215.

90 Saint Justin Martyr, 'The Monarchy or The Rule of God,' trans. Thomas B. Fall (New York: Christian Heritage, 1948), 455.

is, that they are filled with the working of those spirits to whose service they have subjected themselves.[91]

In the writings of the second-century Church philosopher, Clement of Alexandria, however, a new interpretation of the 'divine connection' is given. The connection now is Reason and in illustration he quotes a comic poet, Epicharmus.

> There is in man reasoning; and there is a divine Reason.
> Reason is implanted in man to provide for life and sustenance,
> But divine Reason attends the arts in the case of all.
> Teaching them always what it is advantageous to do.
> For it was not man that discovered art, but god brought it;
> And the Reason of man derives its origin from the divine Reason.[92]

A final interesting aesthetic principle, given by Clement, seems to be yet another reflection of the Church's hostility to pagan entertainments.

> We must not aspire to please the multitude. For we do not practice what will please them, but what we know is remote from their disposition.[93]

[91] Origen, 'De Principiis,' trans. Frederick Crombie, in *The Writings of Origen* (Edinburgh: T. & T. Clark, 1871), III, iii.

[92] Clement of Alexandria, 'The Miscellanies,' trans. Alexander Roberts, in *Ante-Nicene Christian Library* (Edinburgh: T. & T. Clark, 1869), XII, bk. V, p. 290. In bk. VI, Clement quotes Plato and Democritus regarding the 'divine conection' of poets.

[93] Clement of Alexandria, *The Miscellanies*, trans. William Wilson (Edinburgh: T. & T. Clark, 1884), I, 378.

ON THE AESTHETICS OF MUSIC

Among the Church philosophers of the first three centuries, one finds little discussion of the aesthetics of music in general, apart from church music. The third-century writer, Lactantius, however, makes some observations which probably reflect the views of most of his colleagues. While he presumes 'pleasure of the ears' has the capacity of leading one to vice, he seems to regard music as not terribly dangerous because what we hear in music does not remain with us, as compared to the words of poetry.

It is worthy of note here that he confirms there is still no generally known system of notation yet.

> Pleasure of the ears is received from the sweetness of voices and melodies, which indeed is as productive of vice as that delight of the eyes of which we have spoken. For who would not deem him luxurious and worthless who should have scenic arts at his houses? But it

> makes no difference whether you practice luxury alone at home, or with the people in the theater. But we have already spoken of spectacles: there remains one thing which is to be overcome by us, that we be not captivated by those things which penetrate to the innermost perception. For all those things which are unconnected with words, that is, pleasant sounds of the air and of strings, may be easily disregarded, because they do not adhere to us, and cannot be written.[94]

It is also worthy of note that he acknowledges, in the above quotation, the power of music to 'penetrate to the innermost' part of us. He mentions this in another place, where he is discussing the tendency of the senses to lead man to vice. One gets the distinct impression that, while he would never speak in favor of music generally, he had observed, and was perhaps disturbed by, the powerful impact of music on the listener.

> But he who is carried away by hearing, to say nothing respecting songs, which often so charm the inmost senses that they even disturb with madness a settled state of the mind.[95]

However, he concludes by revisiting the central philosophies of ancient Greece music education contending that if we are going to listen to music, it should be music which has two aesthetic characteristics, that which nourishes the soul and that which improves you as a person. The only type of music which does this, of course, is music which praises God.

> Let nothing be agreeable to the hearing but that which nourishes the soul and makes you a better man. And especially this sense ought not to be distorted to vice, since it is given to us for this purpose, that we might gain the knowledge of God. Therefore, if it be a pleasure to hear melodies and songs, let it be pleasant to sing and hear the praises of God. This is true pleasure, which is the attendant and companion of virtue.[96]

On Church Music

It is rare to find any mention of music in the writings of the early Church philosophers which are in correspondence with the abundant references to music in the Old Testament. The first reason

[94] Lactantius, 'The Divine Institutes,' trans. William Fletcher in *The Works of Lactantius* (Edinburgh: T. & T. Clark, 1886), I, bk. VI, xxi.

[95] Lactantius, 'Epitome of the Divine Institutes,' trans. William Fletcher in *The Works of Lactantius* (Edinburgh: T. & T. Clark, 1871), II, lxii.

[96] Lactantius, 'The Divine Institutes'.

for this, as one will recall, was that the Church was still an outlaw organization and the 'Praise the Lord with Trumpets' of the Old Testament was therefore not observed as a matter of security. Also, however, it is clear that the new Church was opposed to instrumental music because of its association with 'pagan' music in general, but also because music was often at the heart of pagan religious ritual, as Clement of Alexandria points out.

> If I go on further to quote the symbols of initiation into this mystery (those of Attis, Cybele and Corybantes) they will, I know, move you to laughter, even though you are in no laughing humor when your rites are being exposed. 'I ate from the drum; I drank from the cymbal.' Are not these symbols an outrage?[97]

This, however, left them in the unenviable position of having to justify all the complimentary references to instrumental music in the Old Testament. This they accomplished by maintaining that all references to instrumental music in the Old Testament were only metaphorical figures of speech. Their interpretations of the 'real' meaning of these metaphors seem to the modern reader to be too ridiculous to have been believed even by the faithful![98] A typical example of this official bending of the truth can be seen in this passage by Clement of Alexandria, in which he also offers his explanation for the ban on instrumental music in the new church.

> The Spirit ... sings, 'Praise Him with sound of trumpet;' for with sound of trumpet He shall raise the dead. 'Praise Him on the psaltery;' for the tongue is the psaltery of the Lord. 'And praise Him on the lyre.' By the lyre is meant the mouth struck by the Spirit, as it were by a plectrum. 'Praise with the timbrel and the dance,' refers to the church meditating on the resurrection of the dead in the resounding skin. 'Praise Him on the chords and organ.' Our body He calls an organ, and its nerves are the strings, by which it has received harmonious tension, and when struck by the Spirit, it gives forth human voices. 'Praise Him on the clashing cymbals.' He calls the tongue the cymbal of the mouth, which resounds with the pulsation of the lips ... For man is truly a pacific instrument; while other instruments, if you investigate, you will find to be warlike, inflaming to lusts, or kindling up amours, or rousing wrath.
> In their wars, therefore, the Etruscans use the trumpet, the Arcadians the pipe, the Sicilians the pectides, the Cretans the lyre, the Lacedaemonians the aulos, the Thracians the horn, the Egyptians

97 Clement of Alexandria, *Exhortation to the Greeks*, trans. G. W. Butterworth (Cambridge: Harvard University Press, 1939), 35.

98 Origen, 'Word as Flesh,' in Hans Urs von Balthasar, *Spirit and Fire*, trans. Robert J. Daly (Washington, DC: The Catholic University of America Press, 1984), 150, also says the potentially embarrassing phrase in Song of Solomon 1:2, 'That he would kiss me with the kisses of his mouth,' is also a metaphor for 'that he would pour his words into my mouth and I would hear him speaking and see him teaching.'

the drum, and the Arabians the cymbal. The one instrument of peace, the Word alone by which we honor God, is what we employ. We no longer employ the ancient psaltery, and the trumpet, and timbrel, and aulos, which those expert in war and contemners of the fear of God were wont to make use of also in the choruses at their festive assemblies; that by such strains they might raise their dejected minds.[99]

Even the trumpet, which the Old Testament had always associated with the high priest, is taken over by the new Church writers as a metaphor. Clement of Alexandria, for example, declares, 'The trumpet of Christ is His gospel.'[100]

Most of the early Church writers endorse only vocal music, as Clement of Alexander mentions in a passage where he also uses Music as a metaphor for the creation.

> See how mighty is the new song! ... It is this which composed the entire creation into melodious order, and tuned into concert the discord of the elements, that the whole universe might be in harmony with it ... Yes, and it softened the rage of fire by air, as one might blend the Dorian mode with the Lydian and the biting coldness of air it tempered by the intermixture of fire, thus melodiously mingling these extreme notes of the universe. What is more, this pure song, the stay of the universe and the harmony of all things, stretching from the center to the circumference and from the extremities to the center, reduced this whole to harmony, not in accordance with Thracian music, which resembles that of Jubal, but in accordance with the fatherly purpose of God, which David earnestly sought. He who sprang from David and yet was before him, the Word of God, scorned those lifeless instruments of lyre and harp. By the power of the Holy Spirit He arranged in harmonious order this great world, yes, and the little world of man too, body and soul together; and on this many-voiced instrument of the universe He makes music to God, and sings to the human instrument. 'For thou art my harp and my pipe and my temple'—my harp by reason of the music, my pipe by reason of the breath of the Spirit, my temple by reason of the World—God's purpose being that the music should resound, the Spirit inspire, and the temple receive its Lord.[101]

The most extensive discussion of music by Clement is found in a chapter entitled, 'The Mystical Meanings in the Proportions of Numbers, Geometrical Ratios, and Music.' Although he does not discuss music with respect to numbers here, it is clear he placed

---

99 Clement of Alexandria, *The Instructor*, trans. William Wilson (Edinburgh: T. & T. Clark, 1884), 216.

100 Clement of Alexandria, *Exhortation to the Greeks*, 249.

101 Ibid., 13. The source of Clement's quotation here is unknown. The translator suggests it may have been a line from an early hymn. The text of an actual hymn composed by Clement, quoted in *The Instructor*, 343, contains the following allusion to simply vocal music:

> Thy simple children bring
> In one, that they may sing
> In solemn lays [songs]
> Their hymns of praise.

music in the category of other disciplines based on numbers.[102] Once again he implies that the instruments of the Old Testament were only used metaphorically, concluding that the chief value of music for the new Christian is for the 'composure of manners.'

> The lyre, according to its primary signification, may by the psalmist be used figuratively for the Lord; according to its secondary, for those who continually strike the chords of their souls under the direction of the Choir-master, the Lord. And if the people saved be called the lyre, it will be understood to be in consequence of their giving glory musically, through the inspiration of the Word ... You may take music in another way, as the ecclesiastical symphony at once of the law and the prophets, and the apostles along with the gospel, and the harmony which obtained in each prophet, in the transitions of the persons ...
>
> Music is then to be handled for the sake of the embellishment and composure of manners. For instance, at a banquet we pledge each other while the music is playing; soothing by song the eagerness of our desires, and glorifying God for the copious gift of human enjoyments, for His perpetual supply of the food necessary for the growth of the body and of the soul. But we must reject superfluous music, which enervates men's souls, and leads to variety,—now mournful, and then licentious and voluptuous, and then frenzied and frantic.[103]

The third century Christian was apparently beginning to ask, 'But if music is mentioned in the Old Testament, why may we not enjoy it?' The error the Christian makes, Novatian explains, is in taking these passages literally, and not in their context of religious purpose.

> In Scripture, we also read of nablas, kinnors, timbrels, auloi, citharas, and dancing troupes ... Why, then, should a faithful Christian not be at liberty to be a spectator of things that the divine Writings are at liberty to mention? I can, with reason, state here that it would have been far better for such people to lack knowledge of the Scriptures, than to read them in such a manner. Words and noble deeds which have been put down in writing to stimulate us in the practice of evangelical virtue are misinterpreted by them as so many incentives for the practice of vice. These things were written not to make spectators of us, but to incite our minds to greater enthusiasm for salutary things, given that the pagans show great enthusiasm for things far from salutary ...
>
> And that David danced before the Lord does in no way encourage faithful Christians to take seats in the theater. He did not distort his

---

102 The early Church writers had a particular fascination with the number seven. Clement, in 'The Miscellanies,' trans. Alexander Roberts (Edinburgh: T. & T. Clark, 1869), XII, bk. VI, p. 389, says, 'the whole world revolves in sevens,' pointing to the seven known planets, seven stars in several constellations, seven phases of the moon, seven lyre strings, and seven (!) senses: two eyes, two ears, two nostrils, and the mouth. Victorinus, Bishop of Petau, in *The Writings of Tertullianus* (Edinburgh: T. & T. Clark, 1895), III, 392, makes an interesting observation on the frequency of the number seven in the bible, including seven horns of the Lamb [Revelation 5:6], seven eyes of God [Zechariah 4:10], seven eyes are the seven spirits of the Lamb [Revelation 4:5], seven torches burning before the throne of God [Revelation 4:5], seven golden candlesticks [Revelation 1:13], seven young sheep [Leviticus 23:18], seven women in Isaiah [Isaiah 4:1], seven churches in Paul [Acts 6:3], seven deacons [Acts 6:3], seven angels [Revelation], seven trumpets [Joshua 6, Revelation 8], seven seals to the book, seven periods of seven days and seven weeks in Daniel [Daniel 9:25], seven of all clean things in the ark [Genesis 7:2], seven revenges of Cain [Genesis 4:15], seven years for a debt to be acquitted [Deuteronomy 15:1], the lamp with seven orifices [Zechariah 4:2], and the seven pillars of wisdom in the house of Solomon [Proverbs 9:1].

103 Clement of Alexandria, 'The Miscellanies,' bk VI, xi.

body in obscene movements and dance out the drama of Grecian libido. The nablas, kinnors, auloi, timbrels, and citharas played to the Lord—not an idol. Therefore, no approval whatever is given for spectators of illicit things. Through the devil's artifice, things that were holy are changed into illicit things.[104]

104 Novatian, 'The Spectacles,' trans. Russell J. DeSimone, in *Fathers of the Church* (Washington, DC: The Catholic University of America Press, 1947), II 3ff.

5 THE NEW TESTAMENT

FOR THE MUSICIAN, one of the most interesting aspects of the New Testament is how remarkably different it is in its description of music from that found in the Old Testament. Reflecting the stern attitudes of the early Church fathers and their warnings against pagan entertainment, in particular the theater, we find in the New Testament as well the admonition, 'Let there be no … silly talk, nor levity.'[1] Thus, it is no surprise that there is only one reference to any kind of entertainment music, and this is connected to the important moral story of the prodigal son.[2]

The distinction between the Old and New Testaments is particularly noticeable regarding the use of music in the religious service. The Old Testament has numerous references to the role of singers in the Jewish service, but the vocal form, 'Hymn,' appears only in the New Testament. While there are only two instances in the New Testament of persons singing hymns in the present tense,[3] there are a number of recommendations that hymn singing should be a part of the future observances of the Christians.[4] In one of these cases, singing is specifically recommended when the singer himself *feels cheerful*.[5]

Another of these references is particularly interesting in its unconscious reflection of the function of the twin hemispheres of the brain, 'I will sing with the spirit and I will sing with the mind also.'[6] Ten verses earlier in this same chapter there is another reference to the spirit of the music. Here it is suggested that it is this quality which makes music itself comprehensible.

> If lifeless instruments, such as the aulos or the harp, do not give distinct notes, how will anyone know what is played? And if the trumpet gives an indistinct sound, who will get ready for battle?

The most striking difference between the Old and New Testaments is the treatment of instrumental music. Following the

1 Ephesians 5:4.

2 Luke 15:25.

3 Matthew 26:30, which includes Jesus singing, and Acts 16:25, which describes Paul singing in prison.

4 Romans 15:9, I Corinthians 14:15, 26, Ephesians 5:19, Colossians 3:16 and James 5:13.

5 James 5:13.

6 I Corinthians 14:15.

extensive descriptions of the use of music in the Temple which one finds in the Old Testament, it is somewhat astounding to discover that there is not a single reference to a musical instrument being used in a religious service anywhere in the New Testament. The nearest New Testament correspondence to those exhortations of the Psalms, 'Praise the Lord with Trumpets, Praise the Lord with Cymbals,' is a passage where instruments are not actually named, but a phrase is used which is often a surrogate for instrumental music in early literature.

> Be filled with the Spirit, addressing one another in psalms and hymns and spiritual songs, singing and *making melody* to the Lord.[7]

Perhaps, in view of the hostile comments toward instrumental music in general which we find expressed in the views of the early Church fathers,[8] we should not be surprised. We must also remember, of course, that during much of the first two centuries the Christians were an underground organization holding secret church services. Obviously, if one wishes to hold a secret service, it is not in one's interest to have trumpets playing and cymbals crashing.[9]

Nevertheless, it seems odd that an instrument like the trumpet, an instrument so much a part of every ancient culture, should be entirely absent in this book. Actually, the word appears, but there is no description of a person actually playing the trumpet. It is played by angels (once a septet of angels!),[10] once by God,[11] once as the 'last trumpet' of Judgment Day,[12] once it is heard from City of God,[13] once as a symbol of God's loud voice,[14] and when God will destroy Babylon—then we will finally be rid of all these trumpeters, harp players, aulos players, and 'minstrels.'[15]

Apart from this meagre list, there are no further references to brass players which are not metaphors or symbols. There are two remaining references to woodwind instruments, and one of these is used only in a metaphoric expression complaining that the people are not paying attention to what their religions leaders are saying, 'We piped and you did not dance.'[16]

The remaining woodwind reference is found in the Book of Matthew,[17] where, before he could perform one of his miracles of raising a girl from the dead, Jesus had to first chase the aulos players out of a ruler's house, saying, 'Depart, for the girl is not dead but sleeping.'[18] This is actually a rare example of 'paganism' which escaped the editorial eye of the Church, referring as it does to one of the

---

7 Ephesians 5:19. This same passage appears also in Colossians 3:16, but without the mention of the instrumental music. All quotations are from the Revised Standard Version (1952).

8 The New Testament, as we know it, was assembled somewhat later. In 367 AD Bishop Athanasius of Alexandria selected the books to be included and this was ratified by the Church Council of Hippo in 393 and by the Council of Carthage in 397. Because the New Testament was thus *assembled*, rather than being *rewritten* by a redactor as much of the Old Testament was, a number of curious inconsistencies exist among the various books. For example, in the first four books, books supposedly written by men who knew Jesus, the Jesus of Luke was from a poor family, was born in a manger where he was visited by shepherds. But the Jesus of Matthew was an aristocrat who came to claim the throne, was born in a house where he was visited by other kings. Luke describes Jesus as the gentle shepherd who says, 'turn the other cheek,' while Matthew pictures a Jesus who says, 'Do not think that I have come to bring peace on earth; I have not come to bring peace, but a sword!'

9 Nowhere is this more evident than in Salzburg where one can still visit a church carved out inside a mountain by early Christians as a means of achieving secrecy.

10 Matthew 24:31 and Revelation 8:02.

11 1 Thessalonians 4:16.

12 1 Corinthians 15:52.

13 Hebrews 12:19.

14 Revelation 10:10.

15 Revelation 18:22. .

16 Matthew 11:17.

17 Matthew 9:23.

18 Matthew 9, 24.

Greek myths. Philetaerus, in the fourth century BC, cites a myth that if one goes to Hades, but is a recognized lover of good music, one is permitted 'to revel in love affairs,' whereas 'those whose manners are sordid, having no knowledge of music,' are condemned to spend eternity carrying water in a fruitless effort to fill 'the leaky jar.'[19] Thus Philetaerus exclaims, 'Zeus, it is indeed a fine thing to die to the music of the aulos!' By this he meant arranging to have these musicians playing as one dies so as to demonstrate to the gods that one truly appreciated music.

It is in the context of this myth that we understand a line in Menander's play, *Old Cantankerous*. The character, Getas, enters the stage from a shrine as an aulos player begins to play for him. Getas tells the aulos player to stop playing, 'I'm not ready for you yet!' This is precisely the meaning of the comment by Jesus.

The only reference to percussion instruments in the New Testament does them little credit.

> If I speak in the tongues of men and of angels, but have not love, I am a noisy gong or a clanging cymbal.[20]

19 Philetaerus, *The Aulos Lover*, quoted in Athenaeus, *Deipnosophistae*, XIV, 633.

20 1 Corinthians 13:1.

PART 2

The Triumph of the Church; The Fourth and Fifth Centuries

6 ON THE STATE OF MUSICAL PERFORMANCE IN THE FOURTH AND FIFTH CENTURIES

THE FOURTH AND FIFTH CENTURIES saw the effective demise of the Roman Empire, as every student knows. The long period of economic decline and the constant battles to preserve a continually shrinking empire produced an environment which was hardly conducive to art. Gibbon presents this summary of the climate of civilization at this time.

> It is almost unnecessary to remark that the civil distractions of the empire, the license of the soldiers, the inroads of the barbarians, and the progress of despotism, had proved very unfavorable to genius, and even to learning. The succession of Illyrian princes restored the empire without restoring the sciences. Their military education was not calculated to inspire them with the love of letters; and even the mind of Diocletian, however active and capacious in business, was totally uninformed by study or speculation. The professions of law and [medicine] are of such common use and certain profit that they will always secure a sufficient number of practitioners endowed with a reasonable degree of abilities and knowledge; but it does not appear that the students in those two faculties appeal to any celebrated masters who have flourished within that period. The voice of poetry was silent. History was reduced to dry and confused abridgments, alike destitute of amusement and instruction. A languid and affected eloquence was still retained in the pay and service of the emperors, who encouraged not any arts except those which contributed to the gratification of their pride or the defense of their power.[1]

In another place, Gibbon cites a dramatic symbol of the decline of the arts by the early fourth century.

> The triumphal arch of Constantine still remains a melancholy proof of the decline of the arts ... as it was not possible to find in the capital of the empire a sculptor who was capable of adorning that public monument, the arch of Trajan.[2]

[1] Edward Gibbon, *The History of the Decline and Fall of the Roman Empire* (Philadelphia: Coates), I, 455.

[2] Ibid., 488.

Constantine (306–337 AD) encouraged the arts,[3] but his own conversion to Christianity, together with the failure of Julian (361–363 AD) in his attempt to restore the old pagan religion, effectively handed the victory to the Church, and the Church was no respecter of the arts.

Christianity, meanwhile, which probably represented no more than five per cent of the Roman population at the beginning of the fourth century, was exerting extraordinary influence everywhere. This was due in part to the fact that the Church addressed itself to everyone, while the empire was focused on the single person of the emperor. Some early writers suggest that the Church appealed to the poor and uneducated, but it might be more to the point to say that the Church addressed itself to the *majority*, who were poor and uneducated.

But there were also more concrete reasons for the success of the Church. Gibbon presents five of these.

> I. The inflexible, and, if we may use the expression, the intolerant zeal of the Christians, derived, it is true, from the Jewish religion, but purified from the narrow and unsocial spirit which, instead of inviting, had deterred the Gentiles from embracing the law of Moses. II. The doctrine of a future life, improved by every additional circumstance which could give weight and efficacy to that important truth. III. The miraculous powers ascribed to the primitive church. IV. The pure and austere morals of the Christians. V. The union and discipline of the Christian republic, which gradually formed an independent and increasing state in the heart of the Roman empire.[4]

It should be noted that the Church also had to fight itself, not just Rome. There were many competing sects, which sometimes engaged in bloody battles. It has been said that in the years 342–343 AD, more Christians were killed by Christians than by all the Roman persecutions taken together.[5]

However great was the eventual victory of the Church, it cast at the same time a long shadow over education and the arts, for in the eyes of the early Church these were associated with the pagans. Again, Gibbon summarizes the view of the early Church.

> The acquisition of knowledge, the exercise of our reason or fancy, and the cheerful flow of unguarded conversation, may employ the leisure of a liberal mind. Such amusements, however, were rejected

---

3 Ibid., II, 72. Constantinople, which Constantine tried to name 'New Rome,' was at this time a great Christian capital. However, as the general population was Greek, it played a key role in preserving the ancient Greek culture and transmitting it to the Renaissance.

4 Ibid., I, 508.

5 Will Durant, *The Age of Faith* (New York: Simon and Schuster, 1950), 8.

with abhorrence, or admitted with the utmost caution, by the severity of the [Church] fathers, who despised all knowledge that was not useful to salvation, and who considered all levity of discourse as a criminal abuse of the gift of speech ... The first sensation of pleasure was marked as the first moment of their abuse. The unfeeling candidate for heaven was instructed, not only to resist the grosser allurements of the taste or smell, but even to shut his ears against the profane harmony of sounds, and to view with indifference the most finished productions of human art. Gay apparel, magnificent houses, and elegant furniture, were supposed to unite the double guilt of pride and sensuality; a simple and mortified appearance was more suitable to the Christian who was certain of his sins and doubtful of his salvation. In their censures of luxury the [Church] fathers are extremely minute and circumstantial; and among the various articles which excite their pious indignation we may enumerate false hair, garments of any color except white, instruments of music, vases of gold or silver, downy pillows, white bread, foreign wines, public salutations, warm baths, shaving the beard ...[6]

6 Ibid., I, 546.

Given this well-known historical background, one often is given the impression that art music, in particular, had virtually disappeared. While it is true the references in literature are fewer, they nevertheless reflect that traditional 'pagan' music making continued.

ART MUSIC

Reminding the reader that poetry was still sung, there is one description of a poet which suggests that this art still had representatives of the very highest artistic quality. Sidonius, himself a fifth-century poet, describes the work of the poet Lampidius as being tender, elevated and graceful and characterized by finished artistry. He was technically skilled at handling mixed meters and matched the style with the character of his poems.

> If you examine his poems you find he was tender, a master of many meters, sonorous, and of finished artistry; for he composed verses perfectly constructed with a remarkable variety both of feet and of phrasing—hendecasyllables gliding and smooth; hexameters resounding and majestic; elagiacs now echoic, now palindromic, now with end linked with beginning by duplication.

Further, following the dictates of whatever work he had taken in hand, he would vary the style of his character—drawing in accordance with the nature of the person, the time, and the place, and in so doing he used, not the first words that occurred, but elevated, graceful, and carefully studied expressions.[7]

Perhaps there were more distinguished poets whose works have been lost, and perhaps the art itself was still more respected than the histories remember to say. In Rome, unfortunately, it appears such artists were probably the exception. Marcellinus, the last great historian of the ancient Latin world, through his choice of language, implies that poetry with music was now held in relatively low regard in comparison with other disciplines of the fourth century. Speaking of the self-education of the emperor Julian, he writes,

> It is unbelievable with what great eagerness he sought out the sublime knowledge of all [the best] things, and as if in search of some sort of sustenance for a soul soaring to loftier levels, ran through all the departments of philosophy in his learned discussions. But yet, though he gained full and exhaustive knowledge in this sphere, he did not neglect more humble subjects, studying poetry to a moderate degree.[8]

There are also sufficient references to suggest that Art Music performed by solo instrumentalists was also still in evidence. One such example is given by Marcellinus, in his description of the private music of the emperor Valentinian (364–375 AD).

> He assumed the privilege, when he returned home after a dinner, of having a flute player play soft music before him.[9]

Sometimes there are references to solo players who possessed considerable technique. Paulinus of Nola, for example, mentions 'a musician strumming the strings of the lyre with fluent quill.'[10] This same writer describes a skilled harpist and panpipe player, by way of creating a metaphor for the workings of God. The description of the panpipe player is particularly interesting in its suggestion that the instrument may have been played more like a modern harmonica, rather than as a series of single pipes.

> Think of a man playing a harp, plucking strings producing different sounds by striking them with the one quill. Or again the man who

---

[7] *Sidonius Poems and Letters*, trans. W. B. Anderson (Cambridge: Harvard University Press, 1965), II, 465.

[8] Ammianus Marcellinus, *Constantius et Gallus*, trans. John C. Rolfe (London: Heinemann, 1935), I, 219.

[9] Ibid., II, 583.

[10] *The Poems of St. Paulinus of Nola*, trans. P. G. Walsh (New York: Newman Press, 1975), Poem 27, 93ff.

rubs his lips by blowing on woven reeds; he plays one tune from his one mouth, but there is more than one note, and he marshals the different sounds with controlling skill. He governs the shrill-echoing apertures with his breathing and his nimble fingers, closing and opening them, and thus a tuneful wind with haste of airy movement successively passes and returns along the hollow of the reed, so that the wind instrument becomes alive and issues forth a tune unbroken. This is how God works. He is the Musician who controls that universal-sounding harmony which he exercises through all the physical world.[11]

[11] Ibid., Poem 27, 72.

The emperor Julian mentions a relatively new solo instrument, the water organ, as well as concerts. Judging by his reference to 'swift fingers,' virtuoso repertoire pieces must have been also heard on this instrument at this time.

I see a new kind of reeds. Are they, perchance, the wild product of some strange brazen soil? They are not even moved by our winds, but from a cave of bull's hide issues a blast and passes into these hollow reeds at their root. And a valiant man with swift fingers stands touching the notes which play in concert with the pipes, and they, gently leaping, press the music out of the pipes.[12]

[12] Julian, in *The Greek Anthology* (London: Heinemann, 1925), III, 365.

Finally, a comment by the emperor Julian clearly suggests that the solo singer of epic poetry, who sang of great men and deeds, was still familiar at this time.

For you are already surfeited with them, your ears are filled with them, and there will always be a supply of composers of such discourses to sing of battles and proclaim victories with a loud clear voice, after the manner of the heralds at the Olympic games.[13]

[13] Julian, 'The Heroic Deeds of Constantius,' in *The Works of the Emperor Julian*, trans. Wilmer Wright (London: Heinemann, 1913), I, 209.

One finds relatively few descriptions of choral performances accompanied with dance movements by the singers, in the ancient Greek tradition, but one comment by the fifth-century poet, Sidonius, suggests such performances were still extant. From an aesthetic viewpoint, his comment is especially interesting from the implication of fine singers, for he criticizes those choirs who, through good singing, make bad compositions appear good.[14]

[14] *Sidonius Poems & Letters*, II, 445.

According to a Roman historian contemporary to these times, Ammianus Marcellinus, the productions of the theater were extraordinary and employed enormous numbers of musicians.

The vast and magnificent theaters of Rome were filled by three thousand female dancers, and by three thousand singers, with the masters of the respective choruses. Such was the popular favor which they enjoyed, that, in a time of scarcity … the merit of contributing to the public pleasures exempted them from a law, which was strictly executed against the professors of the liberal arts.[15]

We have some valuable insights regarding the use of music in the theater of the fourth century, found in the fragment of a treatise, 'On Comedy and Tragedy,' by Aelius Donatus. First, he implies meter when he says the music, 'arranged in measures,' was not composed by the author of the play, but by 'some one skilled in music of this sort.' We might judge that in some cases the composer was not only skilled, but famous, for Donatus mentions that the composer's name was placed above that of the author of the play and even the name of the play.

He indicates the music during the play was quite varied and that excerpts were performed before the play began, permitting many people, who recognized the music, to know what play was to be given even before it was announced.

Finally, there seems to have been subtleties associated with the instruments themselves which far surpass any such practice today.

> [Songs] were, moreover, played on 'equal' or 'unequal' flutes, and right- or left-handed. The right-handed, or Lydian, ones proclaimed the production of a comedy of serious and solemn character; the left-handed, or Serranian, ones announced humor in the comedy in the lightness of its catastrophe. In cases, though, where a 'right' and 'left' ceremony was required, it meant that the play combined seriousness and gaiety combined.[16]

The general impression one receives is that the theaters remained popular, but that the quality of production had declined greatly. Gibbon remarks, 'the theaters might still excite, but they seldom gratified.'[17] The emperor Julian now saw them in the same category of low entertainment found in all kinds of public shows and states that he wished he could bring back the theater of old. These productions, as we have seen in previous pages, were strongly criticized by the Church, but we gain the impression in a letter by Julian that individual priests were nevertheless joining the public in attending.

---

15 Quoted in Gibbon, *The History of the Decline and Fall of the Roman Empire*, III, 32.

16 Aelius Donatus, 'On Comedy and Tragedy,' trans. Barrett H. Clark in *European Theories of the Drama* (New York: Crown, 1959), 45. Donatus defines Comedy as, 'a story treating of various habits and customs of public and private affairs, from which one may learn what is of use in life, and, on the other hand, what must be avoided.'

17 Gibbon, *The History of the Decline and Fall of the Roman Empire*, III, 226.

Julian, taking the Church at its word, commands that no priest should go there!

> No priest must anywhere be present at the licentious theatrical shows of the present day, nor introduce one into his own house; for that is altogether unfitting. Indeed if it were possible to banish such shows absolutely from the theaters so as to restore Dionysus those theaters pure as of old, I should certainly have endeavored with all my heart to bring this about; but as it is, since I thought that this is impossible, and that even if it should prove to be possible, it would not on other accounts be expedient, I forebore entirely from this ambition. But I do demand that priests should withdraw themselves from the licentiousness of the theaters and leave them to the crowd. Therefore let no priest enter a theater or have an actor or a chariot-driver for his friend; and let no dancer or mime even approach his door. And as for the sacred games, I permit anyone who will to attend those only in which women are forbidden not only to compete but even to be spectators. With regard to the hunting shows with dogs which are performed in the cities inside the theaters, need I say that not only priests but even the sons of priests keep away from them?[18]

[18] Julian, 'Letter to a Priest,' in ibid., II, 335.

FUNCTIONAL MUSIC

In the older cities, such as Athens, Alexandria and Rome, the ancient pagan religious-cults continued until the end of the fourth century, with more than seven hundred pagan temples still standing in Rome alone by the end of that century.[19] But by the fifth century there are very few remaining descriptions of these ceremonies, although we read of various attempts to revive them, which in itself suggests their general decline.

[19] Will Durant, *The Age of Faith*, 33.

The emperor Julian desired to reestablish these cults, especially that of Cybele and the worship of the Sun, for which he composed a hymn. Gibbon also discusses a brief revival of the festival of the Lupercalia, a festival of arts and agriculture, but there is no mention of music.[20]

We may be sure traditional wedding music continued to be heard, similar to the description recorded by the poet Ausonius. It is interesting that this music, and the ceremony itself, seems very much in the ancient tradition and reflects no Christian influence.

[20] Gibbon, *The History of the Decline and Fall of the Roman Empire*, III, 239ff.

> Hymns do they chant, they beat the ground in dances, and songs repeat. Withal, a long-robed Thracian priest accompanies on his seven strings their various tones. But on another side the aulos breathes song from its twin mouths.[21]

The more affluent 'barbarians' appear to have imitated the Roman wedding customs. Gibbon cites the lavish wedding of the Goth, Adolphus, which included a chorus singing the Hymeneal songs.[22]

While these Eastern peoples are beyond the scope of this book, we should also quote Gibbon's account of the funeral of the famous Attila the Hun. We wish we had a more complete account of the music described here.

> His body was solemnly exposed in the midst of the plain, under a silken pavilion; and the chosen squadrons of the Huns, wheeling round in measured evolutions, chanted a funeral song to the memory of a hero, glorious in his life, invincible in his death, the father of his people, the scourge of his enemies, and the terror of the world.[23]

In view of the nearly constant battles of this period, we are not surprised to find many references to military music. Accounts of the Roman armies mention primarily the use of the trumpet. The historian, Marcellinus, mentions the existence of specific musical signals, including calling the ranks together,[24] to attack ('having ordered the horns to sound the war-note'[25]) and reveille ('the day had ended and the trumpet sounded'[26]). This same writer also includes some rare references to the style of the trumpet music, as in a mention of the trumpets of the Batavians, which 'pealed savagely,'[27] in another place, the 'blare' of the trumpets,[28] and an interesting reference to 'slow' notes by the trumpets.

> And day was now dawning, when mail-clad siege-works veiled almost the entire sky, and the dense forces moved forward, not as before in disorder, but led by the slow notes of the trumpets and with no one running forward.[29]

He is less complimentary of the enemy trumpets, once referring to them as,

> The bands of raging savages, blaring some ferocious tune on their barbaric trumpets.[30]

---

21 *Ausonius*, trans. Hugh G. Evelyn White (London: Heinemann, 1961), I, 379.

22 Gibbon, *The History of the Decline and Fall of the Roman Empire*, III, 62.

23 Ibid., III, 202.

24 Marcellinus, *Constantius et Gallus*, II, 475. Even more information on the use of the trumpet in the military can be found in the Dead Sea Scrolls.

25 Ibid., I, 265, and II, 75.

26 Ibid., I, 299.

27 Ibid., I, 289.

28 Ibid., III, 71

29 Ibid., I, 503.

30 Ibid., III, 269.

It is with this prejudice, that on one occasion he gives us a direct comparison of the military songs of the Roman and barbarians (Goths).

> The light of day had hardly appeared, when the trumpets on both sides sounded the call to take up arms ...
>
> So, when both armies after advancing cautiously remained unmoved, the opposing warriors stared at each other with savage and sidelong glances. The Romans in unison sounded their war-cry, as usual rising from a low to a louder tone, of which the national name is *barritus*, and thus roused themselves to mighty strength. But the barbarians sounded the glories of their forefathers with wild shouts, and amid this discordant clamor of different languages skirmishes were first tried.[31]

We can also see that a broad spectrum of society continued to use music in their occupations for the purpose of relieving the burden of toil. St. John Chrysostom gives a broad sampling of professions using music for this purpose.

> Travelers also, driving at noon the yoked animals, sing as they do, lightening by their songs the hardships of the journey. And not only travelers, but also peasants often sing as they tread the grapes in the wine press, gather the vintage, tend the vine, and perform their other tasks. Sailors do likewise, pulling at the oars. Women, too, weaving and parting the tangled threads with the shuttle, often sing a certain single melody, sometimes individually and to themselves, sometimes altogether in concert. This they do, the women, travelers, peasants, and sailors, striving to lighten with a song the labor endured in working, for the mind suffers hardships and difficulties more easily when it hears songs and chants.[32]

To this list, Paulinus of Nola adds the sailors joyfully singing their usual rowing-songs[33] and Capella the trumpets which 'sharpen the keen edge of wrestlers and other competitors in public games.'[34]

Capella also provides a rare and extensive history of the use of music in physical therapy, including aiding in the cure of drunkenness, deafness, gout, and mental illness! It suggests a broad practice of early music therapy, of which we have by this date only fragments of information. Here, the allegorical character, Music, is speaking.

> I have frequently recited chants that have had a therapeutic effect upon deranged minds and ailing bodies; I have restored the mad to

31 Ibid., III, 431.

32 St. John Chrysostom, 'Exposition of Psalm XLI,' quoted in Oliver Strunk, *Source Readings in Music History* (New York: Norton, 1950), 68.

33 *The Poems of St. Paulinus of Nola*, trans. P. G. Walsh (New York: Newman Press, 1975), Poem 17, 101.

34 *Martianus Capella and the Seven Liberal Arts*, trans. William Harris Stahl and Richard Johnson (New York: Columbia University Press, 1977), II, 358.

health through consonance, a treatment which the physician Asclepiades learned from me. When an unruly mob of common people were raging at the city fathers as they were deliberating, the sound of music that rose above their obstreperous clamor held them in check. Some young men in a drunken condition who were behaving in a rowdy manner were brought to their senses by the musicianship of Damon, one of my disciples. He ordered them to sing some spondaic measures to the accompaniment of an aulos, and brought their noisy brawling to an abrupt halt. Have not I myself brought healing to diseased bodies by prolonged therapy? The ancients were able to cure fever and wounds by incantation. Asclepiades healed with the trumpet patients who were stone deaf, and Theophrastus used the aulos with mentally disturbed patients. Is anyone unaware that gout in the hip is removed by the sweet tones of the aulos? Xenocrates cured insane patients by playing on musical instruments. Thales of Crete is known to have dispelled diseases and pestilence by the sweetness of his cithara playing. Herophilus checked the pulse of his patients by comparing rhythms.[35]

ENTERTAINMENT MUSIC

The historian, Marcellinus, writes that entertainment, and in particular music, had replaced serious endeavors by the mid-fourth century.

> The few houses that were formerly famed for devotion to serious pursuits now teem with the sports of sluggish indolence, re-echoing to the sound of singing and the tinkling of flutes and lyres. In short, in place of the philosopher the singer is called in, and in place of the orator the teacher of stagecraft, and while the libraries are shut up forever like tombs, water-organs are manufactured and lyres as large as carriages, and auloi and huge instruments for gesticulating actors.[36]

The large-scale public shows apparently continued, judging by the continuing objections of the Church. In Rome there were 175 holidays each year, each of which was celebrated with fights in the arena, contests in the Circus, and by theatrical shows. Even naval spectacles were included among these broad public entertainments, one of which is mentioned, unfortunately without description, by Sidonius.[37]

---

35 Ibid., 358. This passage is followed by an extensive description of the effects of music on animals.

36 Marcellinus, *Constantius et Gallus*, I, 47.

37 *The Letters of Sidonius*, trans. O. M. Dalton (Oxford: Clarendon Press, 1915), I, 12. In another place, Sidonius mentions that his education began in the arts [I, 63].

Early literature often mentions the music performed at private banquets, but never so extraordinary an association with music as Marcellinus describes. Here the guest of honor, a young king, is actually murdered while the musicians played!

> The king came, fearing no hostility, and took his place in the seat of honor granted him. And when choice dainties were set before him, and the great building rang with the music of strings, songs, and wind instruments, the host himself, already heated with wine, went out, under pretense of a call of nature. Then a rude barbarian, fiercely glaring with savage eyes and brandishing a drawn sword, one of the class called scurrae, was sent in to kill the young man, who had already been cut off from any possibility of escape.
>
> At this sight the young king, who, as it happened, was leaning forward beyond his couch, drew his dagger and was rising to defend his life by every possible means, but fell disfigured, pierced through the breast like some victim at the altar, foully slain by repeated strokes.[38]

[38] Marcellinus, *Constantius et Gallus*, III, 305.

Sidonius, a French born writer of the fifth century, describes the dinner music of Theodoric, the king of the Goths. While Roman literature always refers to the Goths as 'barbarians,' here we have the descriptions of a highly discerning taste in music.

> Withal there is no noise of hydraulic organ, or choir with its conductor intoning a set piece; you will hear no players of lyre or aulos, no master of the music, no girls with cithara or tabor; the king cares for no strains but those which no less charm the mind with virtue than the ear with melody.[39]

[39] Sidonius, *The Letters of Sidonius*, I, 6.

Marcellinus makes two brief references to military entertainment, the first to the dancing of the 'pyrrhic dance, in which music accompanied the gestures of the performers.'[40] He also mentions, in uncomplimentary language, soldiers singing popular songs.

[40] Ibid., I, 453.

> To these conditions, shameful as they were, were added serious defects in military discipline. In place of the war-song the soldiers practiced effeminate ditties.[41]

[41] Ibid., II, 199.

7 POETS OF THE FOURTH AND FIFTH CENTURIES

If worms and decay must needs by thy lot, my sheet, begin to perish under my verses first. 'Rather,' thou sayest, 'the worms.' Wisely, my woeful little book, dost thou choose to endure the lesser evil. But I like not to lose the leisure given to the wasteful Muse, who causes loss of slumber and lamp-oil too. 'It had been better to sleep than to lose both slumber and oil.'[1]

This conversation between a poet and his blank sheet of paper, an introduction to a collection of epigrams by the fourth-century poet, Ausonius, bemoans the fact that neglect is worse than decay to the poet, reflecting his age when there was relatively little poetry remaining in the ancient Greek tradition. His comment on the hard work necessary to composition is a complaint often voiced by poets before him.

In the tradition of the ancient lyric poets of Greece,[2] Ausonius acknowledges the old gods, the Muses. It is interesting that he has the god of music, Phoebus, the apparent leader. It is in examples such as the following that we are reminded that the essential association of music and the emotions was still understood. It is a topic the Church writers carefully fail to emphasize.

Clio, singing of famous deeds, restores times past to life. Euterpe's breath fills the sweet-voiced auloi. Thalia rejoices in the loose speech of comedy. Melpomene cries aloud with the echoing voice of gloomy tragedy. Terpsichore with her lyre stirs, swells, and governs the emotions. Erato bearing the plectrum harmonizes foot, song and voice in the dance. Urania examines the motions of the heaven and stars. Calliope commits heroic songs to writing. Polymnia expresses all things with her hands and speaks by gesture. The power of Apollo's will enlivens the whole circle of these Muses: Phoebus sits in their midst and in himself possesses all their gifts.[3]

And like the poetry of the lyric poets, the poetry of this age was still considered as music and was sung in performance. This is

---

1 *Ausonius*, trans. Hugh G. Evelyn White (London: Heinemann, 1921), II, 155.

2 We may presume he knew this repertoire, for he mentions Sappho in ibid., II, 53.

3 Ausonius, ibid., II, 281.

evident in one of the poems by St. Paulinus of Nola, who, being a Church poet, also refers to the 'divine connection' which poets were believed to enjoy.

> This is no new or original song I shall sing. The prophets proclaimed it all before … I have merely committed myself to unfolding the words in tuneful rhythms, and to give relaxation to the minds of readers by my verses. It was thus … that David, a name worthy of veneration, adapted to his lyre all that earlier men had said under god's inspiration, and sang harmonious songs to his heavenly lyre.[4]

This same poet takes another ancient and traditional metaphor, the 'harmony' of the body as represented by the lyre, and gives us a new Christian interpretation.

> So let all nine of us, parents and affectionate children together, live with harmonious hearts like a single lyre; let all of us form a lyre assembled from different strings to sing the same song. Aemilius must join us as the tenth [string], and then at last the mystical law will sound in us with full complement. With this number of persons the living strings on the harp of peace will sound forth a work which brings salvation. For this lyre Felix will be the plectrum; with Felix as quill, Christ will delightedly pluck this ten-stringed lyre. This harp in us will resound to Christ's playing in full harmony, once our thoughts are made perfect, if only our peace is at one with God to the depths of our being, so that we are united in body, mind, and faith. The man who by pursuing upright laws personifies this lyre, and orders his life well in all measures, must live a life which harmonizes with the sacred law in all things, for every string will sound forth unbroken.[5]

Another theme of ancient poetry was the tragic wedding in which either the bridegroom or the bride died just before the ceremony. We have a representative of this subject in the famous mid-fifth century poem, 'Hero and Leander,' by Musaeus, which bemoans the absence of one of the central features usually found in descriptions of ancient weddings, the music.

> Wedding it was, but without a dance; bedding, but hymnless.
> None glorified in song Hera the union-maker,
> Nor did the attendant gleam of torches flash on the bed
> Nor was there any who gamboled and sprang in leaping dance,
> Nor father nor lady-mother intoned the hymenael;

---

4 'Poem 6, in Praise of St. John,' in *The Poems of St. Paulinus of Nola*, trans. P. G. Walsh (New York: Newman Press, 1975). 39.

5 Ibid., Poem 21, 326.

> But laying ready the couch in the hour of consummation
> Silence made fast the bed; Gloom was the bride's attendant,
> And it was a marriage afar from the singing of hymenaeals.[6]

6 Musaeus, *Hero and Leander*, trans. Cedric Whitman (Cambridge: Harvard University Press, 1975), 381.

THE AESTHETICS OF MUSIC

On the Nature of Music

Ausonius, in his poetry, expresses a number of important ideas regarding the nature of music. First, unlike paintings and sculpture which can be owned for the private viewing of an individual, music belongs to everyone and cannot be owned. He refers to this in the course of advising a young poet.

> For it is easier to hold hot coals in one's mouth than to keep the secret of a brilliant work. Once you have let a poem out of your hands, you have renounced all your rights: a speech delivered is common property.[7]

7 *Ausonius*, II, 5.

This poet mentions two more characteristics which he considered fundamental to music, the first being that music is Truth, 'Phoebus bids us speak Truth.'[8] But, Truth in music is not found in the externals.

> Because with purchased books thy library is crammed, dost think thyself a learned man and scholarly, Philomusus? After this sort thou wilt lay up strings, keys, and lyres, and, having purchased all, tomorrow thou wilt be a musician.[9]

8 Ibid., II, 17. One fifth-century poet, Julianus, City Prefect of Rome, found, on the other hand, that the public did not always want the truth.

> The flame that gives life to Art was my gift, and now from Art and fire I get the semblance of ceaseless pain. Ungrateful of a truth is the race of mankind, since in return for his benefit to them this is what Prometheus gets from workers in bronze. [*The Greek Anthology*, trans. W. R. Paton (London: Heinemann, 1918), V, 87.]

The second characteristic, which the ancients gave much more psychological importance to than we do today, is that music, unlike all other arts, cannot be seen. Speaking of both music and the voice, heard in the form of an echo, in this poem he reminds us that the painter cannot portray sound.

9 'To Philomusus a Grammar Master,' in ibid., II, 161.

> Fond painter, why dost thou essay to limn my face, and vex a goddess whom eyes never saw? I am the daughter of Air and Speech, mother of empty utterance, in that I have a voice without a mind. From their dying close I bring back failing melodies and in mimicry repeat the words of strangers with my own. I am Echo, dwelling in the recesses of your ears: and if thou woudst paint my likeness, paint sound.[10]

10 Ibid., II, 175.

Finally, Ausonius, believed that a characteristic of good poetry is that it have a variety of moods and that even serious poetry should have lighter moments.

> I have mingled grave with gay, each to give pleasure at its season. Life wears not one hue, nor has my verse one reader only; each page has its due season; mitred Venus approves this, helmed Minerva that; the Stoic loves this part, Epicurus that.[11]

11 Ibid., II, 169.

A fifth-century poet, Palladas, also recommends that poetry must be cheerful, but for a different reason.

> All life is a stage and a play: either learn to play laying your gravity aside, or bear with life's pains.[12]

12 *The Greek Anthology* (London: Heinemann, 1918), IV, 72.

In an intimate revelation in a letter to a friend, the fifth-century poet, Sidonius, reveals that there must have also been some poetry which was more emotionally intense.

> But if by chance you do accept with a measure of indulgent approval these silly trifles of mine, written amid mental tortures, then you will convince me that they were like the songs of swans, whose cry is more tuneful in moments of agony, and like a lyre-string strung more forcible than is wont, which is the more musical the more it is tensed. But if verses lacking ease and cheerfulness cannot be favorably received, then you will find nothing to please you in the sheet I have attached below.[13]

13 *Sidonius Poems and Letters*, trans. W. B. Anderson (Cambridge: Harvard University Press, 1965), II, 443.

This association between the emotions of the author and his poetry, leads Sidonius to state his personal belief that the quality of poetry will reflect the quality of the composer.

> As for me, my anxiety absolutely forbids me to make the content of my poetry different from the content of the life I lead.[14]

14 Ibid.

But an aesthetic such as this never includes all poets, as we see in an extant poem from the fifth century, which suggests that there were some poets who simply wrote for money.

> What good do you do to the city by writing verses, getting so much gold for your slanders, selling iambic verses as a shopman sells oil?[15]

15 *Greek Anthology*, IV, 291.

On the Listener

In a letter to his grandson, the poet Ausonius makes some interesting observations on how poetry was heard by the listener, including the critics. Perhaps the idea most worthy of contemplation is his contention that what the eye sees is retained longer than what the ear hears. It is also interesting that, in his discussion of the role of poetry in education, he classifies poetry is a leisure, and not a basic, study.

> Being about to come myself, I send on ahead a booklet which I have amused myself by writing in the form of an exhortation to my little grandson. For this I prefer to reciting it myself, in order that you may feel less restraint in your criticism—a faculty which is usually hampered by two circumstances: first that what is heard passes over the ears more quickly than what is read; and the second the presence of the reciter handicaps the frankness of the critic. As it is, you have nothing to fear on either score, because both as you read you are free to linger, and as you come to criticize your feelings for me do not stand in your way.
>
> But look you, my dearest son, I have a caution to add. If any passages in these verses shall appear to you (and I fear that there are many such) to be composed with more brilliance than truth, and have more color than vigor, know that I deliberately allow them to run on smoothly, so that these little bits may be attractive rather than forceful, like those marriageable daughters—
>
> *whom their mothers seek to make*
> *Low-shouldered and tight-laced, to seem more trim.*
>
> —you know the rest.
>
> It only remains, then, for you to say: 'Why do you wait for my criticism on what you yourself proclaim to be a faulty piece of work?' My answer, of course, will be that I blush for verses of this sort in public, but am less ashamed of them when between you and me; for I write them to suit his years rather than my own—or perhaps to suit mine also: old men are twice children! ...
>
> The Muses also have their own sports: hours of ease find place among the Camenae, my honey-sweet grandson; nor does the sour schoolmaster's domineering voice always harass boys, but spells of rest and study keep each their appointed times. As for an attentive boy to have read his lessons willingly is enough, so to rest is lawful. 'School' has been called by that Greek name, that the laborious Muses may be allowed due share of leisure. Wherefore the more, assured

that play follows work in turn, learn willingly: to beguile the weariness of long toil we grant spells of leisure. Boyish zeal flags unless serious work is interspersed with merriment, and workaday with holiday. Learn readily, and loathe not, my grandson, the control of your grim teacher. A master's looks need never cause a shudder. Though he be grim with age and, ungentle of voice, threaten harsh outbursts with frowning brows, never will he seem savage to one who has tutored his face to habitual calm ... You also be not afraid, though the school resound with many a stroke and the old master wear a lowering face: 'fear proves a spirit degenerate.' But to yourself be true, mocking at fear, and let no outcry, nor sound of stripes, nor dread, make you quake as the morning hours come on. That he brandishes the cane for scepter, that he has a full outfit of birches, that he has tawse artfully hidden in innocent washleather, that scared confusion sets your benches abuzz, is but the outward show of the place and painted scenery to cause idle fears. Your father and mother went through all this in their day, and have lived to soothe my peaceful and serene old age.[16]

A poem of Paulinus of Nola pictures a fourth-century listener who is not only respectful, but eager.

Then I shall pronounce you truly a poet divinely inspired, and I shall drain your songs like a draught of sweet water.[17]

In another poem he requests enthusiastic applause.

Brethren, I beg you, associate yourselves with my verses, applaud, and pour out your hearts with chaste abandon.[18]

MARTIANUS CAPELLA

Martianus Capella, of whom little is known, composed in the middle of the fifth century a remarkable allegorical work describing a heavenly wedding called 'The Marriage of Mercury and Philology,' or the Marriage of Eloquence and Learning, in which the seven bridegrooms were the seven disciplines of the liberal arts and the guests were various Greek gods, together with a dozen famous earlier philosophers. While the work is not actually poetry (it has been called 'prose-verse,' or 'chantefable fiction'), the beginning part

---

16 Ibid., II, 73ff.

17 Paulinus, *The Poems of St. Paulinas of Nola*, Poem 22, 157.

18 Ibid., Poem 18, 8.

is in the spirit of ancient poetry. Therefore we will quote some of this material here and the more philosophical comments on music in the following chapter.

In the beginning section, 'The Betrothal,' Capella mentions the ancient Greek concept of the 'Music of the Spheres,' observing that some spheres produce melody [harmony] while other provide the accompaniment.[19] Here he also describes another form of natural music, the music of trees. It is a passage which reminds us of Shakespeare's description of dogs with various pitched voices, in *A Midsummer Night's Dream* (act 4, scene 1).

[19] *Martianus Capella and the Seven Liberal Arts*, trans. William Harris Stahl and Richard Johnson (New York: Columbia University Press, 1977), II, 10.

> Amidst these extraordinary scenes and these vicissitudes of Fortune, a sweet music arose from the trees, a melody arising from their contact as the breeze whispered through them; for the crests of the great trees were very tall and, because of this tension, reverberated with a sharp sound; but whatever was close to and near the ground, with drooping boughs, shook with a deep heaviness of sound; while the trees of middle size in their contacts with each other sang together in fixed harmonies of the duple, the sesquialtera, the sesquiteria also, and even the sesquioctave without discrimination, although semitones came between.[20]

[20] Ibid., 9.

In the following chapter, 'The Marriage,' Capella describes wedding music of extensive size, which we would like to think reflects performances he may have heard at some extravagant Roman wedding. If that were the case, then it is important to note here the mention of the well-trained choir and the concerted ensemble of a number of instruments playing together.

> Before the door, sweet music with manifold charms was raised, the chorus of assembled Muses singing in well-trained harmony to honor the marriage ceremony. Auloi, lyres, the grand swell of the water organ blended in tuneful song and with melodious ending as they became silent for an appropriate interval of unaccompanied singing by the Muses. Then the entire chorus with melodious voices and sweet harmony outstripped the beauty of all the instrumental music.[21]

[21] Ibid., 40.

In another place he mentions the dancing, accompanied by tambours and cymbals, was 'to some extent drowned by the booming sound of the tambours.'[22]

[22] Ibid., 46.

Next come 'solos' by each of the nine muses, of whom only Calliope, the Muse of Epic Poetry, describes music in detail, mentioning the lyre, sacred songs, and music used for prophecy.[23]

23 Ibid., 41.

A final poetic passage describes an extraordinary concert by the gods.

> For Eratine, daughter of the Cyprian, and Himeros, attendant of Cupid, and Terpsis, one of the household servants of Dione, were the first to enter, singing in pleasing harmony; but the lad [Hymen?] was playing on a single aulos. Next came Persuasion, Pleasure, and the Graces, singing to the accompaniment of a lyre and dancing hither and thither with the rhythmic beat. At the same time companies of heroes and of philosophers with flowing locks were moving along in the vanguard, to the left and the right, all chanting in soft and sweet tones, many of them singing hymns and praises of the gods, others singing melodies they had just learned. In the middle were some rustic and tuneful demigods, playing on appropriate instruments, the Goat-Footed one [Pan] on a pandura, Silvanus on a reed pipe smoothed of knots, and Faunus on a rustic flute. A company of heroes that followed after, attracted great wonder and surprise; for Orpheus, Amphion, and Arion, most skillful musicians, were harmoniously playing a moving melody on their golden lyres.[24]

24 Ibid., 351.

Two things in this passage are particularly interesting. First, in ancient Greek literature the entertainment instrument which prostitutes played at banquets was always called a 'single-pipe,' which has been assumed to be a relative of the double pipe aulos. Here, for the first time, the prostitute (a boy) is identified as performing on a 'single aulos.' Second it is most interesting to read in the final sentence of three gods playing 'in harmony,' which must surely be taken as music of more than the single line that modern texts so often assume ancient music to have consisted of.

8 PHILOSOPHERS OF THE FOURTH AND FIFTH CENTURIES

The ideas of Plato and Aristotle had not completely died out by the fourth century, being preserved in a few schools dedicated to traditional 'pagan' philosophy. In particular, Athens had a university of sorts which was supported even by the Christian emperor, Constantine. The final important philosopher in the ancient tradition was Libanius, born in 314 AD, whose students included such important future Church leaders as St. Basil and St. John Chrysostom. Indeed, there were elements of pagan philosophy which clearly influenced the Christian doctrine.[1]

One who wanted to study with Libanius, but was not allowed to, was the young man who became the emperor Julian. Banished to Athens, he enjoyed an introduction to the teachings of the ancient philosophers. He, himself, defined philosophy as follows:

> In philosophy the end and the beginning are one, namely, to know oneself and to become like the gods. That is to say, the first principle is self-knowledge, and the end of conduct is the resemblance to the higher powers.[2]

Even as emperor, his private passion remained books and philosophy and a wish to restore the ancient cults. If we can believe his self-portrait, even his appearance resembled the stereotype pagan philosopher which the Church so often ridiculed.

> Though nature did not make my face any too handsome, nor give it the bloom of youth, I myself out of sheer perversity added to it this long beard ... I put up with the lice that scamper about in it as though it were a thicket for wild beasts ... My head is disheveled; I seldom cut my hair or my nails, and my fingers are nearly always black with ink.[3]

---

1 See W.R. Inge, *Philosophy of Plotinus* (London: Longmans Green, 1929), I, 11.

2 Julian, 'To the Cynic Heracleios,' in *The Works of the Emperor Julian*, trans. Wilmer Wright (London: Heinemann, 1913), II, 127. In this same oration, Julian defines Natural philosophy as consisting of theology and mathematics and Practical philosophy as ethics, economics and logic. Music is not named.

3 Julian, 'Misopogon,' 338B.

ON THE PHILOSOPHY OF AESTHETICS

On Beauty

Perhaps reflecting the daily trials of life, with general economic decay and the constant fear of invasion, Beauty, as an aesthetic concept, was rarely discussed during this period. We do have, however, an interesting definition by Julian which stresses that Beauty is the sum of all its parts.

> All who aspire to virtue and the beautiful must study in their words, deeds, conversation, in short, in all the affairs of life, great and small, to aim in every way at beauty.[4]

He expands on this concept of unity in a passage in which he stresses that the language, in all its parts, must be appropriate to the subject.

> When we invent myths about sacred things our language must be wholly dignified and the diction must be as far as possible sober, beautiful, and entirely appropriate to the gods; there must be nothing in it base or slanderous or impious, for fear we should lead the common people into this sort of sacrilegious rashness; or rather for fear we should ourselves anticipate the common people in displaying impiety towards the gods. Therefore there must be no incongruous element in diction thus employed, but all must be dignified, beautiful, splendid, divine, pure, and as far as possible in conformity with the essential nature of the gods.[5]

On Imitation

Julian makes an observation frequently found in ancient literature, that art can never be as beautiful as nature.

> And a lusty wild vine bloomed about her dwelling, with bunches of excellent grapes, laden with clusters. And at the Phaeacian court there were the same things, except that they were more costly, seeing that, as I suppose, they were made of art, and hence had less charm and seemed less lovely than those that were of natural growth.[6]

---

4 Julian, 'Panegyric in Honor of Constantius,' in ibid., I, 9.

5 Julian, 'To the Cynic Heracleios,' in ibid., II, 107.

6 Julian, 'Panegyric in Honor of Eusebia,' in ibid., I, 301.

In one of his extant poems, Julian makes the point again.

> Bear with it, Myron: Art is too strong for thee: the work is lifeless.
> Art is the child of Nature, for Art did not invent Nature.[7]

[7] Julian, in *The Greek Anthology* (London: Heinemann, 1925), III, 798.

ON THE AESTHETICS OF MUSIC

The most important book on music by a 'pagan' philosopher of this period is the allegorical description of 'The Marriage of Philology and Mercury,' by Martianus Capella, written in the fifth century. This work is a defense of the importance of the seven liberal arts, which were by this time established in the Roman schools. These were the *Trivium*, consisting of Grammar, Dialectic, and Rhetoric, and the *Quadrivium*, consisting of Geometry, Arithmetic, Astronomy, and Music [here called Harmony]. The book was written at a time when Christianity had not yet won its final battle against the 'pagans' and might well be thought of as an attempt to fight back against the efforts of the new Church to shut down traditional education and knowledge. Although this book did not have the far-reaching influence of the writings of men like Cassiodorus, whom we shall discuss below, nevertheless it represents one of the efforts which helped keep the liberal arts alive during the 'Dark Ages.'

In this poetic passage, surely Capella is actually making reference to the dampening influence of the stern Church philosophers, as he refers to teachers who kill all pleasure and enthusiasm in education. There can be little doubt that the reference to instrumental music being stilled reflects the Church's constant attacks.

> Will learned teachers ever thwart conjugal pleasures? Lovely Pleasure, used to pampering, sits benumbed, and Cupid has a pale and glowering look. Comely Flora, whose wont it is to deck the marriage couch with garlands, sits anxiously with the Graces three. Sweet Melpomene has grown quiet; she plays no lyric tune upon her flute, nor tries to sings. In short, all revelry and youthful mirth that customarily prevail, are muffled now in awe of learned utterance.[8]

[8] *Martianus Capella and the Seven Liberal Arts*, trans. William Harris Stahl and Richard Johnson (New York: Columbia University Press, 1977), II, 345.

The observations on the decay of music by philosophers, beginning several centuries before the Christian era, is joined by Capella. He clearly believed the music of the past was better.

> Having long since taken her departure from earth, harmony has rejected mortals and their desolated academies.[9]

Similarly, in another place, 'Harmony' says,

> I could mention countless benefactions that I have given to mankind to show you that I did not leave the earth merely because of a desire to get away, but because I was justified in censuring ungrateful mankind for their apathetic attitude.[10]

On the Nature and Purpose of Music

The emperor Julian states that instrumental music was invented by man for the purpose of pleasure and entertainment.

> It seems likely that myth was originally the invention of men given to pastoral pursuits, and from that day to this the making of myths is still peculiarly cultivated by them, just as they first invented instruments of music, the aulos and the lyre, for their pleasure and entertainment.[11]

On the other hand, he seems to suggest that the enjoyment of music does not mean one need actually learn to play an instrument. In an oration, he addresses the famous Greek maxim, 'Know thyself,' which he says is divinely inspired. First, one must contemplate on the relationship of body and soul, especially, he says,

> whatever exists in us nobler and more divine than the soul, that something which we all believe in without being taught and regard as divine …

Next, he considers two kinds of study, subjects related to the body and those related to the emotional part of man. Here he clearly is thinking of music and suggests that noble persons would not want to devote the effort necessary to accomplish this, for 'persistent study is disgraceful!'

> And in the next place he will also observe the first principles of certain arts by which the body is assisted to that permanence, for instance, medicine, husbandry and the like. And of such arts as are useless and superfluous he will not be wholly ignorant, since these

---

9 Ibid., 349.

10 Ibid., 359.

11 Julian, 'To the Cynic Heracleios,' in ibid., II, 77.

too have been devised to humor the emotional part of our souls. For though he will avoid the persistent study of these last, because he thinks such persistent study disgraceful, and will avoid what seems to involve hard work in those subjects; nevertheless he will not, generally speaking, remain in ignorance of their apparent nature and what parts of the soul they suit.[12]

In another place, Julian is much more specific in saying that the noble class now considered it degrading to study music, and especially singing.

> The fashion of education that now prevails among the well-born deprives me of the use of the music that consists in song. For in these days men think it more degrading to study music than once in the past they thought it to be rich by dishonest means.[13]

Capella begins his discussion of music, in 'The Marriage of Philology and Mercury,' by saying the purpose of music is 'to delight the mind' and to 'banish boredom.'[14] He divides music into high and low pitches, of which he says the latter has the more soothing effect.[15]

Perhaps the most interesting descriptions of music itself by Capella, are his comments on rhythm. Reminding the reader that rhythm was still thought of sequentially, having its origin in the rhythmic structure of poetry, and not yet a system based on pulse, it is interesting that Capella defines a tone as something 'stretched over a space.'[16] All rhythm, he says, falls into three categories: visual, auditory, or tactual.

> An example of the visual is in bodily movements; of auditory, in an appraisal of a vocal performance; of tactual, when a doctor looks for symptoms by feeling the pulse.[17]

For the modern reader, perhaps his most curious contention is that rhythm is 'masculine,' melody is 'feminine,' and that it is rhythm which produces form.[18] But one must understand the association with the feminine to be really a reference to the emotions and the relationship of rhythm and form to be meaning rhythm in the meaning of time in space.

12 Julian, 'To the Uneducated Cynics,' in ibid., II, 11.

13 Julian, 'Misopogon,' in ibid., II, 421.

14 Capella, *Martianus Capella and the Seven Liberal Arts*, 345.

15 Ibid., 361.

16 Ibid., 370.

17 Ibid., 373.

18 Ibid., 381.

On Performance

There is extant a lengthy and interesting discussion of the aesthetics of performance by the emperor Julian which makes several very important points. His principal contention is that while some members of the audience, who have superficial taste, will respond to the outward appearance of the performance, one can be assured that the majority of the audience, even if uneducated, will respond to the genuine musical values in the performance. He also suggests that there were recognized aesthetic principles of music itself which were commonly understood by good musicians. Perhaps most important, he defines the artistic performance as one which is genuine and inspired.

> If one were to judge the best of two musicians, and were to clothe him in the raiment suited to his art, and were then to bring him into a theater full of men, women, and children of all sorts, varying in temperament and age and habits besides, do you not suppose that the children and those of the men and women who had childish tastes would gaze at his dress and his lyre, and be marvelously smitten with his appearance, while the more ignorant of the men, and the whole crowd of women, except a very few, would judge his playing simply by the criterion of pleasure or the reverse; whereas a musical man who understood the rules of the art would not endure that the melodies should be wrongly mixed for the sake of giving pleasure, but would resent it if the player did not preserve the modes of the music and did not use the harmonies properly, and conformably to the laws of genuine and inspired music? But if he saw that he was faithful to the principles of his art and produced in the audience a pleasure that was not spurious but pure and uncontaminated, he would go home praising the musician, and filled with admiration because his performance in the theater was artistic and did the Muses no wrong. But such a man thinks that anyone who praises the purple raiment and the lyre is foolish and out of his mind.[19]

19 Julian, 'Misopogon,' I, 299.

Capella provides two very interesting descriptions of performance. The first, clothed in his poetic allegorical style, appears to reflect ensembles performing in multi-part harmony at the same time.

> Immediately a sweet new sound burst forth, like the strains of auloi; and echoing melodies, surpassing the delight of all sounds, filled the

ears of the enchanted gods. For the sound was not a simple one, monotonously produced from one instrument, but a blending of all instrumental sounds creating a full symphony of delectable music.[20]

20 Capella, *Martianus Capella and the Seven Liberal Arts*, 351.

The other description is of the style of vocal performance falling in between speaking and singing, the quasi-singing style of the ancient Rhapsodists and those who 'sang' poetry. One wonders if the highly melodic speech of Chinese opera, which can still be heard today, is not a remnant of this ancient technique.

> Let us now deal with the voice as the parent of all sound, so to speak. All voice production is divided into two categories: continuous and discrete. The continuous is found in flowing conversation; the discrete is used in music. There is an intermediate form, having elements of both; for it neither adheres strictly to the continuous variation of the one nor is discretely varied in modulation like the other. It is the form which is used in the recitation of all poetry.[21]

21 Ibid., 363.

Capella provides a fine definition of catharsis in the Aristotelian sense when he says that the effect of music on the listener is 'to delight,' 'to goad and stimulate emotions,' and then to 'gently soothe them.'[22]

22 Ibid., 354.

Finally, he again refers to catharsis when he writes after 'Harmony' has sung at this allegorical wedding, some of the guests wondered at the 'pains and labor involved in the production of the music and the effort and unabated concentration that must have gone into the mastery and attainment of harmonies so soft and caressing as to enthrall the innermost emotions of their hearts.' It was a subject much discussed in ancient literature. The answer provided by 'Harmony' is a virtual 'pagan' history of music.

> A loathsome and detestable creature to earthborn mortals, I have been striking against the star-studded heavenly spheres, where I am forbidden to discourse on the precepts of my art—this despite the fact that the swirling celestial mechanism, in the swiftness of its motion, produces a harmony which it recognizes as concordant with the gamut of all proportions. But inasmuch as a maiden has risen up from the earth who is about to be wed, it behooves me now with my celestial powers to dispel the darkness, which is beginning to lift after a long intermission. I shall run through my precepts in accordance with your request, if you will first permit me to call to

your attention the boons accruing to ungrateful mankind from the knowledge that is being restored.

From the time that the limitless universe of the ineffable Creator begot me as the twin sister of heaven, I have not forsaken numbers; I followed the courses of the sideral spheres and the whirling motion of the entire mass, assigning tones to the swiftly moving celestial bodies. But when the Monad and first hypostasis of intellectual light was conveying to earthly inhabitations souls that emanated from their original source, I was ordered to descend with them to be their governess. It was I who designated the numerical ratios of perceptible motions and the impulses of perfect will, introducing restraint and harmony into all things, a subject which Theophrastus elaborated upon as a universal law for all mankind. The Pythagoreans too assuaged the ferocity of men's spirits with pipes and strings and taught that there is a firmly binding relationship between souls and bodies. I deigned to have the numbers underlie the limbs of human bodies, a fact to which Aristoxenus and Pythagoras attest. At last, with a generous outpouring of my favor, I revealed the concepts of my art to men, in a manner which they could understand. For I demonstrated the use of stringed instruments at Delphi, through the Delian's cithara; auloi were blown by my companion the Tritonian and by the Lydian Marsyas; the Mariandynians and Aonians blew upon the reed pipes their hymns to the heavenly deities; I permitted the Egyptians to try their skill with the pandura; and I did not deny myself to shepherds imitating on their pipes the calls of birds or the rustling of trees or the gurgling of rivers. I invented the art of cithara players, of players on stringed instruments, on sambukes, and on water organs throughout the world, for the benefit of lowly mankind. Through me, in fact, men have inveigled the support of your deities and have quelled the anger of the underworld deities through mournful songs.[23]

23 Ibid., 356ff.

9 CHURCH PHILOSOPHERS OF THE FOURTH AND FIFTH CENTURIES

With the Roman empire clearly in decline of its own accord, the Church fathers appear to have felt it was no longer necessary to attack the 'pagan' institutions with the same fervor as in the previous three centuries. In its place they seem now to turn some of their attention more toward the Jews. The following example, which we quote because of its musical analogy, will serve to illustrate this emergence of a stronger expression of anti-Semitism.

> Again, the Jews, the most miserable and wretched of all men, are going to fast, and again we must make secure the flock of Christ. As long as no wild beast disturbs the flock, shepherds, as they stretch out under an oak or pine tree and play their flutes, let their sheep go off to graze with full freedom. But when the shepherds feel that the wolves will raid, they are quick to throw down the flute and pick up their slingshots; they cast aside the pipe of reeds and arm themselves with clubs and stones …
>
> Today the Jews, who are more dangerous than any wolves, are bent on surrounding my sheep; so I must spar with them and fight with them so that no sheep of mine may fall victim to those wolves.[1]

Compared to these 'wolves,' the description of the ideal Christian offered by St. Basil is one of a rather bland personality.

> The Christian should not murmur either because of the meager care of his needs or because of fatiguing labors, since those entrusted with authority in these matters have the final decision over each. There should be no outburst, nor any angry demonstration or commotion, nor should there be any distraction of mind from the realization of the presence of God. The Christian ought to control his voice according to circumstances. He should neither give retort nor act boldly or contemptuously, but in everything show moderation and respect toward all. He should not wink his eye shyly, nor use any other posture or gesture which grieves his brother or shows disdain.[2]

---

[1] St. John Chrysostom, *Discourses Against Judaizing Christians*, trans. Paul W. Harkins (Washington, DC: The Catholic University of America, 1988), 71. In another place, ibid., 92, St. John observes, 'To go to the synagogue is a greater crime than going to the theater.'

[2] St. Basil, 'Letter Concerning the Perfection of the Monastic Life,' in *Letters of Saint Basil*, trans. Sister Agnes Way (New York: Fathers of the Church, 1951), I, 57.

ART MUSIC

We have quoted many examples where the Church fathers condemn the productions of the theater, with its musical accompaniment. St. John Chrysostom forbids the Christian from imitating the characteristics of the actors and, in a typical Church attack, says the new Christian does not need instrumental music.

> He is not taking part in a play, or concealing his head by a mask (for he will not discourse on topics suited to this). He is not mounting the platform, or beating time on the stage floor with his foot, nor is he decked out in golden raiment ...
>
> It is not as one playing a part that this man now appears to us, for there is no pretense in him, or make-believe, or legend, but with head uncovered he preaches the naked truth. He is not trying to persuade his listeners that he is something different from what he is, by means of his bearing, his glance, his voice. He does not need instruments such as the harp or lyre, or anything of the kind, to accompany his declaiming, but he effects everything by his speech alone, which is sweeter and produces a more beneficial sound than any harper or any music.[3]

A fifth-century Church writer, Salvian, pours much stronger invective on the theater. Some indication of the depths to which serious theater must have fallen may be seen in the other kinds of entertainments which he associates with the theater. Of particular interest to us is both his testimony that concert halls still existed, and their inclusion in this list of 'monstrosities.'

> The demons have prepared so many treacherous lures in this life for the human race that even though one escapes many of them, he is finally caught by one or another.
>
> And since indeed it would take too long to tell of all these snares, that is, the amphitheaters, the concert halls, games, parades, athletes, rope dancers, pantomimes and other monstrosities of which one is ashamed to speak, since it is shameful even to know of such wickedness, I shall describe only the vices of the circuses and theaters. For the evils that are performed in these are such that no one can mention them, or even think of them without being polluted ... In the theaters no part of our bodies is free from guilt, for our minds are polluted by evil desires, our ears by hearing and our eyes by what they see, and all these are so disgraceful that a man cannot even describe them without loss of decency.[4]

3 St. John Chrysostom, *Commentary on Saint John, Homilies 1–47*, trans. Sister Thomas Aquinas Goggin (New York: Fathers of the Church, 1957), 4.

4 Salvian, *On the Government of God*, trans. Eva Sanford (New York: Columbia University Press, 1930), 162.

The spectators who attend the theater will be sorry some day, warns Salvian, quoting Luke 6:21, 25.

> Is this the example Christ left for us? We read that he wept, not that he laughed ... For this reason he said: 'Woe unto you that laugh now, for you shall weep.'⁵

5 Ibid., 166.

A passing mention of secular choral performance by St. Gregory Nazianzus is particularly interesting in its details which throw light on the role of the conductor and the placement of the singers.

> I thought, in my vain imaginings, that once I had control of this throne (outward show carries great weight) I could act like a chorus leader between two choruses. Putting the two groups chorus-fashion, one on this side of me, the other on that, I could blend them with myself and thus weld into a unity what had been so badly divided.⁶

6 Saint Gregory of Nazianzus, *Concerning his Own Life*, trans. Denis Meehan (Washington, DC: The Catholic University of America Press, 1987), 119. Gregory was born in 329 or 330 AD.

Performances by choral ensembles such as these were given in public musical festivals, both in ancient Greek times and apparently still in the fourth century. St. John Chrysostom finds a passage in the Old Testament where, he warns us, God did not like festivals of any kind—not to mention instrumental music!

> But do their festivals have something solemn and great about them? They have shown that these, too, are impure. Listen to the prophets; rather, listen to God, and with how strong a statement he turns his back on them. 'I have found your festivals hateful, I have thrust them away from myself.'⁷
>
> Does God hate their festivals and do you share in them? He did not say this or that festival, but all of them together. Do you wish to see that God hates the worship paid with percussion, lyres, harps and other instruments? God said: 'Take away from me the sound of your songs and I will not hear the canticle of your harps.'⁸ If God said: 'Take them away from me,' do you run to listen to their trumpets?⁹

7 Amos 5:21. The Revised Standard Version reads, 'I hate, I despise your feasts, and I take no delight in your solemn assemblies.'

8 Amos 5:23. The Revised Standard Version reads, 'Take away from me the noise of your songs; to the melody of your harps I will not listen.'

9 St. John Chrysostom, *Discourses Against Judaizing Christians*, trans. Paul W. Harkins (Washington, DC: The Catholic University of American Press, 1988), 26.

FUNCTIONAL MUSIC

One expects the Church fathers to lash out against the music of the pagan cult-religious ceremonies, but it is most surprising to find St. John Chrysostom attacking the contemporary Jews based on a passage in the Old Testament, Numbers 10, in which God specifically instructs the high priests on the construction and use of trumpets. He criticizes them for giving preference to the trumpet over other traditional articles of worship, such as the golden altar of incense, the holy of holies, etc.

> Did you lose all those and keep only the trumpets? Do you Christians not see that what the Jews are doing is mockery rather than worship.[10]

Some stern and strict Church fathers now condemn even the use of music at weddings. St. John Chrysostom, for example, referring to the marriage of Rebecca and Isaac, pleads,

> Consider, I ask you, dearly beloved, how there was no sign of superfluities and inanities, no sign of devilish rites, no sign of cymbals and pipes and dances, nor those dreadful satanic orgies and the utter obscenity that marks their screaming—instead, complete dignity, complete wisdom, complete restraint.[11]

And again, regarding the wedding of Jacob,

> Surely there's no place for auloi? Surely there's no place for cymbals? Surely there's no place for satanic dances? Why is it, tell me, that you introduce such a nuisance into the house and call in people from the stage and the theater so as to undermine the girl's chastity with this regrettable expenditure and make the young person shameless?[12]

ENTERTAINMENT MUSIC

The Church leaders continue to denounce the great public entertainments of the circus and forbid the Christian to attend. It appears, however, that it was not easy to take away these pleasures from the faithful and that many preferred to go to the circus rather than to church. St. John Chrysostom complains,

---

10 St. John Chrysostom, *Discourses Against Judaizing Christians*, 93.

11 St. John Chrysostom, *Homilies on Genesis 46–67*, trans. Robert C. Hill (Washington, DC: The Catholic University of America Press, 1992), 40.

12 Ibid., 119.

Again there are chariot races and satanic spectacles in the hippodrome, and our congregation is shrinking … See how some who heard my previous instruction have today rushed away. They gave up the chance to hear this spiritual discourse and have run off to the hippodrome.[13]

St. Basil reveals that some of the monks themselves were even participating in musical performances. In criticizing one such monk for abandoning 'your common sense,' he adds,

> Moreover, you will also separate yourself from God with your songs and your robes, by which you are leading young maidens, not to God, but to the pit.[14]

St. John Chrysostom even condemns music and dance in the celebration of private occasions in the home. He tells of Herod who had his wife dance as part of his celebration of his birthday. But this was wrong!

> He ought to have honored the day with hymns and thankfulness to the Master, but he honored it with dishonor. For what is more dishonorable than dancing?
>
> Listen, you men and women who celebrate your own greatest days with such dances and songs. There are no small evils, even though they seem to be neither good nor bad; it is because they seem to be neither good nor bad that they are great evils … Does someone have the boldness to bring dancing into the house of one of the faithful, and is he not afraid that a thunderbolt will sweep down from above to consume all things with its flames? I say this also to the women, that they may also correct the men and lead them away from such pleasure.[15]

What are the entertainments of the Devil, this writer asks?

> Every form of sin, spectacles of indecency, horse racing, gatherings filled with laughter and abusive language.[16]

Having in mind the evils associated with music at festive banquets, St. John Chrysostom recommends that the Christian teach his family to sing sacred music instead at the table.

> This I say, not only that you may yourselves sing praises, but also that you may teach your wives and children to do so … especially

---

13 St. John Chrysostom, *Baptismal Instructions*, trans. Paul W. Harkins (Westminster, MD: The Newman Press, 1963), 93.

14 St. Basil, 'Letter to Glycerius,' in *Letters of Saint Basil*, trans. Sister Agnes Way (New York: Fathers of the Church, 1951), I, 333.

15 St. John Chrysostom, *Baptismal Instructions*, 157.

16 Ibid., 168.

at the table. For since Satan, seeking to ensnare us at feasts, for the most part employs as allies drunkenness, gluttony, immoderate laughter, and an inactive mind; at this time, both before and after table, it is especially necessary to fortify oneself with the protection of the psalms and, rising from the feast together with one's wife and children, to sing sacred hymns to God …

What if drunkenness or gluttony does make our minds dull and foolish? Where psalmody has entered, all these evil and depraved counsels retreat.

And just as not as a few wealthy persons wipe off their tables with a sponge filled with balsam, so that if any stain remain from the food, they may remove it and show a clean table; so should we also, filling our mouths with spiritual melody instead of balsam, so that if any stain remain in our mind from the abundance, we may thereby wipe it away …

And as those who bring comedians, dancers, and harlots into their feasts call in demons and Satan himself and fill their homes with innumerable contentions (among them jealousy, adultery, debauchery, and countless evils); so those who invoke David with his lyre call inwardly on Christ.[17]

The Church father who wrote most extensively about the evils of public entertainment was Salvian, in his book, *On the Government of God*. Here one finds that even in the fifth century the worst examples of the 'games' still continued.

> There is almost no crime or vice that does not accompany the games. In these the greatest pleasure is to have men die, or, what is worse and more cruel than death, to have them torn in pieces, to have the bellies of wild beasts gorged with human flesh; to have men eaten, to the great joy of the bystanders and the delight of onlookers, so that the victims seem devoured almost as much by the eyes of the audience as by the teeth of beasts.[18]

And, in spite of five centuries of admonitions, the Christians themselves were still enjoying these public entertainments and, according to Salvian, attending in greater numbers than those found in church.

> Whenever it happens, as it does only too often, that on the same day we are celebrating a feast of the church and the public games, I ask it of everyone's conscience, which is it that collects greater crowds of Christians, the rows of seats at the public games or the court of God?[19]

---

17 St. John Chrysostom, 'Exposition of Psalm XLI,' quoted in Oliver Strunk, *Source Readings in Music History* (New York: Norton, 1950), 68ff.

18 Salvian, *On the Government of God*, trans. Eva Sanford (New York: Columbia University Press, 1930), 160.

19 Ibid., 169.

Finally, it is interesting that Salvian notes that these kinds of entertainments are no longer given with the frequency of earlier times. The reasons for this he cites is that the cities outside Rome have been destroyed, whereas in Rome it is because of the worsening economy.

> I shall even go so far as to say that they are not now being done in all places where they have been hitherto. For instance, no shows are given now in Mayence, but this is because the city has been destroyed and blotted out; nor at Cologne, for it is overrun by the enemy. They are not being performed in the most noble city of Trèves, which has been laid low by a destruction four times repeated, nor finally in many other cities of Gaul or Spain …
>
> Moreover, the only reason for the cessation of the games themselves [in Rome] is that they cannot be given at the present time because of the misery and poverty in which we live … For the collapse of the imperial fiscus and the beggary of the Roman treasury do not permit money to be lavished on trifling matters that make no return.[20]

[20] Ibid., 170ff.

ON EDUCATION

Since the Church had taken such a clear position against 'pagan' philosophy, one does not expect to find any reference to the power of music to influence and improve the character—indeed, that is now the Church's role. However, when it came to the Church's *own* music, suddenly the ancient Greek question of the role of music on character become relevant. St. John Chrysostom, for example, writes,

> From strange chants harm, ruin, and many grievous matters are brought in, for those things that are lascivious and vicious in all songs settle in parts of the mind, making it softer and weaker; from the spiritual psalms, however, proceeds music of value, much utility, much sanctity, and every inducement to philosophy, for the words purify the mind.[21]

[21] Ibid.

In referring to David, St. Ambrose uses a number of musical metaphors. Of particular interest are the ones he chooses to represent the impact of matters of faith on character. While only speaking metaphorically, the passage does suggest a familiarity with the long-held beliefs of the Greeks in this regard.

> This is the song that holy David, the instrument of God's word and interpreter of the Lord's speech, sang on a spiritual cithara. With such measures of grace he calmed his noble soul and spirit. With such song he smoothed the roughness of this world, with such sound he softened its hardness, with such a psaltery he crushed the dread fear of death, with such sweet chords he trampled underfoot the regions that are below.[22]

As the Church denounced pagan philosophy, including Socrates, Plato and Aristotle, the Church forever changed education. In the new Church it was the message of the Lord, not the message of music, which changed character. Plato and Aristotle would re-emerge, but the idea that music can shape character has never returned to the classroom.

St. Jerome was concerned about priests themselves reading 'the philosophers, the orators, the poets,' for fear it would set an example for the 'weak.'[23] He admits he reads the philosophers and suggests that 'if we find anything useful in them, we apply it to our own doctrine.' But the other literature, anything having to do with idols, love, or secular things, these he says must be cut off like finger nails. And certainly, he says, priests should not read poetry or comedies, which only children read, and then because they are forced to in school.

> But as it is, we see even priests of God slighting the Gospels and the prophets, reading comedies, reciting love passages from bucolic verse, cherishing Virgil and voluntarily making themselves guilty of that which in the case of children is done under compulsion.

St. John Chrysostom argues for a similarly limited acceptance of philosophy. Philosophy is good, he says, as long as its *our* philosophy!

> Philosophy is a very good thing—I mean, of course our philosophy. Pagan philosophy, to be sure, is merely talk and fables, and not even the fables themselves possess any trace of true wisdom. In fact, all their teachings are uttered with a view to worldly repute.[24]

---

[22] Saint Ambrose, 'Jacob and the Happy Life,' in *Seven Exegetical Works*, trans. Michael P. McHugh (Washington, DC: The Catholic University of America Press), 171. Another lengthy use of music as a metaphor can be found in ibid., 419.

[23] St. Jerome, 'Letter to Damasus,' trans. Charles C. Mierow in *The Letters of St. Jerome* (Westminster, MD: The Newman Press, 1963), I, 118.

[24] St. John Chrysostom, *Commentary on Saint John*, trans. Sister Thomas Aquinas Goggin (New York: Fathers of the Church, 1960), 179.

Arts Education

One finds only a few interesting comments addressed to the subject of education in the arts at this time. St. Basil comments on the benefits of having educational ideas presented through singing. The reader should note, as an example of the general suspicion of the Church toward music, that when Basil says it is nice that we can learn something *useful* while singing, he is talking about the words and not about the music!

> Oh! the wise invention of the teacher who contrived that while we were singing we should at the same time learn something useful; by this means, too, the teachings are in a certain way impressed more deeply on our minds. Even a forceful lesson does not always endure, but what enters the mind with joy and pleasure somehow becomes more firmly impressed upon it.[25]

In another place, Basil speaks at greater length on the educational power of singing psalms. While he contends here that it may appear to be music, but it is really education which is important, at least he appears to give some credit to the contributing educational power of melody.

> For when the Holy Spirit saw that mankind was ill-inclined toward virtue and that we were heedless of the righteous life because of our inclination to pleasure, what did He do? He blended the delight of melody with doctrines in order that through the pleasantness and softness of the sound we might unawares receive what was useful in the words, according to the practice of wise physicians, who, when they give the more bitter draughts to the sick, often smear the rim of the cup with honey. For this purpose these harmonious melodies of the Psalms have been designed for us, that those who are of boyish age or wholly youthful in their character, while in appearance they sing, may in reality be educating their souls ... If somewhere one who rages like a wild beast from excessive anger falls under the spell of the psalm, he straightaway departs, with the fierceness of his soul calmed by the melody.[26]

Regarding genuine musical education, St. Gregory Nazianzus acknowledges the period of practice necessary to becoming an instrumental musician.

---

[25] St. Basil, 'Homily 10,' in *Exegetic Homilies*, trans. Sister Agnes Way (Washington, DC: The Catholic University of America Press, 1981), 153.

[26] St. Basil, 'Homily on the First Psalm,' quoted in Oliver Strunk, *Source Readings in Music History* (New York: Norton, 1950), 65.

There aren't any boxers who haven't had previous training and made a study in good time of contests. Do you find a track runner who hasn't exercised his legs? Did anyone in his senses ever cut pipes, shape them, and enter a contest all on the same day?[27]

On the other hand, when St. Basil poses the question, 'How should instructors in the arts correct the blunders of the children?,' he is not thinking of the blunders of art, but the blunders of behavior.

It is the duty of those themselves who teach the arts to reprimand the faulty technique of their pupils and correct their mistakes. All offenses, however, which arise from perversity of character, such as disobedience and the spirit of contradiction, laziness in performing tasks, idle talking, lying, or any other act forbidden to those who lead a religious life, should be referred to the person in charge of general discipline.[28]

Finally we are attracted to the humble Christian idea of St. Basil regarding giving credit to one's teacher.

One should receive instruction modestly and teach graciously. If he has learned anything from another, he should not conceal the fact after the manner of degraded wives who palm off as belonging to their husbands their baseborn children, but he should candidly declare the father of his idea.[29]

[27] Saint Gregory of Nazianzus, 'Concerning Himself and the Bishops,' trans. Denis Meehan (Washington, DC: The Catholic University of America Press, 1987), 66.

[28] St. Basil, 'The Long Rules,' in *Ascetical Works*, trans. Sister Monica Wagner (New York: Fathers of the Church, 1950), 329.

[29] St. Basil, 'Letter to Gregory of Nazianzus,' in *Letters of Saint Basil*, trans. Sister Agnes Way (New York: Fathers of the Church, 1951), I, 9.

ON THE PHYSIOLOGY OF AESTHETICS

In all literature before the discoveries of modern brain research, one finds in ordinary expressions a favoritism for the right hand, which reflects an unconscious preference for the left hemisphere of the brain. The left hemisphere is the only one which can speak and it denies the existence of the right hemisphere, which some believe may make music itself difficult for humanity at large to accept as being equal to, for example, normal language. Thus we know expressions such as, 'The favored one sits at the *right* hand of the king,' or, to turn it around, we make negative reference to a, '*left-handed* compliment.' It is in this regard that our attention is drawn to St. John Chrysostom's paraphrase of Matthew 25:31–46,

But when the Son of Man shall come in the glory of his Father, he will set the sheep on his right hand, but the goats on the left, and the former will go into everlasting life, while the others, into everlasting punishment.[30]

30 St. John Chrysostom, *Commentary on Saint John, Homilies 1–47*, 269.

All musicians (and lovers) know how impossible it is for left hemisphere speech to do justice to the emotions of the right hemisphere of the brain. St. Basil makes the interesting observation that speech can also fail in representing the thoughts of the left hemisphere.

Even when I was writing to your Eloquence, I knew well that every theological expression is less than the thought in the mind of the speaker and less than the interpretation desired by whim who seeks, because speech is in some way too weak to serve perfectly our thoughts.[31]

31 St. Basil, 'Letter to Gregory of Nazianzus,' in *Letters of Saint Basil*, trans. Sister Agnes Way (New York: Fathers of the Church, 1951), I, 20.

Many Christian philosophers simply ignored some of the subjects so often debated by the pagan philosophers, such as the nature of the soul and the senses. For the Christian philosophers the soul was no longer an enigma of man's bodily function, but now the essence of the man which must be saved. For St. Basil this process begins with silence—no listening to music, no looking around at pretty girls, etc.

Silence, then, is the beginning of purification in the soul, since the tongue is not busied with the affairs of men, nor the eyes looking around at fair complexions and graceful forms, nor the ears lessening the harmony of the soul by listening to melodies made for fleeting pleasure.[32]

32 St. Basil, 'Letter to Gregory of Nazianzus,' in ibid., I, 7.

Beginning with the age of Pythagoras, in the sixth century BC, philosophers had struggled to explain the entire question of the senses and where they are located. We find an interesting report in St. Ambrose that some doctors had finally by this day arrived at the correct answer, although he is quick to point out that others disagree.

Those skilled in the art of medicine maintain, in fact, that the brain is placed in a man's head for the sake of the eyes and that the other senses of our bodies are housed close together on account of the brain ... Many are of the opinion that this starting point is the heart.[33]

33 Saint Ambrose, 'Six Days of Creation: Six,' in *Hexameron, Paradise, and Cain and Abel*, trans. John J. Savage (New York: Fathers of the Church, 1961), 200, 273.

St. Ambrose acknowledges the strong impression rendered by the senses, by way of an admonition to instrumental musicians. While this passage is somewhat ambiguous, he seems to be calling for musicians to be responsible for their choice of repertoire.

> Sometimes the musician has compassion on his instrument. Therefore play what is honorable, that your compassion may be honorable. For one who sees is much affected by what he sees, and one who hears by what he hears.[34]

34 Saint Ambrose, 'Death as a Good,' in *Seven Exegetical Works*, 89.

ON THE PSYCHOLOGY OF AESTHETICS

The Church fathers also had little desire to discuss the traditional pagan questions regarding pleasure and pain or the nature of the emotions. For the Church of the fourth century, the word 'Pleasure' was heard not in a discussion of aesthetics so much as of deportment. Most public entertainments were declared bad and the new Christian was not even supposed to laugh. St. Basil simply admonishes the Christian, 'Flee pleasures!'[35]

When it came to the Christian feeling pleasure, especially aesthetic pleasure, the demand of the Church was 'control,' meaning not to give evidence of pleasure. St. Basil speaks of it in this way:

> He who is master of every passion and feels no excitement from pleasure, or at least, does not give it outward expression, but is steadfastly inclined to restraint as regards every harmful delight, such a one is perfectly content—but, clearly, he is also at the same time free from all sin.[36]

35 St. Basil, 'Letter to his Pupil, Chilo,' in *Letters of Saint Basil*, trans. Sister Agnes Way (New York: Fathers of the Church, 1951), I, 107.

36 St. Basil, 'The Long Rules,' in *Ascetical Works*, trans. Sister Monica Wagner (New York: Fathers of the Church, 1950), 272.

The entire subject of the emotions was one the Church considered inappropriate to the life of the Christian. Consequently, we also find no discussion of the emotions with respect to the enjoyment of art. But we don't entirely believe what we read, for even these stern Church fathers were human and possessed emotions, as we can see in an instance when St. Basil cried out,

> Why, how could I even refrain from declaring aloud the emotions of my soul?[37]

37 St. Basil, 'Letter to the Governor of Neo-Caesarea,' in *Letters of Saint Basil*, trans. Sister Agnes Way (New York: Fathers of the Church, 1951), I, 157.

ON THE PHILOSOPHY OF AESTHETICS

The entire question of aesthetics was also somewhat outside the perspective of the Church writers. First, the Church believed one should not value art above the artist, who was made by God. Second, according to St. John Chrysostom, the Christian cannot love art—for to love art is to love the present life, which is inconsistent with believing in the future life.

> Why, even now we shall find men gladly enduring every kind of suffering, for the sake of enjoying this present life, even though they have this belief in the life to come? When they see buildings, and works of art, and mechanical devices, they weep and cry out: 'What great things man devises, and yet will he become dust?' So strong is their attachment to the present life.[38]

38 St. John Chrysostom, *Commentary on Saint John*, 227.

Among the writings of the authors we have been studying here, we find only a single mention of a traditional topic of aesthetics, a reference by St. Ambrose to Imitation. He discusses this with respect to painting and comments on the importance of the artist being faithful to nature.

> The shadow adheres and stays close to the body in accordance with nature, so much so that artists strive to depict the shadows of objects in their paintings. They maintain that it is the province of art not to ignore a quality inherent in nature. An artist whose painting does not represent the requisite shadows may be likened to one who contravenes the natural law.[39]

39 Saint Ambrose, 'Six Days of Creation: Four,' trans. John J. Savage, in *Hexameron, Paradise, and Cain and Abel* (New York: Fathers of the Church, 1961). 134.

ON THE AESTHETICS OF MUSIC

With the exception of Augustine, most Church fathers of this period confined their discussion of the aesthetics of music to church music. There are, nevertheless, a few interesting observations of a more inclusive nature.

One of the most fascinating contentions by one of the Church philosophers is that the pleasure deriving from music is genetically part of mankind. For St. John Chrysostom, it was in recognition of this, and to thus compete with the devil, that God gave man psalms to sing.

> Inasmuch as this kind of pleasure is thoroughly innate to our mind, and lest demons introducing lascivious songs should overthrow everything, God established the psalms, in order that singing might be both a pleasure and a help.[40]

In a passage in which St. Ambrose is discussing a variety of arts and crafts, he observes that the work of the artist remains after the artist is gone. But he is critical of the arts which lack this asset, namely music, noting that when the sounds stop, 'nothing survives or remains.'

> The arts may be considered in various aspects. There are those which are practical. These relate to the movement of the body or to the sound of the voice. When the movement or sound has passed away, there is nothing that survives or remains for the spectators or the hearers. Other arts are theoretical. These display the vigor of the mind. There are other arts of such a nature that, even when the processes of operation cease, the handiwork remains visible. As an example of this we have buildings or woven material which, even when the craftsman is silent, still exhibit his skill.[41]

While the Church writers rarely are complimentary of the music made by man, they do not hesitate to admire 'natural' music. St. Ambrose remarks on the songs of birds, 'some of which learn by nature, others by training,'[42] as well as the cricket, for which he advances a strange theory.

> How sweet is the song from the tiny throat of a cicada! In the heat of midsummer 'they rend the thickets' with their songs. The greater the heat at midday, the more musical become their songs, because the purer the air they breathe at that time, the clearer does the song resound.[43]

Finally, it is somewhat surprising to find St. Ambrose implying a belief in the ancient Greek theory of the 'Music of the Spheres,' a notion which nearly every philosopher had long since abandoned.

> By the impact and motion of these spheres there is produced a tone full of sweetness, the fruit of consummate art and of the most delightful modulation, inasmuch as the air, torn apart by such artful motion, combines in even and melodious fashion high and low notes to such a degree that it surpasses in sweetness any other musical composition.[44]

---

40 St. John Chrysostom, 'Exposition of Psalm XLI,' quoted in Oliver Strunk, *Source Readings in Music History* (New York: Norton, 1950), 68.

41 Saint Ambrose, 'Six Days of Creation: One,' in *Hexameron, Paradise, and Cain and Abel*, 16.

42 Saint Ambrose, 'Six Days of Creation: Five,' in *Hexameron, Paradise, and Cain and Abel*, trans. John J. Savage (New York: Fathers of the Church, 1961), 200.

43 Ibid., 217.

44 Saint Ambrose, 'Six Days of Creation: Two,' in *Hexameron, Paradise, and Cain and Abel*, 50.

Church Music

There are very few references to the use of instrumental music in any association with the Church by these writers. One interesting exception regarding instrumental music is found in St. Ambrose when he speaks of the lyre. Perhaps the fact that he himself was a distinguished composer gave him a broader perspective than his contemporaries.

> For while the tortoise is alive, it is sunk in the mire; but when it has died, its covering is adapted to the uses of song and the gift of holy instruction, to sound forth the seven changing notes in rhythmic measures.[45]

45 Saint Ambrose, 'The Prayer of Job and David,' in *Seven Exegetical Works*, 419.

St. Basil, although his object is to discuss the true purpose of church music, also makes the suggestion that the harp was 'adapted for the hymns.'

> The physical structure of the body is, speaking figuratively, a harp and an instrument harmoniously adapted for the hymns of our God; and the actions of the body, which are referred to the glory of God are a psalm, whenever in an appropriate measure we perform nothing out of tune in our actions. Whatever pertains to lofty contemplation and theology is a canticle. Therefore, the psalm is a musical sermon when it is played rhythmically on the instrument with harmonic sounds.[46]

46 St. Basil, 'Homily 10,' in *Exegetic Homilies*, trans. Sister Agnes Way (Washington, DC: The Catholic University of America Press, 1981), 152.

In the view of St. John Chrysostom, however, there was simply no need for instrumental music in the Church; no need for the long-practiced skill of these players.

> Here there is no need for the cithara, or for stretched strings, or for the plectrum, or for art, or for any instrument; but, if you like, you may yourself become a cithara, mortifying the members of the flesh and making a full harmony of mind and body ...
>
> Here there is no need for art which is slowly perfected; there is need only for lofty purpose, and we become skilled in a brief decisive moment.[47]

47 Ibid., 70.

The general ban on instrumental music, by the fourth century, was more likely due to the performers of these instruments, and no doubt the musical styles associated with them, being identified with the pagan entertainments to which the Church so strongly objected.

Choral music, on the other hand, could not be banned, because a choir of angels had sung at the birth of Christ. As we can see in St. Basil, this was not forgotten.

What, then, is more blessed than to imitate on earth the choirs of angels.[48]

[48] St. Basil, 'Letter to Gregory of Nazianzus,' in *Letters of Saint Basil*, trans. Sister Agnes Way (New York: Fathers of the Church, 1951), I, 7.

But a theological problem remained for the Church fathers: How does one justify the numerous references to musical instruments in the Old Testament? St. Basil, writing of the Psalms, seeks to make the point that the appearance of the harp here, played by David, had the specific purpose of illuminating sacred ideas from above, and, therefore, one should concentrate on these and not the instruments for their earthly musical value.

> To it, although there are many musical instruments, the prophet adapted the so-called harp, showing, as it seems to me, that the gift from the Spirit resounded in his ears from above. With the cithara and the lyre the bronze from beneath responds with sound to the plucking, but the harp has the source of its harmonic rhythms from above, in order that we may be careful to seek the things above and not be borne down by the sweetness of the melody to the passions of the flesh.[49]

[49] St. Basil, 'Homily 10,' in *Exegetic Homilies*, trans. Sister Agnes Way (Washington, DC: The Catholic University of America Press, 1981), 153.

Usually the Church writers explain the Old Testament musical instruments as metaphors, as we have indicated in a previous chapter. Several fourth-century examples of this can be seen in Basil.

> The aulos is a musical instrument which needs wind for the melody. Wherefore, I think that every holy prophet was called figuratively a aulos because of the inspiration of the Holy Spirit.[50]

[50] Ibid., 'Homily 14,' 224.

In another place he refers to the ten-string psaltery as being a metaphor for the 'ten principal precepts, written according to the first teaching of the Law.'[51]

[51] Ibid., 'Homily 15,' 230.

The most striking explanations of the musical instruments in the Old Testament are those which are anti-Semitic. Theodore of Cyrus (died ca. 460), for example portrays the Jews as almost childlike.

> If old Levities used those instruments in the Temple of God to praise Him, not because it pleased Him ... Once it happened, however, He tolerated it, wishing to take them from the error of idolatry. Since they were fond of play and laughter, and since all this sort of thing took place in the temples of the idols, He allowed it, thus to lead them, and by the smaller evil to avoid the greater.[52]

[52] James W. McKinnon, 'Musical Instruments in Medieval Psalm Commentaries and Psalters,' *Journal of the American Musicological Society* 21, no. 1 (Spring 1968), 7.

The origin of Church music, according to St. John Chrysostom, was to lessen the toil of religious contemplation. Here, again, there is a certain anti-Semitic tone, as John seems to suggest that God only gave the Jews music because they were basically lazy and could not otherwise concentrate.

> When God saw that many men were rather indolent, that they came unwillingly to Scriptural readings and did not endure the labor this involves, wishing to make the labor more grateful and to take away the sensation of it, He blended melody with prophecy in order that, delighted by the modulation of the chant, all might with great eagerness give forth sacred hymns to Him. For nothing so uplifts the mind, giving it wings and freeing it from the earth, releasing it from the chains of the body, affecting it with love of wisdom, and causing it to scorn all things pertaining to this life, as modulated melody and the divine chant composed of number [rhythm].[53]

The most frequently mentioned form of music in the new Church is the singing of hymns, although musically we know little about these early forms. Undoubtedly they were sung in unison, as indeed St. Gregory Nazianzus, a fourth-century writer implies, 'while they harmonize many mouths into a single voice.'[54] This would make plausible the resultant effect when St. Paulinus of Nola speaks of the congregation of the faithful engaging in 'lusty rendering of holy hymns.'[55]

It has long been recognized that some of the Psalms seem to indicate an antiphonal or responsorial form of singing, and Basil mentions such two-part antiphonal singing in the fourth century. This account is unusually interesting in suggesting that some of the original musical traditions may have come from older religious practice, the Church's protestations against the 'pagans' notwithstanding.

> As to the charge regarding psalmody, by which especially our slanderers terrify the more simple, I have this to say, that the customs now prevalent are in accord and harmony with those of all the churches of God. Among us the people come early after nightfall to the house of prayer, and in labor and affliction and continual tears confess to God. Finally, rising up from their prayers, they begin the chanting of psalms. And now, divided into two parts, they chant antiphonally, becoming master of the text of the Scriptural passages, and at the same time directing their attention and the recollectedness of their hearts. Then, again, leaving it to one to intone the melody,

53 St. John Chrysostom, 'Exposition of Psalm XLI,' quoted in Oliver Strunk, *Source Readings in Music History* (New York: Norton, 1950), 67.

54 Saint Gregory of Nazianzus, *Concerning his Own Affairs*, trans. Denis Meehan (Washington, DC: The Catholic University of America Press, 1987), 34.

55 *The Poems of St. Paulinus of Nola*, trans. P.G. Walsh (New York: Newman Press, 1975), Poem 27, 542ff.

the rest chant in response; thus, having spent the night in a variety of psalmody and intervening prayers, when day at length begins to dawn, all in common, as with one voice and one heart, offer up the psalm of confession to the Lord, each one making His own the words of repentance. If, then, you shun us on this account, you will shun the Egyptians, and also those of both Libyas, the Thebans, Palestinians, Arabians, Phoenicians, Syrians, and those dwelling beside the Euphrates—in one word, all those among whom night watches and prayers and psalmody in common have been held in esteem.[56]

In another place, St. Basil describes at greater length the style of the fourth-century psalms. It is not entirely clear, however, whether the special attributes he recognizes here are due to the style of the music or the text.

> A psalm implies serenity of soul; it is the author of peace, which calms bewildering and seething thoughts. For, it softens the wrath of the soul, and what is unbridled it chastens. A psalm forms friendships, unties those separated, conciliates those at enmity ... So that psalmody, bringing about choral singing, a bond, as it were, toward unity, and joining the people into a harmonious union of one choir, produces also the greatest of blessings, charity.[57]

The chief value of singing psalms, according to Basil, is 'to calm and soften the wicked spirits which trouble souls.'[58] But he makes a curious distinction here in saying that a 'bad' person cannot properly sing the psalms.

> Not if someone utters the words of the psalm with his mouth, does that one sing to the Lord; but, all who send up the psalmody from a clean heart, and who are holy, maintaining righteousness toward God, these are able to sing to God, harmoniously guided by the spiritual rhythms. How many stand there, coming from fornication? How many from theft? How many concealing in their hearts deceit? How many lying? They think they are singing, although in truth they are not singing. For, the Scripture invites the saint to the singing of psalms. 'A bad tree cannot bear good fruit,' nor a bad heart utter words of life.[59]

We have another detailed description of the new Church music from St. Jerome, in his 'Commentary on the Epistle of Paul to the Ephesians.' Interestingly enough, he takes as his point of departure

---

56 St. Basil, 'Letter to the Clergy of Neo-Caesarea,' in *Letters of Saint Basil*, trans. Sister Agnes Way (New York: Fathers of the Church, 1955), II, 83.

57 St. Basil, 'Homily 14,' in *Exegetic Homilies*, trans. Sister Agnes Way (Washington, DC: The Catholic University of America Press, 1981), 213.

58 Ibid., 214. In Homily 21, ibid., 341, Basil says the purpose of psalm singing is to 'correct the passions of the soul.' He then quotes, without comment, references to many musical instruments in Psalm 61.

59 Ibid., 217.

the only passage in the New Testament which even hints at the use of instrumental music in the service

> Be filled with the Spirit, addressing one another in psalms and hymns and spiritual songs, singing and *making melody* to the Lord with all your heart.[60]

'Making melody' is a phrase found in the Old Testament and in late Medieval and Renaissance literature which is used as a synonym for some form of instrumental music. We believe this phrase simply slipped by unnoticed by the committee which assembled the New Testament, as we know it, in the fourth century. Jerome neatly sidesteps any implicit approval of instrumental music by mistranslating the final part as 'in your heart,' instead of 'with all your heart,' rendering the phrase 'making melody' a metaphor.

It is of further interest that St. Jerome, while recognizing here three basic kinds of Church music, psalms, hymns, and songs, returns to the ancient Greek concept of *ethos*.

> How the psalm, the hymn, and the song differ one from another we learn most fully in the Psalter. Here let us say briefly that hymns declare the power and majesty of the Lord and continually praise his works and favors, something which all those psalms contain to which the word 'Alleluia' is prefixed or appended. Psalms, moreover, properly affect the seat of the *ethos* in order that by means of this organ of the body we may know what ought to be done and what ought not to be done. The subtle moralist, however, who inquires into these things and examines the harmony of the world and the order and concord of all creatures, sings a spiritual song. To express our opinion more clearly to the simple-minded, the psalm is directed toward the body, the song toward the mind. We ought, then, to sing and to make melody and to praise the Lord more with the heart than with the voice.[61]

By this last sentence, Jerome means that it is not music itself, but the person, which praises God. Further, it is not the music which is important, but the *words* of the music which one sings.

> Let the servant of Christ sing so that he pleases, not through his voice, but through the words which he pronounces ... [so that one does not] make of the house of God a popular theater.

60 Ephesians 5:19. This same passage appears also in Colossians 3:16, but without the reference to 'making melody.'

61 Quoted in Oliver Strunk, *Source Readings in Music History* (New York: Norton, 1950), 72.

St. John Chrysostom makes this same point: it is the words of church music which are most important, adding that one must not be inattentive when singing, 'but so the mind may hear the tongue.'[62] Even if you don't understand the words, they are still the most important thing!

> Even though the meaning of the words be unknown to you, teach your mouth to utter them meanwhile. For the tongue is made holy by the words when they are uttered with a ready and eager mind.[63]

[62] St. John Chrysostom, 'Exposition of Psalm XLI,' quoted in Oliver Strunk, *Source Readings in Music History* (New York: Norton, 1950), 68.

[63] Ibid., 69.

10 SAINT AUGUSTINE (354 AD–430 AD)

In Augustine we come to the most important Christian philosopher of the first five centuries. No one else was so influential in the future development of the Church and even today his impact can still be measured in the Roman Catholic Church.

He had a broad education in the liberal arts, including music, and enough study of 'pagan' philosophy to make him believe in Reason almost as much as he believed in God. His intelligence is evident in his ability to form some very important questions, and for this we join in his standing ovation. But it is when we read his answers that we must take our seat and offer only that polite applause which signifies the death of art, for his answers are too often simply wrong. It is for this reason that we cannot join those who think of Augustine as a kind of Christian Plato.

His powerful, rational mind did not seem to be accompanied by any genuine appreciation of the subjective, the arts, or the contribution made to life by the emotions. Since he describes having had a very full range of life experiences before he joined the Church, we are astonished that his writings suggest that he completely failed to understand the point and purpose of music. We prefer to believe that the views he left are restricted by his role as a Church leader and that we are not seeing the true scope of his thought.

Augustine reveals in his *Confessions* that he had had some experience in acting and in the composition of poetry. But what little he later tells us of this experience only reflects a lack of sympathy with the arts and his subsequent feelings of emptiness.

> [From my nineteenth year to my twenty-eighth] hunting after the emptiness of popular praise, down even to theatrical applause, and poetic prizes, and strifes for grassy garlands, and the follies of shows, and the intemperance of desires.[1]

Neither were these feelings of emptiness filled by music, books or entertainment.

1 *The Confessions*, trans. Edward B. Pusey (New York: Collier, 1909), bk. IV. This last reference included, in his youth, a lusty appreciation of the female sex, which resulted in one of the most memorable prayers of the Middle Ages, 'Give me chastity—but not yet!'

> For I bore about a shattered and bleeding soul, impatient of being borne by me, yet where to repose it, I found not. Not in calm groves, not in games and music, nor in fragrant spots, nor in curious banquetings, nor in the pleasures of the bed; nor in books or poetry, found it repose.[2]

2 *The Confessions*, bk. IV.

The man should have left us a much more vivid description of early medieval aesthetics than we have. If the perspective he left is a limited one, it is nevertheless one of the most interesting discussions of its kind.

ART MUSIC

From a passing admission by Augustine, we know there were listeners who appreciated music purely for music's sake in the fourth century. He is speaking of various things which make men happy, when he contributes the following illustration.

> Many decide that for them the happy life is found in vocal music and in the sounds of string instruments and auloi. Whenever these are absent, they account themselves unhappy, whereas when they are at hand, they are thrilled with joy.[3]

3 *The Free Choice of the Will*, trans. Robert P. Russell (Washington, DC: The Catholic University of America Press, 1968), xiii i.

Never does Augustine himself admit such enthusiasm for secular music. In his *Confessions*, he mentions only that as a youth he found some poetry (which he documents was still sung) became part of him, while in other cases it did not stay with him.

> For verses and poems I can turn to true food, and 'Medea flying,' though I did sing, I maintained not; though I heard it sung, I believed not.[4]

4 *The Confessions*, bk. III.

Augustine has left a humorous account of an artist–composer, no doubt a friend, which perhaps reveals some of his own concerns about Art Music. Augustine seems bothered that this artist prefers to withdraw from his friends to work and does not want to be disturbed when composing. Augustine worries that his friend will thus lose his ability for *intellectual* communication. Writing this later, as a Christian writer, Augustine naturally expresses a preference here for contemporary composition to the older 'pagan' repertoire.

When we had returned, we found Licentius eagerly striving to compose verses. But Helicon would never have relieved him of his thirst, for—although only one course was served at our lunch—he had quietly withdrawn when we had reached about the middle, and he had drunk nothing.

I said to him: 'I wish that some day or other you would master that poetics, since you have become so ardently attached to it: not that this kind of perfection would afford me any great pleasure, but because I see you have become so eager for it that you can be alienated from it only by disgust, and this readily happens after perfection has been reached. Furthermore, since you are quite musical, I should prefer to have you inflict your own verses on our ears, rather than have you—like the little birds we see enclosed in cages—singing words you do not understand in those Greek tragedies. But I advise you to go for a drink, if you have any regard for Hortensius and philosophy. In fact, in that disputation between yourself and Trygetius, you have already offered her your first fruits as a most pleasing libation, and she, far more than poetics, has enkindled in you a glowing desire for the knowledge of great and truly profitable things. But, while I wish to invite both of you back to the arena of those intellectual exercises that impart refinement to the mind, I fear lest it become a labyrinth for both of you.'[5]

In another treatise, Augustine mentions this poet again, now expressing even more concern that his poetry might separate him from reality.

Here, fearing that his running to extremes on poetics might take him away from philosophy, I said: 'I am vexed somewhat because, singing and crooning in all kinds of meter, you pursue that verse-making of yours which may be erecting between yourself and reality a wall more impenetrable than they are trying to rear between your lovers (Pyramus and Thisbe), for they used to sigh to each other through a tiny natural crevice.'[6]

Regarding the theater, Augustine particularly objected to the use of plot and song to glorify the pagan gods, many of whom, in their very myths, were guilty of a variety of crimes.

I must confess that the better educated pagans reject such stories about their gods …
[But], however much they may protest, they cannot wholly clear their gods of crime if they have to stage for them, on demand, shows

[5] *Answer to Skeptics*, trans. Ludwig Schopp (New York: CIMA Publishing Co., 1948), IV, 7

[6] *Divine Providence and the Problem of Evil*, trans. Ludwig Schopp (New York: CIMA Publishing Co., 1948), 247.

in which they basely depict the very stories they so loftily deny. For, so long as the gods are so greatly appeased by these false and filthy goings-on, even if the burden of the legendary song is a divine sin which never happened, it is still a real sin for the gods to be delighted with it.[7]

<small>7 *The City of God*, trans. Gerald G. Walsh (New York: Fathers of the Church, 1954), XVIII, xii.</small>

In another place, Augustine blames the pagan gods themselves for the introduction of theater.

> The stage plays, those exhibitions of depravity and unbounded license, were not introduced in Rome by men's vices, but by the command of your gods … If your mind retains enough sense to esteem the soul more than the body, then choose whom you should worship.[8]

<small>8 Ibid., I, xxxii.</small>

FUNCTIONAL MUSIC

For fourth-century Romans the ancient cult-religious ceremonies were now more of a ritual than theology to govern their lives. Augustine focuses on one of the most popular, the 'obscene rites of the Phrygian goddess Cybele,' in his *The City of God*, where he criticizes the Roman citizen who participates in this festival.

> Why, then, now that disaster has laid a heavy hand on you, do you complain about Christian civilization, if it be not that you desire to wallow securely in voluptuousness and, free from all restraint, give free rein to your profligate conduct? For, you do not desire to have peace and abundance of all things, in order to use these goods like decent men, that is, with measure, sobriety, temperance, and piety. No, your purpose is rather to pursue every kind of pleasure with insane extravagance; thus, out of your prosperity, you conjure up that corruption of morals which is more deadly than the fury of your enemies.[9]

<small>9 Ibid., I, xxx.</small>

Now Augustine provides a first-hand description of the cult-religious celebrations as he knew them in the fourth century.

> I myself, in my younger days, used to frequent the sacrilegious stage plays and comedies. I used to watch the demoniacal fanatics and listen to the choruses, and take delight in the obscene shows in honor of their gods and goddesses, of the virgin Caelestis and the

Berecynthian Cybele, mother of the gods. Before the latter's couch on the day of her solemn bathing, ribald refrains were publicly sung about her by lewd actors that were unfit for the ear of the mother of the gods, and of the mother of any Senator or decent man—so unspeakably bestial, in fact, that even the mothers of the players themselves would have been ashamed to listen …

Surely, the comedians themselves would have blushed to rehearse at home before their mothers the obscene words and actions which they uttered and performed in public before the mother of the gods and in the presence of a vast assemblage of both sexes. If curiosity could entice such numbers to come, a shocked sense of decency surely should have hurried them home. If these enormities are religious service, what can sacrilege be? If that bathing is purification, what is pollution?[10]

10 Ibid., II, iv.

As much as the Church philosophers condemned the 'pagan' philosophers, Augustine suggests that a temple dedicated to Plato would be better than what he had witnessed in the celebration of Cybele.

How much more sensible and proper would it be to have Plato's writings read in a temple dedicated to him than to have the mutilation of the priests of Cybele, the consecration of eunuchs, the slashing of insane men, in the temples of the demons, the perpetration of every cruel and foul, or foully cruel and cruelly foul, abomination that is wont to pass for a religious rite.[11]

11 Ibid., II, vii.

ON EDUCATION

Augustine follows the lead of his Church colleagues in dismissing 'pagan' philosophy. In one place he mentions reading the *Hortensius* of Cicero,[12] of whom he makes the interesting observation, 'whose language almost all admire, not so his heart.' In condemning earlier philosophy, he quotes, as many Church writers did, from Colossians 2:8.

12 *The Confessions*, bk. III.

But the love of wisdom is in Greek called 'philosophy,' with which that book inflamed me. Some there be that seduce through philosophy, under a great, and smooth, and honorable name coloring and disguising their own errors: and almost all who in that and former ages were such, are in that book censured and set forth: there also is made plain that wholesome advice of Thy Spirit,

> See to it that no one makes a prey of you by philosophy and empty deceit, according to human tradition, according to the elemental spirits of the universe, and not according to Christ.

Regarding his own education in the liberal arts, including music, Augustine maintains that in his youth he studied and understood them all without the benefit of a teacher.

> Whatever was written, either on rhetoric, or logic, geometry, music, and arithmetic, by myself without much difficulty or any instructor, I understood.[13]

Understanding the liberal arts was, for the fourth-century Church fathers, somewhat of an irrelevant concept. Faith was what mattered. Only later did some Church philosophers come to believe that the liberal arts might have a value in helping the Christian understand this message. For Augustine, education had one central purpose: to help man understand the difference between himself and God!

> All instruction in wisdom, the purpose of which is the education of men, is for distinguishing the creator and the creature, and worshiping the one as Lord and confessing the other as subject.[14]

In another place, speaking to a poet, he takes a broader view.

> You must return to those verses, for instruction in the liberal arts, if only it is moderate and concise, produces devotees more alert and steadfast and better equipped for embracing truth.[15]

Perhaps because he sensed that the mysteries of music lay outside the realm of Reason, Augustine unfortunately fails to accept that the study of music can make any positive contribution to the mind.

> Studies that are taken up with things that are more curious than solidly worthwhile—granted even that on occasion they are not entirely useless—dissipate the mind and hence must be put in our second category. Just because one aulos player so delighted the ears of the populace, according to Varro, that they made him a king is no reason for supposing that we can effect enlargement of the mind by aulos playing.[16]

---

13 Ibid., bk. IV.

14 *Eighty-Three Different Questions*, trans. David L. Mosher (Washington, DC: The Catholic University of America Press, 1981), 81.

15 *Divine Providence*, 261.

16 *The Magnitude of the Soul*, trans. Ludwig Schopp in *Writings of Saint Augustine* (New York: CIMA, 1947), II, xx.

The only value he can recommend in the study of music is a secondary one, for learning 'order.' And even in this case only moderate study is recommended.

> Now in music, in geometry, in the movements of the stars, in the fixed ratios of numbers, order reigns in such manner that if one desires to see its source and its very shrine, so to speak, he either finds it in these, or he is unerringly led to it through them. Indeed, such learning, if one uses it with moderation—and in this matter, nothing is to be feared more than excess—rears for philosophy a soldier ... so competent that he sallies forth wherever he wishes and leads others as well, and reaches that ultimate goal, beyond which he desires nothing else, beyond which he neither ought nor can seek anything.[17]

17 *Divine Providence*, 289.

ON THE PHYSIOLOGY OF AESTHETICS

Augustine's contemplation about how the mind works begins with an observation which baffled him. Why is it, he says,[18] that when the mind orders the body to do something, such as a hand movement, the body obeys immediately. But when the mind wills itself to do something, as in the example of will itself, the mind does not always obey? 'Whence this monstrousness?,' he asks.

18 *The Confessions*, bk. VIII.

He follows this rhetorical question by a brief reference to the New Testament passage, Titus 1:10, 'For there are many insubordinate men, empty talkers and deceivers.' We fail to understand how he derives the following statement from this text, but the statement itself is quite extraordinary.

> Who observing that in deliberating there are two wills, affirm that there are two minds in us of two kinds, one good, and the other evil.

For the modern reader, of course, this statement suggests that perhaps Augustine was one of small number of philosophers who deduced through observation the existence of our twin brain hemispheres. One of the characteristics of the left brain is to attribute somewhat sinister motives to its mute right twin, as in the example we have mentioned earlier of the expression, 'a left-handed compliment.'[19] Similar expressions are found in all cultures and spanning many centuries. There can be no question that this is the connotation Augustine had in mind for 'evil,' for in a sermon on John 21:1–14,

19 We remind the reader that the right hemisphere controls the left side of the body, etc.

he explains what Jesus meant when he directed how his disciples should cast their fishing nets.

> Notice this: in the first fishing episode He did not say to them: 'Lower the nets to the right or to the left,' because, if He were to specify 'to the left' only evil persons would be signified, and, if He were to specify 'to the right,' only the good would be indicated.[20]

20 'Sermon 248,' trans. Sister Mary Muldowney in *Sermons on the Liturgical Seasons* (New York: Fathers of the Church, 1959), 302.

The latest thinking among some psychologists is that, while we have two hemispheres, we have many minds, that is individual depositories of genetic and learned information which takes over various tasks while 'we' are doing something else. Therefore, it is curious to also find a thought of this nature in this same discussion.

> For if there be so many contrary natures as there be conflicting wills, there shall now be not two only, but many.

On the Senses

Following a long line of philosophers who put Reason above any other form of perception, Augustine incorrectly concludes that understanding derived through the senses is somehow outside the mind.

> All things that are perceived through one of the senses are sensed as existing outside of us and are contained in space, which, we affirm, makes possible their perception. Those things that are comprehended by the intellect, however, are comprehended as existing nowhere else but in the comprehending mind itself and, at the same time, as not contained in space.[21]

21 *The Immortality of the Soul*, trans. Ludwig Schopp in *Writings of Saint Augustine* (New York: CIMA, 1947), II, vi.

But if the senses are perceived outside the mind, how do they come to be understood by the mind? Augustine, employing a little personal weird science, supposed a third sense, an inner sense, in some way translates this information.

> I acknowledge that this power, whatever it is, does exist, and I do not hesitate to call it the inner sense. But unless the impression brought to us by the bodily senses pass beyond even this inner sense, they cannot result in knowledge. For it is by reason that we grasp

whatever we know. To mention but a few instances, we know that color cannot be perceived by hearing nor sound by sight. And this is something that we do not know by sight or hearing or by that inner sense which is not lacking in beasts. We are not to suppose that beasts know that light is not perceived by the ear or sound by the eye, since we discern this only by rational reflection and thought.[22]

22 *The Free Choice of the Will*, iii.

Curiously enough, Augustine was aware that each person perceives through the senses in an individual way, but he failed to associate this phenomenon with personal experience. He seemed to simply believe that each person has personal, that is to say, different perceptions of sense, as he suggests in the following dialogue with a student.

> AUGUSTINE. First I shall ask you whether my bodily senses are the same as yours, or whether mine are mine alone and yours are yours alone. If this latter were not so, I would be unable to see anything with my eyes which you would not see.
> STUDENT. I fully agree that though the senses are of the same nature, yet each one of us has his own sense of sight or hearing, and so forth. One man cannot only see but also hear something that another man does not hear, and one man can perceive by any one of the senses something different from what another perceives. So it is obvious that your senses are yours alone and mine are mine alone.
> AUGUSTINE. Would you give the same or a different answer concerning the inner sense?
> STUDENT. Not a different answer, certainly. My inner sense perceives my bodily sensations and your inner sense perceives yours.[23]

23 Ibid., vii.

Augustine makes a number of additional interesting observations about the nature of the senses. First, that since we can love the objects of our senses, therefore the senses themselves cannot be separated from the soul.

> My soul was sickly and full of sores, it miserable cast itself forth, desiring to be scraped by the touch of objects of sense. Yet if these had not a soul, they would not be objects of love.[24]

24 *The Confessions*, bk. III.

He seemed particularly fascinated that while we have separate avenues by which the five senses enter our consciousness, it is not the object itself, as the actual sound in hearing, for example, that is retained in our memory, but the image of that sense. He further observed that when we concentrate on this image of one or the other of the senses, images retained from the other senses tend not to intrude on the concentration—a phenomenon we understand by the separate storage points in the hemispheres.

> Nor yet do the things themselves enter in; only the images of the things perceived are there in readiness, for thought to recall. Which images, how they are formed, who can tell, though it doth plainly appear by which sense each hath been brought in and stored up? For even while I dwell in darkness and in silence, in my memory I can produce colors, if I will, and discern betwixt black and white, and what others I will: nor yet do sounds break in and disturb the image drawn in by my eyes, which I am reviewing, though they also are there, lying dormant, and laid up, as it were, apart. For these too I call for, and forthwith they appear. And though my tongue be still, and my throat mute, so can I sing as much as I will; nor do those images of colors, which notwithstanding be there, intrude themselves and interrupt, when another store is called for, which flowed in by the ears. So the other things, piled in and up by the other senses, I recall at my pleasure.[25]

This last reference to the pleasure associated with the senses is the aspect of the senses which troubled this Christian philosopher, for the pure pleasure of the senses was inevitably associated with evil. Thus, with regard to hearing church music, the danger lay in being caught up in the beauty of the music, rather than the conceptual message of the words of the hymns. When he does this, Augustine says, he feels he has sinned.

> The delights of the ear had more firmly entangled and subdued me; but Thou didst loosen and free me. Now, in those melodies which Thy words breathe soul into, when sung with a sweet and attuned voice, I do little repose; yet not so to be held thereby, but that I can disengage myself when I will …
>
> Yet again, when I remember the tears I shed at the Psalmody of Thy Church … and how at this time I am moved not with the singing, but with the things sung, when they are sung with a clear voice and modulation most suitable, I acknowledge the great use of this institution. Thus I fluctuate between peril of pleasure and approved wholesomeness; inclined the rather (though not as pronouncing an irrevocable opinion) to approve of the usage of singing in the church that so by the delight of the ears the weaker minds may rise to the feeling of devotion.[26] Yet when it befalls me to be more moved with the voice than the words sung, I confess to have sinned penally, and then had rather not hear music.[27]

---

25 *The Confessions*, bk. X.

26 An unbelievable purpose of church music, also found by some other early Christian writers!

27 Ibid., bk. X.

The sense of sight had for Augustine a similar dangerous tendency toward pleasure, as for example in appreciating art.

> What innumerable toys, made by divers arts and manufactures in our apparel, shoes, utensils, and all sort of works in pictures also in divers images, and these far exceeding all necessary and moderate use and all pious meaning, have been added to tempt their own eyes withal; outwardly following what they themselves make, inwardly forsaking Him by whom themselves were made![28]

For himself, Augustine declares, 'These seductions of the eyes I resist.' In another place, he says the Christian must resist all the senses, for the same reason.

> Therefore, it is clear that the senses are to be resisted with the whole force of the mind. But, what if sensible things give us too much pleasure? They must be prevented from giving pleasure. How? By the practice of renouncing them, and aiming at higher things.[29]

Augustine also observed that the senses stimulate our curiosity. It seems odd to us to read here that curiosity is a 'disease,' and that, even in science, man does not need this desire to know for the mere sake of knowing. But one must remember that the Church leaders were building an institution based not on knowledge but on faith, and if one had faith in the Church and its pronouncements, then there is no appropriate need to seek further knowledge. This attitude was the father of the 'Dark Ages.'

> But by this may more evidently be discerned, wherein pleasure and wherein curiosity is the object of the senses; for pleasure seeketh objects beautiful, melodious, fragrant, savory, soft; but curiosity, for trial's sake, the contrary as well, not for the sake of suffering annoyance, but out of the lust of making trial and knowing them. For what pleasure hath it, to see in a mangled carcass what will make you shudder? and yet if it be lying near, they flock thither, to be made sad, and to turn pale. Even in sleep they are afraid to see it. As if when awake, any one forced them to see it, or any report of its beauty drew them thither! Thus also in the other senses, which it were long to go through. From this disease of curiosity are all those strange sights exhibited in the theater. Hence men go on to search out the hidden powers of nature, which to know profits not, and wherein men desire nothing but to know.[30]

28 Ibid.

29 'Letter to Nebridius,' trans. Sister Wilfrid Parsons in *Letters of Saint Augustine* (New York: Fathers of the Church, 1951), Nr. 3.

30 *The Confessions*, bk. X.

On Reason and the Intellect

Whereas Augustine has stated that in the case of the senses it is not the object but the image of the object that is stored in the memory, with regard to conceptual knowledge he holds the reverse is true: it is the things themselves which are retained. He is incorrect, of course, for they too are images, symbolic descriptions, not the real things, which are stored in our left hemispheres.

> Here [in the memory] also is all learnt of the liberal sciences and as yet unforgotten; removed as it were to some inner place, which is yet no place: nor are they the images thereof, but the things themselves.[31]

Curiously enough, in another place he seems to understand the true symbolic nature of conceptual knowledge.

> The memory containeth also reasons and laws innumerable of numbers and dimensions, none of which hath any bodily sense impressed; seeing they have neither color, nor sound, nor taste, nor smell, nor touch. I have heard the sound of the words whereby when discussed they are denoted: but the sounds are other than the things. For the sounds are other in Greek than in Latin; but the things are neither Greek, nor Latin, nor any other language.[32]

Augustine does not seem to associate memory with the mind, for regarding its location he says above, 'there is no place.' He offers only the explanation, or rather his incorrect deduction, is that all knowledge is innate, 'they were already in the memory, but thrown back and buried as it were in deeper recesses,' which some suggestion draws to the surface.[33]

[31] *The Confessions*, bk. X.
[32] Ibid.
[33] Ibid.

ON THE PSYCHOLOGY OF AESTHETICS

On Pleasure and Pain

Regarding the nature of pleasure, Augustine first makes the very important observation that the perception of pleasure is entirely dependent on personal experience. Second, he adds the observation, frequently mentioned in 'pagan' philosophy, that pleasure is often accompanied by pain.

The conquering commander triumphant; yet had he not conquered unless he had fought; and the more peril there was in the battle, so much the more joy is there in the triumph. The storm tosses the sailors, threatens shipwreck; all wax pale at approaching death; sky and sea are calmed, and they are exceedingly joyed, as having been exceeding afraid. A friend is sick, and his pulse threatens danger; all who long for his recovery are sick in mind with him. He is restored, though as yet he walks not with his former strength; yet there is such joy, as was not, when before he walked sound and strong. Yea, the very pleasures of human life men acquire by difficulties, not those only which fall upon us unlooked for, and against our wills, but even by self-chosen, and pleasure-seeking trouble. Eating and drinking have no pleasure, unless there precede the pinching of hunger and thirst. Men, given to drink, eat certain salt meats, to procure a troublesome heat, which the drink allaying, causes pleasure …

Every where the greater joy is ushered in by the greater pain.[34]

In another place, Augustine points out that sometimes we experience pleasure at another's pain, citing the case of the spectators of gladiators.[35]

It follows, therefore, that pleasure must properly be judged in relation to the virtue associated with it. Augustine discusses this relative to bodily pleasure.

Pleasure is subordinate to virtue when it is a means to the practice of virtue. For example, it is a part of virtue to live in one's native land and to beget children for the sake of the fatherland—neither of which is possible without bodily pleasure, since we cannot eat to live without pleasure nor, without pleasure, take the means to propagate a family. On the other hand, when pleasure is preferred to virtue, it is sought for its own sake and virtue is pursued as a means for the sake of pleasure. This is to say that virtue makes no effort save to procure or to make secure some bodily pleasure. Strange life, indeed, where pleasure is the mistress and virtue is the handmaid![36]

Finally, in an argument which will be astonishing to animal lovers, Augustine produces the following logic regarding the perception of pleasure in animals: Animals lack reason; without reason an animal cannot have knowledge; without knowledge there can be no happiness.

It therefore does not belong to animals … to be happy.[37]

34 *The Confessions*, bk. VIII.

35 Ibid., bk. III.

36 *The City of God*, XIX, 185.

37 *Eighty-Three Different Questions*, 5, 7.

On the Emotions

The emotions represent a subject rarely discussed by Church philosophers by this date, primarily because in their minds emotions were associated with various sins. Augustine, at least, seemed to understand that it was a much more complicated question, observing, 'Yet are the hairs of [a man's] head easier to be numbered than are his feelings.'[38]

Augustine numbers the basic emotions as four: desire, joy, fear, and sorrow, each of which can be divided into 'subordinate species.' However, he is at a loss to explain how the perception of the emotions actually occurs. He understood the *real* emotions to be felt in the body, but yet he was aware that there exists some kind of recall of these emotions located in the memory—wherever that is located. One senses his frustration in not understanding these various relationships.

> The same memory contains also the affections of my mind, not in the same manner that my mind itself contains them, when it feels them; but far otherwise, according to a power of its own. For without rejoicing I remember myself to have joyed; and without sorrow do I recollect my past sorrow. And that I once feared, I review without fear; and without desire call to mind a past desire. Sometimes, on the contrary, with joy do I remember my fore-past sorrow, and with sorrow, joy. Which is not wonderful, as to the body; for mind is one thing, body another. If I therefore with joy remember some past pain of body, it is not so wonderful. But now seeing this very memory itself is mind ... this being so, how is it that when with joy I remember my past sorrow, the mind hath joy, the memory hath sorrow; the mind upon the joyfulness which is in it, is joyful, yet the memory upon the sadness which is in it, is not sad? Does the memory perchance not belong to the mind? Who will say so? The memory then is, as it were, the belly of the mind, and joy and sadness, like sweet and bitter food; which, when committed to the memory, are, as it were, passed into the belly, where they may be stowed, but cannot taste. Ridiculous it is to imagine these to be alike; and yet are they not utterly unlike.[39]

A further frustration for Augustine, was his inability to explain, once something is in the memory, how it can be forgotten, as in the example of someone's name.[40]

---

38 *The Confessions*, bk. IV.

39 Ibid., bk. X.

40 Ibid.

But, if Augustine cannot explain where the perception of emotions are located, it is interesting that he says that in the case of the arts, the emotions are felt in 'their actual presence,' and not as images of emotions. It is a very important truth, from which much of the power of music derives.

> Behold in the plains, and caves, and caverns of my memory, innumerable and innumerably full of innumerable kinds of things, either through images, as all bodies; or by actual presence, as the arts.[41]

41 Ibid.

Failing our knowledge that reason lies in the left hemisphere and emotions in a separate, but equal, right hemisphere, Augustine follows the assumption of all earlier philosophers in saying that Reason must rule over the emotions.

> Do you think that the power of passion is greater than the mind, which we know has been given mastery over the passions? Personally, I do not think so. For there could be no perfect order if the weaker should lord over the stronger. Consequently, I feel that the power of the mind must be greater than desire for the very reason that it is only right and just that it should hold sway over desire.[42]

42 *The Free Choice of the Will*, x.

ON THE PHILOSOPHY OF AESTHETICS

Augustine states very clearly that by 'Art' we mean not the art object itself but the artistic impression in the mind of the artist.

> A human artisan, for example, a woodworker, though he is almost nothing in comparison with the wisdom and power of God, nonetheless cuts and handles the wood for a long while, turning, sawing, planing, or shaping and polishing it, until it is brought, as far as possible, in conformity with the norms of the art and pleases the artisan. Did he, therefore, not know what was good, just because he is pleased by what he made? Of course, he knew it interiorly in his mind, where the art itself is more beautiful than the things which are produced by the art. What the artist sees interiorly in the art, he tests externally in his work, and it is finished when it pleases the artisan.[43]

43 *On Genesis*, trans. Roland Teske (Washington, DC: The Catholic University of America Press, 1990), 61.

Similarly, Augustine's understanding of art was clearly influenced by the Church's position that the artist is greater than the art, because God made the artist. Since art is, therefore, of secondary importance, the observer of art should focus not on the art, but on the artist.

> The artist through the beauty of his work, intimates in a way to the viewer of it that he should not fasten his attention there completely but should so scan the beauty of the artistic work that he will turn his thoughts back fondly upon him who made it. Those who love the things you make instead of yourself are like the men who listen to the eloquence of a wise man. In their overeagerness to hear his beautiful voice and the skillful cadence of his words, they neglect the primary importance of his thoughts for which the spoken words were to serve as signs.[44]

Despite this demeaning view of art, Augustine is the earliest philosopher who comes to understand that art is not a craft and expresses this point clearly and directly. In the following passage, he returns to one of the subjects which intrigued him most—the nature of memory. If the art of music is in the mind, where does it go when the musician is thinking of something else? He concludes with a truly extraordinary insight, a fact we would express today by saying that the rational mind, the left hemisphere, knows nothing of the 'mind,' the right hemisphere, which understands the experience of music.

> It is evident not only that art is in the mind of the artist, but also that it cannot be but in his mind, and inseparable from it …
>
> If art exists at one time in the mind and at another time does not, a state sufficiently known through forgetting and ignorance, the logic of this argument in no way supports the immortality of the mind, unless the antecedent is invalidated in the following manner: Either there is something in the mind that is not actual in present thought, or the art of music is not in a trained mind while, and as long as, it is concerned only with geometry. This latter statement, however, is false; hence, the former is true. But, the mind is not aware that it possesses something, except what has entered its thought. Therefore, something may be in the mind of whose presence there the mind itself is not aware.[45]

44 *The Free Choice of the Will*, xvi.

45 *The Immortality of the Soul*, II, iv.

On Imitation

Regarding the process of the artist, Augustine again says the highest art is that which is *within* the artist, 'who causes first the superior beauties of the soul and then the inferior beauties of physical things.' Whatever technical understanding is given the artist, however, is a gift from God.

> Those numbers and the harmony of lines which they impress upon matter with material tools are received in their minds from that supreme Wisdom, which has impressed the very numbers and harmony itself in a far more artistic way upon the whole physical universe.[46]

46 *Eighty-Three Different Questions*, 45, 78.

By 'inferior beauties,' Augustine is thinking of the imitation of nature. In another place he suggests that imitation will always be inferior because the senses themselves deceive us. The passage in this discussion which touches on music reads as follows:

> We must contain ourselves patiently until all the other senses inform us that falsity dwells in the resemblance to the true. In the sense of hearing, for example, almost as many types of resemblances occur: as, when we hear the voice of someone we do not see, we judge it to be someone else whose voice is similar. Likewise, in the class of inferior resemblances: the echo is a case in point, or the ringing of the ears, or a certain imitation of the blackbird or the crow in clocks, or the sounds which dreaming persons or the insane think they hear. It is unbelievable how closely falsetto voices, as they are called by musicians, bear witness to this truth. It is enough for the present to say that they are not without a resemblance to the voices which are called true …
> It is evident, then, that in all our senses we are deceived.[47]

47 *Divine Providence*, 394.

Augustine, in a dialog with Reason, elaborates on the nature of this deception in the theater and the arts.

> AUGUSTINE. I wonder why you should think that those poems and jokes and other things that are not true ought not to be included in this class of false things.
> REASON. Because it is one thing to want to be false; it is quite different to be unable to be true. So, we can group the works of men, like comedies, tragedies, farces, and other things of that type with the works of painters and sculptors. A man in a painting cannot be as true, even though it tends toward the appearance

of a man, as those things which are written in the works of the comic authors. Such things do not choose to be false nor are they false, through their own desire to be so, but they are compelled by a kind of necessity to conform as much as they are able to the artist's will. On the other hand, the actor Roscius was by choice a false Hecuba on the stage, through, by nature, a true man; he was by choice a true tragedian in that he fulfilled his purpose, and a false Priam because he played the part of Priam though he was not Priam. From this fact arises something remarkable, which nevertheless nobody denies is a fact.

AUGUSTINE. What is that?

REASON. What else do you think but that all these things are in some respect true precisely because they are in other respects false. To establish their truth, the only thing in their favor is that they are false in some other regard. Hence, they never succeed in being what they want or ought to be, as long as they refuse to be false. How could that man I just mentioned be a true tragedian, if he were unwilling to be a false Hector, a false Andromache, a false Hercules, and others without number? Or how would it be a true picture, if the horse in it were not false? How could it be a true image of a man in a mirror, if it were not a false man? If, therefore, in order to be something true it is to the advantage of some things that they be something false, why should we have such a dread of falsities and desire truth as if it were a great good?

AUGUSTINE. That I do not know, and I will be very much surprised if it is not because I find in these examples nothing worthy of imitation. To the end that we may be true to our nature, we should not become false by copying and likening ourselves to the nature of another as do the actors and the reflections in a mirror and the brass cows of Myron. We should, instead, seek that truth which is not self-contradictory and two-faced so that it is true on one side, false on another.

REASON. The things which you require are great and divine. Yet, if we find them, shall we not admit that it is from these that Truth itself is derived and, as it were, fused—that Truth from which everything which by any title is called true gets its name?

AUGUSTINE. I agree willingly.[48]

Augustine at length concludes, 'it … cannot be doubted that nothing is false except by some imitation of the true.'[49]

[48] Ibid., 401ff.
[49] Ibid., 416.

On Beauty

Augustine finds Beauty in an art work to be, of necessity, both in the whole and in the parts. He mentions in this passage having written two or three books on this subject, which unfortunately were lost during his lifetime.

> Do we love any thing but the beautiful? What then is the beautiful? And what is beauty? What is it that attracts and wins us to the things we love? For unless there were in them a grace and beauty, they could by no means draw us unto them. And I marked and perceived that in bodies themselves, there was a beauty, from their forming a sort of whole, and again, another from apt and mutual correspondence, as of a part of the body with its whole, or a shoe with a foot, and the like. And this consideration sprang up in my mind, out of my inmost heart, and I wrote 'On the fair and fit,' I think, two or three books. Thou knowest, O Lord, for it is gone from me; for I have them not, but they are strayed from me, I know not how.[50]

50 *The Confessions*, bk. IV.

In another place, Augustine provides a brief view of the organization of these lost books.

> 'Fair,' I defined and distinguished what is so in itself, and 'fit,' whose beauty is in correspondence to some other thing: and this I supported by corporeal examples. And I turned to the nature of the mind, but the false notion which I had of spiritual things, let me not see the truth.[51]

51 Ibid., bk. IV.

In his book, *The City of God*, Augustine, reflecting the general hesitation of the Church toward the senses and emotions, states that it is Reason which allows us to create an image of an object in our mind and to judge the beauty of that object. It follows, he says, that this capacity we have is superior the art work. Perhaps he felt it was the only justification of art which the Church could admit, but from our perspective the conclusions are entirely wrong.

> Now, whatever can be so imagined in the mind's eye is certainly not a body but only the likeness of a body, and that power of the mind which can perceive this likeness is itself neither a body nor an image of a body. Moreover, that faculty which perceives and judges whether this likeness is beautiful or ugly is certainly superior to the object judged.

Now, this faculty is a man's reason, the essence of his rational soul.[52]

52 Augustine, *The City of God*, trans. Gerald G. Walsh (New York: Fathers of the Church, 1954), VIII, 31.

On the other hand, in a passage which seems characteristic of anything but Reason, Augustine provides a remarkable personal illustration of Aristotle's theory of catharsis, by which the observer identifies with the character and through this empathy is affected at a deep level. It would appear he did not actually know of Aristotle's explanation, for here Augustine wonders how it is possible that experiencing sorrow in the theater can be pleasurable.

> Stage plays also carried me away, full of images of my miseries, and of fuel to my fire. Why is it, that man desires to be made sad, beholding doleful and tragical things, which yet himself would by no means suffer? Yet he desires as a spectator to feel sorrow at them, and this very sorrow is his pleasure. What is this but a miserable madness? For a man is the more affected with these actions, the less free he is from such affections. Howsoever, when he suffers in his own person, it is styled misery; when he compassionates others, then it is mercy. But what sort of compassion is this for feigned and scenical passions? For the auditor is not called on to relieve, but only to grieve: and he applauds the actor of these fictions the more, the more he grieves. And if the calamities of those persons (whether of old times, or mere fiction) be acted in such a way, that the spectator is not moved to tears, he goes away disgusted and criticizing; but if he be moved to passions, he stays intent, and weeps for joy …
>
> I, miserable, then loved to grieve, and sought out what to grieve at, when in another's and that feigned and personated misery, that acting best pleased me, and attracted me the most vehemently, which drew tears from me.[53]

53 *The Confessions*, bk. III.

One of the strange and important functions which our brain produces with respect to time, is that as time recedes, it is shortened in our memory of it. It is for this long observed phenomenon that composers, for example, created the repeat of the exposition section in the sonata form. When we hear the recapitulation, our brain has already 'reduced' the memory of the repeated exposition sections to approximately one-half their actual duration in time, thus making the recapitulation seem to be truly balanced in time. Perhaps Augustine was thinking of something like this when he wrote,

Times lose no time; nor do they roll idly by; through our senses they work strange operations on the mind.[54]

54 Ibid., bk. IV.

In another place, Augustine states this phenomenon even more precisely.

For what is not found in the memory after a year, for instance, is also already less after a day's time.[55]

55 Augustine, 'On Music,' trans. Robert Taliaferro in *Writings of Saint Augustine* (New York: Fathers of the Church, 1947), VI, iv.

ON THE AESTHETICS OF MUSIC

When Augustine seeks to define Music, he reveals a very curious misunderstanding of its nature. He almost never speaks of music as an emotional language, which is its true essence. Rather he continually refers to its rational characteristics, reflecting his own period when music was closely associated with grammar and mathematics as a member of the liberal arts. Still, to the modern reader, a definition of music such as the following seems to entirely miss the point.

Music, that is the science or perception of rhythm, is granted by the liberality of God to mortals having rational souls, to teach a great truth. Hence, if a man who is skilled in composing a song knows what lengths to assign to what tones, so that the melody flows and progresses with beauty by a succession of slow and rapid tones, how much more true it is that God permits no periods of time in the birth and death of His creatures—periods which are like the words and syllables in the measure of this temporal life—to proceed either more quickly or more slowly than the recognized and well-defined law of rhythm requires, in this wonderful song of succeeding events, for the wisdom through which He made all things is to be esteemed far above all the arts.[56]

Rarely does Augustine admit the relationship of music and emotions. In the following passage, and here it may only be a figure of speech, he refers to the ability of music to sooth the feelings, a virtue enumerated by almost all earlier philosophers.

Thereupon, this recollection brought to my mind a way in which I could soothe your feelings, in case I had irritated you, namely, to

56 'Letter to Jerome,' in *Letters of Saint Augustine*, trans. Sister Wilfrid Parsons (New York: Fathers of the Church, 1955), Nr. 166. In a letter (Nr. 26) to the poet, Licentius, Augustine, using music as a metaphor for good speech, says music can have charm, but not excite one to action.

If I sing and you dance to another tune, it will not bother me, for my song has its own charm, even if it does not stir feet to the dance.

summon you to the Lord, the Creator of every sort of harmony, by the music of poetry.[57]

In his book, *On Music*, Augustine is attempting to define good composition, when he rather inadvertently uses an example which reflects the emotional nature of music and has nothing to do with Reason. It is possible, he says, for music to be pleasing when it shouldn't.

> For example, if one should sing sweetly and dance gracefully, wishing thereby to be gay when the occasion demanded gravity …[58]

In all other discussions of music, however, Augustine's emphasis is on the rational or conceptual qualities he finds in music. It is from this same perspective that Augustine gives us a glimpse into his views of the aesthetic purpose of music, in a passage in which he is discussing the association of Reason and the arts. First, he says, Reason is innate, planted by God. In infancy it appears to be asleep, but is awakened with education. He then remarks on the 'astonishing achievements' which Reason has made possible, including those in the arts.

> Or think of the originality and range of what has been done by experts in ceramics, by sculptors and by painters; of the dramas and theatrical spectacles so stupendous that those who have not seen them simply refuse to believe the accounts of those who have.[59]

It is interesting that he does not include music in this listing of the arts, but rather includes it in the category of human communication. And that's right—music is basically a language of feelings. It is curious that on some level he understood this role of music, even though in his writings he attempts to make music a rational (left-hemisphere) entity.

> It was human ingenuity, too, that devised the multitude of signs we use to express and communicate our thoughts—and, especially, speech and writing. The arts of rhetoric and poetry have brought delight to men's spirits by their ornaments of style and variety of verse; musicians have solaced human ears by their instruments and songs.

---

57 'Letter to Paulinus and Therasia,' trans. Sister Wilfrid Parsons in *Letters of Saint Augustine* (New York: Fathers of the Church, 1951) Nr. 32.

58 *On Music*, I, iii.

59 *The City of God*, XXII, 484.

However, in yet another place he suggests that the appreciation of music is one of rational reflection of its beauty, not a response to its emotional content.

> Consideration of beauty, even corporeal beauty, whether visible as in colors and shapes, or audible as in songs and melodies, a consideration proper only to a rational mind, is not the same as the stirring of lust, which must be restrained by reason.[60]

One can see a clear pattern here, the highest aesthetic in music is that in which Reason participates. In the following passage he makes the distinction that pleasure in music is music which is reasonably organized. A mere beautiful chord is not 'reasonable.' It is also interesting that we find here additional hints of multi-part music, something which standard music texts refuse to believe.

> I see, therefore, two things wherein the faculty and power of reason can even be brought before the senses: namely, the works of man which are seen and his words which are heard. In each case the mind uses a twin messenger, the eye and the ear, according to the needs of the body. Thus, when we behold something formed with well-fitting parts, not absurdly do we say that it appears reasonable [fashioned]. In like manner, when we hear a melody harmonized well, we do not hesitate to say that it sounds reasonably [harmonized] ...
>
> In so far as we have been able to investigate, we now detect certain traces of reason in the senses, and, with regard to sight and hearing, we find it in pleasure itself ... With regard to the eyes, that is usually called *beautiful* in which the harmony of parts is wont to be called reasonable; with regard to the ears, when we say that a harmony is reasonable and that a rhythmic poem is reasonably composed, we properly call it *sweet*. But, we are not wont to pronounce it reasonable when the color in beautiful objects allures us or when a vibrant chord sounds pure and liquid, so to speak. We must therefore acknowledge that, in the pleasure of those senses, what pertains to reason is that in which there is a certain rhythmic measure.[61]

Augustine continues this thought by explaining where he finds reason with respect to three classes of music, by way of a virtual history of the development of mind and sound, seen through the eyes of a rational Christian philosopher. Sound itself has little value, he says, unless it is organized by reason.

60 *Against Julian*, trans. Matthew A. Schumacher (New York: Fathers of the Church, 1957), XIV, 73.

61 *Divine Providence*, 309ff.

Reason, being endowed with the keenest powers of discernment, quickly saw what difference there was between sound itself and that of which it was a symbol. It saw that to the jurisdiction of the ears pertained nothing more than sound, and that this was threefold: sound in the utterance of an animate being, or sound in what breath produces in musical instruments, or sound in what is given forth by percussion. It saw that to the first class pertained actors of tragedy and comedy or stage players of this kind, and in fact all who give vocal renditions; the second class was restricted to flutes and similar instruments; and that to the third class were attributed the cithara, the lyre, cymbals, and everything that would be tonal on being struck.

Reason saw, however, that this material was of very little value, unless the sounds were arranged in a fixed measure of time and in modulated variation of high and low pitch. It realized that it was from this source that those elements came which it had called *feet* and *accents*, when, in grammar, it was treating of syllables with diligent consideration. And, because in words themselves it was easy to notice the syllabic *longs* and *shorts*, interspersed with almost equal frequency in a discourse, reason endeavored to arrange and conjoin them into definite series. At first it followed the sense of hearing itself in this, and superimposed measured link-units, which it called *segments* and *members*. Then, lest the series of feet be carried further than its discernment could continue, it set a limit at which *reversion* to the beginning should be made, and, precisely on this account, called it *verse*. But, whatever was not restricted by a definite limit, and yet ran according to methodically arranged feet—that, it designated by the term *rhythm*. In Latin this can be called nothing other than *number*. Thus, poets were begotten of reason. And, when it saw in them great achievements, not in sound alone, but in words also and realities, it honored them to the utmost, and gave them license for whatever reasonable fictions they might desire. And yet, because they took origin from the first of the liberal disciplines, it permitted grammarians to be their critics.

Reason understood, therefore, that in this fourth step of ascent—whether in particular rhythm or in modulation in general—numeric proportions held sway and produced the finished product. With the utmost diligence it investigated as to what their nature might be, and, chiefly because by their aid it had elaborated all the aforesaid developments, it concluded that they were divine and eternal. From then onwards, it most reluctantly endured their splendor and serenity to be clouded by the material stuff of vocal utterances. And, because whatever the mind is able to see is always present and is acknowledged to be immortal, numeric proportions seemed to be of this nature. But, because sound is something sensible, it flows away into the past and is imprinted on the memory. By a reasonable fiction it was fabled that the Muses were the daughters of Jupiter and Memory. Now, with reason bestowing its favor on the poets, need it be asked what the offspring likewise contained? Since this branch of learning partakes as well of sense as of the intellect, it received the name of *music*.[62]

In another book, *The Teacher*,[63] Augustine gives yet another example of his personal belief that reason is at the heart of music appreciation. He states that the act of speaking words is a form of teaching. His pupil, Adeodatus, answers, 'But what about singing, which also uses words?' Augustine says, 'There is a form of teaching by way of recalling,' and this is what music does. Adeodatus responds, 'No, I don't sing to recall something, I sing only for pleasure.' Augustine's response once again suggests he fails to understand the pleasure of music for music's sake. Pleasure for him must be something rational, here in the ordering of sound.

> I see what you mean. But you notice, do you not, that what pleases you in singing is a certain melodious ordering of the sound?

Augustine maintains that to some degree the rational understanding which lies behind musical performance is innate. He first gives the example of birds, which although lacking reason, nevertheless give forth music which is 'most accurately and aptly proportioned.'[64] A singer untrained in music is genetically analogous to the bird.

> What good singer, even though he be unskilled in the art of music, would not, by the same natural sense, keep in his singing both the rhythm and the melody known by memory? And what can become more subject to measure than this? The uninstructed man has no knowledge of it. Nevertheless, he does it by nature's doing.

This misplaced emphasis on the importance of Reason in understanding music also led Augustine to place music itself in a lesser category of importance than Reason. What man understands through Reason, he says, can never be taken away from him. Music, however, is fleeting and disappears. The listener cannot keep music!

62 Ibid., 316ff.

63 *The Teacher*, trans. Robert Russell (Washington, DC: The Catholic University of America Press, 1968), i.

64 *Divine Providence*, 326.

Even if the beautiful singing of a vocalist were to last forever, his admirers would vie with one another to come to hear him; they would press about each other, and, as the crowd became larger, would fight over seats so that each might be closer to the singer. And as they listened, they could not take any of the sound to keep for themselves but could only be caressed by all the fleeting sounds.[65]

Now we come to somewhat of a paradox. After so many detailed examples of the association of Reason and music for the listener, Augustine, in another place, suggests that listeners (and singers!) need not know anything about the conceptual nature of music, or what we would call today the 'theory' of music. While we certainly agree with him, with respect to the listener, it does seem odd, given his views presented above, that he did not connect the conceptual with Reason. At the end of the following passage he qualifies this by saying this pertains to common people. 'Great men' may listen to music this way sometimes, or for the purpose of relaxation, but they are never really absorbed by music, for that would be 'disgraceful.'

> AUGUSTINE. Now tell me, then, don't [singers] all seem to be similar to the nightingale, all those which sing well under the guidance of a certain sense, that is, do it harmoniously and sweetly, although if they were questioned about the numbers or intervals of high and low notes they could not reply?
> STUDENT. I think they are very much alike.
> AUGUSTINE. And what's more, aren't those who like to listen to them without this science to be compared to beasts? For we see elephants, bears, and many other kinds of beasts are moved by singing, and birds themselves are charmed by their own voices. For, with no further proper purpose, they would not do this with such effort without some pleasure.
> STUDENT. I judge so, but this reproach extends to nearly the whole of human kind.
> AUGUSTINE. Not as much as you think. For great men, even if they know nothing about music, either wish to be one with the common people who are not very different from beasts and whose number is great; and they do this very properly and prudently. But this is not the place to discuss that. Or after great cares in order to relax and restore the mind they very moderately partake of some pleasure. And it is very proper to take it in from time to time. But to be taken in by it, even at times, is improper and disgraceful.[66]

65 *The Free Choice of the Will*, xiv.

66 *On Music*, I, iv.

Instrumental musicians Augustine places in a different category, in this regard, because of the obvious conceptual and technical skill one must acquire in order to play an instrument. This discussion leads him to return to the subject of imitation, whereby he concludes that the art of the instrumental performer is not imitation.

> AUGUSTINE. Those who play on auloi or lyres or any other instrument of this kind, they can't be compared to the nightingale, can they?
> STUDENT. No.
> AUGUSTINE. How, then do they differ?
> STUDENT. In that I find a certain art in these instrument players, but only nature in the nightingale.
> AUGUSTINE. That's true. But do you think it ought to be called an art even if they do it by a sort of imitation?
> STUDENT. Why not? For imitation seems to be so much a part of the arts that, if it is removed, nearly all of them are destroyed. For masters exhibit themselves to be imitated, and this is what they call teaching.
> AUGUSTINE. But don't you think art is a sort of reason, and those who use art use reason?
> STUDENT. It seems so.
> AUGUSTINE. Therefore, whoever cannot use reason does not use art.
> STUDENT. I grant that, too ...
> AUGUSTINE. I have asked you whether you would say lyre players and aulos players or any other men of this sort had an art, even if what they do in singing they do by imitation. You have said it is an art, and you have affirmed this so true it seems to you that, if imitation were done away with, nearly all the arts would be destroyed. And from this it can be concluded that anyone who does something by imitating uses an art, although, perhaps not everyone who uses an art acquired it by imitating. But if all imitation is art, and all art reason, all imitation is reason. But an irrational animal does not use reason; therefore, it does not posses an art. But it is capable of imitation; therefore, art is not imitation.[67]

67 Ibid.

On the surface, this seems a contradiction to Augustine's views, quoted above, on the *creative* artist and imitation. However, in the following discussion it is revealed that what Augustine means by 'imitation,' with respect to the art of the instrumental player, is the experiential understanding that the player learns by ear. Having declared, above, that this skill is not imitation, Augustine now doubts that it is a true conceptual knowledge.

Nor do I affirm that all those who handle such instruments lack science, but I say they do not all have science. For we are considering this question for the following purpose: to understand, if we can, how correct it is to include science in the definition of music. And if all pipers, flute players, and others of this kind have science, then I think there is no more degraded and abject discipline than this one.[68]

[68] Ibid.

Today we would probably call the acquisition of technique by the instrumental player a form of knowledge attained by experience, and furthermore neurologists can cite the precise part of the brain in which this learning takes place. Augustine, however, while continuing to deny such experiential understanding has anything to do with 'science,' interestingly enough provides the correct explanation in the words of the student, which he then overrules with an incorrect explanation.

> AUGUSTINE. I believe you attribute the greater or less mobility of the fingers not to science but to practice, don't you?
> STUDENT. Why do you believe so?
> AUGUSTINE. Because just now you attributed science to the mind alone. But, although in this case the mind commands, you see the act belongs to the body.
> STUDENT. But, since the knowing mind commands this of the body, I think the act ought to be attributed to the mind rather than the servile members.
> AUGUSTINE. But, don't you think it is possible for one person to surpass another in science, even though the other person move his fingers much more easily and readily?
> STUDENT. I do.
> AUGUSTINE. But, if the rapid and readier motion of the fingers were to be attributed to science, the more science anyone had the more he would excel in the rapidity of the motion.
> STUDENT. I concede that.[69]

[69] Ibid.

Having denied that rational knowledge is involved in learning to play an instrument, how then does Augustine account for the process of learning? His answer is an important recognition of genetic understanding of music, as he says, that it is a kind of rote repetition committed to memory, made possible by a very interesting premise that a kind of innate understanding is shared by both players and listeners.

AUGUSTINE. How do you explain the fact that an ignorant crowd hisses off an aulos player letting out futile sounds, and on the other hand applauds one who sings well, and finally that the more agreeably one sings the more fully and intensely it is moved? For it isn't possible to believe the crowd does all this by the art of music, is it?
STUDENT. No.
AUGUSTINE. How then?
STUDENT. I think it is done by nature giving everyone a sense of hearing by which such things are judged.
AUGUSTINE. You are right. But now consider this, too, whether the aulos player himself is also endowed with this sense. And if it is so, he can, by following his own judgment, move his fingers when he blows on the aulos, and can note and commit to memory what he decides sounds well enough; and by repeating it he can accustom his fingers to being carried about without hesitation or error, whether he gets from another what he plays or whether he finds it himself, led and abetted as he is by the nature we spoke of. And so, when memory follows sense, and the joints, already subdued and prepared by practice, follow memory, the player sings as he wishes, the better and more easily the more he excels in all those things which reason just now taught us we have in common with the beasts: that is, the desire of imitating, sense, and memory.[70]

[70] Ibid., I, v.

Augustine now questions whether it isn't the case that most artists performed for money and not in the service of their art. But, he concedes, in the voice of his student, that it must be possible to do both.

When he accepts applause or when money is given him, he doesn't give up his science, if he chanced to have any, to please the people with. But, heavier with pennies and happier with the praise of men, he returns home with the same discipline entire and intact. But he would be a fool if he despised these advantages. For, if he hadn't gotten them, he would be much poorer and more obscure; having gotten them, he is no less skilled.[71]

[71] Ibid., I, vi.

Augustine also observes that some musicians value applause higher than their music itself. The highest art, he concludes, is found in the artist who learns and exhibits his art without respect to applause or money, but 'who loves his art for itself'—although he expresses doubt that such an artist exists.[72]

[72] Ibid.

ON CHURCH MUSIC

Augustine commends the Church of Milan for its effective employment of congregational singing of hymns for the purpose of 'consolation and exhortation,' and adds the very interesting comment that the tradition had begun in the Eastern Churches.

> Then it was first instituted that after the manner of the Eastern Churches, Hymns and Psalms should be sung, lest the people should wax faint through the tediousness of sorrow: and from that day to this the custom is retained, divers (yea, almost all) Thy congregations, throughout other parts of the world, following herein.[73]

In hearing such singing, Augustine experienced the catharsis he was unable to experience in Art Music.

> How did I weep, in Thy Hymns and Canticles, touched to the quick by the voices of Thy sweet-attuned Church! The voices flowed into mine ears, and the Truth distilled into my heart, whence the affections of my devotion overflowed, and tears ran down, and happy was I therein.[74]

This is a rather remarkable reaction to the music, especially if one remembers that the Church fathers gave the greatest emphasis to the idea that it is the *words* of the hymn, and not the music itself, which the Christian should concentrate on. In an Easter sermon, Augustine seems to emphasize this same idea. When he speaks of 'the voice of the inner man,' he means, as we shall see in retrospect, the Christian's heart-felt concentration on the meaning of the words.

> What is expressed in the Hebrew language by 'Alleluia' is, in Latin, *Laudate Dominum*, or 'Praise the Lord.' So, let us praise the Lord our God, not only with our voice, but also with our heart, since he who praises from the heart praises with the voice of the inner man.[75]

Augustine immediately follows this with a very extraordinary statement. While man is thinking left-brained [language] as he sings, God is hearing it right-brained!

> As far as men are concerned, the voice is a sound; as far as God is concerned, it expresses an emotion.

[73] *The Confessions*, bk. IX.

[74] Ibid.

[75] 'Sermon 257,' trans. Sister Mary Muldowney in *Sermons on the Liturgical Seasons* (New York: Fathers of the Church, 1959), 362.

In any case, this kind of vocal church music was sufficient for Augustine, who saw no need for additional instruments.

> We sing praises to God, we chant our 'Alleluias' with hearts attuned to harmony far better than with the chords of the lyre.[76]

And, like many of his Church contemporaries, he appears to have been content to explain away the Old Testament references to musical instruments in the service as having been only metaphors. He says, for example, that the famous 'Praise the Lord with cymbals,' in Psalm 150, is really talking about good neighbors.

> Cymbals touch each other in order to play and therefore some people compare them to our lips. But I think it better to think of God as being praised on the cymbals when someone is honored by his neighbor rather than by himself.[77]

In this regard, we should mention that Augustine refers to the passage, Ephesians 5:19, which, correctly translated, is possibly the only reference to sacred instrumental music in the New Testament, 'making melody,' being in the later Middle Ages a synonym for such music.

> Be filled with the Spirit, addressing one another in psalms and hymns and spiritual songs, singing and making melody to the Lord with all your heart.

Like other early Church writers, Augustine mistranslates[78] this as 'making melody *in* your hearts,' thus assuming the reference is to singing.

> But, not everyone who sings with his lips sings a new canticle, but only one who sings in the way advised by the Apostle, when he says: 'singing and making melody in your hearts to the Lord.' For this joy is within, where the voice of praise sings.[79]

Considering the fact that Augustine has discussed music itself at such length, it is surprising that we have relative few comments by him regarding Church music. This is explained in part by the fact that many of his writings are lost, in particular an entire book on Church music entitled, 'Against Hilary.' This was an answer against a layman who had attacked the Church fathers for a recently introduced custom in Carthage of singing hymns at the altar.[80]

---

76 'Sermon 243,' in Ibid., 278.

77 Translated by James W. McKinnon, 'Musical Instruments in Medieval Psalm Commentaries and Psalters,' *Journal of the American Musicological Society* 21, no. 1 (Spring 1968): 7.

78 In 'Letter Nr. 100,' trans. Sister Wilfrid Parsons in *Letters of Saint Augustine* (New York: Fathers of the Church, 1953), Augustine confesses he neither understands the Hebrew language nor anything of the meters of which the Psalms are composed.

79 'Letter to Honoratus,' Nr. 140.

80 This lost book is mentioned by Augustine in *The Retractions*, trans. Sister Mary Bogan (Washington, DC: The Catholic University of America Press, 1968), XXXVII, 'At the urging of my brethren, I answered him; the book is called Against Hilary.'

On the Nature of Music

In his book, *On Music*, Augustine defines music as the science of modulating [*modulandi*] well.[81] If we take this word in its modern, if alternate, meaning of 'to adjust to or keep in proper measure or proportion,'[82] we can see that it is similar in intent to the definition of music given above in Augustine's letter to Jerome. In any case, it seems clear that to Augustine the science of composition had to do with the organization of conceptual materials and not with the communication of emotional ideas. Augustine points out that similar organizational structures are found in oratory and dance, although he was hesitant to associate them with music.

> Many things in singing and dancing are reprehensible, and that, if we take the word *modulatio* from them, the almost divine art becomes degraded.

The element of music which was most susceptible to rational discussion, under the definition given above, is rhythm. For Augustine, the rhythm of music was still closely tied to the rhythms of poetry and, indeed, he says what grammarians teach is 'the difference between long and short syllables.'[83] He contends that it is at this level that the listener is delighted by the rhythmic organization of music, that it is these 'short interval lengths which delight us in singing and dancing.' Here he also makes the interesting observation that we cannot retain the perception of music which lasts an hour or more.

> All well measured movements admittedly belong to the rationale of this discipline, if indeed it is the science of mensurating well ... keeping within themselves their end of ornament and delight, yet even in proper ratios these movements ... cannot be suited to our senses when accomplished in a long space of time, an hour or more.[84]

Augustine also notes that when historical poetry is set to music these long and short syllables are sometimes altered according to the 'rationale of the measure,' the music having precedence. The grammarian objects to this, he says, but 'the science of music is not outraged in the least.'[85] He provides an interesting example of this kind of alteration in the lengthening of a final syllable with music, when followed by a rest. He suggests there is a natural desire for the

81 *On Music*, I, ii.

82 *Webster's Ninth New Collegiate Dictionary*.

83 *On Music*, II, i.

84 Ibid., I, xiii.

85 Ibid., II, i and II, ii.

ear to hear a longer note in such a circumstance, even as long as twice its indicated length.[86]

> Why, too, is a short syllable taken for a long one when followed by a rest—and not by convention, but by natural consideration directing the ears … The nature of hearing and passing over in silence allows the lengthening of a syllable beyond two times: so what is also filled with rest can be filled with sound.[87]

The phrase, 'rationale of the measure,' suggests that the old system of rhythm based on syllabic modes is developing into the modern practice of meter organized on pulse. Augustine, in the following, seems to define this in a way which appears to the modern reader very much like music with and without bar lines.

> Since it is not the same thing to roll forward, although in legitimate feet [the 'longs' and 'shorts'], yet without any definite end, and to progress likewise in legitimate feet, but to be bounded by a fixed end, these kinds, therefore, had to be distinguished by names. So the first was called only by the name proper to it, rhythm, but the other by meter as well as rhythm.[88]

An even stronger suggestion of a modern concept of meter can be seen in his implication that a conductor was responsible for the control of this aspect of time.

> Now, fix your ears on the sound and your eyes on the beats. For the hand beating time is not to be heard but seen, and note must be taken of the amount of time given to the arsis and to the thesis.[89]

Finally, Augustine suggests that this delight which one takes in organized time has its origin in the innate organization of the 'laws of equality, unity, and order,' of the universe, which in turn are created by God.[90]

Augustine follows this thought immediately by observing that God has also given man an innate ability to perceive form. In a poem, for example, our pleasure derives from the whole, not the individual rhythms alone as they are heard.

> In a poem, if syllables should live and perceive only so long as they sound, the harmony and beauty of the connected work would in no way please [the listeners]. For they could not see or approve the

[86] It is tempting to wonder if this represents the beginning of the psychological need that becomes the *Eingang* in later music.

[87] Ibid., VI, x.

[88] Ibid., V, i.

[89] Ibid., II, xiii.

[90] Ibid., VI, xi.

whole, since it would be fashioned and perfected by the very passing away of these singulars.[91]

The first five books of Augustine's *On Music* consist of lengthy discussions of the old rhythmic modes of poetry, a discourse he understands most readers will find rather dull.

Let's hope a dutiful labor will readily excuse our triviality in the eyes of benevolent men.[92]

In Book Six he proceeds to a more philosophic level, which he presumes those 'with tumultuous tongues taking vulgar delight in the noise of rhythm-dancers' will probably not read.

Augustine now engages in a detailed consideration of the essence of music. He begins by asking, 'Where is music?' Is it [1] in the sound itself, [2] in the perception of the listener, [3] in the performer, or [4] in the memory?

Regarding the first, he suggests that everyone would accept the possibility of a sound, such as a drop of liquid, existing where there is no listener to hear it. The second, of necessity, requires the first.

Number three, the performance, Augustine does not consider as fundamental as the first two, for we can hear music in our minds where there is no sound or performance at all. This kind of listening is, of course, closely related to the fourth, memory.

Consider, too, the fourth class, that is, the class of those numbers[93] in the memory. For, if we draw them out by recollection, and, when we are carried away to other thoughts, we again leave them as if hidden in their own hiding places, I don't think it is difficult to see they can exist without the others.[94]

Before proceeding, Augustine now brings up a fifth possibility, regarding the perception of music, one he mentions in several other places, a kind of innate template for judging music.

I believe, while we were discussing these things, a fifth kind appeared from somewhere, a kind in the natural judgment of perceiving when we are delighted by the equality of numbers or offended at a flaw in them.[95]

Augustine concludes that of the four forms of music mentioned above, the fourth, memory, is to be preferred. This is because it not

---

91 Ibid.

92 Ibid., VI, i.

93 Among the writers of this period, this is a frequently used synonym for music.

94 Ibid., VI, iii.

95 Ibid., VI, iv.

only can exist without sound or performance, but it also lasts indefinitely, whereas 'live' music quickly disappears.[96]

Now he proposes, of the remaining three, which is the most important? Augustine, in words assigned to his student, says that performance must be the most important, 'according to the rule that things making are to be preferred to those made.' But, for a Christian philosopher, there is a problem in admitting this, for it implies that the corporeal is more important than the incorporeal (soul).[97] At the same time, this is the essential question for Augustine: Should one value music, or art in general, so highly, in view of the fact that it is *man* made.

Augustine's solution to this problem is again based on his suspicion of genetic understanding of music, a concept of a kind of innate template, a God given music, against which man-made music is to be judged. He quotes from the Scriptures[98] a passage which he says refers to this God given template and not to earthly music.

> So it is truly said in the Holy Scriptures, 'I have gone the rounds, to know and consider and seek wisdom and number.' And you are in no way to think this was said about those numbers shameful theaters resound with, but about those, I believe, the soul does not receive from the body [the ears], but receiving from God on high it rather impresses on the body.[99]

But, if music is in the soul, implanted by God, can we say we hear the music outside the soul at all?

> It must be carefully considered if there is really nothing called hearing unless something is produced in the soul by the body. But it is very absurd to subordinate the soul like a matter to the body as an artisan. For the soul is never inferior to the body, and all matter is inferior to the artisan. The soul, then, is in no way a matter subordinated to the body as an artisan. But it would be, if the body worked numbers in it. Therefore, when we hear, [music is] not made in the soul by [music] we know in sounds.

His student asks, 'What happens, then, when a person hears?' Before attempting to answer, Augustine admits doubt and suggests it might be better to answer it some other time.

96 Ibid.

97 Ibid.

98 The edition of Augustine we are using cites, '2 Eccle. 7:26,' but we cannot find this quotation.

99 *On Music*, VI, iv.

> Whatever it is—and perhaps we cannot find or explain it—it won't result, will it, in our denying the soul's being better than the body? … But if, because of the infirmity of either or both of us, the [answer] should be less than we wish, either we ourselves shall investigate it at another time when we are less agitated, or we shall leave it to more intelligent people to examine, or, unworried, we shall leave it unsolved.

Nevertheless, Augustine says, 'I shall say right away what I think.' His essential point seems to be his belief that when we hear music, the soul hears the sensory input, but without emotion. Upon the sensory perception, it is the soul which produces the emotions in the body.

> I think the soul, then, when it senses, produces these actions on the passions of the body, but does not receive these passions.[100]

Augustine concludes this discussion by observing that of these, now five, possible descriptions of music only the God-given template form, which he now names 'the judicial,' is undying. The others 'either pass away when they are made or are stricken out of the memory by forgetfulness.'[101]

In a later book called *The Retractions*, Augustine mentions his book, *On Music*, and finally suggests that the value of music to the Christian is to see God. It was this fortunate thought, that secular knowledge can lead one to understanding the Christian message, which saved the liberal arts from extinction during the Dark Ages.

> I wrote six books On Music. The sixth of these became especially well known because in it a subject worthy of investigation was considered, namely, how, from corporeal and spiritual but changeable numbers, one comes to the knowledge of unchangeable numbers which are already in unchangeable truth itself, and how, in this way, 'the invisible attributes' of God, 'being understood through the things that are made, are clearly seen.'[102]

---

100 Ibid., VI, iv, 10.

101 Ibid., VI, vii.

102 *The Retractions*, trans. Sister Mary Bogan (Washington, DC: The Catholic University of America Press, 1968), X. Augustine quotes here, Romans 1:20.

Part 3
The Dark Ages; The Sixth Through The Eighth Centuries

11 ON THE STATE OF MUSIC AND THE LIBERAL ARTS IN THE SIXTH THROUGH EIGHTH CENTURIES

The 'Dark Ages,' which are dated from the sixth century, take this name primarily from the general disappearance in Western Europe of secular letters, in particular philosophy, history and science. As Cassiodorus observed already at the beginning of the sixth century,

> Arithmetic, Theoretical Geometry, Astronomy, and Music are discoursed upon to listless audiences, sometimes to empty benches.[1]

In another place, Cassiodorus mentions that teacher's salaries were being cut back and argues that instead they should be increased.

> I have referred disputes involving sons to the senators, that they may take thought for the careers of those affected by the advancement of education at Rome. For it is incredible that you should lack concern for something which brings honors to your offspring, and gives your assembly the counsel that comes from constant reading. Now recently I came to know by discreet reports from various people, that the teachers of eloquence at Rome are not receiving the constituted rewards for their labors, and that the trafficking of certain men has caused the sums assigned to the masters of the schools to be diminished.
>
> Therefore, since it is clear that rewards feed the arts, I have judged it abominable that anything should be stolen from the teachers of youth; they should instead be incited to their noble studies by an increase in their fees.
>
> For the school of grammar has primacy: it is the fairest foundation of learning, the glorious mother of eloquence, which has learnt to aim at praise, to speak without fault. As good morals view an alien crime, so it views a dissonant error in the course of declamation. For, as the musician creates the sweetest song from a choir in harmony, so, by well ordered modulations of sound, the grammarian can recite in meter.

[1] Cassiodorus, 'Letter to the Illustrious Consularis,' III, lii, in *Variae*, trans. Thomas Hodgkin (London: Frowde, 1886).

Grammar is the mistress of words, the embellisher of the human race; through the practice of the noble reading of ancient authors, she helps us, we know, by her counsels.[2]

[2] 'Letter to the Senate in Rome,' in ibid., IX, xxi.

Because the Church was now effectively uncontested, it has been tempting for historians to lay the blame for the Dark Ages on that institution itself. Contributing to this viewpoint is the fact that the foundation of the Church was faith, and not knowledge. Even the study of grammar was considered unnecessary by some Church leaders, as we can see in the example of Pope Gregory the Great's letter criticizing Desiderius, the Bishop of Vienne.

A report has reached us which we cannot mention without a blush, that thou expoundest grammar to certain friends; whereat we are so offended and filled with scorn that our former opinion of thee is turned to mourning and sorrow.[3]

[3] Quoted in Nan Cooke Carpenter, *Music in the Medieval and Renaissance Universities* (Norman: University of Oklahoma Press, 1958), 15.

With regard to the sufficiency of Faith, we have quoted a number of examples by various Church fathers during the first five centuries who said, in effect, 'Just accept what we say, and look no further.' Indeed, in the sixth century, we find pronouncements which seem to reflect a similarly narrow perspective. Cassiodorus, for example, writes,

The most holy Fathers, moreover, not tolerating harm to upright faith, have preferred to establish ecclesiastical rules at [church] councils and have destroyed the stubborn contrivers of new heresies with the divine sword, decreeing that no one ought to trouble them with new questions, but that, content with the authority of the excellent men of old, they ought to obey the wholesome decrees without evasion and treachery.[4]

[4] *Divine Letters*, trans. Leslie W. Jones (New York: Octagon Books, 1966), XI, 1.

And, in another place,

… if anything happens to be found out of harmony and inconsistent with the rules of the Fathers, let us decide that it should be avoided.[5]

[5] Ibid., XXIV, 1.

However, quotations such as these are misleading, for the struggle of the Church leaders was now *within* the Church, it no longer having a strong pagan adversary to argue against. In fact, Cassiodorus was one of several important Church philosophers who understood the importance of preserving the liberal arts. Indeed, one modern writer states that were it not for Cassiodorus, no Latin classic except the works of Virgil would have come down to us in complete form.[6] For Church men such as Cassiodorus, the great value of the liberal arts, including music, was to produce in the Christian the intelligence necessary to understanding the Scriptures.

> Beyond any doubt knowledge of [the liberal arts], as it seemed to our Fathers, is useful and not to be avoided, since one finds this knowledge diffused everywhere in sacred literature, as it were in the origin of universal and perfect wisdom. When these matters have been restored to sacred literature and taught in connection with it, our capacity for understanding will be helped in every way.[7]

The Venerable Bede, another enlightened Churchman, presents this same argument for the contribution of the liberal arts to Christian understanding.

> We are to be initiated in *grammatica*, then in *dialectia*, afterward in *rhetorica*. Equipped with these arms, we should approach the study of philosophy. Here the order is first the quadrivium, and in this first *arithmetica*, second *musica*, third *geometria*, fourth *astronomia*, then holy writ, so that through knowledge of what is created we arrive at knowledge of the Creator.[8]

On the question of the Church's culpability, then, we get a more accurate picture if we remember that the Church was also composed of individuals. In the spirit of the Church's attacks against the pagan writers, there were some, such as Theophilus, Archbishop of Alexandria, who destroyed all the ancient manuscripts he could find.[9] But there were other individuals who saved ancient manuscripts and their Church buildings offered the manuscripts some chance of survival during centuries of turmoil. And we must not forget the lowly monks, the scribes, who expended a good part of their lives making copies, thereby increasing the odds for survival of individual works of literature. Perhaps it was they who really transmitted these works across the gulf of the Dark Ages. Their tired backs and cramped hands were driven by superiors who told them God would forgive one of their sins for each line they copied. One monk, his superior reported, escaped Hell by the margin of a single letter! It is no wonder that we find a scribe has written at the end of one of his volumes,

---

6 M. R. James, quoted in William Harris Stahl, *Martianus Capella and the Seven Liberal Arts* (New York: Columbia University Press, 1977), I, 7, fn. 12.

7 Cassiodorus, *Divine Letters*, XXVII, 1.

8 De elementis philosophiae, quoted in Carpenter, *Music in the Medieval and Renaissance Universities*, 20, fn. 12.

9 For this and the following two quotations, see Will Durant, *The Age of Faith* (New York: Simon and Schuster, 1950), 907.

> This completes the whole;
> For Christ's sake give me a drink!

And another,

> For the work of the pen,
> Let the writer receive a beautiful girl.

The real reason for the decline of culture during the Dark Ages was a decline in culture. With the fall of Rome and the pulling back of Roman soldiers, who had functioned as the police force of Western Europe, towns of all sizes were now left exposed to slaughter by tribes from the North and East. Consider, for example, that Paris was pillaged in 856, 861, and burned in 865. Tours was pillaged in 853, 856, 862, 872, 886, 903, and 919. It is no wonder that Gregory of Tours, in his *History of the Franks*, wrote,

> In fact in the towns of Gaul the writing of literature has declined to the point where it has virtually disappeared altogether. Many people have complained about this, not once but time and time again. 'What a poor period this is!' they have been heard to say. 'If among all our people there is not one man to be found who can write a book about what is happening today, the pursuit of letters really is dead in us!'[10]

How could there be culture? Culture requires peace, as Cassiodorus points out, 'Peace is the fair mother of all liberal arts, the softener of manners.'[11]

What else, but the 'Dark Ages,' can we call a Europe which one writer described in 909.

> The cities are depopulated ... the country reduced to solitude ... As the first men lived without law ... so now every man does what seems good in his own eyes, despising laws human and divine ... The strong oppress the weak; the world is full of violence against the poor ... Men devour one another like the fishes in the sea.[12]

Rome, itself, was in total decay by 700, its great institutions forgotten (the Forum was used as a cow pasture already in the seventh century) and the great public buildings and temples were dismembered to provide building material for Christian churches and palaces.

---

10 Gregory of Tours, *The History of the Franks*, trans. Lewis Thorpe (Harmondsworth: Penguin Books, 1974), 63.

11 Letter to Emperor Anastasius, in *Variae*, I, i.

12 H.W.C. Davis, *Medieval England* (Oxford: Clarendon Press, 1928), 266.

We have an eye-witness description of the city during the period of the first emperor of the sixth century, Justinian, who was certainly one of the strangest of all Roman emperors. He lived and dressed like a monk, fasting, praying, and discussing philosophy. As he wanted to become a musician and poet, we must assume his neglect of the educational institutions reported here was due more to his inclination to hoard money (he once increased his income by putting ashes in the peasant's bread).

> [Justinian] caused doctors and teachers of gentlemen's sons to go short of the elementary necessities of life. For the free rations which earlier emperors ordered to be issued to members of these professions Justinian took away altogether. Moreover, the whole of the revenues which all the municipalities had raised locally for communal purposes and for entertainments he took over and shamelessly pooled with the revenues of the central government. From then on doctors and teachers counted for nothing: no one was now in a position to plan any public building projects; no lamps were lit in the streets of the cities; and there was nothing else to make life pleasant for the citizens. Theaters, hippodromes, and circuses were almost all shut ... Both in private and in public there was grief and dejection, as if yet another visitation from heaven had struck them, and all laughter had gone out of life.[13]

13 Procopius, *The Secret History* (Harmondsworth: Penguin Books, 1981), 169.

Gibbon adds that this Christian emperor also closed the schools of Athens.

> Justinian suppressed the schools of Athens and the consulship of Rome, which had given so many sages and heroes to mankind ...
> The Gothic arms were less fatal to the schools of Athens than the establishment of a new religion, whose ministers superseded the exercise of reason, resolved every question by an article of faith, and condemned the infidel or skeptic to eternal flames.[14]

14 Edward Gibbon, *The History of the Decline and Fall of the Roman Empire* (Philadelphia: Coates), III, 466ff.

Once the schools had been closed, the clergy remained the principal portion of the population which was literate and they served as the official scribes attending to the needs of the nobles. This became a self-perpetuating problem, for why should a noble learn to write, for example, when an inexpensive scribe was available to do the work. Consequently, for centuries most lay persons in Western Europe, including kings and emperors, could neither read or write.[15]

15 Kenneth Clark, *Civilisation* (New York: Harper & Row, 1969), 17.

The first break in this chain of illiteracy came with the court of the greatest of medieval kings, Charlemagne (742–814), who learned to read but never quite mastered writing. A naturally brilliant man, Charlemagne, observing the appalling illiteracy of his age, called leading scholars to his court for the purpose of restoring the schools of France. In 787 he issued an historic document, *Capitulare de litteris colendis*, urging the Church to establish schools. In another document of 789, he urged these schools to,

> take care to make no difference between the sons of serfs and of freemen, so that they might come and sit on the same benches to study grammar, music, and arithmetic.[16]

The result of his efforts saw the founding of numerous schools in France and Western Germany.[17] Among these were the first examples in history of free public education.[18]

As a consequence of Charlemagne attracting so many scholars to his court, we are fortunate to have historical portraits of this man and the music of his immediate circle which are unique for these three centuries. One of these scholars, Einhard, writes of Charlemagne's personal interest in the liberal arts.

> He paid the greatest attention to the liberal arts; and he had great respect for men who taught them, bestowing high honors upon them. When he was learning the rules of grammar he studied with Peter the Deacon of Pisa … but for all other subjects he was taught by Alcuin … a man of the Saxon race who came from Britain and was the most learned man anywhere to be found.[19]

Another member of the court tells of Greek envoys who came to visit the court and brought a number of musical instruments. His account includes some of the most interesting details extant regarding the early organ.

> These Greek envoys brought with them every kind of organ, as well as all sorts of other instruments. These were all examined by the craftsmen of the most sagacious Charlemagne to see just what was new about them. Then the craftsmen reproduced them with the greatest possible accuracy. The chief of these was that most remarkable of organs ever possessed by musicians which, when its bronze wind chests were filled and its bellows of ox-hide blew through its pipes of bronze, equaled with its deep note the roar of thunder, and

---

16 Quoted in Durant, *The Age of Faith*, 466.

17 Carpenter, *Music in the Medieval and Renaissance Universities*, 17ff.

18 An account of Charlemagne visiting one of these schools includes an example of the right and left hand prejudice we have mentioned several times above. In this case he placed the outstanding students on his right hand, praising them, and the unsuccessful students on his left, condemning them. Einhard and Notker the Stammerer, *Two Lives of Charlemagne*, trans. Lewis Thorpe (Harmondsworth: Penguin Books, 1981), 95.

19 Ibid., 79.

yet which, for very sweetness, could resemble the soft tinkle of a lyre or a cymbal.[20]

A description of music heard at a banquet suggests that even on such occasions this court heard a high level of aesthetic music.

> The bishop ordered skilled choristers to advance: they were accompanied by every musical instrument one could think of, and by the sound of their singing they could have softened the hardest hearts or turned to ice the limpid waters of the Rhine.[21]

Charlemagne also took an interest in jongleurs, the first of the wandering minstrels, and even rewarded them with gifts of land in Provence. One scholar points to this court as the birth of what would become the *chansons de geste*.[22] An attractive anecdote tells of a jongleur who guided Charlemagne over Mt. Cenis in 773 and was then given as a reward all the land over which his *tuba* [trumpet] could be heard when played from a hill.[23]

According to another source, Charlemagne even had prepared a collection of his hunting signals, called, *Frohliche Jagd*.[24] While this music is not extant, iconographic clues suggest it was performed by various animal horns, trumpet-types, flute-types, drums and bells.

Charlemagne also took an active interest in Church music. Einhard describes his actual singing.

> He made careful reforms in the way in which the psalms were chanted and the lessons read. He was himself quite an expert at both of these exercises, but he never read the lesson in public and he would sing only with the rest of the congregation and then in a low voice.[25]

It was in this regard that Charlemagne once requested that the pope send him two singers who were expert in the approved style of singing to instruct the various churches of his realm. These two came, but deviously instructed each congregation in a separate style. When Charlemagne discovered this he sent them back to Rome, where they were punished with life imprisonment. Thereupon, the pope wrote Charlemagne,

> If I send you some more they will be just as blind with envy as the first ones, and they will cheat you in their turn ... Send me two of the most intelligent monks whom you have in your own entourage ...

20 Ibid., 143.

21 Ibid., 112.

22 E. K. Chambers, *The Mediaeval Stage* (Oxford, 1903), I, 37, who quotes Philippe Mouskes, *de Poetis Provincialibus*,

> Quar quant li buens
> Rois Karlemaigne
> Ot toute mise à son demaine
> Provence, qui mult iert plentive
> De vins, de bois, d'aigue, de rive,
> As lecours, as menestreus,
> Qui sont auques luxurieus,
> Le donna toute et departi.

23 Chambers, ibid., I, 37, fn. 2.

24 Gottfried Veit, *Die Blasmusik* (Bozen: Verband Sudtiroler Musikkapellen, 1972), 20.

25 Einhard and Notker, *Two Lives of Charlemagne*, 80.

With God's help they will acquire the proficiency in this art which you are looking for.[26]

> [26] Ibid., 103ff.

There are two interesting anecdotes regarding Charlemagne and his Church music. In the first,[27] a choir member appeared at an important feast somewhat drunk and intoned the final response instead of the first. This monk was fired on the spot. The monk in the second anecdote was considerably more fortunate.

> [27] Ibid., 98ff.

One day when Charlemagne was on a journey he came to a great cathedral. A certain wandering monk, who was unaware of the Emperor's attention to small detail, came into the choir and, since he had never learned to do anything of the sort himself, stood silent and confused in the middle of those who were chanting. Thereupon the choir-master raised his baton and threatened to hit him, if he did not sing. The monk, not knowing what to do or where to turn, and not daring to go out, twisted and contorted his throat, opened his mouth wide, moved his bottom jaw up and down, and did all that he could to imitate the appearance of someone singing. The others present had not the self-control to stop laughing. Our valiant Emperor, who was not to be moved from his serenity by even the greatest events, sat solemnly waiting until the end of the Mass, just as if he had not noticed this pretense at singing. When it was all over, he called the poor wretch to him and, taking pity on his struggles and the strain he had gone through, consoled with these words: 'My good monk, thank you very much for your singing and your efforts.' Then he ordered him to be given a pound of silver to relieve his poverty.[28]

> [28] Ibid., 100ff.

Aside from this rich account of the musical environment surrounding Charlemagne, the reports of the few remaining historians contain very little information regarding secular musical performance during these three centuries. While their references may be few, they are of such a nature as to suggest that the traditional uses of music continued. The 'Dark Ages,' therefore, may have more to do with a lack of literature, than a lack of art.

ON THE PHYSIOLOGY OF MUSIC

Boethius, for all the insight with which he discusses music, could not quite bring himself to validate music as belonging to the realm of the senses. It was rather to be associated with Reason. We will present here his views on the nature of Reason itself, and discuss his views on music and Reason below, in chapter 14.

He first observes that God is 'understanding, memory, and the rational will.' Whatever, and however little, man has of these is the divine in him, for he thus reflects his maker.[29]

Boethius, who wrote his *Consolatione Philosophiae* while in prison, awaiting his unjust execution, concludes that Reason is the only happiness in life, for it alone cannot be taken away.

> Therefore I advise thee, that thou learn, that there is no happiness in this present life. But learn that nothing is better in this present life than reason: because man cannot by any means lose it.[30]

He observes further that, 'No man can injure the rational mind, or cause it that it should not be what it is.' He illustrates this with a startling anecdote.

> This is very evidently to be known by a certain Roman nobleman, who was called Liberius. He was put to many torments because he would not inform against his associates, who conspired with him against the king who had with injustice conquered them. When he was led before the enraged king, and he commanded him to say who were his associates who had conspired with him, then bit he off his own tongue, and immediately cast it before the face of the tyrant.[31]

It seems clear that Boethius would have simply concluded that man *is* Reason, were it not for one troublesome problem. He recognized that there was something else to man, something he called the 'spirit,' which did not seem to act according to Reason. He observed the evidence of this primarily in the subsequent dreams when man sleeps.

The soul of man, according to Boethius, has three natures, the power of willing, anger [emotions?], and the rational. Of these, he observes that lower animals have the first two, but only man has Reason.[32]

In another place, however, he states that Wisdom is the best part of the soul.

---

29 Boethius, *Consolatione Philosophiae*, trans. Samuel Fox (London: George Bell, 1895), XIV, ii.

30 Ibid., XI, ii. He adds here, that since death brings the end to both man and his riches, 'I wonder why men are so irrational as to think that this present life can make man happy whilst he lives.'

31 Ibid., XVI, ii.

32 Ibid., XXXIII, iv.

Indeed, wisdom is one single faculty of the soul, and yet we all know that it is better than all the other faculties, which we have before spoken about.³³

Wisdom, observes Boethius, comes from experience. He illustrates this by pointing out that the wise man understand he profits from a hard life, and therefore does not wish for an easy life.

> Then replied Wisdom sharply, and said: Therefore no wise man ought to fear or lament, in whatever wise it may happen to him, or whether severe fortune or agreeable may come to him; any more than the brave man ought to lament about this, how often he must fight. His praise is not the less; but the opinion is, that it is the greater. So is also the wise man's reward the greater, if more adverse, and severer fortune comes to him. Therefore no wise man should be desirous of a soft life, if he makes account of any virtues, or any honor here in the world, or of eternal life after this world.³⁴

Finally, in spite of his adamant belief in Reason, Boethius curiously admits that it is through *experience*, together with knowledge, that one learns.

> We very well know that no man doubts of this, that he is powerful in his strength, who is seen to perform laborious work: any more than if he be anything, any one doubts that he is so. Thus the art of music causes the man to be a musician, the medical knowledge to be a physician, and rhetoric causes him to be a rhetorician.³⁵

Alcuin, the famous English scholar who was a member of the court of Charlemagne, also mentions experience, in quoting an observation by Tullius that, 'Memory is the storehouse of all our experiences.'³⁶

Another writer who comments at length on Reason and the senses is known as Pseudo-Dionysius Areopagite, whose existence cannot be accurately documented, but apparently falls within our present time frame. In his *Divine Names*, he begins by quoting from I Corinthians 2:4, 'my speech and my message were not in plausible words of wisdom, but in demonstration of the Spirit,' to suggest that we should not trust the intelligence of man, but only the word of God as revealed through theologians.³⁷ At the same time, he says, we cannot trust our senses, 'what is intelligible is incomprehensible and unseen to the senses.'³⁸

---

33 Ibid., XXXII, ii.

34 Ibid., XL, iii.

35 Ibid., XVI, iii.

36 Alcuin, *Rhetoric*, trans. Wilbur Howell (New York: Russell & Russell, 1965), 137.

37 Pseudo-Dionysius Areopagite, *The Divine Names and Mystical Theology*, trans. John Jones (Milwaukee: Marquette University Press, 1980), 585B.

38 Ibid., 588B.

In one of his poems, addressed to 'Timothy,' he again recommends abandoning both the intellect and the senses.

> And you, dear Timothy,
> in the earnest exercise of
> mystical contemplation, abandon
> all sensation and all intellectual activities
> all that is sensed and intelligible,
> all non-beings and all beings;
> thus you will unknowingly be elevated,
> as far as possible,
> to the unity of that beyond being and knowledge.[39]

[39] Ibid., 998B.

If, then, we are not to use either the intellect or the senses, where does this leave us? The reader will quickly perceive the convoluted mind of this writer in his answer.

> Once we cease our intellectual activities, we are thrust upon the ray beyond being as far as the divine law permits. In this ray the limits of all knowledge have pre-subsisted in a more than ineffable way. It is not possible to conceive, to speak, or in any way to contemplate this ray; for, it is apart from all, beyond unknowing, and at once the completing ends of all essential knowledge and powers.[40]

[40] Ibid., 592D.

In another place, he suggests the purpose of the senses is to contribute to Reason and that Reason will always be more valuable than anything perceived by the senses.

> Clearly, when the intellect is seriously raised up through the senses toward a contemplative intellection, clearer interpretation will be wholly more honored than sensations and the most distinct and clear reasons will be wholly more honored than what is visible.[41]

[41] Ibid., 709A.

ON THE PSYCHOLOGY OF AESTHETICS

Boethius begins his discussion of Pleasure with a rather pessimistic summary of the point made by so many philosophers before him, that with pleasure comes pain.

Very narrow, and very worthless, are human enjoyments: for either they never come to a man, or they never constantly remain there such as they first came ...

With very much bitterness is the sweetness of this world mingled. Though it seem pleasant to any one, he will be unable to hold it, if it begin to fly from him.[42]

42 Boethius, *Consolatione Philosophiae*, XI, i.

He continues with a rather Epicurean conclusion that happiness is the absence of pain.

Do we not know that no anxiety, or difficulties, or trouble, or pain, or sorrow, is happiness? What more, then, need we say?[43]

43 Ibid., XXIV, iv.

But he does have more to say, namely that there are five things which are indispensable to happiness: wealth, power, dignity, renown, and pleasure. These, he says, are like five members of a man, yet all of the same body.[44]

44 Ibid., XXXIII, ii, and XXXIV, vi.

Near the end of this same book, Boethius inadvertently admits that music gives pleasure.

For it is near the time when I had intended to begin other work, and I have not yet finished this: and methinks, too, thou are rather weary, and these long discourses appear to thee too lengthy, so that thou art now desirous of my songs. I know, too, that they give thee pleasure.[45]

45 Ibid., XXXIX, iv.

He speaks of musical pleasure again, in retelling the myth of Orpheus, the source of the expression, 'Music tames the savage beast.' Whereas in his *De Musica* he said that in man it is Reason which produces pleasure, in the case of the animals in this tale, Boethius says they were calmed, 'for the pleasure in the sound.'[46]

46 Ibid., XXXV, vi.

ON AESTHETICS

Only one writer of this period, Pseudo-Dionysius Areopagite, speaks in any length of Beauty as an abstract quality. He appears to be defining here an ideal Beauty apart from anything which could be achieved on this earth. But, since we freely admit to a certain dizziness when reading this man's books, we will simply quote the essence of his argument and pray the reader will experience greater understanding than we.

Now the beautiful and beauty are not to be distinguished with respect to the cause which gathers the whole into one. For with respect to all beings this whole is divided into participations and participants. What is beautiful is said to be a participant in beauty; beauty is said to be the participating in the beauty producing cause of all that is beautiful.

> That, beautiful beyond being, is said to be
> Beauty—for it gives beauty from itself in a manner appropriate to each,
> it causes the consonance and splendor of all,
> it flashes forth upon all, after the manner of light, the beauty producing gifts of its flowing ray,
> it calls all to itself, whence it is called beauty,
> it brings all together into the same;
>
> Beautiful—as
> At once all-beautiful and beyond-beautiful, always be-ing beautiful according to the same and in like manner; thus
> not coming to be, not passing out of being,
> not increasing or decreasing,
> not beautiful to some and ugly to others,
> not beautiful at one time and ugly at another,
> not beautiful in one relation and ugly in another,
> It is not beautiful to some and ugly to others, but
> itself—always be-ing uniformly beautiful in virtue of itself and with itself,
> preeminently before-having in itself the flowing beauty of what is beautiful;
> before subsisting,
> in the simple nature beyond nature of the whole of what is beautiful and in its cause:
> all beauty and all that is beautiful.[47]

Cassiodorus, in a comment on aesthetics, transforms the traditional phrase, 'Art imitates Nature,' into 'Art conquers Nature.' While he is speaking only of sculpture, this observation nevertheless implies that the appreciation of Beauty had not died.

> From Art proceeds this gift, which conquers Nature. And thus the discolored surface of the marble is woven into the loveliest variety of pictures; the value of the work, now as always, being increased by the minute labor which has to be expended on the production of the Beautiful.[48]

[47] Pseudo-Dionysius Areopagite, *The Divine Names and Mystical Theology*, 701Cff.

[48] Cassiodorus, 'Letter to Agapitus, Praefectus Urbis,' in *Variae*, I, vi.

Boethius, in speaking of predestination, uses an analogy which reveals that his definition of art is that it exists first in the mind, and then in the art object.

> As every artist considers and marks out his work in his mind before he executes it, and afterwards executes it all ... [49]

For Alcuin, a member of the court of Charlemagne, the primary characteristic of art seems to have been precision. He defines elequence in rhetoric as that which 'observes the rules of grammar, and is supported by the authority of the ancients.'[50] In another place he states an aesthetic principle, which he says is of the greatest importance, that what is unbecoming can give no pleasure. Here he again quotes Tullius.

> The cardinal precept of art is that the sense of propriety must regulate the activity of the artist.[51]

Finally, in a dialog with Charlemagne, Alcuin sets forth his concept of the Four Virtues which he associated with rhetoric, and presumably art in general.

> ALCUIN. Virtue is perfection of mind, dignity of character, reasonableness of life, excellence of habits.
> CHARLEMAGNE. How many aspects does it have?
> ALCUIN. Four: Prudence, Justice, Courage, Temperance.
> CHARLEMAGNE. What is Prudence?
> ALCUIN. Prudence is the knowledge of things and of natures ... [Its attributes are] Memory, Intelligence, Foresight.
> CHARLEMAGNE. Explain now the concept of Justice.
> ALCUIN. Justice is a disposition of the mind to render to each what is his due ... [Its attributes are] Religion, Duty, Gratitude, Retribution, Respect, Truthfulness.
> CHARLEMAGNE. Now I entreat you to consider Courage and its special attributes.
> ALCUIN. Courage is the capacity to endure danger and hardship with an undaunted spirit. Its attributes are High-Mindedness, Confidence, Forbearance, Perseverance ...
> CHARLEMAGNE. It remains for you to speak of Temperance ...
> ALCUIN. Temperance may be defined as the firm and moderate rule by the reason of our desires and the other wayward passions of our souls. Its attributes are Restraint, Clemency, Moderation.[52]

---

49 Boethius, *Consolatione Philosophiae*, XXXIX, vi.

50 Alcuin, *Rhetoric*, trans. Wilbur Howell (New York: Russell & Russell, 1965), 133. In his poem, *The Bishops, Kings, and Saint of York*, ed. Peter Godman (Oxford: Clarendon Press, 1982), 113, 121, Alcuin mentions that his own teacher, Aelberht, owned the works of both Cassiodorus and Boethius and taught his students not only rhetoric and grammar, but music.

> Some he polished with the whetstone of true speech, teaching others to sing in Aonian strain, teaching some to blow on the Castalian pipe, and run with lyric step over the peaks of Parnassus. To others this master taught the harmony of the spheres.

51 Ibid., 141.

52 Ibid., 147ff.

Pope Gregory the Great makes a curious argument against the Christian applauding in the theater, which can only be understood in the light of several centuries of earlier Church leaders forbidding attendance at all. In making a distinction between the 'kindly-disposed' person and one who is envious,[53] Gregory stipulates that the Christian must applaud and imitate the good deeds they see in others. Indeed, to not do so, 'they stand to be smitten the more severely with punishment at the end of time.'

On the other hand, one should not applaud the actor, whom one would not actually desire to imitate.

> The kindly-disposed must, therefore, be told that if they do not bestir themselves to imitate what they approve and praise, the holiness of virtue pleases them in the same manner that the vain art of public performers pleases foolish spectators; for these extol with favors the performance of charioteers and actors, yet do not wish to be like those whom they applaud. They admire people for the pleasing exhibition they give, but decline to please others in like manner.

[53] Gregory the Great, *Pastoral Care*, III, X, trans. Henry Davis (New York: Newman Press, 1978).

ON THE AESTHETICS OF MUSIC

We have an extraordinary survey of the aesthetics of music by Cassiodorus in a letter to the famous Boethius. His purpose in writing was to ask Boethius to find a harp player to fulfill a request by Clovis, king of the Franks, whom Cassiodorus suggests has 'heard of the fame of my banquets.' He requests Boethius to find someone 'who is skilled in musical knowledge,' who with his 'sweet sound can tame the savage hearts of the barbarians.' Cassiodorus then digresses to compose a tribute to the power of music to move men and to affect their character, even recalling the ancient Greek beliefs on the specific influences of various modes. He also suggests that oratory and poetry achieve their success through their relationship with music and concludes with a reference to the 'Music of the Spheres' and praise of string music. It is a stunning testimonial to the recognition of art music in the sixth century.

> For what is more glorious than music, which modulates the heavenly system with its sonorous sweetness, and binds together with its virtue the concord of nature which is scattered everywhere? For

any variation there may be in the whole does not depart from the pattern of harmony. Through this we think with efficiency, we speak with elegance, we move with grace. Whenever, by the natural law of its discipline, it reaches our ears, it commands song.

The artist changes men's hearts as they listen; and, when this artful pleasure issues from the secret place of nature as the queen of the senses, in all the glory of its tones, our remaining thoughts take to flight, and it expels all else, that it may delight itself simply in being heard. Harmful melancholy he turns to pleasure; he weakens swelling rage; he makes bloodthirsty cruelty kindly, arouses sleepy sloth from its torpor, restores to the sleepless their wholesome rest, recalls lust-corrupted chastity to its moral resolve, and heals boredom of spirit which is always the enemy of good thoughts. Dangerous hatreds he turns to helpful goodwill, and, in a blessed kind of healing, drives out the passions of the heart by means of sweetest pleasures.

Through bodily means he softens the bodiless soul, and leads it where he wills by hearing only, while unable to control it by speech. In silence, he cries aloud through his hands; he speaks without a mouth; and, by the service of insensible matter, he is strong to govern the senses.

Among men all this is achieved by means of five modes, each of which is called by the name of the region where it was discovered. Indeed, the divine compassion distributed this favor locally, even while it assuredly made its whole creation something to be praised. The Dorian mode bestows wise self-restraint and establishes chastity; the Phrygian arouses strife, and inflames the will to anger; the Aeolian calms the storms of the soul, and gives sleep to those who are already at peace; the Ionian sharpens the wits of the dull, and, as a worker of good, gratifies the longing for heavenly things among those who are burdened by earthly desire. The Lydian was discovered as a remedy for excessive cares and weariness of the spirit: it restores it by relaxation, and refreshes it by pleasure. This one a corrupt age perverted to cabaret performances, making an immoral invention out of a decent remedy …

But all this was evidently achieved by the human art of [instrumental] music. Yet, as we know, the living voice has a natural rhythm: it preserves an exquisite melody when it is silent at the right moment, speaks suitably, and steps with careful elocution, on musical feet, down the path of intonation. The sweet and forceful speeches of orators were likewise invented to move men's souls, so that judges would pity the erring, and be enraged with the criminal. Whatever an eloquent man may achieve clearly belongs to the glory of this discipline.

To the poets also, as Terentianus bears witness, two original meters are ascribed: the heroic and iambic, the one devised to arouse, and the other to quieten men. From these, various ways of delighting the souls of an audience have been born; and, as with the tones of an instrument, so in the human voice, the pregnant meters have brought forth different passions of the soul.

The researches of the ancients have revealed that the Sirens sang to a miracle; and, though the waves drove on the sailors, and the wind filled their sails, under the pleasant deception they preferred to run on the rocks, rather than forgo such sweetness. Only the man of Ithaca [Ulysses] escaped, who was quick to stop up the seductive hearing of his crew. Against the poisonous sweetness, that craftiest of men thought up the device of a fortunate deafness: what they could not overcome by their judgment, they conquered instead by insensibility …

But, that I may follow the example of the wise Ithacan, and pass on, let me speak of that psaltery which came down from heaven, which a man to be sung throughout the world so composed and modulated for the soul's deliverance that, by these hymns, the wounds of the mind might be healed, and God's special grace implored. Let the world wonder at this and believe: David's lyre drove out a devil; its sound commanded the spirits; and, as the cithara played, the king [Saul] whom an inward enemy had evilly enthralled returned to his freedom.

For, although many instruments of this delight have been discovered, nothing has been found more effective to move the soul than the sweet resonance of the hollow cithara. Hence, we suppose that the strings of the instrument were called chords because they easily move the heart [corda]. So great is the concord of the diverse notes assembled there that a string, once struck, makes it neighbor vibrate spontaneously, although itself untouched. For such is the power of harmony that it makes a lifeless object move spontaneously because it so happens that its fellow is in motion.

Hence different notes emerge without a tongue; hence some sweet chorus is formed from a variety of sounds: one is high through great tension, another low through a certain slackening of the string, a third mezzo, through a mellow adjustment of the instrument's back. Human beings cannot achieve a unison to equal the social concord that unreasoning objects have attained. For there all notes which are tuneful or flat, harsh or most clear, and so on, are gathered, as it were, into one glory; and, as a diadem delights the eyes by the various light of its gems, so does the cithara delight the ears by the diversity of sound.

It is the talking loom of the Muses, with speaking wefts and singing warps, on which the plectrum shrilly weaves sweet sounds. Now this instrument Mercury is said to have discovered, modeling it on the mottled tortoise. As the bringer of such benefits, astronomers have believed it should be sought among the stars, urging that music must be heavenly, since they can detect the shape of a lyre placed among the constellations.

Yet, the harmony of heaven cannot be fittingly described by human speech, as nature has not revealed it to human ears, but the soul knows it through reason only. For they say that we should believe that the blessedness of heaven enjoys those pleasures which have no end, and are diminished by no interruption. They maintain, indeed, that things above are absorbed by that same perception, that heavenly beings enjoy those same pleasures, and that those who are engrossed by such contemplations are constantly enfolded in blessed delights.[54]

Boethius, in his *Consolatione Philosophiae*, written in prison, makes the interesting observation that while he could freely compose happy poetry and music, when composing in a tragic style he had difficulty finding words to match the emotions of his music.

> The lays [songs] which I, an exile, formerly with delight sung, I shall now mourning sing, and with very unfit words compose. Though I formerly readily invented, yet I now, weeping and sobbing, wander from appropriate words.[55]

One of his extant poems expresses this same theme.

> Lo! I sang cheerily
> In my bright days,
> But now all wearily
> Chaunt I my lays;
> Sorrowing tearfully,
> Saddest of men,
> Can I sing cheerfully,
> As I could then?
>
> Many a verity
> In those glad times
> Of my prosperity
> Taught I in rhymes;
> Now from forgetfulness
> Wanders my tongue,
> Wasting in fretfulness
> Meters unsung.

54 'Letter to Boethius,' in *Variae*, II, xl.

55 Boethius, *Consolatione Philosophie*, II.

ART MUSIC

We need not be disappointed if few references to specific performances of art music are to be found among the historians of this period, for that which we have, such as the extraordinary testimonial to music by Cassiodorus, bears clear witness to its existence.

During the reign of Justinian, Procopius recalls one, Gelimer, the object of a siege, who requested a lyre to perform for himself alone what must be regarded as art music.

> Being a skillful harpist he had composed an ode relating to his present misfortune, which he was eager to sing to the accompaniment of a lyre while he wept out his soul.[56]

A letter by Cassiodorus mentions that singers and dancers were rewarded by the Consul.[57] In another letter he mentions a gift to the court of 'musical instruments of ebony,' which were no doubt used for Art Music.[58]

We have supplied numerous references, in previous chapters, to the decay of the theater productions, which had a fundamental participation of music. Another letter of Cassiodorus also comments on the decline of this art.

> When farmers, on the holidays, celebrated the rites of various deities in groves and villages, the Athenians were the first to raise this rustic beginning into an urban spectacle. To the place where they looked on, they gave the Greek name of theater, since the gathered throng, separated from the bystanders, could look on with no hindrance.
>
> But the back-drop of the theater was called the *scaena* from the deep shade of the grove where, at the start of spring, the shepherds sang various songs. Musical performances flourished there, and the precepts of a wise age. But it gradually came about that the respectable arts, shunning the company of depraved men, withdrew from that venue out of modesty.[59]

Cassiodorus continues with an enlightening and rare description of the use of music in Comedy and Pantomime.

> Comedy ... is where the rustic actors made fun of human doings in merry songs. To these were added the speaking hands of dancers, their fingers that are tongues, their clamorous silence, their silent

[56] Procopius, *History of the Wars*, IV, vi.

[57] 'Letter to Maximus, Illustris, Consul,' in *Variae*, V, xlii.

[58] 'Letter to the King of the Vandals,' in *Variae*, V, i.

[59] 'Letter to the Patrician Symmachus,' in ibid., IV, li. In a document found in ibid., VII, x, Cassidorus expresses particular concern for the problem of the itinerant stage actor.

exposition. The Muse Polymnia is said to have discovered this, showing that humans could declare their meaning even without speech ...

Again, there is the pantomime actor, who derives his name from manifold imitations. When first he comes on stage, lured by applause, bands of musicians, skilled in various instruments, support him. Then the hand of meaning expounds the song to the eyes of melody, and, by a code of gestures, as if by letters, it instructs the spectator's sight; summaries are read in it, and, without writing, it performs what writing has set forth.

He makes a passing reference to a musical instrument, the *acetabula*,[60] which 'yields such pleasure that, of all the senses, men think their hearing is the highest gift conferred on them,' and concludes by again commenting on the decline of these arts.

The succeeding age corrupted the inventions of the ancients by mingling obscenities; their headlong minds drove towards bodily lusts an art devised to give decent pleasure.

FUNCTIONAL MUSIC

In the literature of the period, we have found only one reference to one of the ancient cult-religious ceremonies which specifically mentions the music. This is found in a passage in the writings of Gregory the Great, in which he is discussing the 'barbarians' of Germany.

It was during this same period that the Lombards, holding as prisoners some 400 other persons, were performing their customary rite of sacrificing the head of a goat to the Devil, dedicating to him by running around, singing sacrilegious songs.[61]

Procopius provides an interesting description of Roman army music during the early sixth century. From this account one would have to believe there had been a decline in the organization of military signals, the number of recognizable signals, and in the instruments used. In the case of the latter, only the trumpet and lituus are mentioned, with no reference to the most important military instrument of earlier Roman armies, the cornu, although he does include some interesting comments on the actual signals. In

60 Presumed to be an instrument like the glockenspiel, but with metal cups instead of bars.

61 Gregory the Great, *Dialogue Three*, 28, trans. Odo Zimmerman (New York: Fathers of the Church, 1959).

this account, Procopius himself is speaking to the famous Roman general, Belisarius.

> The men, General, who blew the trumpets in the Roman army in ancient times knew two different strains, one of which seemed unmistakably to urge the soldiers on and impel them to battle, while the other used to call the men who were fighting back to the camp, whenever this seemed to the general to be for the best. And by such means the generals could always give the appropriate commands to the soldiers, and they on their part were able to execute the commands thus communicated to them. For during actual combat the human voice is in no way adapted to give any clear instructions, since it obviously has to contend with the clash of arms on every side, and fear paralyzes the senses of those fighting. But since at the present time such skill has become obsolete through ignorance and it is impossible to express both commands by one trumpet, do you adopt the following course hereafter. With the cavalry trumpets urge on the soldiers to continue fighting with the enemy, but with those of the infantry call the men back to the retreat. For it is impossible for them to fail to recognize the sound of either one, for in the one case the sound comes forth from leather and very thin wood, and in the other from rather thick brass.[62]

Gibbon mentions that during the winter, when not engaged in battle, the Roman troops maintained their skills by practicing the Pyrrhic dance.

> They repeated each day their military exercise on foot and on horseback, accustomed their ear to obey the sound of the trumpet, and practiced the steps and evolutions of the Pyrrhic dance.[63]

62 Ibid., VI, xxiii. Gregory of Tours, in *The History of the Franks*, 243, mentions a certain Sigulf, who, in 573 AD, chased Clovis, son of King Chilperic, 'as if he were chasing a hunted deer,' with these same two instruments.

63 Gibbon, *The History of the Decline and Fall of the Roman Empire*, III, 626.

ENTERTAINMENT MUSIC

While Cassidorus bemoans the decline in serious theater, in a letter answering some complaint about the behavior of the audience at entertainment spectacles, he seems much more tolerant.

> As to their complaints of rudeness against the mob, you must distinguish between deliberate insolence and the license of the theater. Who expects seriousness of character at the spectacles? It is not

exactly a congregation of Catos that comes together at the circus. The place excuses some excesses.[64]

On the same topic, another letter makes a curious suggestion.

> The Circus, in which the King spends so much money, is meant to be for public delight, not for stirring up wrath. Instead of uttering howls and insults like other nations, whom they have despised for doing so, let them tune their voices, so that their applause shall sound like the notes of some vast organ, and even the brute creation delight to hear it.[65]

Modeled on an ancient tradition, apparently among the nobles there was a popular tradition during banquets to pass a lyre around the table for each guest to sing in turn. Bede mentions this custom in reference to the poet, Caedmon, whose serious approach to poetry prevented him from participating.

> Others after him attempted, in the English nation, to compose religious poems, but none could ever compare with him, for he did not learn the art of poetry from men, but from God; for which reason he never could compose any trivial or vain poem, but only those which relate to religion suited his religious tongue; for having lived in a secular habit till he was well advanced in years, he had never learned anything of versifying; for which reason being sometimes at entertainments, when it was agreed for the sake of mirth that all present should sing in their turns, when he saw the instrument come towards him, he rose from the table and returned home.[66]

Finally, Gibbon paints a rather grim scene in describing banquets in 590 AD.

> The restoration of Chosroes was celebrated with feasts and executions; and the music of the royal banquet was often disturbed by the groans of dying or mutilated criminals.[67]

---

64 'Letter to Speciosus,' in *Variae*, I, xxvii.

65 'Letter to the Roman People,' in ibid., I, xxxi.

66 The Venerable Bede, *Ecclesiastical History of England*, trans. J. A. Giles (London: Bohn, 1849), XXIV.

67 Gibbon, *The History of the Decline and Fall of the Roman Empire*, IV, 62.

12 POETS OF THE SIXTH THROUGH EIGHTH CENTURIES

DURING THIS PERIOD A FUNDAMENTAL CHANGE in the nature of sung poetry takes place. First, during the sixth century, we find the very last of the poets in the Greek tradition, who sung of pastoral scenes, myths and gods. Second, as a direct result of the earliest period of jongleurs, a new kind of poetry emerges, poetry which reflects contemporary life. This new poetry, of course, is much more revealing with regard to aesthetic ideas of this period.

We might begin our brief look at the poets of the older style with a quotation from Agathias Scholasticus, who in fact speaks in tribute to the old traditions.

> So now that the whole earth is full of beloved peace, now that the hopes of disturbers at home and abroad have been shattered by our Emperor, come, blest Theodorus, and let us institute a contest of poetic skill and start the music of the singer's dance …
>
> I will first select for you, competing with men of old time, all that the parents of the new song wrote as an offering to the old gods. For it was meet to adhere to the wise model of the ancient writers.[1]

Another poet of the sixth century, Paulus Silentiarius, retells the old story of the cricket which substitutes for the missing tone of a lyre, here also in the setting of a music contest.

> To Lycorean Apollo doth Locrian Eunomus dedicate the brazen cicada, in memory of his contest for the crown. The contest was in lyre playing, and opposite him stood his competitor, Parthis. But when the Locrian shell rang to the stroke of the plectrum, the string cracked with a hoarse cry. But before the running melody could go lame, a cicada lighted on the lyre chirping tenderly and caught up the vanishing note of the chord, adapting to the fashion of our playing its wild music that used to echo in the woods.[2]

1 *The Greek Anthology*, trans. W. R. Paton (Cambridge: Harvard University Press, 1939), I, iv.3.

2 Ibid., I, vi, 54.

As if in recognition of this fading style of poetry, several poems speak of aged players. First, Macedonius, writes of a retiring lyre player.

> Eumpolpus, finding fault with his aged hands, laid his lyre on the tripod as an offering to Phoebus. He said, 'May I never touch a lyre again or carry the instrument of the music I made of old. Let young men love the lyre-string, but I, instead of holding the plectrum, support my shaky hands on a staff.'[3]

Macedonius sings a particularly lovely poem of resignation by an elderly panpipe player.

> I, Daphnis the piper, in my shaky old age, my idle hand now heavy, dedicate, now I have ceased from the labors of the fold, my shepherd's crook to rustic Pan. For still I play on the pipes, still in my trembling body my voice dwells unshaken. But let no goatherd tell the ravenous wolves in the mountains of the feebleness of my old years.[4]

Similarly, there are poems in honor of deceased musicians. Paulus Silentiarius wrote a poem in honor of a deceased lyre player, which includes an interesting association of music and grammar.

> Damocharis passed into the final silence of Fate; alas! the Muses' lovely lyre is silent; the holy foundation of Grammar has perished. Sea-girt Cos, thou are again in mourning as for Hippocrates.[5]

A poem by Agathias Scholasticus, is unusual, being written in honor of a deceased *female* singer and lyre player.

> Alas! alas! this earth covers the tenth Muse, the lyric chanter of Rome and Alexandria. They have perished, the notes of the lyre; song hath perished as if dying together with Joanna. Perchance the nine Muses have imposed on themselves a law worthy of them—to dwell in Joanna's tomb instead of on Helicon.[6]

We even find such a poem by Pope Gregory the Great remembering a deceased choir member.

> O founts of ears, O knees, O hands of Carterius, that appeased Christ by most pure sacrifices. How like all mortals has he ceased to be. The choir there in heaven required a hymn singer.[7]

---

3 Ibid., I, vi, 83.

4 Ibid., I, vi, 73.

5 Ibid., I, vii, 588.

6 Ibid., II, vii, 612.

7 Ibid., II, viii, 144. A poem by Gregory, in ibid., 22, speaks of the panpipe in a metaphorical sense.

A poem by Agathias Scholasticus was inspired by a painting of a Satyr holding a panpipe to his ear. We find two aesthetic observations here: first, that he is listening with 'his whole soul,' and second, the reference to such delight in listening that all other thoughts disappear.

> 'Does thy pipe, little Satyr, send forth sound of its own accord, or why dost thou bend thine ear and put it to the reed?' But the Satyr smiled and spoke not; perchance he would have uttered words, but his delight held him in forgetfulness. For it was not the wax that hindered him, but he chose of his own will to be silent, turning his whole soul to his occupation with the pipe.[8]

[8] Ibid., V, 244.

Another composition by this same poet speaks of a cymbal-playing statue, with a strange emotion we cannot interpret.

> The sculptor set up a statue of a Bacchant, yet ignorant of how to beat the swift cymbals with her hands and ashamed. For so does she bend forward, and looks as if she were crying, 'Go ye out, and I will strike them with none standing by.'[9]

[9] Ibid., V, 59.

Additional aesthetic insights by this poet are found in a poem which speaks of a harp-playing tragic actress, named Ariadne. The poet voices his fear that this player of art music might be taken over for use in the Bacchus ceremonies.

> Whenever she strikes her harp with the plectrum, it seems to be the echo of Terpsichore's strings, and if she tunes her voice to the high tragic strain, it is the hum of Melpomene that she reproduces. Were there a new contest for beauty too, Cypris herself were more likely to lose the prize than she, and Paris would revise his judgment. But hush! let us keep it to our own selves, lest Bacchus overhear and long for the embraces of this Ariadne too.[10]

[10] Ibid., I, v, 222.

These poets, as those ancient ones whom they imitate, also speak of the association of music and love. A poem of Macedonius, for example, sings,

> Thy mouth blossoms with grace and thy cheeks bloom with flowers, thy eyes are bright with Love, and thy hands aglow with music. Thou takest captive eyes with eyes and ears with song; with thy every part thou trappest unhappy young men.[11]

[11] Ibid., I, v, 231.

And, similarly, in a poem by Paulus Silentiarius, we find,

> Meliscus would dedicate his reed-flute to Pan, but Pan says he will not accept the gift in these words: 'It was from the reeds I was infected with love-madness.'[12]

A phenomenon often remarked on by early writers is the sympathetic vibrations of the string instruments. A poem by Agathias Scholasticus reminds us that the true explanation for this was not yet understood.

> Some one questioned the musician Androtion, skilled in what concerns the lyre, on a curious piece of instrumental lore. 'When you set the highest string on the right in motion with the plectron, the lowest on the left quivers of its own accord with a slight twang, and is made to whisper reciprocally when its own highest string is struck; so that I marvel how nature made sympathetic to each other lifeless strings in a state of tension.' But he swore that Aristoxenus, with his admirable knowledge of plectra, did not know the theoretical explanation of this. 'The solution,' he said, 'is as follows. The strings are all made of sheep's gut dried all together. So they are sisters and sound together as if related, sharing each other's family voice. For they are all legitimate children, being the issue of one belly, and they inherit those reciprocal noises. Just so does the right eye, when injured, often convey its own pain to the left eye.'[13]

The last important poet of the old Greek lyric poetry style, Fortunatus, died in the seventh century, bringing the end to an artistic tradition more than a thousand years old. His poem, 'Time,' seems almost to be announcing the final curtain.

> Where!—I ask—is the song?
> Orpheus, cajoling with his tenor & the stout cry of his lute lies dead!
> What of the poem? of Virgil? Ovid? Menander? Homer?
> Whose sepulchers shelter their fleshless corpses in mildew.
> When the last day arrives, verses to the Muses are worthless
> neither can pleasure be found in elongating the eloquence of a song [lay].[14]

The new kind of poetry which takes the place of that of the old style is more important in providing insights into performance practice, for it sings of contemporaries rather than ancient mythical characters and gods. This new tradition had its roots among the

---

12 Ibid., I, vi, 82.

13 Ibid., IV, 352.

14 Fortunatus, *The Miscellanea*, VII: 12, trans. Geoffrey Cook (Rhinebeck, NY: Open Studio, 1981).

fellow travelers, the jugglers, story-tellers, actors, musicians and performers of magic, who accompanied the large groups of people fleeing the 'barbarians' spreading into the West after the fall of the Roman empire.

The earliest musician–entertainers we call today 'jongleurs,' after the medieval Latin, *Ioculator*, 'one who makes merry.' These early folk who tried to make a living as entertainers were not yet specialists, but probably learned every possible skill which might be useful. The 'resume' of one of them, no doubt speaks for them all.

> I can play the lute, vielle, pipe, bagpipe, panpipes, harp, fiddle, guittern, symphony, psaltery, organistrum, organ, tabor and the rote. I can sing a song well, and make tales to please young ladies, and can play the gallant for them if necessary. I can throw knives into the air and catch them without cutting my fingers. I can jump rope most extraordinary and amusing. I can balance chairs, and make tables dance. I can somersault, and walk doing a handstand.[15]

No music is extant from the earliest jongleurs, but we can see his contribution and it is an important one. As he traveled during centuries of migration with the homeless, with merchants, students, pilgrims and knights, he wove a unified cultural language that laid the way for a truly European music. It is through him that so many European countries have a common popular foundation to their music and legends, and that the same instruments appear in all countries.

As a class, we begin to call these entertainers minstrels only as they begin to specialize as musicians. The first of these appear in the eighth century, the Spielmann of Germany and Bards of the British islands.

Ancient literature tells us the Bards were poet–musicians who specialized in singing of the deeds of their illustrious countrymen to the accompaniment of the lyre. One clue to their social status can be seen in their robes of six colors, surpassed only by kings, who had seven. Lords were entitled to five, governors of fortresses four, officers and gentlemen three, soldiers two and common people only one color.[16]

Gibbon describes the local renown of the Bards of Wales.

15 Anonymous, quoted in Howard D. McKinney and W. R. Anderson, *Music in History* (New York: American Book Co., 1940), 170.

16 Edmondstoune Duncan, *The Story of Minstrelsy* (Detroit: Singing Tree Press, 1968), 4.

Their rank and merit were ascertained by solemn trials, and the strong belief of supernatural inspiration exalted the fancy of the poet, and of his audience.[17]

This poet–musician, he says,

> Sung in the front of battle, excited their courage, and justified their depredations; and the songster claimed for his legitimate prize the fairest heifer of the spoil.[18]

The Romans ceased to rule Britain in 409 AD and by the eighth century we have a considerable body of extant poetry. One of these poems is an actual autobiographical description of a poet–musician named, Widsith. First, he tells us that he is very widely traveled.

> Thus I traveled through many foreign lands
>   over the wide earth …
> So I can sing and tell my story,
>   declare before the company in the banquet hall
>   how men of high rank were nobly generous to me.
> I was among the Huns and among the Goths,
>   among the Swedes and among the Geats and among the South Danes.
> I was among the Gepids and among the Wends and among the Vikings.
> I was among the Angles and among the Swabians and among the Aenenes.
> I was among the Saxons and Seggs and among the Swordmen.
> I was among the Whalemen and among the Deans and among the Heathoreams.
> I was among the Thuringians and among the men of Drontheim
>   and among the Burgundians, where I received a bracelet;
>   there Guthhere gave me the shining jewel
>   as a reward for my song—that was no niggardly king.[19]

He speaks of his skill in recounting a performance before Queen Ealhhild, the daughter of Eadwine.

> Her praise extended through many lands
> when it was my duty to tell in song
> where I knew the best example under heaven
> of a gold-decked queen distributing gifts.
> When Scilling and I with clear voice

---

[17] Gibbon, *The History of the Decline and Fall of the Roman Empire*, III, 360.

[18] Ibid., III, 359.

[19] *The Exeter Book* (London: Oxford University Press, 1958), II, xi, 50ff.

raised the song before our victorious lord
(loud to the harp our speech made music),
then many men bold of heart, who well knew, declared in words
that they had never heard a better song.[20]

Another poem is by a minstrel who concludes by bemoaning the fact that he lost his position to a better singer.

With regard to myself I will tell
that for a long time I was minstrel of the Heodenings
and dear to my prince. My name was Deor.
For many years I had a good office
and a gracious lord, till now Heorrenda,
a man skilled in song, has received the estate
which the ruler of men once gave to me.
That passed over, so can this.[21]

An anonymous poem, 'The Endowments of Men,' which lists every then-known profession and skill, mentions 'one skilled in songs,' and separately, the singer of church music.

One hath skill in many functions of the church;
he can loudly glorify with songs of praise
the Lord of life; he hath in rich degree
a clear-resounding voice.[22]

The lonely sailor, we learn in another poem, was one professional who was not a musician, as 'He has no mind for the harp.'[23] We hear of him again in another poem called, 'The Wanderer.'

Then the wounds of his heart become the heavier,
in grief for the loved one; his sorrow is renewed,
when the memory of kinsmen passes through his mind;
he greets them with snatches of song, he scans them eagerly,
comrades of heroes: soon they swim away;
the sailor-souls do not bring thither
many old familiar songs; his grief is renewed,
who must too often send forth
his weary spirit o'er the frozen waves.[24]

Christianity was well established by the eighth century in Britain and several extant poems are on its themes. The most popular image was the Day of Judgment, when, as one poem tells us, 'A horn is never sounded so loudly or a trumpet blown, but that the word of

---

20 Ibid., 99ff.

21 'The Song of Deor,' ibid., II, xviii, 35ff.

22 Ibid., I, vii, 52 and 91ff.

23 'The Seafarer,' in ibid., II, ix, 44.

24 Ibid., I, vi, 49ff.

the Lord, that clear voice, is not louder to men all over the world.'[25] Musically it is going to be quite a day, according to these poets, for one tells us that on this day angels shall sound their trumpets from the four corners of the earth.

> Then from the world's four corners,
> from the uttermost regions of the realm of earth,
> resplendent angels shall loudly, with one accord,
> sound their trumpets, and mid-earth shall quake,
> and the region under men. Boldly and gloriously
> shall they blow together toward the stars' career,
> and sing and chant from south and north,
> from east and west, o'er all creation.[26]

While another poet adds that all the humans will join in a great choir!

> and righteous souls shall raise a song,
> and the pure and chosen shall praise their Sovran's majesty;
> strain on strain shall mount to glory,
> sweetly perfumed with their goodly deeds.[27]

Several poems describe musical instruments and among these is a charming riddle song which describes an instrument which the reader will surely guess.

> I was an armed warrior. Now a gallant young bachelor
> covers me with gold and silver,
> with twisted wires. Sometimes men kiss me,
> Sometimes, by means of my sound, I summon
> good comrades to battle. Sometimes a horse
> carries me over the march. Sometimes the steed of the sea
> bears me, bright with ornaments, over the waves.
> Sometimes a woman, ring-adorned,
> fills my bosom. Sometimes I must lie stripped,
> hard and headless, on the boards of a table.
> Sometimes, decked with trappings, and beautiful,
> I hang on the wall where men are drinking.
> Sometimes warriors carry me on horseback,
> a noble ornament in an army, when, treasure-adorned,
> I must swallow the breath from some one's breast.
> Sometimes, by means of my notes, I invite
> gallant men to their wine. Sometimes, by my voice,
> I must rescue from foes what has been stolen
> and put enemies to flight. Discover what I am called.[28]

---

[25] 'The Day of Judgment,' ibid., II, xxii, 109ff.

[26] 'Christ,' ibid., I, i, 878ff. Angel choirs of singers are also mentioned in this poem in lines 102 and 1342.

[27] 'The Phoenix,' ibid., I, iv, 540ff.

[28] Riddle 14, describing a primitive trumpet, ibid., II.

A poem called 'The Phoenix,' which describes a fanciful bird, provides us with a broad list of musical instruments known to the eighth-century English.

> The music of its voice
> is sweeter and more beauteous than any craft of song,
> winsomer than any melody;
> nor trumpets, nor horns, may equal that sound,
> nor strain of harp, nor the voice of man,
> of any man on earth, nor organ's tone,
> nor harmonious lay, nor feather of swan,
> nor any of the sounds that the Lord hath created
> for men's delight in this sad world.[29]

29 Ibid., 131ff.

This last line is one of several which provides us with insights into the aesthetic ideas of these poet–musicians, in this case regarding the purpose of music itself—to offer delight. A poem which mentions the German gleeman makes a similar observation, that a man is less sad,

> who knows many poems
> or can greet the harp with his hands;
> he has his gift of music which God has granted him.[30]

30 'Gnomic Verses,' ibid., II, xiii, 169ff.

There are two poems which mention a virtue of music pointed out by earlier philosophers, that music is associated with Truth. The poem, 'The Wonders of Creation,' refers to this and also attributes to music the ability to help man understand life.

> It is, thinking man, an obvious example
> to every one who by wisdom
> can comprehend in his mind all the world,
> that long ago men, well-advised people,
> could often utter and say a Truth
> in the art of song, by means of songs [lays],
> so that most of mankind, by always asking
> and repeating and remembering,
> gained knowledge of the web of mysteries.[31]

31 Ibid., II, xiv, 8ff.

Another poet declares,

> Let none of human kind imagine,
> that I of lying words compose my song [lay],
> or write my verse![32]

32 'The Phoenix,' ibid., II, iv, 546ff.

It may have been for this reason, in part, that the minstrel was welcome in the home of the noble. One poem observes that, 'It is fitting that men have a good minstrel,'[33] and lists among the attributes of a 'good man,' he that 'sings poems.'[34]

Perhaps we may also find a clue to the 'good' in music in a poem which associates 'song with the Lord,' but discord with the devil.[35]

33 'Gnomic Verses,' ibid., II, xiii, 127.

34 Ibid., 139.

35 'Christ,' ibid., I, 594.

BEOWULF

The greatest English poem of this period is the anonymous epic 'Beowulf.' In this famous composition we also find numerous aesthetic clues.

First, we are struck by the range of emotions which the musicians conveyed to their listeners. We read of an elderly musician who, with an instrument associated with delight, first soothed and then brought sadness to his audience.

> The gray-haired Scylding,
> much tested, told of the times of yore.
> Whiles the hero his harp bestirred,
> wood-of-delight; now songs [lays] he sang
> of sooth and sadness.[36]

In another place we are told, 'Oft minstrels sang blithe'[37] and in still another a minstrel fills the hall with joy.[38] This last reference is particularly interesting for the phrase 'song *and* music,' which we believe may suggest the presence of independent instrumental music in addition to the usual epic songs.

36 'Beowulf,' trans. Francis Gummere in *Epic and Saga*, vol. 49, *The Harvard Classics* (New York: Collier, 1909–10), XXVII.

37 Ibid., VII.

38 Ibid., XVI.

> Then song and music mingled sounds
> in the presence of Healfdene's head-of-armies
> and harping was heard with the hero-song [lay]
> as Hrothgar's singer the hall-joy woke
> along the mead-seats, making his song
> of that sudden raid on the sons of Finn.

There is an unusual emphasis in this poem on situations and songs reflecting sadness. One person is described as singing songs of grief in private.

39 Ibid., XXXV.

> Then he goes to his chamber, a grief-song chants alone for his lost.[39]

We also read of 'sorrowful songs,'⁴⁰ and in yet another place,

40 Ibid., II.

> A rime he makes,
> sorrow-song for his son there hanging
> as rapture of ravens; …
> no harp resounds,
> in the courts no wassail, as once was heard.⁴¹

41 Ibid., XXXIV.

In particular, the absence of the harp, as in the quotation just given, seems to be associated with the environment of sadness. One line, for example, reflects, 'No harp's delight, no glee-wood's gladness!'⁴² A reference to a funeral mentions no 'lilt of harp.'⁴³ This may refer to a happier, lilting, style associated with harp music, for when it is present we find a completely different mood.

42 Ibid., XXXII.

43 Ibid., XLI.

> he heard each day the din of revel
> high in the hall: there harps rang out,
> clear song of the singer.⁴⁴

44 Ibid., I.

One passage suggests the maintenance of the tradition that some music, even at the table, was listened to carefully and not as 'background' music. Here, for example, it is only after a gleeman sings his song that the 'revel' begins.

> The song [lay] was finished,
> the gleeman's song. Then glad rose the revel;
> bench-joy brightened.⁴⁵

45 Ibid., XVII.

Attentive listening must surely have been the norm when the epic songs were sung, for here the words themselves, telling of the deeds of the great, would be the point of the song. This seems clearly implied in the description of the following singer. This passage is additionally interesting in its suggestion that the repertoire included older music.

> From time to time, a thane of the king,
> who had made many vaunts, and was mindful of verses,
> stored with sagas and songs of old,
> bound word to word in well-knit rime,
> welded his song [lay]; this warrior soon
> of Beowulf's quest right cleverly sang,
> and artfully added an excellent tale,
> in well-ranged words, of the warlike deeds
> he had heard in saga of Sigemund.⁴⁶

46 Ibid., XIII.

The remaining references to music in this poem deal with the use of the primitive trumpet. There must have been some form of music played by this instrument which represented a specific noble, as an aural representation in the way a coat of arms would be a visual symbol. In the following passage the noble is clearly recognized by the music of his personal trumpet.

> But rescue came
> with dawn of day for those desperate men
> when they heard the horn of Hygelac sound,
> tones of his trumpet …[47]

47 Ibid., XL.

For the most part, however, this instrument is mentioned only in battle. The nearest aesthetic description of this kind of music comes in the following.

> These started away,
> swollen and savage that song to hear,
> that war-horn's blast.[48]

48 Ibid., XXI.

13 CHURCH MUSIC OF THE SIXTH THROUGH EIGHTH CENTURIES

THE WRITINGS OF THE CHURCH PHILOSOPHERS of the first five centuries generally speak of the purpose of hymn singing as simply for praising God, in the manner of the language of the Old Testament. Among the extant works of a man known as Dionysius the Pseudo-Areopagite[1] we find two new explanations which are quite interesting. The first is a variant of the 'divine connection' we have referred to many times in these volumes. Numerous early philosophers attributed to the poet–musicians a divine connection, in large part, we believe, because of similarities music shares with religion, but not the other arts. In the case of both religion and music, the principal mysteries cannot be seen,[2] but the effect on the observer is apparent to all. Dionysius writes that the first purpose of hymn singing is to create a kind of reverse divine connection, to prepare the participant to be able to communicate with God. The second purpose, he seems to suggest, is that the singing of unison hymns brings a unity, a 'consensus,' in the congregation itself.

> The sacred description of the divine songs, whose purpose is to praise all the divine words and works of God and to celebrate the holy words and works of godly men, forms a universal hymn and exposition of divine things, conferring on those who recite it in a divine and holy fashion a power capable of receiving and distributing all the mysteries of the hierarchy.
>
> Thus, when the chant resuming most holy things has harmoniously prepared the faculties of our souls for the rites to be celebrated a little later, and when it has established through the unison of the divine songs a consensus regarding divine things, ourselves, and others, as if in one harmonious chorus of sacred things ...[3]

From the sixth century we begin to read of a much broader use of hymns and psalms outside the Church by the faithful. Gregory of Tours mentions the singing of hymns during meals, replacing the traditional entertainment music.[4] He also recalls that after a

---

1 No one knows when this man lived, although most scholars agree that it was before the ninth century. We have placed him here, rather than earlier, for reasons of the quality of his intellectual arguments.

2 Only the instruments of performance of each can be seen.

3 Dionysius the Pseudo-Areopagite, *The Ecclesiastical Hierarchy*, III, ivff., trans. Thomas Campbell (Washington, DC: University Press of America, 1981).

4 Gregory of Tours, *The History of the Franks*, VIII, iii, trans. Lewis Thorpe (Harmonsworth: Penguin Books, 1974).

great flood, Gregory the Great ordered the faithful to sing psalms for three days, including in the streets, as a means of asking the forgiveness of God.[5] Adomnan also describes singing hymns and praises as they led a visitor through the streets.[6]

There are several references during this period to the singing of hymns throughout the night. Once, for example, during a vigil accompanying the placing of the relics of St. Julian on an altar, 'They passed the night by singing the sacred hymns and the celestial melodies.'[7] On the death of King Chilperic, we are told Mallulf, Bishop of Senlis, 'passed the night singing hymns.'[8]

There are several references to the singing of hymns as part of the funeral service. The seventh-century writer, Adomnan, recalls the service for St. Columba in Ireland.

> After the departure of the holy soul, when the matin hymns were ended, the sacred body was carried back from the church, with the brothers' tuneful psalmody, to the lodging from which alive, he had come a little while before.[9]

Gregory the Great writes of the brothers' singing psalms as one of their own was actually dying, recalling the ancient Greek myth of the importance of departing to music.[10]

One of the factors which helped establish the new Church during the first centuries was the retelling of the miracles of Jesus, stories such as the restoring of life to persons, accomplishments which no pagan god could claim. Thus, perhaps to keep the momentum continuing, one encounters numerous stories of miracles during the subsequent years. By the period of which we speak these tales of miracles begin to include music. Adomnan, for example, tells of an occasion when the singers were spared, but the non-singers were killed.

> This also seems to be a thing that should not be passed unnoticed: that certain lay people of the same blessed man [Columba], though they were guilty men and blood-stained, were through certain songs of his praises in the Irish tongue, and the commemoration of his name, delivered, on the night in which they had sung those songs, from the hands of their enemies who had surrounded the house of the singers; and they escaped unhurt, through flames, and swords, and spears. A few of them had refused to sing, as if valuing little the singing of the holy man's commemoration, and miraculously those few alone had perished in the enemies' assault.[11]

---

5 Ibid., X, i.

6 Adomnan, *Life of Columba*, trans. Alan Anderson and Marjorie Anderson (London: Nelson, 1961), 14a.

7 Gregory of Tours, 'The Suffering and Miracles of the Martyr St. Julian,' V, xxxvi, trans. Raymond Van Dam, in *Saints and their Miracles in late Antique Gaul* (Princeton: Princeton University Press, 1993).

8 Gregory of Tours, *The History of the Franks*, VI, xlvi.

9 Adomnan, *Life of Columba*, 133a.

10 Gregory the Great, *Dialogue Four*, trans. Odo Zimmerman (New York: Fathers of the Church, 1959).

11 Adomnan, *Life of Columba*, 10a.

This same writer tells of another miracle by which St. Columba, a man with a normal speaking voice, could, when he sang a hymn, be heard more than a mile away, 'so clearly that they could distinguish every syllable in the verses that he sang.'[12]

The Venerable Bede tells of an occasion when St. Cuthbert spent the entire night, standing up to his neck in the sea, singing hymns, two otters came to his rescue.

> When daybreak was at hand, he went up on to the land and began to pray once more, kneeling on the shore. While he was doing this, there came forth from the depths of the sea two four-footed creatures which are commonly called otters. These, prostrate before him on the sand, began to warm his feet with their breath and sought to dry him with their fur.[13]

Perhaps we should include here one of several tales of those who heard choirs of angels singing, a powerful Church image since the time they reportedly sung at the birth of Jesus. Gregory of Tours relates the following:

> The blessed Severinus, bishop of Cologne, lived an honorable life and was praiseworthy in all respects. One Sunday, while he and his clerics were as usual visiting the holy shrines, he heard a chorus of singers on high at the hour when the blessed man died. He summoned his archdeacon and asked whether the voices that he heard so attentively were also striking his ears. The archdeacon replied: 'Certainly not.' Then Severinus said: 'Listen carefully.' The archdeacon began to stretch his neck up, pricked up his ears, and with the assistance of a staff stood on his tiptoes. But I believe that this man who did not deserve to hear these songs was not of equal merit. Then the archdeacon and the blessed bishop together knelt on the ground and prayed to the Lord that divine mercy might allow this man to hear the singing. They stood up, and again the old bishop asked: 'What do you hear?' The archdeacon replied: 'I hear the voices of men chanting Psalms, as if in heaven; but I do not know at all what it is.' Severinus said to him: 'I will tell you what this is. My lord bishop Martin has migrated from this world, and now the angels are escorting him on high with their singing.[14]

In the Venerable Bede's famous *Ecclesiastical History of England*, he reports that the introduction of Church music occurred in England, in Kent, in approximately 635 AD.[15] He tells of one singer sent by the pope in Rome, in 680 AD, to instruct the congregations on

12 Bede, 'Life of St. Cuthbert,' in *Two Lives of Saint Cuthbert*, trans. Bertram Colgrave (New York: Greenwood Press, 1969), 191.

13 Gregory of Tours, 'The Suffering and Miracles of the Martyr St. Julian,' 206.

14 Bede, *Ecclesiastical History of England*, trans. J. A. Giles (London: Bohn, 1849), II, xx.

the 'method of singing throughout the year, as it was practiced at St. Peter's at Rome,' which is a reference to the new body of Gregorian Chant. Bede writes that many Church men came to hear him sing and many others invited him to their towns.[16] Similarly, another singer came in 710 AD.

> He in like manner invited to him a celebrated singer, called Maban, who had been taught to sing by the successors of the disciples of the blessed Gregory in Kent, for him to instruct himself and his clergy, and kept him twelve years, to teach such ecclesiastical songs as were not known, and to restore those to their former state which were corrupted either by want of use, or through neglect.[17]

Bede, himself, sometimes betrays a lack of personal enthusiasm for congregational singing, once using the expression, 'the tediousness of psalm singing.'[18] On another occasion, he attributes to St. Cuthbert the admonition that one should lift up 'the heart rather than the voice, sighing rather than singing.'[19]

One notices during this period a striking absence of the attacks on instrumental music, which were found so regularly in the writings of earlier Church fathers. We can only conclude that these instruments had finally been forced out.

While there is reference to a much broader use of hymn singing, now in the streets, at meals and in funerals, it is all reported in a matter of fact style. No longer do we find the enthusiasm for hymn singing which accompanies earlier accounts, not to mention examples of listener's crying, as we found, for example, in Augustine. Now that the Church was firmly established, and perhaps to some degree taken for granted, we wonder if the Church's music had simply become another part of the ritual. Or perhaps it had become too serious, for Columba administered six stripes by flogging to any monk who coughed when beginning a psalm![20]

15   Ibid., IV, xviii.

16   Ibid., V, xx.

17   Bede, 'Life of St. Cuthbert,' 211.

18   Ibid., 213.

19   F. H. Dudden, *Gregory the Great* (London: Longmans, Green & Co., 1905), I, 86.

14 COMMENTS ON AESTHETICS IN THE MUSIC TREATISES OF THE SIXTH AND SEVENTH CENTURIES

BEFORE THE FULL IMPACT OF THE DARK AGES HAD SET IN, three men managed to write specialized works on the subject of music. They were Boethius (475–524 AD), Cassiodorus (480–573 AD) and Isidore of Seville (560–636 AD) and the existence of their works in manuscript copies made possible the education of musicians for centuries, not to mention helping to preserve the liberal arts through the Dark Ages. The book by Boethius, in particular, was the most influential music treatise of the Middle Ages. This work was still a commonly studied text in the fourteenth century, though yet unpublished.

While all of these works concern themselves primarily with the grammar of music, that which we call today, 'music theory,' we shall consider them only for their insights into aesthetics.

BOETHIUS, *DE INSTITUTIONE MUSICA*

Boethius was born to a wealthy Roman family and enjoyed the best possible education, including eighteen years in the schools of Athens. The breadth of his education can be appreciated by a survey of it found in a letter written to him by Cassiodorus.

> You have thoroughly imbued yourself with Greek philosophy. You have translated Pythagoras the musician, Ptolemy the astronomer, Nicomachus the arithmetician, Euclid the geometer, Plato the theologian, Aristotle the logician, and have given back the mechanician Archimedes to his own Sicilian countrymen. You know the whole science of Mathematics.[1]

He entered politics and unfortunately became caught up in a plot against the king. Although he maintained his innocence, he was arrested and sent to prison where he composed his last works while awaiting execution.

---

[1] 'Letter to Boethius,' in *The Letters of Cassiodorus* (London: Frowde, 1886), 169.

Four centuries after Boethius, a writer commented, 'If there is someone interested in profound and perplexing subtlety, let him read the *De institutione* by Boethius … and he will be able to test his genius.' And it *is* tough reading, filled to overflowing with sleep-inducing prose such as the following:

> But since the nete synemmenon to the mese (3,456 to 4,608) holds a sesquitertian ratio—that is, a diatessaron—whereas the trite synemmenon to the nete synemmenon (4,374 to 3,456) holds the ratio of two tones.[2]

But, as we said, we shall leave all this to the professors of theory and confine ourselves to the lines of thought which we have been following in previous chapters.

True to the spirit of the Greek philosophy, Boethius could not quite justify music without bringing it into the realm of Reason. No doubt from his perspective it was a tribute to music, among the other arts, that it *could* be correlated with Reason. Lacking our modern understanding of the twin hemispheres of the brain, and the full equality of both experiential and conceptual information, Boethius thought music was too important to belong to the senses—it had to be Reason which made the senses understandable.

> Harmonics is the faculty that weighs differences between high and low sounds using the sense of hearing and reason. For sense and reason are, as it were, particular instruments for the faculty of harmonics. The sense perceives a thing as indistinct, yet approximate to that which it is; reason exercises judgment concerning the whole and searches out ultimate differences. So the sense discovers something confused, yet close to the truth, but it receives the whole through reason. Reason itself comes to know the whole, even though it receives an indistinct and approximate likeness of truth. For sense brings nothing whole to itself, but arrives only at an approximation. Reason makes the judgment.[3]

To support his contention that Reason correctly judges where the senses cannot, he offers the following illustration.

> To see how the sense gathers confused information and by no means attains the fullness of reason, let us consider the following. Given a line, it is not difficult for the sense [of vision] to tell what is longer or what is shorter. But if the goal is to determine a measure some

---

2 Boethius, *Fundamentals of Music*, trans. Calvin Bower (New Haven: Yale University Press, 1989), IV, ix.

3 Ibid., V, ii.

precise degree larger or smaller, the first impression of the sense will not be able to do it, but the clever skill of reason will.[4]

The role that Reason, therefore, must play in the perception of music, Boethius summarizes as follows:

> The entire judgment is not to be granted to the sense of hearing; rather, reason must also play a role. Reason should guide and moderate the erring sense, inasmuch as the sense—tottering and failing—should be supported, as it were, by a walking stick.[5]

He is wrong, of course. We understand today that music is its own form of truth and requires no conceptional understanding whatsoever. Were it not so, ordinary people would find no pleasure in music. But Boethius, having the perspective that he does, believes the pleasure we obtain from music also derives in part from Reason.

> Judgment should be exercised with respect to all these consonances which we have discussed; one ought to decide by the reason, as well as by the ear, which of them is the more pleasing. For as the ear is affected by sound or the eye by a visible form, in the same way the judgment of the mind is affected by numbers or continuous quantity.[6]

Thus, Boethius concludes, the noble in music is personified by the person who understands it as a rational concept, not the composer or the performer. Anyone today who understands the true essence of music would regard the following as an incredible statement.

> Now one should bear in mind that every art and also every discipline considers reason inherently more honorable than a skill which is practiced by the hand and the labor of an artisan. For it is much better and nobler to know about what someone else fashions than to execute that about which someone else knows; in fact, physical skill serves as a slave, while reason, rules like a mistress. Unless the hand acts according to the will of reason, it acts in vain. How much nobler, then, is the study of music as a rational discipline than as composition and performance![7]

Regarding aesthetics, Boethius first ranks types of music into three species, in an apparent descending order of aesthetic importance.[8] The most important, presumably representing God directly, is Cosmic Music, in particular the 'Music of the Spheres.'[9]

---

4 Ibid.

5 Ibid, and I, ix.

6 Ibid., I, xxxii.

7 Ibid., I, xxxiv.

8 Ibid., I, ii.

9 This is discussed further in I, xxvii.

Next, in order of importance, is Human Music.

> Whoever penetrates into his own self perceives human music. For what unites the incorporeal nature of reason with the body if not a certain harmony and, as it were, a careful tuning of low and high pitches as though producing one consonance? What other than this unites the parts of the soul, which, according to Aristotle, is composed of the rational and the irrational? What is it that intermingles the elements of the body or holds together the parts of the body in an established order?

The third kind of music is Instrumental Music, music which he curiously seems to suggest exists in the instruments themselves. Again, for the modern person, the thought that music exists anywhere but in the ear of the listener is quite odd.

> The third kind of music is that which is said to rest in various instruments. This music is governed either by tension, as in strings, or by breath, as in the aulos or those instruments activated by water, or by a certain percussion, as in those which are cast in concave brass, and various sounds are produced from these.

With regard to consonance and dissonance, one would expect Boethius to present a detailed conceptual description, yet he seems content to observe that consonance is that which falls 'pleasantly' on the ear, while dissonance is heard as 'harsh and unpleasant.'[10]

For the modern reader, perhaps the most important discussion regarding the aesthetics of music by Boethius is found in his discussion of the nature of pleasure in music. Here, finally, he leaves the world of Reason and begins to approach the true essence of music, feeling. He begins, literally in the first sentence of his book, by admitting that our ability to perceive through the senses is innate, it is not the product of reason. Indeed, he correctly observes, the senses are something quite apart from the 'mind.'

> Perception through all the senses is so spontaneously and naturally present in certain living creatures that an animal without them cannot be conceived. But knowledge and clear perception of the senses themselves are not so immediately acquired through inquiry with the mind.[11]

10 Ibid., I, ix.

11 Ibid., I, i.

Next, he again correctly observes that the first source of pleasure in music is found in the musical materials themselves.

> Now the same can be said with respect to other sensible objects, especially concerning the witness of the ears: the sense of hearing is capable of apprehending sounds in such a way that it not only exercises judgment and identifies their differences, but very often actually finds pleasure if the modes are pleasing and ordered, whereas it is vexed if they are disordered and incoherent.[12]

Boethius, in his most eloquent testimony to the role of feeling in music concludes that this relationship is so strong that we 'cannot be free from it even if we so desired.' He also returns here to the idea that music is innate, observing that even someone who 'cannot sing' nevertheless expresses his emotions in song.

> Why is it that mourners, even though in tears, turn their very lamentations into music? This is most characteristic of women, as though the cause for weeping might be made sweeter through song …
> Someone who cannot sing well will nevertheless sing something to himself, not because the song that he sings affects him with particular satisfaction, but because those who express a kind of inborn sweetness from the soul—regardless of how it is expressed—find pleasure. Is it not equally evident that the passions of those fighting in battle are roused by the call of trumpets? If it is true that fury and wrath can be brought forth out of a peaceful state of mind, there is no doubt that a more temperate mode can calm the wrath or excessive desire of a troubled mind. How does it come about that when someone voluntarily listens to a song with ears and mind, he is also involuntarily turned toward it in such a way that his body responds with motions somehow similar to the song heard? How does it happen that the mind itself, solely by means of memory, picks out some melody previously heard?
> From all these accounts it appears beyond doubt that music is so naturally united with us that we cannot be free from it even if we so desired.[13]

Then, as if surprised that he finds himself so removed from Reason, Boethius immediately follows this by noting that it is not enough for a musician to know *music*, he must know *about* it.

> For just as in seeing it does not suffice for the learned to perceive colors and forms without also searching out their properties, so it

12 Ibid.

13 Ibid.

does not suffice for musicians to find pleasure in melodies without also coming to know how they are structured internally by means of ratio of pitches.

Boethius now goes beyond feeling to the subject he touches on above, the apparent ability of music to affect character. In his review of this subject it is particularly interesting that he clearly separates music from the other liberal arts, stating that only music and not math or geometry or astronomy can affect morals. It is also fascinating that he uses the expression, 'that we ourselves are put together in its likeness.' One of the latest discoveries in physics, in research conducted in England, is that all organs of the body vibrate to specific pitches. One of these physicists has stated that we have evolved to look as we do, due to the combination of these harmonies and gravity. Boethius discusses the effect of music as follows:

> There happen to be four mathematical disciplines [arithmetic, music, geometry, and astronomy], the other three share with music the task of searching for truth; but music is associated not only with speculation but with morality as well. For nothing is more characteristic of human nature than to be soothed by pleasant modes or disturbed by their opposites. This is not peculiar to people in particular endeavors or of particular ages. Indeed, music extends to every endeavor; moreover, youths, as well as the aged are so naturally attuned to musical modes by a kind of voluntary affection that no age at all is excluded from the charm of sweet song. What Plato rightfully said can likewise be understood: the soul of the universe was joined together according to musical concord. For when we hear what is properly and harmoniously united in sound in conjunction with that which is harmoniously coupled and joined together within us and are attracted to it, then we recognize that we ourselves are put together in its likeness. For likeness attracts, whereas unlikeness disgusts and repels.
>
> From this cause, radical transformations in character also arise. A lascivious disposition takes pleasure in more lascivious modes or is often made soft and corrupted upon hearing them. On the other hand, a rougher spirit finds pleasure in more exciting modes or becomes aroused when it hears them. This is the reason why musical modes were named after certain peoples, such as 'Lydian' mode and 'Phrygian,' for in whatever a particular people finds pleasure, by that same name the mode itself is designated. A people finds pleasure in modes because of likeness to its own character, for it is not possible for gentle things to be joined with or find pleasure in

rough things, nor rough things in gentle. Rather, as has been said, similitude brings about love and pleasure. Thus Plato holds that the greatest care should be exercised lest something be altered in music of good character. He states that there is no greater ruin of morals in a republic than the gradual perversion of chaste and temperate music, for the minds of those listening at first acquiesce. Then they gradually submit, preserving no trace of honesty or justice—whether lascivious modes bring something immodest into the dispositions of the people or rougher ones implant something warlike and savage.

Indeed no path to the mind is as open for instruction as the sense of hearing. Thus, when rhythms and modes reach an intellect through the ears, they doubtless affect and reshape that mind according to their particular character.[14]

He adds that this is exactly what has happened in his own time.

> Since the human race has become lascivious and impressionable, it is taken up totally by representational and theatrical modes. Music was indeed chaste and modest when it was performed on simpler instruments. But since it has been squandered in various, promiscuous ways, it has lost its measure of dignity and virtue; and, having almost fallen into a state of disgrace, it preserves nothing of its ancient splendor.

14 Ibid. Recent clinical research demonstrates that the brain actually changes *physically* according to the music it listens to.

CASSIODORUS, *INSTITUTIONES DIVINARUM ET HUMANARUM LECTIONUM*

Cassiodorus, like Boethius, was born to a wealthy Roman family, well-educated and active in politics. At the age of sixty, or so, he retired from politics and founded a monastery where for the next thirty years he directed the copying of manuscripts by his monks. Thus, as we have mentioned in an earlier chapter, many scholars consider Cassiodorus the individual most responsible for saving the classics of Greek literature for posterity. His book, *Institutiones*, the object of our comments here, was a very influential book which includes chapters on all the seven liberal arts, including music. The chapter on music is rather brief, but because the book traveled everywhere in Europe his remarks were well-known.

With Cassiodorus we need to begin by considering his outline of the divisions of philosophy, for music's placement in this organization is, at the same time, an aesthetic comment. Philosophy, he says, is divided into two main branches, Speculative Philosophy and Practical Philosophy. Practical Philosophy, 'is that which seeks to explain advantageous things,' and includes only Moral, Economic and Political subject matters.[15]

Speculative Philosophy is 'that by means of which we surmount visible things and in some degree contemplate things divine and heavenly, surveying them with the mind alone, inasmuch as they rise above corporeal eyes.' This main branch of philosophy is made up of three sub-branches, Natural, Theoretical, and the Divine. Music is found under 'Theoretical,' together with Arithmetic, Geometry, and Astronomy.

Thus we see he thought of music not as a 'practical,' but as a 'speculative' art, 'something we contemplate with the mind,' and that it is clearly included in the category of mathematical-based disciplines. He saw music most closely related to arithmetic, indeed it is together with this subject that he defines it.

> *Arithmetic* is the science of numerable quantity considered in itself.
> *Music* is the science which treats measure in relation to sound.

His chapter on music is, as we noted, not lengthy and is concerned again with an explanation of 'music theory.' There is little, therefore, which pertains to the subject of this book. He begins by defining music as being innate to man, related to the organization of the heavens, and fundamental to religion.

> Musical science, then, is diffused through all the acts of our life if we before all else obey the commands of the Creator and observe with pure hearts the rules which he has established. For whatever we say or whatever inward effect is caused by the beating of our pulse is joined by musical rhythms to the power of harmony. Music is indeed the science of proper modulation; and if we observe the good way of life we are always associated with this excellent science. When we sin, however, we no longer have music [we are not in 'harmony']. The sky and the earth and everything which is accomplished in them by the supernal stewardship are not without the science of music; for Pythagoras is witness to the fact that this world was founded through the instrumentality of music and can be governed by it.
>
> Music also freely permeates religion itself: witness the ten-stringed instrument of the Decalogue, the reverberations of the harp, timbrels, the melody of the organ, the sound of cymbals. There is no doubt,

15 Cassiodorus, 'On Dialectic,' in *An Introduction to Divine and Human Readings*, trans. Leslie Jones (New York, Octagon Books, 1966).

moreover, that the Psalter itself was named after a musical instrument because it contains the exceedingly pleasant and agreeable modulation of the heavenly virtues.[16]

[16] 'On Music,' in ibid, 1.

Cassiodorus discusses the various modes with respect to their theoretical relationships. It is only regarding Hypodorian, 'the lowest of all,' that he mentions the influence of music on the state of the listener.

> These tones ... have been shown to possess such great usefulness that they calm excited minds and cause even wild animals and serpents and birds and dolphins to approach and listen to their harmony.[17]

[17] Ibid., 8.

The purpose of music, he says, is to educate and 'to soothe.'

> Most pleasant and useful, then, is the branch of learning which leads our understanding to heavenly things and soothes our ears with sweet harmony.[18]

[18] Ibid., 10.

ISIDORE OF SEVILLE, *ETYMOLOGIRARUM*

Isidore, Bishop of Seville, is the only writer known today representing Gothic Spain. His twenty-volume *Etymologiarum*, which is really the first encyclopedia, has the goal of presenting all the information a Christian needs to know. Its practical importance lies in the fact that it treats the seven liberal arts, including music, and thus was one more powerful weapon for preserving traditional knowledge throughout the Dark Ages.

Once again, we will only consider the comments which reflect on aesthetics, from a book which primarily deals with Greek theoretical principles.

In his initial definition of music, Isidore mentions a notion which many early writers seemed to find a particularly significant characteristic of music, that once a performance is finished the music is gone, it has disappeared and does not exist anymore except in the memory. This is probably one of the reasons the ancient writers could not accept music as a rational discipline. That is, since the music cannot be seen, and cannot be written down, and disappears after the performance, it is as if they considered it as almost an illusion, or as Isidore calls it, an impression.

> The sound of [music], since it is an impression upon the sense, flows by into the past and is imprinted upon the memory ... Unless sounds are remembered by man, they perish, for they cannot be written down.[19]

Isidore next provides a brief summary of the importance given to music by the Greeks, the Music of the Spheres, the use of music in the Old Testament, and its employment in battle and various occupations. He summarizes all of this by concluding, 'Without music there can be no perfect knowledge, for there is nothing without it.'[20]

The performance of music, Isidore organizes into three types: *harmonica*, *organica*, and *rhythmica*. By *harmonica* he means vocal music, and he reminds us that singing still belonged as much to the actor as to the singer.

> Harmonica is the modulation of the voice, it is the affair of comedians, tragedians, and choruses and all who sing. It produces motion of the mind and body, and from this motion sound. From this sound comes the music which in man is called voice.[21]

He also introduces the word *Symphonia* here, by which he means harmony in the modern usage. He also maintains that 'melody' comes from the Greek, *mel* [honey] reflecting the 'sweetness' of music. Finally, he presents the most extensive discussion of texture by any early writer to this date, in a catalog of the various qualities of the human voice.

> Sweet voices are fine, full, loud, and high.
> Penetrating voices are those which can hold a note an unusually long time, in such a way that they continuously fill the whole place, like the sound of trumpets.
> A thin voice is one lacking in breath, as the voice of children or women or the sick. This is as it is in string instruments, for the finest strings emit fine, thin sounds.
> In fat voices, as those of men, much breath is emitted at once.
> A sharp voice is high and thin, as we see in strings.

---

19 'Etymologiarum,' III, xv, trans. W. M. Linsay, quoted in Oliver Strunk, *Source Readings in Music History* (New York: Norton, 1950). This important work, published a dozen times in the fifteenth century, has never been translated into English.

20 Ibid., III, XVII.

21 Ibid., III, xx.

> A hard voice is one which emits sound violently, like thunder, like the sound of an anvil whenever the hammer is stuck against the hard iron.
> A harsh voice is a hoarse one, which is broken up by minute, dissimilar impulses.
> A blind voice is one which is choked off as soon as produced, and once silent cannot be prolonged, as in crockery.
> A pretty voice [*vinnola*] is soft and flexible; it is so called from *vinnus*, a soft curling lock of hair.
> The perfect voice is high, sweet, and loud: high, to be adequate to the sublime; loud, to fill the ear; sweet, to soothe the minds of the hearers. If any one of these qualities is absent, the voice is not perfect.[22]

22 Ibid.

In terms of aesthetics, the most interesting comment in this list is the last—that the high voice is associated with the sublime, perhaps in a divine sense, 'on high.' But we must remember that in instrumental music the entire Middle Ages is characterized by high sounds, for it was only in the sixteenth century that the technology became available to produce the bass instruments. Thus, for these people it is possible that the most aesthetically pleasing register was one placed higher than that which we would find pleasing today.

The second category of performance, *organica*, includes all instrumental music, except percussion. 'Organ,' he says, 'is the generic name of all musical vessels.'[23] Here he provides an interesting observation on the aulos, called *tibiae* in Latin.

23 Ibid., III, xxi.

> They were long used only in funerals, and afterward in the sacred rites of the heathen. It is thought that they are called tibiae because they were first made from the leg bones of deer and fawns.

The third category, *rhythmica*, are the percussion instruments, 'sounds produced by the beat of the fingers.' These, he finds, 'yield an agreeable clanging.'[24]

24 Ibid., III, xxii.

All three of these writers are still thinking of music as one of the seven liberal arts, and in particular as a discipline closely related to arithmetic, geometry and astronomy. Isidore, in fact, treats all four in Book III, which he titles, 'On the Four Mathematical Sciences.' It follows, then, that the bulk of their discussion deals with the theoretical proportions and relationships of tones.

While all three men acknowledge the power of music to affect the state of mind of the listener, only Boethius explores this subject at length. None attempts an explanation for how this occurs.

Regarding the aesthetic purpose of music, for Boethius it seems merely 'to be pleasing,' and for Cassiodorus and Isidore, to 'soothe' the mind of the listener. It is an inadequate definition from our perspective, but we must remember that music was, for these men, something secondary in nature. For Boethius it was only part of the senses, to be understood by Reason, and for Isidore it was but a fleeting impression of the senses. One has the feeling that they included music as one of the important 'mathematical sciences' out of tradition, but could not explain its significance to the degree they could with arithmetic, geometry and astronomy.

Part 4

The First Dawnings of the Restoration; The Ninth Through The Eleventh Centuries

15 THE STATE OF MUSIC AND AESTHETICS IN THE NINTH THROUGH ELEVENTH CENTURIES

BEGINNING WITH THE NINTH CENTURY one can see the clouds of ignorance of the Dark Ages begin to part. We take our title for Part 4 from this summary by Gibbon, who describes the change in climate at this time in Constantinople.

> The seventh and eighth centuries were a period of discord and darkness: the library was burnt, the college was abolished, the Iconoclasts are represented as the foes of antiquity; and a savage ignorance and contempt of letters has disgraced the princes of the Heraclean and Isaurian dynasties.
>
> In the ninth century we trace the first dawnings of the restoration of science. After the fanaticism of the Arabs had subsided, the caliphs aspired to conquer the arts, rather than the provinces, of the empire: their liberal curiosity rekindled the emulation of the Greeks, brushed away the dust from their ancient libraries, and taught them to know and reward the philosophers, whose labors had been hitherto repaid by the pleasure of study and the pursuit of truth.[1]

1 Edward Gibbon, *The History of the Decline and Fall of the Roman Empire* (Philadelphia: Coates), IV, 587.

In Western Europe as well, by the eleventh century one can clearly discern a new enthusiasm for life and culture. Perhaps the most notable symbol of this new civic spirit was the beginning, after the year 1000, of the construction of the great Gothic cathedrals.

The leaders of the Church were moving more slowly, but we continue to read, here and there, of more enlightened prelates. A letter of 1051 by Peter Damian, for example, praises the bishop of Numana for his study of the liberal arts.[2] There is one Church leader of this period who was quite extraordinary, the tenth century pope, Sylvester II. He was one of those enlightened Churchmen who privately paid to have manuscripts copied. In a letter of 985, for example, we read,

2 *The Letters of Peter Damian*, trans. Owen Blum (Washington, DC: The Catholic University of America Press, 1990), II, Letter 38.

> Just as a short time ago in Rome and in other parts of Italy, in Germany also, and in Lorraine, I used large sums of money to pay copy-

ists and to acquire copies of authors, permit me to beg that this be done likewise in your locality.[3]

In another letter he observes, 'I offer to noble scholars the pleasing fruits of the liberal disciplines to feed upon.'[4]

This man was also an accomplished musician, an organist apparently, who offered to give lessons in music[5] and proved himself capable of explaining some of the most difficult passages found in Boethius.[6]

ON PHILOSOPHY

During the Dark Ages traditional secular philosophy had almost completely disappeared. Only one important thinker from this period is familiar to us today, the ninth-century Irishman, Joannes Scotus Eriugena. In his *Periphseon on the Division of Nature*, he discusses a number of topics dealing with the philosophy of aesthetics. His point of view is still one in which music is a member of the seven liberal arts and primarily associated with mathematics. Consequently, he not only defines music in this perspective, but associates with it motion and Reason.

> Music is the discipline which, through natural ratios, discerns by the light of reason the harmony of all things endowed with being, whether they are in motion or in a knowable state of stability.[7]

In another place, he rejects the possibility that man can be both rational and irrational, which, of course, we know today to be precisely the case.[8] It is also interesting that he regarded the liberal arts themselves as being innate, something implanted genetically in the soul.

> We see that the Liberal Arts established in the soul are one thing and the soul itself, which is a kind of subject of the arts, is something else; while the arts appear to be, in effect, inseparable and natural accidents of the soul ... They do not come from another source, either, but are naturally implanted in the soul.[9]

Art, following the logic of the Church, can only truly be understood if one first attempts to understand God, who made the artist, who made the art object.

---

3 *The Letters of Gerbert*, trans. Harriet Lattin (New York: Columbia University Press, 1961), Letter 50.

4 Ibid., Letter 105.

5 Ibid.

6 Ibid., Letters 3 and 5.

7 Joannes Scotus Eriugena, *Periphyseon on the Division of Nature*, trans. Myra Uhlfelder (Indianapolis: Bobbs-Merrill, 1976), I, 27.

8 Ibid., IV, 5.

9 Ibid., I, 44.

As the understanding [*intellectus*] of the artist precedes the understanding of the art, and the understanding of the art precedes the understanding of what is in it and made by it, so the understanding of the Father, the Artificer, precedes the understanding of His Art, i.e., His Wisdom, in which He created all things. Next the knowledge of everything made in and by that Art follows the understanding of the Art itself. Whatever true reasoning finds prior in any sense must precede according to natural sequence.[10]

10 Ibid., III, 3. In another place, III, 14, he contends that the pure objects of the senses, as color relative to the eye, are incorporeal and can be understood only when they exist in a form.

In a problem related to the above, Joannes Scotus now considers the relationships of mind, skill and discipline. He seems to arrive at two conclusions: first, that knowledge is formed from the arts, and not arts formed from knowledge, and second, that the mind, the knowledge by which it knows itself and the discipline necessary to that knowledge are all one and the same.[11]

11 Ibid., IV, 7.

The philosopher Psellus reports that at the time of Constantine IX (1042–1055) there was still no discernible lifting of the Dark Ages in this field.

Today, in fact, neither Athens, nor Nicomedia, nor Alexandria in Egypt, nor Phoenicia, nor even the two Romes (the ancient and lesser Rome, and the later, more powerful city[12]), nor any other State glories any longer in literary achievement. The golden streams of the past ... all are blocked and choked up: their damming is complete.[13]

12 Constantinople.

13 Michael Psellus, *Chronographia*, trans. E. R. A. Sewter (Baltimore: Penguin Books, 1966), VI, 43.

Three decades later, however, Psellus was employed by the emperor, Michael VII (1071–1078), who was in every way a 'Renaissance man.' Psellus describes this ruler as well-read in several areas of science, philosophy and interested in a wide variety of spiritual and literary subjects. He engaged in extemporaneous poetry, which Psellus characterizes, 'if the rhythm is generally defective, at least the sentiments are sound.'[14] There is one intriguing passage, relative to Michael VII, of which we can only wish Psellus had supplied more detail.

14 Ibid., VII, 4.

It is agreed that certain standards of behavior, certain manners of speaking are appropriate to an emperor, others to a philosopher, others to an orator, others to a musician.

We have given numerous examples in these volumes of the close association held by ancient philosophers between music and movement, some of them even describing dance as visible music. Psellus makes a revealing statement, in this regard, relative to his description of Michael VII.

> A musician, who from the nature of his vocation must understand the regulated succession of notes, would praise his movements.[15]

15 Ibid., VII, 5.

ON THE MILIEU OF THE CHURCH

As we have pointed out in a previous chapter, the singing of the hymns by fervent, even tearful, Christians had given way to professional singers of sombre chant. Popular enthusiasm had been replaced by ritual. No musical performances sound so grim as those described in the many small monasteries. Peter Damian, the leader of such a group of hermits, complains about monks who hurry the singing of their psalms at night in order to get to bed sooner and worries that evil thoughts will creep into the minds of monks who may daydream while singing.[16] There is no pleasure in singing here! Time and time again, Damian warns his monks against the sins of pleasure, with such exhortations as, 'In every struggle with titillating pleasure try always to evoke the memory of the grave.'[17] He even went so far as to prescribe exercises in crying, in order that the monks could develop suitably somber demeanors.

16 *The Letters of Peter Damian*, II, Letter 50.

17 Ibid.

Regarding specific performance practices, in one place he recommends the practice of a monk, named Dominic, of singing twelve psalms twenty-four times with his hands extended above the head in the form of a cross. This, he says, would compensate for one year of penance.[18] In another place, he mentions instrumental music in an interesting distinction between canticles and psalms.

18 Ibid., Letter 53.

> That a canticle is daily added to the psalms in the office of Lauds, seems to be redolent with mystery, namely, the mystery of both the contemplative and the active life. For the psaltery, an instrument made in the shape of a delta, vibrates through its ten strings when struck by the plectrum; a song, however, is produced only by the voice. Wherefore, the former, because it needs the use of the hands, denotes work and hence the active life, while the latter, because it related to a song of joy, indicated the contemplative life. And because we are able to experience contemplation only briefly and interruptedly, and that, scarcely for a moment, but are always engaged in the business of the active life, it is proper that we employ several psalms but only one canticle.[19]

19 Ibid., I, Letter 17.

On Church Literature

The Church literature of this period remains filled with tales of new miracles and other extraordinary stories to support the faith. Music is almost never mentioned in such literature, although we find in the *Life of Mary Magdalene,* by the ninth-century writer, Rabanus Maurus, the assertion that Mary, Martha and Lazarus were in their youth highly educated, not only in Hebrew, but 'the gifts of arts.'[20] In this romantic biography, by the way, Martha, after the death of Christ, goes to France and fights a dragon![21]

A more significant work, the play, *Paphnutius,* by the tenth-century nun, Hrotswitha, contains an extensive dialog on the subject of music.[22] The passage begins with a Disciple asking, 'What *is* music?' Paphnutius answers with a brief description of the place held by music among the liberal arts. The Disciples beg for more information and Paphnutius relents, 'since it is knowledge which monks don't have.'

Paphnutius, following the definition by Boethius, begins by telling the students that music is divided into three species: the celestial, the human, and that made with instruments.

> DISCIPLES. What does celestial music consist of?
> PAPHNUTIUS. Of the seven planets and the celestial sphere.
> DISCIPLES. How do you mean that?
> PAPHNUTIUS. Because, you see, they produce the same harmonious music as the strings of stringed instruments; For just as in the case of instruments, we find the same concordances and intervals of like number and length.
> DISCIPLES. And what are these 'intervals' you speak of?
> PAPHNUTIUS. They are the distances which exist between the planets, as between the notes of strings.

Upon further questions about the 'notes' just mentioned, Paphnutius begins to speak in the complex mathematical language of Boethius. The students object to this conceptual language and respond, 'What has this got to do with *music*?,' implying, we presume, that music has instead to do with feelings and emotions, not mathematics. The teacher's answer, like that of so many theory teachers today, is, 'But that is how you *talk* about music!' The reader will notice that he introduces here the word 'symphonia,' which the Greeks had used in place of our term 'harmony.'

20 *The Life of Saint Mary Magdalene and of her Sister Saint Martha*, trans. David Mycoff (Kalamazoo: Cistercian Publications, 1989), I, 29.

21 Ibid., XL, 2365.

22 *The Plays of Hrotswitha of Gandersheim*, trans. Larissa Bonfante (New York: New York University Press, 1979), 108ff.

PAPHNUTIUS. A tone is formed of two sounds, of which the proportion is that of an *epothos* number, a sesquioctave: that is of nine to eight.

DISCIPLES. (Discouraged.) The faster we try to keep up with you and follow the basic notions you give us, and technical terms of this discussion, the more you go on adding more difficult concepts for us to take in.

PAPHNUTIUS. But that is how this kind of discussion is carried on.

DISCIPLES. Well at least tell us something—but only the simplest account—about what they mean by concordances, just so we will know what the word means.

PAPHNUTIUS. A concordance or 'symphonia' is a proper combination of sounds.

The students now ask the difficult question, 'Why can't we hear the music of the spheres?' Of all early philosophers, Paphnutius now gives the most complete answer, indeed four possible explanations.

DISCIPLES. Well, why can't we hear them, then?

PAPHNUTIUS. Many different reasons are given to explain why we can't hear the music of the heavenly spheres. Some assert it can't be heard because the music never stops, and we become accustomed to its sound. Others say it is the density of the air, while there are some who claim that a sound of such grand volume cannot physically be taken in by the narrow passages of our human ears. And there are some who say that the spheres give forth a sound so sweet, of such great joy, that if men ever heard it, they would all join together, of one common accord, forget about themselves and any other interest, and be intent only on following this sound as it led them from the East to the Western regions.

Well, say the students, we have heard enough of the music of the spheres. Now tell us about 'human' music, and how it is produced.

PAPHNUTIUS. Not only, as I said before, in the harmonious connection between body and soul, and in the deep bass or high pitched soprano voices, but even in the rhythmic throbbing of our veins, and in the measure and proportion of each of our limbs, as for example in the joints of our fingers, for which we find the same proportions when we measure off their sections. These are the same proportions, if you remember, which we talked of in our discussion of the meaning of 'symphonias,' because music is in fact an agreeable combination not only of voices, but of other unlike elements as well.

DISCIPLES. (The have been looking at the joints of their fingers. They are quite frankly lost.) If we had only known before we asked, how knotty all these problems were for laymen like us, and how difficult to follow or resolve, we would have preferred never to have known about the 'lesser world' than try to learn such difficult lessons.

PAPHNUTIUS. It did you no harm to try, for now you have learned things you did not know before.

DISCIPLES. That's true. But we are exhausted from this philosophical lecture, since we are not able to understand the details of your explanation.

Perhaps because of the student's professed exhaustion, this discussion never continues on to the subject of instrumental music. The teacher brings the topic to a close by reminding the students of the true purpose of the acquisition of knowledge—to understand God.

PAPHNUTIUS. For to whose praise does knowledge of all the arts redound more worthily and justly, if not to His, since He is the One who created all things knowable and gave us knowledge of them?

ON CHURCH SCHOOLS

During its first eight centuries the Church, as we have seen in previous chapters, argued strenuously against traditional secular, 'pagan,' education, especially philosophy, and only gradually came to accept the liberal arts for the purpose of creating a Christian capable of understanding the sacred literature. The Church's principal interest in education was to prepare the Christian for the next life.

Thanks to the enlightenment of Charlemagne, the Church began to engage in a broader educational role in the ninth century. These monastic schools, particularly in France, joining together with the Church's need to teach the new official body of Church music, developed into the first real schools of music of modern Europe. Because of the great flourishing of monasteries famous for the cultivation of music during the ninth through eleventh centuries, one can say that music education emerged out of the Dark Ages before almost any other discipline.[23]

One result of the development of music pedagogy in these monastic schools is the extant treatises on music, to which we shall devote a later chapter. Several of these treatises hint at the formidable discipline which accompanied the teaching of music in these schools. In the *Enchiridion musices*, by Odo of Cluny, when the teacher promises an effective new system of learning sight-singing, the student replies with relief,

> he will never [again] torment me with blows or abuse when provoked by the slowness of my sense.[24]

Similarly, Guido, in *Prologus antiphonarii sui*, remarking on the success of his new method of teaching music reading, challenges the reader,

> Should anyone doubt that I am telling the truth, let him come, make a trial, and see what small boys can do under our direction, boys who until now have been beaten for their gross ignorance of the psalms.[25]

We get another glimpse of the rigid discipline of these monastic schools when we see the unvarying daily schedule which these young music students had to observe. Here is the schedule of one of these schools.[26]

23:30	Waken
24:00–2:00	Sing Matin Service
2:00	Sleep
4:30	Waken
5:00–6:30	Sing Laudes and First Mass
7:00–9:00	School Studies
9:00–10:00	Sing Mass
11:00–15:00	Sing *Hora sexta* Service
	Lunch
	Rest Period
15:00–18:00	Sing *Hora nona* Service
	School Studies
	Dinner
18:00–19:00	Sing Vesper Service
19:30	Sleep

---

23 The growth of these monastic schools is summarized in Nan Cooke Carpenter, *Music in the Medieval and Renaissance Universities* (Norman: University of Oklahoma Press, 1954), 13–31.

24 Quoted in Oliver Strunk, *Source Readings in Music History* (New York: Norton, 1950), 109.

25 Quoted in ibid., 118.

26 Given in Joseph Smits van Waesberghe, *Musikerziehung, Lehre und Theorie der Musik in Mittelalter* (Leipzig: VEB Deutscher Verlag für Musik, 1949), III, Lfg. 3, 28.

We believe these young music students would have applauded the phrase by which Gibbon described their Church superiors:

The vices of the clergy are far less dangerous than their virtues.²⁷

27 Gibbon, *The History of the Decline and Fall of the Roman Empire*, IV, 301.

ART MUSIC

There had been, by this time, a long tradition of the solo art singer who sang epic poetry extolling the deeds of the great. The philosopher, Psellus, makes an interesting reference to choral music in this style, during the reign of the empress, Theodora of Constantinople, in 1042 AD.

> Some made thanks-offerings to God for their deliverance, others acclaimed the new empress, while the common folk and the loungers in the market joined in dancing. The revolution was dramatized and they composed choral songs inspired by the events that had taken place before their eyes.²⁸

28 Psellus, *Chronographia*, V, 39.

It is during this period that we see the more proficient of the wandering jongleurs hired in the courts of the aristocracy. When William the Conqueror made his historic voyage in 1066 to conqueror England, he was accompanied by a famous jongleur named Taillefer. It is recalled that Taillefer led the army in the Battle of Hastings, singing heroic tales of Roland, Charlemagne, and Roncesvalles.²⁹

29 Wace, d. 1170, *Roman de Brut*.
  Taillefer, ki mult bien chantout,
  Sor un cheval ki tost alout,
  Devant le duc alout chantant
  De Karlegaigne et de Rolant
  Et d'Oliver de des vassals
  Qui morurent en Rencevals.

In the famous *Domesday Book*, of 1086, a census taken at the request of William the Conqueror, we find the name of one of his jongleurs, Berdic, as well as a female jongleur named Adelinda, who was in the service of Earl Roger.³⁰

30 E. K. Chambers, *The Mediaeval Stage* (Oxford: Clarendon Press, 1903), I, 43–44.

Finally, our attention is drawn to a poem by Peter Damian. Although he is speaking of heaven, he seems to us to be describing 'kingly' music he has heard on earth, and perhaps there is even a reference here to the kings who saved musical instruments during the Dark Ages.

> Ever more the voice melodic makes new harmonies to ring;
> Instruments of heavenly music their exultant concord bring;
> Worthy of the King who saves them are the praises that they sing.³¹

31 Peter Damian, *On the Joyes & Glory of Paradise*, trans. Stephen Hurlbut (Washington, DC: St. Albans Press, 1928), 17.

FUNCTIONAL MUSIC

Among the annals of the Eastern Christian Church of the ninth century there is an extraordinary occasion when the emperor, Leo V, was actually murdered during a church festival service. The signal for the perpetrators of this deed was when the emperor began to sing.

> On the great festivals, a chosen band of priests and singers was admitted into the palace by a private gate to sing matins in the chapel; and Leo, who regulated with the same strictness the discipline of the choir and of the camp, was seldom absent from these early devotions. In the ecclesiastical habit, but with swords under their robes, the conspirators mingled with the procession, lurked in the angles of the chapel, and expected, as the signal of murder, the intonation of the first psalm by the emperor himself. The imperfect light, and the uniformity of dress, might have favored his escape, whilst their assault was pointed against a harmless priest; but they soon discovered their mistake, and encompassed on all sides the royal victim. Without a weapon and without a friend, he grasped a weighty cross, and stood at bay against the hunters of his life; but as he asked for mercy, 'This is the hour, not of mercy, but of vengeance,' was the inexorable reply. The stroke of a well-aimed sword separated from his body the right arm and the cross, and Leo the Armenian was slain at the foot of the altar.[32]

Gibbon also describes the music heard in a procession honoring a tenth-century emperor in Constantinople.

> From either side they echoed in a responsive melody the praises of the emperor; their poets and musicians directed the choir, and long life and victory were the burden of every song.[33]

An interesting account of religious functional music in Italy dates from the occupation of Milan by the Franconian king, Conrad II, in 1037. The Archbishop of Milan, Aribert, seeking a means of organizing the resistance of the town's people, created a civic symbol called the *carroccio*. This was a large wagon which contained an altar, the civic flag, and at the rear eight trumpeters who played a fanfare to assemble the people. The priests, also on the wagon, read a field mass and gave the last rites for those killed in the resistance. An Italian scholar describes it as,

32 Gibbon, *The History of the Decline and Fall of the Roman Empire*, IV, 201.

33 Ibid., IV, 569.

a curious emblem of superstition and faith, of popular poetry and military discipline, of fantastic images of religion and the nation; a wagon of victory and later of peace around which you would fight with energy and die with enthusiasm.[34]

By the eleventh century in England we read of well-organized military music, including established repertoire, relative to the siege of Rochester in 1088.

When Bishop Eudes was forced to surrender, he obtained the king's permission to quit the city with all arms and horses. Not satisfied with this, he further endeavored to seek the favor, that the king's military music should not sound their triumphant fanfares during the capitulation. But William [the Conqueror] angrily refused, saying that he would not make the concession for a thousand gold marks. So, when the rebellious Normans marched out of Rochester, they did so with colors lowered, and to the sound of the king's trumpets.[35]

Finally, Psellus mentions, in passing, the singing of traditional 'wedding songs' during the eleventh century.[36]

34 R. Bonfadini, 'Le origini del Comune di Milano,' in *Albori della Vita Italiana* (Milano, 1897).

35 Henry G. Farmer, *The Rise and Development of Military Music* (London: William Reeves, 1912), 8.

36 Psellus, *Chronographia*, VII, 9.

ENTERTAINMENT MUSIC

In an early reference to a court banquet, one given for Louis I of France (814–840), we find the later medieval custom of serving food with music already clearly established.

Of the service there must be no question; All of the possible meats to be found were in abundance, and served between trumpets and clarions; and minstrels, lutes, psalterons and followers were many.[37]

37 Chronicle of St-Denis.

The primary observation we wish to make here, as we come to the end of the Dark Ages, is that we can find no evidence that the performance of music ended, or even diminished, during this period. Literature *did* diminish significantly, and with it the abundant references to music which are typical of literature before the Christian era. But we believe only the descriptions become fewer, not the activity itself.

What references there are to musical performance, and the values with which society viewed them, seem no different from earlier times, nor are these performances described as unusual or rare.

We believe any idea that the performance of art or entertainment music declined during the Dark Ages is simply colored by the fact that most of the literature we have from this period is Church literature. We may not know much about secular music, but logic, plus the great flourishing of music during the next two centuries, compels us to believe it was there all along.

16 AESTHETICS OF MUSIC IN THE LITERATURE OF THE NINTH THROUGH ELEVENTH CENTURIES

THE NINTH THROUGH THE ELEVENTH CENTURIES, falling still within the Dark Ages, provide us with an extant literature which is rather small. Indeed, it is in part the small size of this body of literature which makes so astonishing the great outpouring of literature which begins in the twelfth century. At the same time, twelfth- and thirteenth-century literature, especially poetry, being more romantic, devotes far greater attention to music than do these battle weary centuries. Few though the references to music may be at this time, it is important that they be acknowledged for their testimony that the practice of music survived in its traditional forms.

The prose and poetry we will quote here often exists only in manuscripts of the twelfth century, or later, but is material which most scholars consider to have been created in an earlier century.

ART MUSIC

We have an extant body of songs from England known as the 'Cambridge Songs,' which take their name from the libraries where their manuscripts are found. We know these poems were still a sung literature through evidence such as the first line of 'The Lying Hero,' which begins, 'The song of fable that I take up ...'

In the 'Invitation to the Beloved,' is found the most extensive reference to art music, here music performed in a private room. We think of it as art music for the poem seems to suggest an environment in which sweet and happy music is being listened to, rather than being to accompany the serving of food.

> What melodies sweet there abound,
> Much higher the flutes seems to sound!
> Accomplished, both maiden and lad
> Sing songs dulcet and glad.

> With plectrum the cithara he plays,
> She sings to the lyre her melodies,
> While bowls the servants bring up
> With many an overflowing cup.[1]

In the Irish prose masterpiece, 'The Destruction of Da Derga's Hostel,' we find references to both sung lays and instrumental music. One reference, while an analogy, is nevertheless descriptive of indoor music. It is interesting that the only specific musical instruments named in this long work are 'pipes,' which we take to mean bagpipes. This instrument, together with the thirty-string harp and eight-string *timpan* were the most common Irish instruments at this time.

> Sweeter is the melodious sounding of the sword than the melodious sound of the golden pipes that accompany music in the palace.[2]

In the North German literature known as the 'Volsungs and Niblungs' there are a large number of extant epic songs, although, of course, here only the words survive.[3] Of particular interest here is a genuine tribute to the importance of poetry, together with the demand, 'Choose song or silence!'

> There be the book-runes,
> And the runes of good help,
> And all the ale-runes,
> And the runes of much might;
> To whomso they may avail,
> Unbewildered unspoilt;
> They are wholesome to have:
> Thrive thou with these then.
> When thou hast learnt their lore,
> Till the Gods end thy life-days.
>
> Now shall thou choose thee
> E'en as choice is bidden,
> Sharp steel's root and stem,
> Choose song or silence;
> See to each in thy heart,
> All hurt has been heeded.[4]

---

[1] Quoted in *Secular Latin Poems of the Middle Ages*, trans. Edwin H. Zeydel (Detroit: Wayne State University Press, 1966), 103.

[2] 'The Destruction of Da Derga's Hostel,' trans. Whitley Stokes, in *Epic and Saga*, vol. 49, *The Harvard Classics* (New York: Collier, 1910), 242.

[3] 'The Story of the Volsungs and Niblungs,' trans. Eiríkr Magnússon and William Morris in *Epic and Saga*, vol. 49, *The Harvard Classics* (New York: Collier, 1910), 290, 306, 309ff, 317, 320ff, 341, 347, 349, 351ff and 361.

[4] Ibid., 324.

This same body of literature contains an extraordinary tale with echoes of the Greek myth of Orpheus and his ability to 'tame the savage beast' with music. Here a character, with his hands tied, is thrown into a den of snakes. He manages to play such impressive music by using his feet that he tames all but one of the beasts.

> So Gunnar was cast into a worm-close, and many worms abode him there, and his hands were fast bound; but Gudrun sent him a harp, and in such wise did he set forth his craft, that wisely he smote the harp, smiting it with his toes, and so excellently well he played, that few deemed they had heard such playing, even when the hand had done it. And with such might and power he played, that all the worms fell asleep in the end, save one adder only, great and evil of aspect, that crept unto him and thrust its sting into him until it smote his heart; and in such wise with great hardihood he ended his life days.[5]

5 Ibid., 372.

Among the North German poems known as the 'Elder Edda,' which also deals with the Volsungs, there is an account of the solo singer singing art music for the purpose of cheering up a sad young lady.

> No more than this
> They spake methinks;
> Kind sat she down
> By the damsel's knee;
> Mightily sang Oddrun,
> Eagerly sang Oddrun,
> Sharp piercing songs
> By Borgny's side ...[6]

6 'The Lament of Oddrun,' in *Songs from the Elder Edda*, vol. 49, *The Harvard Classics* (New York: Collier, 1910), 458.

Later in this same poem we find a passage describing two singers, one of whom is a king. The other apparently sings at a banquet, but the nature of his song, of 'sore trouble,' suggests music to be listened to.

> There the king, the wise-hearted,
> Swept his harp-strings,
> For the mighty king
> Had ever mind
> That I to his helping
> Soon should come.

> But now was I gone
> Yet once again
> Unto Geirmund,
> Good feast to make;
> Yet had I hearing,
> E'en out of Hlesey,
> How of sore trouble
> The harp-strings sang.[7]

[7] Ibid., 463.

FUNCTIONAL MUSIC

Among the Cambridge Songs we find a very unusual form of Functional Music, early wake-up music.

> His servants stand, they tremble,
> they fear to touch the sleeper,
> and they rescue him
> by arousing him
> with plucking
> of strings
> and then give their master's
> name to the song
> they play.[8]

[8] 'Otto Mode,' in *Secular Latin Poems*, 213,

Among the North German poems known as the 'Elder Edda,' we find a reference to funeral music.

> Din arose from the benches,
> Dread song of men was there
> Noise 'mid the fair hangings,
> As all Hun's children wept …[9]

[9] 'Song of Atli,' in *Songs from the Elder Edda*, vol. 49, *The Harvard Classics* (New York: Collier, 1910), 442.

Most Functional Music of this period is battle music. A typical passage, found in the Volsung and Niblung literature, speaks of the primitive trumpet-types made from animal horns.

> Now the Vikings rushed from their ships in numbers not to be borne up against, but Sigmund the King, and Eylimi, set up their banners, and the horns blew up to battle; but King Sigmund let blow the horn his father erst had had, and cheered on his men to the fight.[10]

[10] 'The Story of the Volsungs and Niblungs,' 298.

A similar instrument is described in another poem in this North German literature, where we read, 'their great horn winded.'[11]

One passage among the Cambridge Songs refers to the soldiers singing to the usual war trumpets.

> follow the standards,
> sing to the horns;
> everywhere tumult arises …[12]

Another reference to war music is found in 'Da Derga's Hostel,' where an unusually large number of nine pipers are said to 'sally forth.'[13]

[11] 'The Lay of Hamdir,' in *Songs from the Elder Edda*, vol. 49, *The Harvard Classics* (New York: Collier, 1910), 454.

[12] Ibid., 217.

[13] 'The Destruction of Da Derga's Hostel,' 261.

17 COMMENTS ON AESTHETICS IN THE MUSIC TREATISES OF THE NINTH THROUGH ELEVENTH CENTURIES

This period is certainly one of the most interesting in music history, with respect to the development of the theory and notation of Western European music. The period begins with a rather distant view of Greek theory, primarily as interpreted by Boethius, and completely transforms itself into the first stage of modern. This is a fundamental and pivotal moment in the history of music for it is at this moment that the musician begins to perform from the page. Music after having been, for eons beyond knowing, something for the ear now becomes something for the eye and it is extraordinary to see how fast the psychological pendulum shifts from valuing what is heard to what is seen. It seems to us that any unbiased observer of the performance of music for the next thousand years must conclude that we lost more than we gained by writing music on paper.

It is true that earlier in the Middle Ages the separation between 'theory' and 'practice' was acknowledged, and that a prejudice toward ranking theory as something higher, more having to do with knowledge, was evident. But it is with these writers at the dawn of music being written on paper that this prejudice becomes very pronounced. They express over and over the idea that the music on paper has to do with math, Reason and knowledge whereas the singer who just sings on the basis of what pleases him is ignorant. It is weighing performance practice against math-based theory and even today for many musicians the concept of 'performance practice' is marginalized as if it were merely a personal preference and not somehow associated with the music itself. Hence, following this kind of prejudice, we have lost so much knowledge of how to perform Renaissance, Baroque and Classic Period music. We are left with only the written form of this music and it is this form which is studied in school even though every musician's ear must tell him that much is missing.

In addition, much of the discussion in these treatises is related to mathematics and grammar and so is not central to our purpose. We therefore restrict our view of this material to observations by the authors which reflect on the general topic of aesthetics and performance.

AURELIAN OF RÉOME
MUSICA DISCIPLINA (CA. 843 AD)

> Whoever reads this, composed in the line of great authority,
> Will know that the most wholesome authors are here;
> Here is the musician Pythagoras, the fountain head of the Greeks;
> Here are the sayings of the Latin fathers.
> I, your Aurelian, have compiled, arranged, and written,
> O Pastor Bernard, this slight gift.[1]

This initial poem might have more properly mentioned Boethius, Cassiodorus, and Isidore of Seville upon whom this work, like nearly all late medieval material on music, draws heavily. In the Preface which follows, also dedicated to Bernard, whom he calls 'the archsinger of the entire Holy Church,' Aurelian makes the interesting observation that present day singers know the rules, but are nevertheless lacking as musicians.

> I know that very noble singers are found, but I confess that I have seen none skilled in this art save you alone; for some of our musicians know many rules of music, yet nowhere, I think, is a musician found like the old ones.[2]

This first music treatise of the centuries which initiate the emergence from the Dark Ages begins by contending that music should not be neglected and by testifying that its power is still evident in both secular and sacred usage.

> There is much authority both in the ancient books, that is, those of the heathen, and in the holy books, affirming that the discipline of music should not be disdained, since there are to be found, both among the heathen and our own people, innumerable acts of efficacious through its power.[3]

---

[1] Aurelian of Réome, *The Discipline of Music*, trans. Joseph Ponte (Colorado Springs: Colorado College Music Press, 1968), 1. Aurelian was a Frankish monk who was expelled from his monastery for some unknown offense. He apparently wrote this treatise as a form of penance and it is dedicated to his superior the Abbot Bernard who later became the bishop of Autun.

[2] Ibid., 3.

[3] Ibid., I.

The foundation for church music he finds both in the Old Testament and in the Church's belief of the existence of choirs of angels. Beyond this, he observes, all of nature seems to be harmoniously organized and man is innately and physically prepared for music.

> Man himself, if he knows that he possesses all the resources customarily associated with this art, will not doubt the great harmony with which he is equipped for this discipline: for in his throat he has a pipe for singing; in his chest, a kind of harp, adorned with strings, as it were, the fibers of the lungs; in the alternations of the beating of his pulse, fluctuating ascents and descents.[4]

[4] Ibid., I.

Aurelian defines music as, 'the science, applicable to sound and song, of correctly controlling variations of sound.'[5] He remarks that music was associated with one of the daughters of Jupiter, who were also goddesses of memory, 'because this art, unless it is imprinted in the memory, is not retained.'

[5] Ibid., II.

Following Boethius, Aurelian categorizes music in the order of importance: celestial music, human music and instrumental music.[6] He admits man cannot actually hear the 'music of the spheres,' but finds evidence for it in a mistranslation of a passage from the Old Testament book, Job 38:37, '... or who can make the harmony of heaven to sleep.'[7]

[6] Ibid., III.

Regarding 'human music,' he says first that it is music which joins 'Reason to the body.' Next he makes an astounding deduction, considering that he could have known nothing of the rational left and the irrational right hemispheres of the brain. It is only music, he believes which unites the rational and the irrational.

[7] Modern translations, such as the Revised Standard Version, make no inference to music.
> Who has put wisdom in the clouds, or given understanding to the mists?
> Who can number the clouds by wisdom?

> What else is it that binds together the parts of the soul and body of man himself, who, as Aristotle is pleased to put it, has been joined together of the rational and the irrational.[8]

[8] Ibid., III. The Aristotle reference is apparently to the *Nicomachean Ethics*, I, 13.

He ranks instrumental music lowest in aesthetic value, on the basis of the curious mistake made by some early philosophers that the music exists in the instruments themselves, rather than in the men playing them. Since the music is in the instrument, this kind of music 'is separated from the science and intellect of music.'[9] He somehow continues in this line of thought by creating a strange dichotomy under which he regards meter as part of performance tradition whereas rhythm, being written on paper, is more 'proper' to his definition of a good musician.

[9] Ibid., III.

> [Another part] of human music, which is called metrics, although it takes its origin from music, should nevertheless be separated from it, since it is applied to song not so much through reasoning and through the rationality of this art as through natural impulse. But rhythmics, because it is totally based on intellect and reasoning, should be considered proper to music. A musician is one who has the faculty of judging without error with regard to reasoning, purposeful reflection, and musical convention, concerning quantities and rhythms, the kind of relationships of melodies, and the songs of the poets.[10]

[10] Ibid., IV.

Aurelian, in another place, carries this separation between the performer and the 'musician' to a much more severe level. He begins by asking the question, 'What is the difference between a musician and a singer?'

> There is as much difference between a musician and a singer as there is between a grammarian and a mere reader, or between physical skill and intellect. For physical skill obeys like a servant, but reason rules like a mistress, because the hands of the worker labor in vain, unless work grows out of the intellect. Every art and discipline has naturally a more honorable character than a handicraft, which is performed by hand and toil. For it is a much greater thing to know what someone does than to do what someone knows. Thus it is that the intellectual contemplation of work does not stand in need of any act of working, but the works of the hands are nothing unless they are directed by reason. How great the glory of the art of music is can be learned from this: that other craftsmen have received their names not from their discipline, but from the instruments themselves, as the hammerer from the hammer, the cithara player from the cithara, and each one of the others who have received their names from the instrument of their employment. But a musician is one who has with well-weighed intellect attained the science of singing not by the servitude of labor, but by the rule of contemplation. We see this antithesis particularly in the works of buildings and of wars. For buildings are inscribed with, and the triumphs of war are called by, the names not of those by whose toil and servitude they were completed, but by the names of those at whose command and inspiration they were begun: hence, the temple is called Solomon's …
>
> Musician and singer seem to differ as much as teacher and pupil. For example, the former creates poems, the latter analyses them; and the least little thing that the pupil accomplishes with time-consuming labor, the teacher discusses and empties of difficulty in the space

of a single moment through the skill of his aptitude. And the singer seems to stand before the musician like a prisoner before the judge. Whoever has any notion of music, however small it may be, can understand this fairly well. As we have said in the foreword, very noble singers are found, yet nowhere, in my opinion, is a musician found like the old ones.[11]

11 Ibid., VII.

Aurelian discusses the aesthetic quality of the human voice by dividing it into fifteen classes, based on the model of Isidore of Seville which we have presented above. Interesting here is the early evidence of vibrato.

> The first of the voices is the hyperlydian kind, which is the newest and the highest; the hypodorian is the second and is the lowest of all.
> The third kind is song and it is an inflection of the voice. The sound is simple and sound precedes song.
> The fourth is arsis, that is, a lifting up of the voice, i.e., a beginning.
> The fifth is thesis, which is a putting down of the voice, i.e., an end.
> The sixth kind is where there are sweet voices. Sweet voices are those that are thin and intense, loud and high.
> The seventh is where there are clear voices, which sustain fairly long, so that they fill all the place around, like a trumpet.
> The eighth is where there are thin voices, as are those in infants or of strings.
> The ninth is fat [*pinguis*], as are the voices of men.
> The tenth is where the voice is sharp, thin, and high, as in strings.
> The eleventh is where there is a hard voice that is emitted violently, like hammers on an anvil.
> The twelfth kind is where the voice is rough; a rough voice is one that is hoarse and is dispersed through minute and dissimilar sounds.
> The thirteenth kind is that in which the voice is blind; a voice is called blind when it stops as soon as it is emitted.
> The fourteenth kind is where the sound is tremulous [*vinnola*]; a tremulous voice is a flexible voice; it is called *vinnola* from *vinno*, that is, a lock of hair gently curled.
> The fifteenth kind is where the voice is perfect; a perfect voice is high, sweet, and loud. If any of these qualities is lacking, the voice will not be perfect.[12]

12 Ibid., V, 13.

As Aurelian begins his review of the old Greek model of music theory, he makes the familiar medieval association between music and mathematics.

> Music has the greatest correspondence to mathematics and encompasses that part of mathematics that compares one quantity with another.[13]

13 Ibid., VI.

In another place, he says if one wishes to become more versed in *music*,

> let him turn his eyes to the harmony of proportions, to the contemplation of intervals, and to the exactitude of mathematics.[14]

14 Ibid., X.

Aurelian summarizes the history of modes by saying there were first eight, named for the muses, then Charlemagne added four more and more recent Greeks still another four. He seems to want to discourage anyone who might want to enlarge the concept of tonality in this way, saying it is simply not necessary to do this, and adding the admonition from Proverbs 22:28,

> Remove not the ancient landmark which your fathers have set.

Regarding the names of some of the new Greek modes, he supplies the interesting suggestion that, in their being named for emotions and not mathematics, reflecting no doubt some relationship with the ancient modes.

> I asked a certain Greek how they would be translated into Latin. He answered that they were untranslatable, but that among the Greeks they were exclamations of one rejoicing.[15]

15 Ibid., IX.

There are a few observations by Aurelian about the performance of chant which we must include here. First, a curious maxim which demonstrates that the spirit of the myth had not completely died.

> We pray the singer to begin concluding all the verses of the nocturnal responses from the fifth syllable before the end; and this is according to the musicians who have maintained that not more than five waves of the sea also remove all storms from the same.[16]

16 Ibid., XIX.

Aurelian finds one moment of true contemplation for the listener of church music to be the music of Communion.

> So long as the faithful people receive heavenly benediction, their minds may be drawn by the sweet melody and suspended in sublime contemplation.[17]

17 Ibid., XX.

Although Aurelian's entire understanding of music is closely tied to Reason, it is interesting that he concludes his treatise on music with a brief reference to the ability of music to affect the emotions.

> The very world and the sky above us, according to the doctrine of philosophers, are said to bear in themselves the sound of music. Music moves the affections of men, stimulates the emotions into a different mood. In war it restores the strength of the combatants; and the stronger the blaring of the trumpet, the braver is the spirit made for battle. It influences beasts also, serpents, birds, and dolphins, at its hearing ... And what more? The art of music surpasses all other arts. If anyone doubts that the angels, too, in the starry sky, render praises to God with the practice of this discipline, he is not a reader of [the book of Revelations].[18]

[18] Ibid.

HUCBALD
DE HARMONICA INSTITUTIONE (CA. 895 AD)

Hucbald (b. ca. 840 AD) was a Benedictine monk who taught at several monastic schools and it seems clear that this treatise is intended for instruction in such a school. The functional premise of treatises such as this was to produce a church singer who understood music on a conceptual level and could read music, as opposed to what seems to have become a traditional singer who learned only by ear. In this case, Hucbald, following the prejudice discussed at the beginning of this chapter, promises such a singer that if he will just study the exercises in this treatise, that is, if he will just sing what is on paper, he,

> may at length be granted entry to the inner regions of this discipline, the darkness being gradually withdrawn from his dull eyes.[19]

Having, therefore, purely a conceptual aim, this treatise contains no real discussion of aesthetics, although there are hints that Hucbald swas aware of something beyond the conceptual in music. For example, we wish he would have expanded his remarks on the distinction between 'judgment' and 'ear.'

> One will generally find that melodies can close on these notes a fifth above without offending either one's judgment or ear.[20]

[19] Hucbald, 'Melodic Instruction' in *Hucbald, Guido, and John on Music*, trans. Warren Babb (New Haven: Yale University Press, 1978), 104a/16.

[20] Ibid., 119b/1.

ANONYMOUS
SCHOLIA ENCHIRIADIS (CA. 900 AD)

This treatise, formerly ascribed to Hucbald, is the earliest which deals with the improvisation of a simple counterpoint over a given chant. This author is still thinking of the old liberal arts definition of Mathematics consisting of Arithmetic, Geometry, Music, and Astronomy. Indeed, he says 'Music is the daughter of Arithmetic.' It is in this context that he defines music.

> [Music is] the rational discipline of agreement and discrepancy of sounds according to numbers in their relation to those things which are found in sounds ... Because everything comprehended by these disciplines exists through reason formed of numbers and without numbers can be neither understood nor made known.[21]

This writer clearly believed that the aim of this knowledge was 'delight,' a term he uses repeatedly. However, it appears that 'delight' for him was not aesthetic delight but the delight of Reason, perhaps an afterthought to avoid straying too far from the Church dogma.

> Whatever is delightful in song is brought about by number through the proportioned dimensions of sounds; whatever is excellent in rhythms, or in songs, or in any rhythmic movements you will, is effected wholly by number. Sounds pass quickly away, but numbers, which are obscured by the corporeal element in sounds and movements, remain.[22]

21 Anonymous, 'Of Symphonies,' in Oliver Strunk, *Source Readings in Music History* (New York: Norton, 1950), 135.

22 Ibid., 137.

AL-FARABI
IHSA AL-ULUM (CA. 900 AD)

This important treatise by one of the greatest scientists and philosophers of the Islamic world while recognizing both performance and the conceptual form of music, by no means considers them equally respected. Indeed, this becomes a new aesthetic measure, for the conceptual is more highly regarded by all of these theorists. Their prejudices still influence much of the educational world today. Nevertheless, it is this division of the art which makes possible the eventual recognition of the aesthetics of music in performance in the Aristotelian model. Al-Farabi's historic new definition reads as follows.

> As for the Science of Music, it comprises, in short, the investigation into the various kinds of melodies, and what they are composed of, and for what they are composed, and how they are composed, and in what forms it is necessary that they should be in order that the performance of them be made more impressive and effective. And that which is known by this name [music] comprises two sciences. One of them is the science of practical music, and the second is the science of theoretical music.
>
> And as for practical music, its concern is the production of the various kinds of perceptible melodies in the instruments adapted for them either by nature or by artifice …
>
> And the science of theoretical music is divided into [two] major parts. The first of them is the discourse about principles and fundamentals … And the second part is the discourse about the rudiments of this art.[23]

23 Quoted in Henry George Farmer, *Al-Farabi's Writings on Music* (New York: Hinrichsen, 1934), 13ff.

AL-FARABI
DE ORTU SCIENTIARUM (CA. 900 AD)

In this Latin treatise we find an important passage which preserves two familiar tenets of Greek philosophy, namely the influence of music on character and the definition of dance as visible music. He concludes with the thought that the educational purpose of music is to make man 'keener' and to prepare him for other studies.[24]

24 The French Doctor Tomasi after an extended study of chant around the world concluded that its purpose served as a kind of start-up engine to warm up the brain to do its best work.

> [Music's] utility lies in tempering the character of living beings that digress from the mean and in perfecting the fitness of those that have not yet been perfected, and in maintaining those that appear to possess the mean and have not yet gone to any of the extremes. It is also of utility to bodily health whenever the body is weakened by a languid soul and is impeded by the existence of its own impediment. Thus the cure of the body is affected by the cure of the soul through the adjustment of its own constitution, and combining this with its own substance of means of effective sounds, such as concordant sounds.
>
> To this science are three roots—meter, melody, and gesture. Meter was devised to regulate a rational comprehension of diction. Melody

was devised to regulate the parts of acuteness and gravity, and to it two roots have been included in the sense of hearing. Gesture has been included in the sense of seeing which, by coincident motions and corresponding proportions, has been arranged to agree with meter and sound. This art, therefore, is included in two particular senses—hearing and seeing.

And in this the educational sciences which are called the dominating sciences are completed. Therefore, it is now manifest whence the art of music emerged, and whence it arose and flowed. And these four sciences are called the dominating because they dominate their investigator, render him keener, and disclose to him the right way to become most accurately acquainted with that which comes after them.[25]

25 Ibid., 49.

ODO OF CLUNY
ENCHIRIDION MUSICES (CA. 935 AD)

This treatise, by the son of a feudal lord who became an important church leader in France, was the first in which letters are used as symbols for pitch in the modern sense, was also written for the purpose of perfecting the ability of church singers to read. With his system, Odo says he has taught boys in a few days to read 'without fault anything written in music,' something which he states that until now ordinary singers could not do even after fifty years experience.[26]

26 Odo, 'Enchiridion musices,' in Strunk, *Source Readings in Music History*, 104.

Given the purpose of this treatise, we are not surprised to find, when the Disciple asks, 'What is music?,' the Master answers, 'The science of singing correctly.' This, of course, means following the rules of music in so far as it was understood as a science. Singing something because it pleases the ear was no justification for Odo.

> Ordinary singers often fall into the greatest error because they scarcely consider the force of tone and semitone and of the other consonances. Each of them chooses what first pleases his ear.[27]

27 Ibid., 110.

On the other hand, following a discussion of the modes, Odo gives as the goal of any changes in the music, that it 'sound better.' When he summarizes the selection of modes, his comments reflect not 'science,' but improvisation and even 'trial and error.' Actually, he is speaking of aesthetics without realizing it, for he is saying the ear must judge where the eye cannot. This view perhaps reflects his contact with music of the courts instead of only the church.

> From this it is understood that the musician who lightly and presumptuously emends many melodies is ignorant unless he first goes through all the modes to determine whether the melody may perhaps not stand in one or another, nor should he care as much for its similarity to other melodies as for regular truth. But if it suits no mode, let it be emended according to the one with which it least disagrees. This also should be observed: that the emended melody either sound better or depart little from its previous likeness.[28]

28 Ibid., 111.

GUIDO OF AREZZO
MICROLOGUS (CA. 1026–1028 AD)

This is a treatise famous for the introduction of a staff of lines and spaces for the notation of music, but it is also one which comments on a broad range of other subjects. This treatise, by a Benedictine monk, is another educational one directed at the training of church singers. He begins his discussion with a little anagram which refers to the disappearance of music in the schools during the Dark Ages.

> Gone from school are the Muses; there may I hope to induce them,
> Unknown yet to adults, to unveil their light to the young ones!
> Ill will's indiscriminate rage let charity frustrate;
> Dire indeed are the blights that else will ravage our planet,
> Opening letters of these five lines will spell you the author.[29]

29 Guido of Arezzo, 'Micrologus,' 80, in *Hucbald, Guido, and John on Music*.

In his Prologue, reflecting the rapidly changing identification of 'music' being that which is on paper, Guido immediately centers on the importance of the ability to sing at sight. If the singer can not do this, he says, 'I do not know with what face he can venture to call himself a musician or a singer.'[30] He declares that he will discuss here only those things important to singing and then adds a comment we can only wish he had elaborated on. He says he will omit those 'things which are said but cannot be understood.'[31] He means, of course, the things related to performance practice which he has heard singers discuss but which 'cannot be understood' as they

30 Ibid., 85.

31 Ibid., 86.

cannot be notated on paper according to his tools of notation. And given his concern with the training of singers he is apparently speaking of those insights which musicians arrive at through experience, rather than through instruction. This same point he makes in another place, where he observes,

> In our times, of all men, singers are the most foolish. For in any art those things which we know of ourselves are much more numerous than those which we learn from a master.[32]

32 Quoted in Strunk, *Source Readings in Music History*, 117.

Among his comments on music theory, we find interesting his explanation for why there are seven tones of the scale as being associated with the seven days of the week.[33] It is also interesting that he gives the origin of the word 'tone' as *intonandus*, 'to be sounded.'[34] That is, the concept came from the experience, whereas in today's world of music education the experience is usually thought to come from the concept. He takes the opposite view with respect to *musica ficta*, which is clearly an appropriate aesthetic concept which grew out of experience. This apparently violated his goal of accurate sight-singing.

33 'Micrologus,' 116, in *Hucbald, Guido, and John on Music*. The number '7' was a very special number in Old Testament mythology.

34 Ibid., 116.

> False notes also creep in through inaccuracy in singing; sometimes performers deviate from well-tuned notes, lowering or raising them slightly, as is done by untrue human voices.[35]

35 Ibid., 134.

Guido's discussion of cadences includes a very curious statement. It strikes our attention especially as so many earlier Church philosophers had commented on the fact that music disappears after it is performed, suggesting that music exists only in its precise moment of performance. Guido presents here a thought which is quite different psychologically.

> The previous notes, as is evident to trained musicians only, are so adjusted to the last one that in an amazing way they seem to draw a certain semblance of color from it.[36]

36 Ibid., 139.

His actual explanation of the importance of the cadence he draws from grammar, a place where ancient philosophers often sought relationships with music.

> It is no wonder that music bases its rules on the last note, since in the elements of language, too, we almost everywhere see the real

force of the meaning in the final letters or syllables, in regard to cases, numbers, persons, and tenses.[37]

37 Ibid., 145.

When Guido turns to his discussion of the impact of music on character, he begins by suggesting that the pleasure in music is found in the senses themselves, rather like the incorrect conclusion of some earlier music theorists that the source of instrumental music was found in the instruments themselves.

> Nor is it any wonder if the hearing is charmed by a variety of sounds, since the sight rejoices in a variety of colors, the sense of smell is gratified by a variety of odors, and the palate delights in changing flavors. For thus through the windows of the body the sweetness of apt things enters wondrously into the recesses of the heart.[38]

38 Ibid., 159.

He provides an illustration of the ability of music to affect character in an anecdote not found elsewhere. As to the explanation how music does this, he cannot say, offering only the observation that this is known only to Divine Wisdom.

> Another man was roused by the sound of the cithara to such lust that, in his madness, he sought to break into the bedchamber of a girl, but, when the cithara player quickly changed the mode, was brought to feel remorse for his libidinousness and to retreat abashed.[39]

39 Ibid., 160.

Guido makes some interesting aesthetic observations in the course of a discussion of composition. First, it is clear that rhythm, for him, is still something bound to poetic textual rhythms. Here he finds variety, and not consistency, an aesthetic goal.

> For just as lyric poets join now one kind of foot, now another, so composers reasonably juxtapose different and various neumes. Diversity is reasonable if it creates a measured variety of neumes and phrases, yet in such a way that neumes answer harmoniously to neumes and phrases, with always a certain resemblance.[40]

40 Ibid., 172.

It is also important, he says, for the composer to create in music emotions which match the emotions of the text.

> Let the effect of the song express what is going on in the text, so that for sad things the neumes are grave, for serene ones they are cheerful, and for auspicious texts exultant, and so forth.[41]

41 Ibid., 174.

Regarding the emotions in performance, Guido makes a curious psychological observation regarding the illusion of hearing pitch.

> We often place an acute or grave accent above the notes, because we often utter them with more or less stress, so much so that the repetition of the same note often seems to be a raising or lowering.[42]

[42] Ibid.

Another curious suggestion has to do with the psychological relationship of the speed of notes at the cadence. Here Guido recommends the concept of the *retard*, a performance practice long used in all but the word itself.

> Towards the ends of phrases the notes should always be more widely spaced as they approach the breathing place, like a galloping horse, so that they arrive at the pause, as it were, weary and heavily.[43]

[43] Ibid., 175.

He concludes this discussion with the aesthetic rule that, in the end, taste must rule.

> Do everything that we have said neither too rarely nor too unremittingly, but with taste.[44]

[44] Ibid., 177.

We know today that music communicates on both a general, genetically understood, level and on an individual level where it is heard in a personal interpretation. Guido was apparently only observant of the latter.

> In accordance with the diversity of people and minds, what displeases one is cherished by another; and, anon, things that blend together delight this man, whereas that one prefers variety; one seeks a homogeneity and blandness in keeping with his pleasure-loving mind; another, since he is serious-minded, is pleased by staider strains; while another, as if distracted, feeds on studied and intricate contortions; and each proclaims that music as much the better sounding which suits the innate character of his own mind.[45]

[45] Ibid., 194.

Finally, in an interesting passage, Guido, because he apparently considered his discussion innovative, refuses to believe that more ancient men could have understood music on any rational level. In other words, now that we can write music on paper we can dismiss everything which came before.

In ancient times there were instruments that we are not clear about and also a multitude of singers who were, however, in the dark, for no man could by any train of thought reason out the differences between notes or a description of music.[46]

[46] Ibid., 288.

GUIDO OF AREZZO
EPISTOLA DE IGNOTO CANTU (CA. 1030–1032 AD)

In this treatise Guido again promises a system which will rapidly produce accurate sight-singers. Here he observes that previously singers learned by rote, after hearing the pitch on a monochord. This he calls, 'childish.'[47]

He refers to the previous treatise, which he says he has simplified for the sake of the young. He makes an implicit reference to the 'practical' versus the 'theoretical' division in music when he points out that he has not followed the model of Boethius, 'whose treatise is useful to philosophers, but not to singers.'[48]

[47] Guido, 'Epistola de ignoto cantu,' in Strunk, *Source Readings in Music History*, 123.

[48] Ibid., 125.

JOHN
ON MUSIC (CA. 1100 AD)

This author, formerly known as 'John Cotton,' has also written a treatise intended for a choir school. His viewpoint is again primarily a conceptual one and he clearly states that it is knowledge, the ability to judge music, which is the highest accomplishment—not that pleasing music played by uneducated jongleurs! We see here the beginning of the correspondence between the grammar of language and the grammar of music, a fallacious notion that has had the most unfortunate influence on young musicians in their score study.

> Music is one of the seven liberal arts—and a natural one, as are the others. Thus we sometimes see jongleurs and actors who are absolutely illiterate composing pleasant-sounding songs. But just as grammar, dialectic, and the other arts would be considered vague and chaotic if they were not committed to writing and made clear by precepts, so it is with music …
>
> For whoever devotes unremitting labor to it, and perseveres without pausing or wearying, can gain from it this reward, that he will

know how to judge the quality of song—whether it is refined or commonplace, true or false—and how to correct the faulty and compose the new.[49]

Indeed, he says, it is knowledge which distinguishes a musician from a mere singer.

> Nor, it seems, should we omit that the musician and the singer differ not a little from one another. Whereas the musician always proceeds correctly and by calculation, the singer holds the right road intermittently, merely through habit. To whom then should I better compare the singer than to a drunken man who does indeed get home but does not in the least know by what path he returns.[50]

He attempts to strengthen this viewpoint by quoting from Guido, that a musician who does not know what he is doing is a 'beast!'

> From the musician to the singer how immense the distance is;
> The latter's voice, the former's mind will show what music's nature is;
> But he who does, he knows not what, a beast by definition is.[51]

In another place he goes even further, refusing to accept performance traditions which derive from that talent which nature provides has an aesthetic value—even if it sounds correct and is agreeable!

> We said 'having a knowledge of music' because even if one unversed in the subject does what he does correctly, still, because he does it unwittingly, he is little esteemed, especially since both actors and precentors of dancing choruses for the most part sing agreeably, which is granted to them not by art but by nature.[52]

John begins his principal discussion of music by admitting that he does not know where the name 'music' actually derives from. If the reader knows, he does not begrudge him, for 'as Paul says, the Holy Ghost apportions to individuals as he sees fit.'[53] He finds two kinds of music, the first being natural and artificial music made by man and the second the 'music of the spheres,' which he says we know only through philosophers.[54]

His principal instrument for teaching pitch was the monochord, an instrument through which he believed true pitch could be

49 John, 'On Music,' 51, in *Hucbald, Guido, and John on Music.*

50 Ibid., 52.

51 John gives the source as the 'Micrologus,' but it actually comes from the beginning of Guido's 'Regulae rhythmicae.'

52 'On Music,' 77.

53 1 Corinthians 12:11.

54 'On Music,' 57.

achieved. This was a goal he apparently found to be not universally appreciated.

> For there are indeed a great many clerics and monks who neither understand this discipline nor wish to understand it, and, what is worse, who avoid and abhor those that do.
> If, as sometimes happens, a musician takes them to task about a chant which they perform either inaccurately or crudely, they get angry and make a shameless uproar and are unwilling to admit the truth, but defend their error with the greatest effort ...
> The monochord serves to silence their wrong-headedness, so that those who will not trust the words of a musician are refuted by the testimony of the sound itself.[55]

[55] Ibid., 65ff.

In discussing cadences, unlike Guido who found confirmation of his logic in grammar, John finds an analogy in business.

> Musicians of judgment have not unreasonably decided to base the decision as to modes on the endings, since in business affairs a single-minded regard for the outcome distinguishes the wise from the heedless.[56]

[56] Ibid., 82.

Regarding the modes, John rejects the expansion of their ranges, which he admits some composers do for aesthetic reasons, 'to tickle the ears.'[57]

[57] Ibid., 96.

In his reflection on performances which he has heard, he makes a statement which is remarkably similar to Mahler's famous definition of 'tradition' as being 'the last bad performance.'

> We do know most assuredly that a chant is often distorted by the ignorance of men, so that we could now enumerate many corrupted ones. These were really not produced by the composers originally in the way that they are now sung in churches, but wrong pitches, by men who followed the promptings of their own minds, have distorted what was composed correctly and perpetuated what was distorted in an incorrigible tradition, so that by now the worst usage is clung to as authentic.[58]

[58] Ibid., 104.

He also has observed that the physical status of the singer can affect the performance, pointing to 'singers weighed down by weariness' singing flat and those of 'high spirits' singing sharp.[59]

[59] Ibid.

John's discussion of the effect which music has on the emotions is quite unlike that of any other philosopher. He begins, like Guido, by pointing out that everyone has different tastes in music. It is an important recognition that the listener holds a different perspective from the theorist.

> Nor should it seem surprising to anyone that we say different men are attracted by different things, for by nature itself men are so endowed that not everyone's senses cherish the same desire. Thus, it often happens that while to one man what is being sung appears most delightful, by another it is pronounced ill-sounding and utterly formless. Indeed I myself remember singing a number of chants for some people, and what one praised to the heights another disliked profoundly.[60]

Therefore, in his view it is not the mode which affects man, rather it is the natural emotional affinity of the man which is attracted to a particular mode—thus, each man like a different mode. We are much more attracted to his unusual description of the aesthetic character of the various modes than we are to his logic.

> Some are pleased by the slow and ceremonious peregrinations of the first, some are taken by the hoarse profundity of the second, some are delighted by the austere and almost haughty prancing of the third, some are attracted by the ingratiating sound of the fourth, some are stirred by the well-bred high spirits and the sudden fall to the final in the fifth, some are melted by the tearful voice of the sixth, some like to hear the spectacular leaps of the seventh, and some favor the staid and almost matronly strains of the eighth.

These differences he finds are so pronounced that a musician recognizes the mode immediately by its character, as one does in the case of national characteristics.

> The modes have individual qualities of sound, differing from each other, so that they prompt spontaneous recognition by an attentive musician or even by a practiced singer. Just as someone who has studied the manners and appearances of various peoples distinguishes expertly the nationality of any man he sees, noting, for instance, that this one is a Greek and that one a German, but that one a Spaniard and that one a Frenchman.

The object of the composer, then, is to fit the character of the music to the character of the listener. How one does this, not

[60] This discussion is found in ibid., 109ff.

to mention what one does in the case of a large congregation of assorted personalities, he does not say.

> Therefore, in composing chants, the duly circumspect musician should plan to use in the most fitting way the mode by which he sees those are most attracted whom he wishes his chant to please.

Later in this same treatise, John takes the opposite, and traditional, view that it is the music itself which affects character. He begins by rhapsodizing on the wide range of purpose available in music.

> It should not pass unmentioned that chant has great power of stirring the souls of its hearers, in that it delights the ears, uplifts the mind, arouses fighters to warfare, revives the prostrate and despairing, strengthens wayfarers, disarms bandits, assuages the wrathful, gladdens the sorrowful and distressed, pacifies those at strife, dispels idle thoughts, and allays the frenzy of the demented …
>
> Music has different powers according to the different modes. Thus, you can by one kind of singing rouse someone to lustfulness and by another kind bring the same man as quickly as possible to repentance and recall him to himself.[61]

John concludes this subject by arguing in favor of two ideas which were contrary to the teachings of the Church. He was in favor of instrumental music and he saw no reason to restrict chant to the Gregorian repertoire.[62]

John now addresses himself to the subject of the composition of chant and begins by listing some specific aesthetic goals. First the composer must fit the music to the meaning of the words, as well as to the occasion which may range from frivolity to grief.[63] As an example of the latter, he recommends the Hypolydian for lamentations because of its 'doleful sound.'

One must have variety and 'not abuse one neume by unduly harping on it.' He also appears to discourage melodic repetition, although he says 'we do not find fault if now and then some appropriate melodic figures are repeated just once.'

Finally, we find a curious observation on the relationship of the character of the singing voice with scale-steps. It is a regret the he does not elaborate on this idea which he calls 'obvious.' One wonders if we are reading here of the application in performance of

61 Ibid., 114ff.

62 Ibid., 115.

63 Ibid., 117ff.

'slurs,' something which will not appear on paper until Praetorius in 1619.

> It is obvious that men with harsh and intractable voices avoid semitones as much as possible, while those who have flexible voices relish them greatly—so much so that they sometimes produce them even where they should not be made.[64]

64 Ibid., 137.

We close by paying tribute to John for his support of instrumental music and venturing to recommend music for the Church other than Gregorian chant. Both views were heresies in the year 1100.

Part 5

The Glory of the Late Middle Ages

18 THE STATE OF MUSIC IN SOCIETY IN THE TWELFTH AND THIRTEENTH CENTURIES

THE TWELFTH AND THIRTEENTH CENTURIES are characterized by the beginnings of Humanism, a final burst of freedom from the dogma of the Dark Ages. The virtual explosion of confidence in man and his works is both the hallmark of these two centuries and the harbinger of the Renaissance. What greater display of this new confidence can there be than the huge cathedrals which began to spring up everywhere. Built in cities which had only a fraction of the population the cathedrals could contain, they remain not only as symbols of faith, but of man himself and of the glorious final two centuries of the Middle Ages.

Many factors contributed to this period of enthusiastic renewal of society. Certainly the great Crusades introduced to the West the more advanced and more cultured civilizations of the East. International trade followed the Crusades and through it not only a dramatic expansion of the general economy resulted, but a great stimulus to all the arts. Consider, for example, the testimony of a priest named Theophilus. From a small monastery near Paderborn, Germany he wrote in 1190,

> Here you shall find all that Greece possesses in the way of diverse colors and mixtures; all that Tuscany knows of the working of enamels ... all that Arabia has to show of works ductile, fusible, or chased; all the many vases and sculptured gems and ivory that Italy adorns with gold; all that France prizes in costly variety of windows; all that is extolled in gold, silver, copper, or iron, or in subtle working of wood or stone.[1]

1 Theophilus, 'Schedule diversarum artium,' in E. Dillon, *Glass* (New York: G.P. Putnam, 1907), 126.

This period saw equally dramatic progress in the intellectual life of Western Europe. Just before the dawn of the twelfth century paper mills in Germany and France began to open. The modern universities were founded at this time and the rediscovery of the works of Aristotle and the ancient philosophers provided them with an immediate challenge: to reconcile these monuments of Reason with a Church long content to rest its case on Faith.

No sooner were the universities founded, than the germ of 'practical' education began to spread. According to the chronicle of Matthew Paris, it appears that by 1254 there was some concern that university students were not so interested in the Liberal Arts as in gaining skills for employment. It is interesting that even pope Innocent IV felt impelled to speak out in defense of traditional values in the Liberal Arts. Paris provides the following background:

> It occurred to the pope, who still remained at Rome, that the liberal arts were almost entirely converted into mechanical arts for the sake of gain, and that it might with justice be said of philosophy: 'She prostitutes herself and sits as a harlot awaiting her hire;' and he also discovered that nearly all scholars neglected the rudiments of grammar, and, deserting the study of authors and philosophers, were hurrying to study the laws, which, it is clear, are not included in the number of liberal arts; for liberal arts are sought after and acquired for their own sake; but the laws are studied for the sake of acquiring salaries. Indeed, as was evident to all, young men, deficient in knowledge, as soon as they have learned to chatter on a few sophisms in noisy assemblages, mount to the chairs of the masters, in order, by usurping the name of master, to swell in their pride, and, being in a position demanding greater respect, to climb to more lofty situations.[2]

2 Matthew Paris, *English History*, trans. J. A. Giles (London: Bohn, 1852), III, 65ff.

The pope responded by sending a papal letter to all the countries under his spiritual guidance.

> We observe with grief how much the formerly pious and holy seminary of clerks, forgetful of its original well-doing, has fallen from the highest sanctity to the lowest depths of vice. Since a shocking report has reached and continually assailed our ears by frequent repetitions, that philosophical studies are abandoned, aye, and long ago cast aside, that all the multitude of the clerks are endeavoring to get a knowledge of secular laws, and what is still more worthy of cognizance of the divine judgment, in the greater number of the countries of the world, no one is elected by the prelates to ecclesiastical dignities, honors, or prebendaries, unless he is either a professor of secular science or a lawyer, although such men ought rather to be rejected by them, unless other things plead for them. Most of all we grieve that the students of philosophy, educated so tenderly in her bosom, so diligently taught, so excellently trained and instructed, are obliged, through want of food and clothing, to avoid the presence of men,

hiding here and there like the owls, while these lawyers, or rather devils, clothed in purple and mounted on richly-caparisoned horses, reflecting the dazzle of the sun with the glare of gold, the brilliancy of silver, the sparkling of gems, with their whole raiments of silk, show themselves not the servants of Him who was crucified, but the heirs of Lucifer, making themselves a spectacle wherever they go, stirring up and incurring the indignation and odium of the laity against themselves, and what is much more grievous, against the whole Church of God.[3]

Perhaps there never was an 'ivory tower.'

Towns and cities take on a stronger sense of identity during these two centuries, as is found expressed in many new civic institutions. It was this period in which the watch towers were built on city walls everywhere and musicians hired to serve as both watchmen[4] and surrogate clocks during hours of darkness. These civic musicians were also available to perform a wide variety of official entertainment music, accompanying the town crier (to attract his crowd) and playing for public punishment of the guilty.

From Italy, in particular, we have much extant documentation for civic wind bands from the twelfth and thirteenth centuries. Documents mention civic 'trombe e i corni' in Milan in 1121,[5] 'jogleurs, chanteors e troubadours' in residence in Genoa in 1180[6] and no fewer than twenty-four civic musicians in Monferrato in 1213.[7] In Florence a document of 1232 speaks of these civic musicians already having both summer and winter uniforms.[8] In this century the first minstrel guild in Florence, 'La Filarmonica dei Laudesi,' was established.[9]

In Siena, a document of 1262 speaks of five 'tabatores e tamburelli' who accompany the city fathers when they leave the town hall and were to perform for all civic celebrations and banquets. These players received clothing, housing and a salary based on the amount of performance.[10]

In Paris, civic musicians are mentioned in a tax roll of 1295,[11] while in England, there appears to have been only civic watchmen by the thirteenth century. In the oldest extant document which mentions these musicians, during the reign of Henry III, we read,

but for a full remedy of enormities in the night ... in the yeere of Christ 1253 Henrie the third comanded Watches in Cities, and Borough Townes to be kept, for the better observing of peace and quietnesse amongst his people.[12]

3 Ibid., III, 440ff.

4 A famous anecdote tells of a tower musician blowing a warning on his trumpet on the approach of the Tartar hordes in 1241. In the middle of the fanfare a Tartar arrow pierced his throat and the fanfare was left unfinished. This fanfare is reproduced in Stephen Mizwa, *Nicholas Copernicus* (New York: Kessinger Publications, 1943), 73.

5 Bernardino Corio, *L'Historia di Milano volgarmente scritta* (Padoa, 1646), 57.

6 Grove, *The New Grove Dictionary of Music and Musicians*, ed. Stanley Sadie (London: Macmillan, 1980), VII, 204.

7 Ibid.

8 Giuseppe Zippel, *I Suonatori della Signoria di Firenze* (Trento, 1892).

9 Ibid.

10 Alessandro Vessella, *La Banda* (Milan: Instituto editoriale nazionale, 1935), 39.

11 Grove, II, 326; VII, 205.

12 Quoted in John Stow, *Survey of London* (London, 1618), 158.

In Germany, fragmentary evidence suggests well-developed civic musical institutions by the twelfth century. In Mulhouse, for example, a statute limits the number of musicians for private weddings to six.[13] By the thirteenth century, both Hamburg and Breslau had permanent four-man civic wind bands and in Köln a street was named 'platea joculatorum,' in 1231.[14] Civic musician guilds were also founded in Germany during the thirteenth century, in particular the Marienbrüderschaft der Musicanten und Spielleute zu St. Catherinen of Lübeck and the Nicolai-Brüderschaft of Vienna, founded in 1288.[15]

Thus, the better of the wandering jongleurs were hired by town governments, thereby enjoying an improved social status by moving from beggar to civic official. Ramón Lull, in 1272, now lists the social status of musicians as being above painters, farm laborers, and artisans, but below the other professions, merchants, and seamen.[16]

Individual noblemen were also hiring the better jongleurs they could find and Lull complains that while the poor shiver in rags outside the palace door, the musicians are clothed in royal clothing. Some of them must have done well indeed, for a jongleur, named Rahere (d. 1144), in the employ of Henry I of England, retired and donated the money to build St. Bartholomew's Hospital in London.

Pedro III (1276–1285) of Aragon maintained an ensemble of trumpets and percussion (*atabale*) and a separate group of minstrels under the leadership of Cerveri de Girona.[17]

When the Emperor Frederick II married his third wife, the English princess, Isabella, she arrived with her own company of musicians. A document relative to the purchase of a sackbut for her ensemble is one of the earliest references to that instrument.[18]

Among the musicians sponsored by the nobles were some of the finest contributors to art music during this period, the singers known as troubadours, trouvères and Minnesingers.

---

13 M. B. Bernhard, *Notice sur la Confrérie des Joueurs d'Instruments d'Alsace* (Paris, 1844), 5, fn. 2.

14 Wilhelm Ehmann, *Tibilustrium* (Kassel, 1950), 8. Today this street is named, 'Nächelsgasse.'

15 Ibid., 28, quotes some of the original charter.

16 Jocelyn N. Hillgarth, *The Spanish Kingdoms* (Oxford: Clarendon Press, 1976), I, 46ff. Lull nevertheless grumbles that he finds no king who rules as he should, few judges not corrupted by gold, and few jongleurs who will not lie for money.

17 Baltasar Saldoni y Remendo, Diccionario biografio-bibliografico de Efemérides de musicos españos (Madrid: Imp. A cargo de A. Perez Dubeull, 1880), I, 334, and Hillgarth, *The Spanish Kingdoms*, I, 54.

18 Georgina Masson, *Frederick II of Hohenstaufen* (New York: Octagon Books, 1973), 270. This document was lost in World War II.

ART MUSIC

The most famous description of art music of this period involves the discovery of Richard I, of England, who was captured on his return from the Third Crusade and was being held captive by Austria for debts owed. He was discovered by Blondel, a fellow member of an aristocratic singing society in England, who heard Richard singing an art song known only to members of this society. In the following version of this tale, written by a jongleur of Reims in 1260, we are told Blondel found a castle which reportedly held a distinguished prisoner. He offered himself as a jongleur to work in the castle, as a means of discovering the identity of the prisoner. The knight in charge of the castle 'said he would keep him gladly.'

> Then was Blondel right glad, and he went and fetched his viol and his other instruments. And he continued to serve the castellan and pleased him well. And he was on good terms with them of the castle and with all the household. So Blondel abode there all that winter; yet never could he find out who the prisoner was, until one day in Eastertide he went all alone into a garden that adjoined the tower. And he looked about him and bethought himself if by any chance he might see the prisoner. And while he was yet thinking of this, the king looked out through a loophole and espied Blondel. And he took thought how he might make himself known to him. Then did he bethink himself of a song that the two of them had made betwixt them, which none other knew save they two. So began he to sing the first words thereof, loud and clear (for he sang passing well); and when Blondel heard him, then knew he of a surety that this was his lord. And he had in his heart the greatest joy that ever yet he had had in all his days. Straightway he left the garden and went into his own chamber, where he slept; and he took his viol and began to play a strain, and as he played he rejoiced over his lord whom he had found.[19]

One purpose often given for Art Music in early literature was to bring joy to the listener. In this regard we have a reference regarding the king of France, who, in 1254, was despondent over his capture by the Saracens during his failed Crusade. In this case, even music failed to bring him joy.

> The king of the French, cast down in heart and look, refused all consolation: musical instruments afforded him no pleasure; no cheerful or consolatory speeches drew a smile from him ...[20]

[19] 'La Chronique de Rains,' quoted in Edward Stone, trans., *Three Old French Chronicles of the Crusades* (Seattle: The University of Washington Press, 1939), 275.

[20] Paris, *English History*, III, 96.

FUNCTIONAL MUSIC

With the towns and cities now engaging musicians as civic employees, we begin to find a wide variety of appearances by these musicians. They are always to be found following the town crier around as he makes his announcements. Such a civic trumpet player is mentioned in a twelfth-century poem by the Goliard poet known as, Archpoet of Cologne.

> Rumor, with its trumpet blowing
> Mid the heralds' voices glowing
> Tells the people far and wide
> That a virtuous man has nighed,
> Friend of peace and champion;
> In Vienne there is a throne
> Which for him the peers prepare.
> Crowds of players rend the air
> Making ready tune on tune,
> Many kinds of jongleurs soon
> Enter, waiting not a week.
> Largess they and presents seek.[21]

Welcoming noble visitors was another important role for civic musicians. We read of the civic band of Milan (*tamburi, ciaramelle e trombe*) riding in a wagon in the procession in 1268 which welcomed the visit of the Queen of Sicily.[22] When the king of England visited Paris in 1254 he was welcomed by the citizens,

> carrying branches of trees and flowers, they went singing, and attended by musical instruments, to meet the approaching visitors.[23]

Departure ceremonies were equally important occasions for music. A typical example is given by Matthew Paris who describes the papal legate leaving England in 1241, 'in great pomp, amidst the sound of trumpets.'[24]

We have an interesting eyewitness account of the Doge leaving Venice to accompany the Fourth Crusade. Pictured here are both the personal musicians of the Doge, together with those of the city itself.

> The Doge of Venice had with him fifteen galleys, all at his own cost. The galley wherein he himself was, was all vermilion-colored, and

---

[21] 'Fama tuba dante sonum,' in Edwin H. Zeydel, *Vagabond Verse* (Detroit: Wayne State University Press, 1966), 251.

[22] Bonanni, *Gabinetto armonico* (Rome, 1723).

[23] Paris, *English History*, III, 106. He describes another welcoming ceremony in 1255 in Dover which included ringing of bells and songs. [III, 135]

[24] Ibid., I, 319.

it had a pavilion stretched above it of vermilion samite, and there
were four silver trumpets which sounded before him, and timbrels
that made a most joyful noise ...

And when the fleet set forth from the haven of Venice ... it was
the goodliest thing to behold that ever hath been since the beginning
of the world. For there were full an hundred pair of trumpets, both
silver and brass, which all sounded for the departure, and so many
timbrels and tabors and other instruments that it was a fair marvel
to hear.[25]

With the formation of civic musician guilds at this time, the civic
musicians took over the role of supplying music for weddings as
an extra source of income. A contemporary describes one of these
joyous occasions.

Then there is a jesting song, the cook shouts, the meal is spread out,
the hall swarms with cheering people and melodious dances; there
is a procession with wedding songs preceding and following.[26]

The musicians employed by private nobles also begin performing a wide variety of services at this time. Most regular performances were surely for meals, although descriptions of the performance of music while people are actually eating are fairly rare in early literature.

While the king and queen were eating, minstrels went to and fro in
the hall singing and playing their instruments.[27]

A more frequent description is of the performance of music
while the food is paraded in from the kitchen. A contemporary
thus describes the scene as the first course enters a banquet by
Richard I of England.

King Richard was set on des
With dukes and eerles, prowde in pres,
Fro keehene com the fyrste cours,
With pypes and trumpes and tabours.[28]

The Emperor Frederick II returned from his Crusade with a
number of Arabic slaves, including some young trumpet players
who performed at meal times.

25 'Li estoires de chiaus qui conquisent Coustantinoble' (1216), quoted in Stone, *Three Old French Chronicles of the Crusades*, 179.

26 Bernard of Cluny, *Scorn for the World: Bernard of Cluny's* De Contemptu Mundi, trans. Ronald Pepin (East Lansing: Colleagues Press, 1991), 111.

27 Ramón Lull, *Libre de Meravelles*, quoted in Christopher Page, *Voices and Instruments of the Middle Ages* (London: Dent, 1987), 183.

28 K. Brunner, ed., *Der mittelenglische Versroman über Richard Löwenherz* (Vienna and Leipzig, 1913), 88, 268.

He selected Negro boys between sixteen and twenty to form a musical corps; they were magnificently clad and taught to blow large and small silver trumpets.[29]

An eyewitness to the marriage of Henry III of England, in 1236, mentions the royal musicians in a performance which he regarded as musically unusual.

… preceded by the king's trumpeters and with horns sounding, so that such a wonderful novelty struck all who beheld it with astonishment.[30]

This same writer describes the wedding celebration of Earl Richard of England in 1243, for which the elaborate banquet included thirty thousand dishes! Among the entertainers were apparently separate ensembles of jongleurs, here called 'gleemen.'

Worldly pomp, and every kind of vanity and glory, was displayed in the different bodies of gleemen, the variety of their garments …[31]

The greatest outdoor events held by the aristocrats were the tournaments, which were part entertainment, but also a form of training for war. A thirteenth-century Romance tells of a noble who took two string players with him on his trip to a tournament.

Gerars Malfillastres, noble, valiant, courteous
and forbearing, went in this magnificent way to
the tournament. He took six companions with him
in whom he put the deepest trust; and he had two
fiddlers with him who sang a *son d'amours* between
themselves, one Sunday morning. They rode straight
along on the first day of May, when the grass is
green, the gladioli are in flower, and everything
takes on a verdant hue. The fiddlers, with loud and
clear voices, sang a *son d'amour*, according themselves
with their fiddles.[32]

There are, of course, many references to the use of trumpets in battle during this period, but with the exception of descriptions of the Crusades little detail is given. A typical example portrays the citizens of Milan as they await an invasion by Frederick I, 'Barbarossa.'

When the emperor went his rounds, tumult arose in the city in expectation of an assault. There was great trepidation; signals

---

[29] Ernst Kantorowicz, *Frederick the Second*, trans. E. O. Lorimer (New York: Frederick Ungar, 1957), 312.

[30] Paris, *English History*, I, 8.

[31] Ibid., I, 461.

[32] Gautier de Tournai, 'Gille de Chyn,' quoted in Christopher Page, *Voices and Instruments of the Middle Ages* (London: Dent, 1987), 181.

sounded, trumpets blew, the strong took up arms, women and feeble old men took to lamentation.[33]

Finally, we mention an unusual reference to a religious trumpeter who was responsible for a moment of religious fanaticism in 1233 known as the 'Great Hallelujah!' This man wore a black beard, a high Armenian cap, and a sack-like robe with a red cross on front and back. He played a copper trumpet from which he produced 'now sweet, now terrifying sounds.' When he played people followed him and when he arrived in a market place or public square it was said,

> all anmosities were suddenly forgotten, and a time of happiness and joy began; knights and people, citizens and peasants struck up hymns and songs in praise of God; people fell on each other's necks, and there was no wrath, no strife, no confusion: only Love and Peace.[34]

[33] Otto of Freising, *The Deeds of Frederick Barbarossa*, III, xlii, trans. Charles Mierow (New York: Columbia University Press, 1953), 216.

[34] Kantorowicz, *Frederick the Second*, 397.

ENTERTAINMENT MUSIC

The most frequently described Entertainment Music in early literature is always associated with the banquet. In a twelfth-century biography of the Englishman, Hereward the Wake, we find an account of a nobleman unusually skilled in performance as well as attentive listeners, even though in an entertainment atmosphere.

> One of the girls offered Hereward a goblet full of wine while the man with the harp was standing by. But he refused to take it from the woman's hand because he and the Irish king's son had just taken a vow to accept nothing until they had received something they had long wanted from the hand of the prince's daughter. The guests immediately condemned him for this severe slight to the cupbearer, and the jongleur described the affair disapprovingly to his mistress … Directing that he should be excused this time since he was unfamiliar with their customs, she promptly conveyed a ring from her hand into a fold of his clothing. But the jongleur, strolling about everywhere, wouldn't keep quiet, and as often as he passed by declared that a man who at a feast would slight the cup-bearer with her cup simply wasn't fit to pluck the harp. Eventually stirred to anger by his conduct, Hereward gave him an answer—which the jongleur stupidly spread about—that given the chance, he could better perform that duty than him. Indignantly, as if he alone were skilled in the art, the

> jongleur pushed the harp into Hereward's arms. Taking it, he touched the strings most adroitly, and for a while produced sounds and strains to the admiration of all, while the other was quite shamefaced at the business, and kept trying to snatch the harp from his hands. But in fact the guests reckoned him well worthy of a reward, and said that he should be allowed to keep the harp for the time being. Since they persisted in plying him with drink he acquiesced singing to the harp in a variety of ways. And he sang in different styles, now by himself now in a trio with his friends in the manner of the Fenland people. Whereupon everyone was greatly delighted.[35]

Matthew Paris describes the visit of the English Earl Richard to Frederick II in 1241. The English visitor was welcomed

> with the greatest joy and honor, the citizens and their ladies coming to meet him with music and singing, bearing branches of trees and flowers, dressed in holiday garments and ornaments.

Frederick himself entertained the visitor with the performance of two Saracen girls, whom he had brought back with him from his Crusade.

> Two Saracen girls of handsome form, mounted upon four round balls placed upon the floor, namely, one of the two on two balls, and the other on the other two. They walked backwards and forwards, clapping their hands, moving at pleasure on these revolving globes, gesticulating with their arms, singing various tunes, and twisting their bodies according to the tune, beating cymbals or castanets together with their hands.[36]

When this English visitor departed to travel through Italy, Frederick ordered that he be welcomed in each town with 'vocal and instrumental musicians.' In Cremona he was welcomed by an elephant,

> bearing a wooden sort of tower, in which the masters of the animal sat, playing on trumpets, and exultingly clapping their hands together.[37]

We also find a very rare reference in early literature to genuine popular music.

> Whenever he saw a gathering of young people
> He would go with his instrument
> And sing them new songs.[38]

---

35 Richard of Ely, 'The Life of Hereward the Wake,' in *Three Lives of the Last Englishmen*, trans. Michael Swanton (New York: Garland Publishing, 1984), 53.

36 Paris, *English History*, I, 369ff.

37 Ibid., I, 385ff.

38 Jacopone da Todi, *The Lauds*, trans. Serge and Elizabeth Hughes (New York: Paulist Press, 1982), 103.

ON THE MUSIC OF THE CRUSADES

Only a period which had the courage to imagine constructing the enormous arches and pillars of the great cathedrals and which had such enthusiasm for the German and French Romances could have seriously considered the incredible idea of driving the Moslems out of Jerusalem and making that city the center of the Christian world.

The First Crusade (1095–1099), urged on by Urban II, was largely a grand adventure led by French nobles. Some 30,000 troops set out and after two years of battles the surviving 12,000 conquered Jerusalem. The Latin chronicles describe the Western armies as using three types of trumpets, 'tubae, buccinae, and lituui,' as well as 'corni.' One would suppose that some of these instruments were used only in battle, as the historian, Fulcher of Chartres (d. 1130), who was present, mentions the English musician, Evrardus Venator, who played 'tuba' during the crusade, but was a horn player at court.[39]

After slaughtering the remaining 70,000 Moslems in the city, burning alive the remaining Jews in their synagogue, throwing babies over the walls and killing their mothers, the Christians paused to sing hymns to God.

> The Christians, having obtained with the wished-for victory ... blessed God with due praises ... raising to heaven hymns of thanksgiving.[40]

Upon establishing the new Latin kingdom of Jerusalem, the victorious leaders soon divided up the major cities into private principalities and began to feud among themselves. Eventually most of the Crusaders returned to Europe, leaving a small number of Christians prey to Moslems eager to avenge their losses. In the report of a speech by King Baldwin of Jerusalem intended to inspire his troops, we know that among those who remained were jongleurs.

> Remember the ten-year siege of Troy, call to mind the marvelous deeds of the heroic lords which your jongleurs chant every day and restore your strength and renew your courage from these.[41]

The Second Crusade (1146–1148) was organized at the insistence of Bernard of Clairvaux ('St. Bernard') and was led by Louis VII of France and Conrad of Germany. The Western troops were virtually annihilated en route leaving Louis and Conrad to arrive in Jeru-

[39] Henry G. Farmer, 'Crusading Martial Music,' *Music & Letters* 30, no. 3 (July 1949): 244.

[40] Ordericus Vitalis, *The Ecclesiastical History of England*, IX, x, trans. Thomas Forester (London: Henry G. Bohn, 1854), III, 141.

[41] Ordericus Vitalis, *The Ecclesiastical History of England*, bk. XI, trans. Marjorie Chibnall (Oxford: Clarendon Press, 1978), VI, 121.

salem without little more than the numerous ladies who had also joined the adventure. Europe was shocked by the total failure of this Crusade, Bernard was widely criticized for his role and Christians wondered how God had permitted so complete a defeat.

The Third Crusade (1189–1192) followed a period of relative peace between Christians and Saracens in the Holy Land which was primarily upset by Reginald of Châtillon who threatened to destroy Mecca. The result of Reginald's adventure was the fall of the Holy City again to the 'infidels.' Ambrose, a jongleur in the Service of Richard I of the Lion Heart writing in 1196, relates that this news was such that the common people of Western Europe were very disheartened, 'forgotten were the dances, the singing of songs [lays] and of ballads, sweet converse, and every earthly joy' until they took the cross on another crusade.[42]

As the respective leaders were the famous Saladin, a man of superior character, and the legendary Richard I of the Lion Heart,[43] this Crusade became the most romantic and best-known. Richard's jongleur, Ambrose, records the king's reception when he arrived in Acre in 1191.

> Great was the joyance ... Nor do I think that ever was any mother's son hath seen or could describe so great a rejoicing as was made in the host over the king. There was heard the sound of timbrels, of trumpets, of horns and pipes and flutes. Then might ye see joy unrestrained, of folk of divers sort—the singing of goodly songs and lays, cupbearers bearing wine through the streets in goodly cups, both to the great folk and to the lowly.[44]

Another chronicle also contains an interesting description of Richard's arrival at Acre. The reference to 'soothing symphonies heard like blended voices' suggests that instrumental jongleurs also traveled with Richard.

> The people testified their joy by shouts of welcome and the clang of trumpets; the day was kept as a jubilee, and universal gladness reigned around, on account of the arrival of the king, long wished for by all nations ... No pen can sufficiently describe the joy of the people on the king's arrival, nor tongue detail it; the very calmness of the night was thought to smile upon them with a purer air; the trumpets clanged, horns sounded, and the shrill intonations of the pipe, and the deeper notes of the timbrel and harp, struck upon the ear; and soothing symphonies were heard like various voices blended

---

42 'L'Estoire de la Guerre Sainte' (1196), quoted in Stone, *Three Old French Chronicles of the Crusades*, 11.

43 Geoffrey de Vinsauf, in 'Itinerary of Richard I to the Holy Land,' quoted in *Chronicles of the Crusades* (London: G. Bell and Sons, 1914), 155, a contemporary, describes Richard:

He was tall of stature, graceful in figure; his hair between red and auburn; his limbs were straight and flexible; his arms rather long, and not to be matched for wielding the sword or for striking with it; and his long legs suited the rest of his frame; while his appearance was commanding, and his manners and habits suitable; and he gained the greatest celebrity, not more from his high birth than from the virtues that adorned him.

44 Ibid., 41.

in one; and there was not a man who did not, after his own fashion, indulge in joy and praise; either singing popular ballads to testify the gladness of his heart, or reciting the deeds of the ancients.[45]

From the writings of scribes who accompanied Richard I on this Crusade we know that his army musical instruments consisted primarily of primitive trumpet-types. Indeed Richard himself is quoted as saying, upon his arrival at Messina, 'at the third day, at the sound of the buccina, let them follow me.'[46] A few days later a scribe mentions another trumpet-type.

> In front came the terrible dragon standard unfurled. Then rode the King. Behind him the clangor of the tuba exited the army.[47]

Another eyewitness describing this same arrival at Messina gives us a much more colorful view of the scene. Of particular interest is the phrase, 'harmoniously blended,' which suggests the possibility of multi-part trumpet music.

> And lo! they beheld the sea in the distance covered with innumerable galleys; and the sound of trumpets and clarions, loud and shrill, strike upon the ear! ... You might behold the sea boiling from the number of oarsmen who plied it, and the ears of the spectators rang with the peals of the instruments commonly called trumpets ... Meanwhile the trumpets blew, and their sounds being harmoniously blended, there arose a kind of discordant concord of notes, whilst the sameness of the sounds being continued, the one followed the other in mutual succession, and the notes which had been lowered were again resounded.[48]

One contemporary chronicle provides a rare glimpse of the use of Richard's trumpets in controlling the movement of his ships. For the purpose of hearing these trumpet signals, the ships sailed in the formation of a pyramid, with three ships in the first row, thirteen in the second, fourteen in the third, twenty in the fourth, thirty in the fifth, forty in the sixth, and sixty in the seventh.

> Between the ships and their ranks there was such care in the spacing of the fleet that from one rank to another the sound of a trumpet could be heard, and from one ship to another [in the same rank] the voice of a man.[49]

[45] Ibid., 200ff.

[46] Richard Devizes, 'The Crusade of Richard Coeur de Lion,' Section 24, in *Chronicles of the Crusades* (London: G. Bell and Sons, 1914), 17.

[47] Ibid., Section 26.

[48] Vinsauf, 'Itinerary of Richard I to the Holy Land,' 164.

[49] John T. Appleby, ed., *The Chronicle of Richard of Devizes* (London: Nelson, 1963), 35.

One of the earliest descriptions of the role of military trumpet signals in the West, an account of the battle of Arsul, in 1191, gives more detail of the use of these trumpets in performing military signals in combat.

> It had been resolved by common consent that the sounding of six trumpets in three different parts of the army should be a signal for a charge, viz. two in front, two in the rear and two in the middle, to distinguish the sounds from those of the Saracens, and to mark the distance of each. If these orders had been attended to, the Turks would have been utterly discomfited; but from the too great haste of the aforesaid knights, the success of the affair was marred.[50]

50 Vinsauf, 'Itinerary of Richard I to the Holy Land,' 238.

In the midst of this Crusade, we have an extraordinary anecdote of a battle of music! While the Western troops were trying to take Jerusalem, some Western leaders apparently became impatient with Richard's hesitation. The jongleur, Ambrose, tells what happened next.

> And Hugo, the Duke of Burgundy, who did much to make the matter worse, with great and exceeding arrogance made a song about the king, and a right villainous song it was—yea, full of villainy; and this song spread throughout the host. What could the king do, save in his turn to make another song concerning them that through envy thus assailed and mocked him?[51]

51 Stone, *Three Old French Chronicles of the Crusades*, 141.

Musically, the most historically significant aspect of the Crusades was the encounter by Western persons of the more sophisticated military bands of the East with much broader types of instruments, most of which rapidly became part of the Western musical scene. Arabic historians identify the instruments of the Saracens at this time as trumpets (*anafir*[52]), horns (*bugat*), shawms (*zumur*), timpani (*kusat*), drums (*tubul*) and cymbals (*kasat*).[53]

52 From which comes the word, 'fanfare.'

53 Farmer, 'Crusading Martial Music,' 243. A contemporary, quoted in ibid., 244, describes the trumpet-types of the Saracens as 'trumpae, tubae, tibiae,' which is the earliest known mention of the cognate form of the trumpet.

An eyewitness describes for us what it must have been like for the Western troops to face their Eastern adversaries with their frightening music.

> They came on with irresistible charge, on horses swifter than eagles, and urged on like lightening to attack our men; and as they advanced, they raised a cloud of dust, so that the sky was darkened. In front came certain of their admirals, as it was their duty, with clarions and trumpets; some had horns, others had pipes and timbrels, gongs,

cymbals, and other instruments, producing a horrible noise and clamor. The earth vibrated from the loud and discordant sounds, so that the crash of thunder could not be heard amidst the tumultuous noise of horns and trumpets. They did this to excite their spirit and courage, for the more violent the clamor became, the more bold were they for the fray.[54]

Another chronicle describes the percussion signals of Saladin's troops as resembling 'the crash in the air caused by thunder and lightning.'[55] Victory and defeat alternated until a three-year peace was signed in 1192.

The Fourth Crusade (1202–1204) is remembered for the involvement of the Venetians, whose investment was repaid in the rape of Constantinople. The incredible loss of art treasures, which a contemporary said represented two-thirds of all the wealth of the world,[56] included the only copies of many plays by Sophocles and Euripides. This reprehensible Crusade led some Europeans to imagine that only the pure of heart would be supported by God in the next attempt. Thus two efforts were attempted by children, resulting in thousands of them being drowned, eaten by wolves, dying of hunger or being sold as slaves.

The pope, Innocent III, called for the Fifth Crusade, which began in 1217 with the goal of attacking through Egypt. The failure of this Crusade was blamed on the young Frederick II, Emperor of Germany and Italy, who did not participate.

Frederick II, however, led the Sixth Crusade in 1228. Frederick, one of the most literate and cultured of early nobles was personally attractive to the Saracens.[57] The peace they organized might have been the basis for a permanent one had it not been for the refusal of then pope Gregory IX to ratify it. Therefore Jerusalem once again fell to Islam.

The Seventh Crusade was organized by Louis IX ('St. Louis') of France in 1248. This Crusade, memorialized by the chronicler, Jean de Joinville, after four years in the Holy Land, basically ran out of health, courage and money.

Joinville describes Louis arriving at the Egyptian port of Damietta to the welcome of 'noisy nacaires and cors sarrazinnois.' He also discusses the Sultan's band, which he calls *Haulequa*, from the Arabic, *Halqa*, 'circle.' This band consisted of 'cors sarrazinnois, tabours and nacaires.'

54 Goeffrey de Vinsauf, *Chronicle of Richard the First's Crusade* [1191] (London, 1914), 234–235.

55 Ibid., 203.

56 Stone, *Three Old French Chronicles of the Crusades*, 226.

57 Frederick spoke nine languages and wrote in seven, wrote a definitive treatise on falconry, studied mathematics and anatomy and founded the University of Naples in 1224.

And with these they made such a noise at the point of day and at nightfall, that those who were near could not hear one another speak; and clearly were they heard throughout the camp.

Nor would the musicians have been rash enough to sound their instruments during the day, save by order of the master of the Halca; whence it happened that if the soldan wished to give an order, he sent for the master of the Halca, and gave the order through him; and then the master caused the soldan's instruments to be sounded, and all the host assembled to hear the order of the sultan.[58]

58 'Joinville's Chronicle of the Crusade of St. Lewis,' in *Memoirs of the Crusades*, trans. Frank Marzials (London: J. M. Dent, 1926), 205ff.

Joinville also mentions the extraordinary impression the sound of the Eastern military bands made on the Western soldiers in battle.

The noise they made with their cymbals and horns was fearful to listen to.[59]

59 Ibid., 172.

Meager efforts by Louis in 1267 and by Edward of England in 1268 represented the final efforts to establish European control of Jerusalem.

We call the twelfth and thirteenth centuries, 'The Glory of the Late Middle Ages.' After so many centuries in which the spirit of man appears so heavily laden under the weight of political strife and Church dogma, civilization seems to burst forth in every direction. The stage was set for the Renaissance, where one finds a virtual explosion of new musical institutions, including permanent civic and private aristocratic ensembles. Church music finally breaks free from the bonds of Pope Gregory and begins to seek to be as interesting, and as genuine, as secular music. The burst of creative activity of this period is further documented in the repertoire of the troubadours, trouvéres, Minnesingers and even in those ever cerebral music theorists, who finally stop talking about mathematics and began to talk about man.

It is through the perspective of the next nine chapters that the reader will see how extraordinary these past two centuries really were.

19 AESTHETICS OF MUSIC IN THE WRITINGS OF THE SCHOLASTIC PHILOSOPHERS OF THE THIRTEENTH CENTURY

THE TWELFTH AND THIRTEENTH CENTURIES saw the conversion of the medieval monastic schools into the first modern universities of Western Europe. This process had its origin in part in a monastic reform movement opposed to the rising secular culture, but also to the climate of intellectual enthusiasm following the relatively recent and wide spread reappearance of the works of the ancient philosophers. The latter, in particular, brought a sense of urgency to reconciling the broad spectrum of natural philosophy with a Church which had been content to rest on Faith. The Liberal Arts, which had long been justified only for their role in preparing the Christian to understand the Scriptures, now received a new impetus. A modern scholar pictures what an exciting period this must have been for the student.

> For the first time in European history students and teachers at Paris and Bologna enjoyed the intoxicating experience of participating in the work of an academic community engaged in solving problems of universal importance, clarifying the principles of the Christian religion, of human behavior, and of correct reasoning, and then of adapting these principles to the organization of society. The students had the stimulus of belonging to a cosmopolitan body of men of varied backgrounds and turbulent instincts, and future importance. The masters had the stimulus of critical pupils and the daily discipline of expounding difficult subjects and solving intricate problems. And they all had the satisfaction of adding to a growing body of important knowledge.[1]

The great university at Bologna was characterized, among other things, by the strong role of the students in its day-to-day administration. Students not only paid the teachers, but hired and fired

1 R. W. Southern, *Robert Grosseteste* (Oxford: Clarendon Press, 1992), 50.

them and allotted their holidays. Students determined when lectures began and ended, their duration and the portions of the texts to be used. One can understand how, for six hundred years, we professors have tried to keep this quiet!

Perhaps related to the student influence in this university, Bologna had a reputation in the thirteenth century for being the only university which was relatively free of Church domination, indeed, there was no theological faculty at all before 1364.[2] It was in this light that a popular joke of the day among students told of a professor from Paris who came to Bologna, where he had to 'unlearn' everything he had learned in Paris and then returned to Paris to 'unteach' it. Perhaps it was the lack of Church interference in Paris which made possible women students there in the thirteenth century and women professors in the following century.

Without question, then or now, the greatest university center of the thirteenth century was Paris. It was truly an international university and it has been suggested that so many German students were in residence that it contributed to the delay in the establishment of universities in Germany.[3]

The curriculum in Paris began with the Liberal Arts,[4] then proceeded to Philosophy and finally to Theology. The professors, clerics usually, were required to speak without notes and were forbidden to read their lectures. It is interesting that as early as the twelfth century one philosopher complained that in Paris some teachers gave easy courses to gain popularity with the students and concluded that permitting the students to choose from a wide variety of teachers and subjects resulted in a lowering of the standard.[5] It is from the question and answer format of these classes, known as *scholastica disputatio*, that we derive the term, Scholastic Philosophy.

The third great university center, Oxford, was based on the Paris model and had by 1209, according to a contemporary, already over three thousand students and teachers.[6]

---

2 Will Durant, *The Age of Faith* (New York: Simon and Schuster, 1950), 918. Durant provides an extensive description of the early universities in Bologna, Paris and Oxford.

3 Ibid., 920.

4 Hence, the students of the Liberal Arts, the undergraduates, so to speak, were called 'art-ists' [*artistae*]. For a discussion of the role of music in the curriculum of the thirteenth-century university, see Nan Cooke Carpenter, *Music in the Medieval and Renaissance Universities* (Norman: University of Oklahoma Press, 1958), 48, 115.

5 Lynn Thorndike, *History of Magic and Experimental Science* (New York: Macmillan, 1929), II, 53.

6 H. Rashdall, *The Universities of Europe in the Middle Ages* (Oxford: Clarendon Press, 1936), III, 29fn.

ON MUSIC AND THE LIBERAL ARTS

We are surprised to find very little discussion of music by the major Scholastic Philosophers of the thirteenth century, especially since we know it was part of the curriculum at the University of Paris.[7] Maybe we should refer to the problem as paradoxical, for this was an atmosphere in which the Liberal Arts were given new impetus and music itself, in so far as performance, was breaking new ground everywhere, in the towns, in the courts and in the Church, yet none of these philosophers wrote extensively on music. It seems, in retrospect, a perfect moment for a new Boethius. It seems Thomas Aquinas should have addressed himself to music as a separate topic, as did Augustine.

It almost seems, judging by the coverage it received, that music had disappeared from the list of the seven Liberal Arts. Perhaps, in the perspective of these philosophers, that is what happened. While they continue to refer to music as one of the Liberal Arts, perhaps hearing music all around them, and especially the wonderful art music of the troubadours and Minnesingers, they had come to realize that music was somehow no longer a 'science' in the way the other disciplines of the Liberal Arts were. We wonder if perhaps this is the point made in an allegorical poem, 'The Battle of the Seven Arts' (*La Bataille des. VII Ars*), composed in about 1236 by a trouvère named Henri d'Andeli. In this work he describes a battle between Grammar and Logic. Music is present here, but stands apart and is not a participant in the 'battle.'

> Madam Music, she of the little bells
> And her clerks full of songs
> Carried fiddles and viols,
> Psalteries and small flutes;
> From the sound of the first fa
> The ascended to cc sol fa.
> The sweet tones diatessaron
> Diapente, diapason,
> Are struck in various combinations.
> In groups of four and three
> Through the army they went singing,
> They go enchanting them with their song.
> These do not engage in battle.[8]

[7] Carpenter, *Music in the Medieval and Renaissance Universities*, 48, 115.

[8] Quoted in Carpenter, *Music in the Medieval and Renaissance Universities*, 71.

There was another characteristic which distinguished Music from the other six Liberal Arts—music,[9] alone, could not be *seen*. We would therefore venture to suggest the following possibility. These philosophers, in their enthusiasm to write commentaries on the newly available works of Aristotle and the other ancient Greek philosophers, and subsequently to reconcile these ideas to those of the Church, were drawn immediately to the subjects of Reason, the Intellect, Understanding, and Metaphysics. These subjects are all of the left-hemisphere domain, a world of writing and language, a world dependent on the eye. Perhaps it should be no surprise that several writers state that the eye is the most important of the senses. And music, of course, has very little to do with either the eye or Reason.

The one philosopher of the thirteenth century whom we might have expected to write extensively about music was Robert Grosseteste (d. 1253).[10] A contemporary, Matthew Paris, tells us Grosseteste was well-grounded in the Quadrivium, which included music.

> Grosseteste was born from the very humblest stock, a man of refined learning in both trivium and quadrivium, unconventional in his manner of life, following his own will and relying on his own judgment.[11]

It has always been assumed that he was a great lover of music, perhaps an inaccurate generalization based on some early poetry. In the following, we are told that he listened to music day and night because it gave him solace and sharpened his mind. When asked why he took such delight in music, he answered that the virtue in music protected one against the devil and that good skill in harp playing was closely associated with the Church.

> Y shall you tell as I have herd
> Of the bysshop seynt Roberd;
> His toname is Grosteste,
> Of Lyncolne, so seyth the geste.
> He lovede moche to here the harpe,
> For mans witte it makyth sharpe;
> Next hys chamber, besyde his study,
> Hys harpers chamber was fast the by.
> Many tymes, by nightes and dayes,
> He hadd solace of notes and layes.
> One askede hem the resun why
> He hadde delyte in mynstrelsy:
> He answered hym on thys manere

---

9   For reasons given in volume 1 of this series, when we use the term Music we always mean the *performance* of Music, not the notated representative of it.

10   Traditional beliefs that he was a Master of Arts of Oxford and a scholar in the Parisian scholastic model are without real evidence. He is perhaps best thought of as an original, and brilliant, thinker associated with a provincial administrative position in Lincoln.

11   Quoted in R. W. Southern, *Robert Grosseteste* (Oxford: Clarendon, 1992), 11. Paris, as quoted in ibid., 10, adds another dimension of Grosseteste's reputation.

Let no one be disturbed by the violent acts which he did in his life-time … his treatment of his canons whom he excommunicated and harassed, his savage attacks on monks, and even more savage against nuns … They arose from zeal.

Why he helde the harpe so dere:
'The virtu of the harpe, thurgh style and ryght
Wyll destrye the fendys myght;
And to the cros by gode skeyl
Ys the harpe lykened weyl.'[12]

But there is no great new philosophical treatise on music by Grosseteste. In his treatise, 'De artibus liberalibus,' he places music at the head of the Quadrivium, but there is nothing new here, only the old discussions about the mathematical basis of music, reference to the 'Music of the Spheres,' and so on.[13] His few remarks about music reveal an interest more in the practical, such as the use of music in healing, which we will return to below.

It was clearly his interest in music which prompted him to attempt to explain the physics of sound production and the nature of hearing. His explanation was all bound up in numbers and the soul, namely that a sound is understood as a number in the ear, which is then compared to numbers stored in the soul-memory, whereupon it is judged harmonious or dissonant. Music, then, was not just a matter of hearing musical tones, but involved a broad range of faculties dealing with numbers, memory and finally Reason.[14]

The one scholar who did contribute original thought on music at this time was another Englishman, Roger Bacon (b. ca. 1214). Bacon studied at Oxford[15] and at the University of Paris, where he received a doctorate in theology and then joined the Franciscan Order in about 1247. Unlike the gentle patron of his order, St. Francis, Bacon was very outspoken and many who read or heard him must have felt somewhat insulted. Youth, he says, has no interest in the perfection demanded by science, indeed they take pleasure in their imperfection, and older people, 'with the greatest difficulty climb to perfection in anything.'[16] He was even more outspoken in his disrespect for the masses, the 'unenlightened throng,' the 'ignorant multitude,' whom he says can never rise to the perfection of wisdom. For this reason, he maintains, the wise have always been an elite segment of society, separated from the masses. He found this true in religion ('as with Moses so with Christ the common throng does not ascend the mountain') and well as in the universities.

We see that such is the case among the professors of philosophy as well as in the truth of our faith. For the wise have always been divided from the multitude, and they have veiled the secrets of wisdom not

12 William de Wadington, *Manuel des Péchés*, trans. Robert Mannyng, quoted in James McEvoy, *The Philosophy of Robert Grosseteste* (Oxford: Clarendon, 1982), 43.

13 Some Latin text is quoted in Carpenter, *Music in the Medieval and Renaissance Universities*, 82.

14 McEvoy, *The Philosophy of Robert Grosseteste*, 258.

15 Bacon is often cited as a student of Grosseteste, but as McEvoy, *The Philosophy of Robert Grosseteste*, 14, points out, there is no foundation for this belief.

16 Opus Majus, 'Causes of Error,' III, in *The Opus Majus of Roger Bacon*, trans. Robert Burke (New York: Russell & Russell, 1962), 9ff.

only from the world at large but also from the rank and file of those devoting themselves to philosophy.[17]

He cites a book by A. Gellius in which the author maintained that the great Greek philosophers had discussions among themselves at night, so as to 'avoid the multitude.'

> In this book he says that it is foolish to feed an ass lettuces when thistles suffice him. He is speaking of the multitude for whom rude, cheap, imperfect food of science is sufficient. Nor ought we to cast pearls before swine.

He was also outspoken about false teaching in the schools and other forms of vice and corruption. One can suppose he did not make many friends and, in fact, he was brought to trial in 1278, condemned and thrown into prison for fourteen years.

But, from our perspective today, he reads much more objectively than most philosophers of his day. We admire him for being honest enough to point out that the famous philosophers were sometimes wrong[18] and that none of us can have perfect knowledge, for what we know is far less than what we don't know.[19] And we believe he was right on the mark when he observed that the greatest barriers to truth are the 'submission to faulty and unworthy authority, influence of custom [and] popular prejudice.'[20]

In his discussion of the Liberal Arts, Bacon first comments that while the ancients knew of the various sciences, they only actually used two: astronomy for the calendar, and music for worship.[21] Mathematics, he calls the 'gate and key' for the other Liberal Arts[22] and he specifically recommends that the study of mathematics should come before the study of music.

> The natural road for us is to begin with things which befit the state and nature of childhood, because children begin with facts that are better known by us and that must be acquired first. But of this nature is mathematics, since children are first taught to sing, and in the same way they can learn the method of making figures and of counting, and it would be far easier and more necessary for them to know about numbers before singing, because in the relations of numbers in music the whole theory of numbers is set forth by example, just as the authors on music teach, both in ecclesiastical music and in philosophy.[23]

---

17 This discussion is found in ibid., 'Causes of Error,' IV.

18 Ibid., 'Causes of Error, VII.
19 Ibid., X.

20 Ibid., I.

21 Ibid., XIV.
22 Ibid., 'Mathematics,' I.

23 Ibid., III. See also XVI for more on the relationship of music to both mathematics and theology.

Sounding very much like those today who attempt to defend music in the schools by suggesting, 'Music helps Reading,' or 'Music helps Math,' Bacon gives a strong endorsement for the importance of music in fully understanding another of the Liberal Arts, Grammar. We find of particular interest his interest in the grammar of both speech and music, something which might reflect the ancient period when music existed before speech.

> Now the accidental parts of philosophy are grammar and logic. Alpharabius makes it clear in his book on the sciences that grammar and logic cannot be known without mathematics. For although grammar furnishes children with the facts relating to speech and its properties in prose, meter, and rhythm, nevertheless it does so in a puerile way by means of statement and not through causes or reasons. For it is the function of another science to give the reasons for these things, namely, of that science, which must consider fully the nature of tones, and this alone is music, of which there are numerous varieties and parts. For one deals with prose, a second with meter, a third with rhythm, and a fourth with music in singing. And besides these it has more parts. The part dealing with prose teaches the reasons for all elevations of the voice in prose, as regards differences of accents and as regards colons, commas, periods, and the like. The metrical part teaches all the reasons and causes for feet and meters. The part on rhythm teaches about every modulation and sweet relation in rhythms, because all those are certain kinds of singing, although not so treated as in ordinary singing ... Therefore grammar depends causatively on music.
>
> In the same way logic ... Alpharabius especially teaches this in regard to the poetic argument, the statements of which should be sublime and beautiful, and therefore accompanied with notable adornment in prose, meter, and rhythm ... And therefore the end of logic depends upon music.[24]

In his discussion of music, as one of the Liberal Arts, Bacon contributes the most precise and interesting definition offered by any philosopher of the thirteenth century. He begins by dividing the world of music into two broad categories, 'one part of music deals with what is audible, the other with what is visible.'[25]

Audible music he recognizes as being of two divisions, vocal music and instrumental music. In vocal music, in turn, Bacon finds four subdivisions.

24 Ibid., II.

25 Ibid., XVI, in Burke, *The Opus Majus of Roger Bacon*, I, 259, for this entire discussion.

For one part concerns melody, as in singing; the second concerns meters, and considers the nature and properties of all songs, meters, and feet; the third concerns rhythm, and considers every variety of relations in rhythms; the fourth concerns prose and considers accents and other aforesaid things in prose discourse. For accent is a kind of singing; whence it is called accent from *accino, accinis* [I sing, thou singest], because every syllable has its own proper sound either raised, lowered, or composite, and all syllables of one word are adapted or sung to one syllable on which rests the principal sound. Thus length and shortness and all other things required in correct pronunciation are reduced to music.

This is a very interesting discussion for several reasons. First, these thoughts come at the end of two thousand years, at least, during which poetry was sung. When Bacon says 'every syllable has its own proper sound either raised, lowered, or composite,' we wonder if there was a commonly recognized, but now lost, tradition in the performance of sung poetry. Did the text, perhaps, 'compose' the music? We also find fascinating his statement, 'For accent is a kind of singing.' This comment, seven hundred years before our age, reminds us that among ancient peoples singing preceded language. Can we not see a trace here of that distant period when pitch fluctuation preceded, and perhaps turned into, the sounds we call consonants?

Bacon is not so expansive on instrumental music, noting only that the subject deals with 'the structure of the instruments and their use.' He also adds that the theologian must also know the 'numberless mystical meanings' of the instruments. We wish he had elaborated more, for he has made it clear in previous passages that he takes the Old Testament references to instruments literally, and not metaphorically as did many earlier medieval Church philosophers.

It is Bacon's recognition of a category of music which he calls 'visual music' which is of great significance. The ancient Greek philosophers never discussed this topic at length, but there are sufficient hints in their descriptions of choral performance to suggest that the inevitable movements by the singers were thought of not as a kind of dance, but as the part of music you could see. One must remember that the Greeks placed considerable significance in the fact that one cannot *see* music and it was for this reason that music was so closely associated with religion (whose principal mysteries also cannot be seen). The significance of Bacon's discussion is that it is the first which supplies important insights into this ancient association of music and movement.

> Music, moreover, consisting in what is visible, is necessary; and that it is such is evident from the book on the Origin of the Sciences. For whatever can be conformed to sound in similar movements and in corresponding formations, so that our delight may be made complete not only by hearing, but by seeing, belongs to music. Therefore dances and all bendings of bodies are reduced to gesture, which is a branch of music, since these are conformed to sound in similar movements and corresponding formations, as the author of the aforesaid book maintains. Therefore Aristotle says in the seventh book of the Metaphysics that the art of dancing is not complete without another art, that is, without another kind of music to which the art of dancing is conformed.

Bacon mentions the Old Testament reference to the dancing by the sister of Moses and recommends that theologians need to study this aspect of music (dance) in order that in preaching on these passages they might,

> know how to express all their properties, so that they may give utterance to all the spiritual senses of an angelic devotion.

In the end, however, Bacon returns to the old Church position that the Liberal Arts have their real value in bringing one to know God.

> I say, therefore, that one science is the mistress of the others, namely, theology, to which the remaining sciences are vitally necessary, and without which it cannot reach its end.[26]

26 Ibid., 'Philosophy,' I.

He adds that whatever cannot be connected with the Gospel is therefore against it and should be shunned by the Christian.

ON THE PHYSIOLOGY OF AESTHETICS

As we have mentioned, the great challenge for the Western European philosophers, after the reintroduction of the works of Aristotle and other ancient thinkers, was to reconcile these works with the teachings of a Church based on Faith. No where is this struggle more evident than in the attempt to explain the relationship and function of the senses and Reason. Because the lower animals also have senses, their distinction with man had to lie in the application of sensory information to higher intellectual use. It was here that these philosophers found God and thereby attempted to make a connection between the 'pagan' philosophy of Aristotle and the Church.

An early twelfth-century writer known as Theophilus, in a famous book, *De Diversis Artibus*, contended that it was Reason which distinguished man from the lower animals and made him capable of understanding the wisdom of God. However, man lost the latter because of his original sin. What he retained was a kind of potential, which Theophilus describes as almost a genetic ability.

> In the account of the creation of the world, we read that man was created in the image and likeness of God and was animated by the Divine breath, breathed into him. By the eminence of such distinction, he was placed above the other living creatures, so that, capable of reason, he acquired participation in the wisdom and skill of the Divine Intelligence, and, endowed with free will, was subject only to the will of his Creator, and revered His sovereignty. Wretchedly deceived by the guile of the Devil, through the sin of disobedience he lost the privilege of immortality, but, however, so far transmitted to later posterity the distinction of wisdom and intelligence, that whoever will contribute both care and concern is able to attain a capacity for all arts and skills, as if by hereditary right.[27]

27 Theophilus, *The Various Arts*, trans. C.R. Dodwell (London: Nelson, 1961), 1.

Grosseteste seems to have been familiar with this argument that original man had greater powers of immediate understanding, which were lost through the Church's concept of original sin. For him, post-original sin man was then left with only the senses which he shares with lower animals upon which he had to rebuild his powers of understanding. At the same time Grosseteste argued that a kind of residual divine knowledge, the potential powers of knowledge of original man, remained, available to those who reached the highest levels of illumination through God and the Church. This kind of understanding did not derive from the senses at all.

> I say that it is possible to have some knowledge without the help of the senses, for in the divine mind all knowledge, not only of universals but also of all particulars, exists eternally ... and intelligences which have received illumination from that source of light see all knowable things, both universal and particular ... and this would be the case with all human beings, if they were not weighed down under the load of the corrupt body.[28]

As to the relationship between the senses and Reason in the normal man, Grosseteste constructs a three-part process. Grosseteste first concentrates not on how we perceive sense images, but on how they travel to us. Thus sight is the highest sense, as its images travel to us by light. Images of hearing arrive not by light, but by a heavier element, air. When an object produces a sound, fine airy elements in the object vibrate and travel to us. Smell is a still lower sense, as now the air is weighed down with vapors, etc.[29]

These sense images, according to Grosseteste, are collected in a kind of temporary staging area, called *imaginatio*, where they are processed by and through some internal sense-related faculties (one being *virtus intellectiva*, a kind of bank of common sense known to all men) before they are ultimately placed at the disposal of Reason. We have greatly simplified an extensive and complex hypothesis by Grosseteste—fortunately God was not so complicated.

The philosopher who came the nearest to deciphering how the brain really works was Roger Bacon. Because he suffered from the lack of modern medical discoveries of brain function, as did all early philosophers, he therefore repeats some nonsense—as for example quoting Aristotle's notion older persons have poor memory because of excessive dryness of their organs, while the young have poor memories because their organs are too moist.[30] Bacon also tends to simply quote others in places where he has no original explanation, but there are nevertheless some moments where he arrives intuitively at truths which had occurred to none of his contemporaries. For this reason one philosopher considers his major work, the *Opus maius*, 'greater than any other in all the literature of this amazing century.'[31]

Like Grosseteste, Bacon begins by ranking the senses in order of their importance, with sight being the highest.

---

28 Quoted in Southern, *Robert Grosseteste*, 165.

29 See McEvoy, *The Philosophy of Robert Grossteste*, 295ff for a more extensive discussion.

30 'De Multiplicatione Specierum,' trans. David Lindberg, in *Roger Bacon's Philosophy of Nature* (Oxford: Clarendon, 1983), 195.

31 Durant, *The Age of Faith*, 1015.

Our experience of things here in the earth we owe to vision, because a blind man can have no experience worthy of the name concerning this world. Hearing causes us to believe because we believe our teachers, but we cannot try out what we learn except through vision. If, moreover, we should adduce taste and touch and smell, we assume a knowledge belong to beasts. For brutes are busied with the things pertaining to taste and touch, and exercise their sense of smell because of taste and touch, but the things are of little value, few in number, and common to us and to brutes concerning which these senses give verification, and therefore they do not rise to the rank of human wisdom.[32]

[32] 'Optical Science,' I, in *Opus Majus*, II, 419.

Bacon understood the images from the senses to be collected in the 'middle cell' of the brain in a storehouse which, like Grosseteste, he calls imagination. Here the sense images are subjected to 'common sense,' which makes judgment on them. This is what gives meaning to the images of the senses, for,

> vision does not perceive that it sees, nor hearing that it hears, but another faculty does, namely, the common sense.[33]

[33] Ibid., 422.

The name he gives to this action conducted in the imagination storehouse is 'cogitation.' This 'cogitative faculty' also works in the opposite direction, using 'all the other faculties as instruments.'[34] This, Bacon says, is the source for Art in humans as well as in animals (the geometrical web of the spider and the hexagonal house of the bee).

[34] Ibid., 426.

Bacon's most important insight was coming to understand intuitively that man has more than one mode of knowing. Whereas all earlier philosophers associated knowing only with Reason, Bacon perceived that there was a form of knowing which was not assembled in the faculty called Reason, but rather was gained through *experience*. Although he recognized that the brain 'has a right and left,'[35] he did not guess that one side dwelt with Reason and the other experience, as we know today. If he did not understand the cerebral geography, he was nevertheless the first to arrive at an understanding of these two separate kinds of knowing.

[35] 'Optical Science,' V, in *Opus Majus*, II, 431.

> For there are two modes of acquiring knowledge, namely, by reasoning and experience. Reasoning draws a conclusion and makes us grant the conclusion, but does not make the conclusion certain, or

does it remove doubt so that the mind may rest on the intuition of truth, unless the mind discovers it by the path of experience.[36]

To these two kinds of knowledge, what we learn from others and what we learn ourselves by experience, Bacon adds a third, 'common sense.' Common sense is that knowledge known in an obvious way to everyone, as in the example he gives that the whole is always greater than the part.[37]

The late thirteenth-century English philosopher, John Duns Scotus,[38] retreated to an older view. Unlike Bacon, who recognizes other faculties as being as important as Reason, Duns Scotus returns to the traditional view that Reason stands supreme above all other faculties. And like earlier philosophers, his principal basis for his belief was the notion that while senses can perceive only specific single information, Reason understands universals.

> One could say that the common distinction made between intellective and sensitive knowledge, namely, that we understand the universal, but we sense the singular, must not be understood as referring to disparate but equal powers such as obtain between sight in seeing colors and hearing in perceiving sounds. Rather the distinction is one between a higher cognitive faculty and one subordinate to it, and hence the superior power can know some object or aspect thereof that the inferior cannot know, but not vice versa.[39]

Part of his distrust in the senses was that they were clearly capable of error, a fact which earlier philosophers had also frequently mentioned. Duns Scotus goes on to point out that Reason knows that the senses are in error and this in itself proves the superiority of Reason.

> But if the judgment of different senses differs in regard to what is seen outside; for instance ... if sight says, as it invariably does, that the sun is smaller in size than it really is, or in general, that everything seen from a distance is smaller than it is in reality, in all such instances we are still certain of what is true and know which sense is in error. This we know by reason of some proposition in the soul more certain than any sense judgment together with the concurrent testimony of several of the senses.[40]

Duns Scotus does recognize the contribution of the senses to the intellect, indeed it is interesting that he refers to this contribution as a 'metaphorical 'transformation,'[41] which is nearly how one might

36 Ibid., 'Experimental Science,' I.

37 Ibid., 'Moral Philosophy,' XXI.

38 Few details of this great thinker's life can be established. We know his ordination as a priest occurred in 1291 and he is found at Oxford in 1300.

39 John Duns Scotus, *God and Creatures*, trans. Felix Alluntis and Allan Wolter (Princeton: Princeton University Press, 1975), 291.

40 John Duns Scotus, 'Concerning Human Knowledge,' trans. Allan Wolter, in *Philosophical Writings of John Duns Scotus* (Indianapolis: Bobbs-Merrill, 1962), 122.

41 *God and Creatures*, 358.

describe what happens through the corpus callosum. In the end, though, it is the intellect which he says defines the man.

> I take 'to know' or 'to understand' in the proper sense of the term as an act of knowledge which transcends every type of sense knowledge.[42]

Indeed, he says, 'the intellective soul is the proper form of man.'[43]

Perhaps the most interesting aspects of Duns Scotus' discussion of the intellect are some special qualities which other philosophers had not proposed. For example, he says that the intellect takes information from the senses, but then has the ability to continue on its own, building more complex propositions without further regard to the senses.[44] Even more interesting is his argument for multiple 'intellections,' which sounds not too distant from modern theories of 'many minds.'

> For every single perfect and distinct intellection existing in the intellect, there can be many indistinct and imperfect intellections existing there. This is evident from the example of vision, the field of which extends as a conical pyramid at the lower base of which one point is seen distinctly, and yet within that same base many things are seen imperfectly and indistinctly; but of these several visions, only one is perfect, namely, that upon which the axis of the pyramid falls. If this is possible in one of the senses, all the more so is it possible in the intellect.[45]

[42] 'Spirituality and Immortality of the Soul,' in *Philosophical Writings*, 148.

[43] Ibid.

[44] 'Concerning Human Knowledge,' 116ff.

[45] *Will and Morality*, trans. Allan Wolter (Washington, DC: The Catholic University of America Press, 1986), 173.

ON THE PSYCHOLOGY OF AESTHETICS

On Pleasure and Pain

Roger Bacon's view of Pleasure is curiously old-fashioned. He reverts to the old Church view that all Pleasure is inevitably associated with some form of sin.

> For the mind grows feeble in the midst of riches and pleasures while it delights itself in these sins. For as regards avarice, pride, luxury, and gluttony it is evident that they are aroused by a strong desire for enjoyment. Envy also springs from the good and the prosperity of another. Sloth, however, owes its being to the fact that the mind is absorbed in pleasures and in the other interests incident to prosperity. For in

such circumstances a man loses interest in the true good which consists in virtue, and finds every virtuous effort disagreeable.[46]

[46] Bacon, 'Moral Philosophy,' in *Opus Majus*, II, 675.

We have mentioned Duns Scotus' thesis that the intellect contains many intellections, a thought which bears some resemblance to modern theories in psychology of 'many minds.' One of these, he says, enables intellection to take pleasure in intellection itself.[47]

[47] *Will and Morality*, 173.

Most of Duns Scotus' reflections on Pleasure, however, are found in his discussion of the Will. He begins with the question, 'Must happiness be desired above everything, and is it the rationale behind all willing?'[48] As he begins to consider this question, he first notes that when it comes to happiness the Will first seeks the 'highest measure' of a particular form of happiness. But then next he presents a definition which we find very interesting. Duns Scotus now contends that the Will, in seeking the highest measure of a form of pleasure, as a matter of course is directed toward a *particular* form of pleasure. Thus, 'real perfection is not something general or universal, but something singular.'[49] What we find of interest is the fact, as we have seen, that many early philosophers conclude that the intellect, or Reason, is the highest form of 'knowing,' because the intellect can know universals while the senses can know only singulars. Happiness, he says, is the other way around.

[48] Ibid., 183.

[49] Ibid., 187.

His answer to his original question is that he finds the Will desires happiness and that in so doing it follows an innate appetite.

The reason why the will wants happiness in most cases, is that the will for the most part follow the inclination of its natural appetite.[50]

[50] Ibid., 189, 191.

His final observation is that Pleasure should be an end. He adds a warning, following Augustine, that we must not 'use as means what is to be enjoyed as an end, and treat as an end what is to be used as a means.'[51]

[51] Ibid., 473. Augustine's reference is found in 'Question 30,' of *Eighty-three Different Questions*.

On the Emotions

The thirteenth-century philosophers speak very little of the emotions. Albertus Magnus (b. 1193)[52] only comments that the distinction between man and the animals is that man, through Reason, has 'the unique ability to control his emotions along the path of virtue and tether the drives of his senses.'[53]

[52] Albert studied at Padua and taught at a number of German Church schools and after about 1245 in Paris. He became Bishop of Ratisbon in 1260.

[53] *De Animalibus*, trans. James Scanlan (Binghamton, NY: Medieval & Renaissance Texts, 1987), 66.

Bacon's only reference to the emotions is with regard to speech, but it is nevertheless interesting as an example of how the emotions can affect the person. He quotes a passage from Seneca in which the inference is that emotion is a form of madness.

> The mind unless stirred cannot utter anything sublime, surpassing the speech of others. It is only when it has spurned all that is common and ordinary and has mounted aloft with divine inspiration that it has uttered something too sublime for human lips. The mind cannot reach the realms of the sublime while it remains sane. It must leave the beaten track, dash forth, take the bit in the teeth, and carry the rider where he would have feared to mount himself.[54]

A mid-thirteenth century contemporary of Bacon, a man known as Bartholomew Anglicus, also comments on emotions with regard to speech. His discussion is interesting primarily because he contends that the proper emotion can 'change the affection of the listener.' In demonstrating the importance of this potential, he contrasts two basic examples.

> A discording voice and an inordinate troubleth the accord of many voices. But according voices sweet and ordinate, gladden and move to love, and show out the passions of the soul, and witness the strength and virtue of the spiritual members, and show pureness and good disposition of them, and relieve travail, and put off disease and sorrow ...
>
> Now it is known by these foresaid things, how profitable is a merry voice and sweet. And contrariwise is of an inordinate voice and horrible, that gladdeth not, nother comforteth; but is noyful and discomforteth and grieveth the ears and the wit.[55]

Duns Scotus' only major reference to emotions in general is one which is again associated with his view on the Will. His contention is that the concept of *deciding* to engage in some 'passion' is in itself synonymous with the Will of the intellect, since the senses have no rational decision capabilities.

> If one understands 'passion' to be something one should avoid if immoderate or should indulge in if moderate, it seems sufficiently clear that as regards such future action it is the will rather than the sense appetite that can do what is right, because the source of the will's knowledge is not the senses but reason, whose role it is to counsel one about future things.[56]

54 Bacon, 'Moral Philosophy,' in *Opus Majus*, II, 786. The Seneca passage is found in *De Tranquillitate Animi*, XVII.

55 Quoted in *Medieval Lore*, trans. Robert Steele (London: Stock, 1893), 64.

56 Duns Scotus, *Will and Morality*, 331.

ON AESTHETICS

Grosseteste recognized a simple, sensuous delight in the objects of the senses, but this alone he did not classify as being aesthetic. The aesthetic experience, for him, was in the combining of this sensual delight with the inner understanding, or vision (*oculus interior*), which recognizes formal and geometrical principles, which in themselves he regarded as having natural beauty.[57]

Roger Bacon's definition of Art is preceded by paraphrasing Aristotle's discussion on Ethics, in particular twelve moral virtues (fortitude, chastity, liberality, munificence, etc.) which result from Reason controlling the senses. Beyond these, according to Bacon, are five virtues belonging to 'pure reason,' which do not depend on the senses.[58] These he identifies as intellect, knowledge, art, prudence, and wisdom. These, in turn, may exist in a speculative form, 'when they are directed to truth alone,' or in a more active form, as when they are directed toward an object of good works. It is from all of this that Bacon arrives at his definition of Art.

> Art is the knowledge of good works in their outcome, and prudence is the acquired mental condition directing such works.[59]

Duns Scotus is similarly interested in the distinction between theoretical and practical knowledge, the former remaining in the mind and the latter being that knowledge carried into practice.[60]

His definition of Beauty is the older Liberal Arts, mathematics oriented one in which the emphasis is on proportion and harmony of the parts.

> Beauty is not some absolute quality in a beautiful body, but a combination of all that is in harmony with such a body (such as size, figure, and color), and a combination of all aspects that pertain to all that is agreeable to such a body and are in harmony with one another.[61]

The earliest Church fathers had had a certain suspicion that Art was too related to mere amusement and hence represented a temptation leading to more serious sins. Duns Scotus' final word on aesthetics makes the same point with regard visual art: delight in what we see can easily lead to the sin of covetousness.

[57] McEvoy, *The Philosophy of Robert Grossteste*, 204.

[58] *Opus Majus*, 'Moral Philosophy,' II.

[59] Ibid.

[60] *Will and Morality*, 127.

[61] Ibid., 207.

> The first sin of the visual appetite would be coveting a vision of what is most beautiful to the eye (which would most perfectly delight and satisfy it), to a will joined to a sense appetite, but unchecked by right reason or justice.⁶²

62 Ibid., 467.

ON AESTHETICS IN MUSIC

As we have seen, the scholastic philosophers do not devote many pages to the emotions, pleasure, or aesthetics in general and so it will be no surprise that there is no extended discussion of aesthetics in music. From our perspective this may seem a curious omission, given the fact that music was still a part of the Liberal Arts in the University of Paris. The answer probably lies in the fact that with the reappearance of the works of the ancient Greek philosophers, and the voluminous commentaries on that literature by the Arab philosophers, these philosophers probably found that the weighty subjects of Metaphysics, Philosophy and the emerging enlightenments in science were subject matter enough for one lifetime.

For Grosseteste, in spite of the love of music attributed to him in his personal life by his contemporaries, we find in his philosophical writings primarily an interest in music therapy. Perhaps, for him, it was the highest purpose of music that it could be employed for healing. As this worked by 'ordering and tempering the spirits,' even the deaf might be treated by music. McEvoy summarizes Grosseteste's explanation of this process.

> The soul follows the body in the latter's affections, and the body follows the soul's actions. When, therefore, the body is affected by sounding numbers, the soul draws out of itself numbers which are of the same proportion, and the spirits adjust the proportions of the numbers to agreement. The wise doctor must therefore have a knowledge of the due proportion of the body as impressed on it by the stars, and must be acquainted with the proportions which induce concord among the elements and the humid parts of the principal spirits, and between the soul and the body. When these proportions are expressed in terms of musical sound, upon the numbers' reaching the soul everything in man returns to a proportioned state. The doctor must also have studied the behavior of the spirits prevailing in different emotional states, such as in joy, when they dilate, and sad-

ness, when they contract; for the states of the soul too can be affected by the knowledgeable employment of musical sound.[63]

Roger Bacon's references to the purpose of music are all in the context of the Church. He cites the use of music for prophesy in the Old Testament citing the example of Elijah who requested that a string instrument be brought to him,

> in order that his soul, stirred by the delight of physical harmony, might be caught up to contemplate divine things.[64]

In his treatise on 'Mathematics,' Bacon adds an educational facet to the purpose of music, in a passage in which he maintains that the theologian must have training in music in order to understand the Scriptures.[65] The first reason, of course, is simply to be able to fully understand the many references to music in the Old Testament.

> According to the judgment of the sacred writers matters pertaining to music are necessary to theology in many ways. For although it is not necessary for an understanding of Scripture that the theologian should have a practical knowledge of singing and of instruments and of other musical things, yet he should know the theory of them, in order to grasp the natures and properties of these things and of the writings on this subject in accordance with their teachings of music theoretical and practical. For Scripture is full of musical terms like rejoice, shout for joy, sing, play upon the cithara, cymbals, and the like of different kinds.

The second reason Bacon gives is relative to the many kinds of meters found in the old Hebrew text. Here he notes that while the grammarian may teach the practical rules, only music gives 'the reasons and theories' for these meters. In the same manner, he points to the issue of pronunciation, as the Scripture is filled with 'accents, longs, shorts, colons, commas, and period.'

> All these belong causally to music, because of all these matters the musician states the reason, but the grammarian merely the fact.

This emphasis by Bacon that the theologian must have some training in instrumental music, for the practical conduct of his work, does not, however, necessarily suggest that he is recommending the actual use of instrumental music in the Church Service. It

---

63 McEvoy, *The Philosophy of Robert Grosseteste*, 257ff. This sounds not too dissimilar to the efforts of some present day physicists who are experimenting with 'tuning' the natural vibrations of organs in the ill.

64 *Opus Majus*, 'Moral Philosophy,' the concluding lines of part 3.

65 This entire discussion is found in *Opus Majus*, 'Mathematics,' trans. Burke, I, 259.

will be the fifteenth century before instruments become common in Church ceremonies and not until the sixteenth century will they become common in the Mass. In the thirteenth century there remained seriously divided opinions on this subject. In a work by Bacon's contemporary, Bartholomew Anglicus, for example, we are told that only the organ is allowed.

> *Organum* is a generall name of all instrumentes of musyk,[66] and is netheless specyally a propryte to the instrument that is made of many pipes, and blowe wyth belowes. And now holy chyrche useth oonly this instrument of musyk, in preses, sequences, and ympnes [hymns]; and forsakyth for men's use of mynstralsye all other instrumentes of musyk.[67]

On the other hand, the poem from the same period, quoted above describing Grosseteste, enthusiastically recommends the use of a broad range of instruments in the Service.

> Therfore, gode men, ye shall lere,
> When ye any Gleman here,
> To worshepe God at your power,
> And Davyd in the Sauter.
> Yn harpe and tabour and symphan gle
> Worship God in trumpes and sautre:
> In cordes, yn organes, and bells ringyng,
> Yn all these worship the hevene Kyng.[68]

Among these thirteenth-century philosophers, only Bartholomew Anglicus provides examples of a more traditional purpose of music, in particular to bring joy to the listener. In a discussion of the needs in planning a proper wedding feast, he recommends that in addition to food, drink, and gifts, one must, 'comforteth and gladeth his guests with songs and pipes and other minstrelsy of music.'[69] A similar passage on feasts in general recommends, 'the guests be gladded with lutes and harps.'[70]

He mentions this same purpose again in writing of the treatment of madness. Those suffering from madness must be tied up, so they will not hurt themselves or others, and then,

> be refreshed, and comforted, and withdrawn from cause and matter of dread and busy thoughts. And they must be gladded with instruments of music, and somedeal be occupied.[71]

---

66 The definition of *Organum* we read in music history texts today is always given as two-part vocal music.

67 *De proprietatibus rerum*, quoted in Carpenter, *Music in the Medieval and Renaissance Universities*, 85, fn. 33.

68 Quoted in Carpenter, ibid., 83.

69 'Medieval Manners,' in Steele, *Medieval Lore of Bartholomew Anglicus*, 48.

70 Ibid., 51.

71 'Medieval Medicine,' Ibid., 58.

This same writer mentions music for the therapy of the ill in another passage, where he says it belongs to the very power of music to bring about changes in men.

> Also by sweet songs of harmony and accord of music, sick men and frantic come oft to their wit again and health of body. Some men tell that Orpheus said,
>
>> Emperors pray me to feasts, to have liking of me; but I have liking of them which would bend their hearts from wrath to mildness, from sorrow to gladness, from covetousness to largeness, from dread to boldness.[72]

[72] Ibid., 64.

Finally, we must mention the book, *De animalibus*, by Albertus Magnus, in which the author discusses many aspects of music relative to animals. We are attracted to his comments because, of necessity, he uses the same language in describing the music of animals which he would use in describing the music of humans. The reader, therefore, may want to consider whether these descriptions are, to any degree, metaphors of the human experience.

First, Albertus describes several animals as listeners. For the deer, its love of music leads to its capture.

> This animal takes delight in all unusual sights and sounds; hence, wanting to be seen by itself and prone to being charmed by the sounds of pipes and song, it often falls into peril of capture or death.[73]

[73] Magnus, *De Animalibus*, trans. Scanlan, 94.

The dragon also, according to this author, can be captured by music. One never knows when one might need this information!

> Dragons are said to be afraid of thunder and prone to be struck by lightning, just as in a contrary sense the eagle among birds and the laurel among plants are said to be impervious to lightening; for this reason they say that when an enchanter seeks to charm a dragon with songs, he causes a great reverberating sound to be made by beating on a drum or stretched leather, and the dragon mistaking this for thunder cowers in fright and meekly allows the enchanter to mount its back.[74]

[74] Ibid., 404.

The horse, on the other hand, becomes excited by 'the sound of martial music.'[75] This writer also makes the interesting observation that, 'for some reason sheep eat better when they are soothed by the pleasant sound of music.'[76]

[75] Ibid., 105.

[76] Ibid., 169.

Albertus retells two ancient stories about music and animals, the first being about the dolphin, which all ancient writers claimed loved music. He cites the story of Arion, a singer who was thrown into the sea and then rescued by a dolphin, and then he provides us with a new anecdote.

> When the king of Caria captured a particular large dolphin, a teeming school of its mates followed the captive to the shore, forming a procession, like a funeral cortege of mourners. Seeing this, the king ordered the dolphin released, whereupon the entire assembly of dolphins welcomed their freed companion and performed a sort of leaping dance as they led it back to sea.[77]

The second story is the most famous ancient tale regarding music and listeners, the story of the Sirens. Best known in Ovid's *Metamorphoses*, these mythological daughters of Phorcys, the sea god, lived on small rock islands off the southwest coast of Campania, where they lured sailors to their death on the rocks through their irresistibly sweet singing. While many ancient philosophers retold this tale, the early Christian writers, focusing on Reason, maintained it was the *words* of the songs, not the music, which captured the sailors! As far as we know, no one before Albertus had ventured to give so detailed a description of these Sirens. In his version it must have been the music, because it clearly was not the physical appearance of these mythical daughters which attracted the sailors!

> SYRENAS (Sirens), popularized in poetic fable, are marine monsters whose upper body has the figure of a woman with long pendulous breasts with which it suckles its young; the face is horrible and it has a mane of long free-flowing hair; below they have eagle's claws, and above are aquiline wings, and behind a scaly tail used as a rudder to guide their swimming. Upon making an appearance, they hold out their young in full view, emit some sweet, alluring sounds by which they lull their hearers to sleep, and then tear the sleepers to pieces.[78]

Of course, no writer on this subject could forget to mention the world of birds. By way of introduction, Albertus offers this general observation on the singing of birds.

> As a general rule, birds emit more vocal sounds than other animals, a manifestation of the levity of their spirits. This is particularly true of the smaller birds, many of whom sing a musical song and display

77 Ibid., 349.

78 Ibid., 373. What reader who has traveled to Italy will not recall that the female gypsy pick-pockets also hold out their young as distractions.

a lightness of spirit reflected in the ease of their melodious outpourings. Birds sing most vocally during the mating season when the males warble in a more tuneful fashion than the females whose natural disposition is colder and more aloof.[79]

79 Ibid., 190.

Among the most melodious of the birds he finds Finches,[80] Birds of Paradise,[81] and above all, the Blackbird.

80 Ibid., 219.
81 Ibid., 207.

In the opinion of some writers, this bird was called 'modula' in ancient times, because it produces melodies [*modulos*] and songs [*melos*]. Some claim a black bird was once trained by human art to reproduce all nine notes of the scale that are used in the composition of every musical piece; moreover, the trained bird gloried so in its talent that it would often sing through its range of notes in melodious sequence for a human audience ...

This bird sings well in the springtime but during the winter makes a stuttering sound.[82]

82 Ibid., 305.

Albertus' most extended, and interesting, discussion of a musical bird is devoted to that virtuoso, the Nightingale.

PHYLOMENA (Nightingale) is a small, well-known bird, named from 'phylos' and 'menos,' which means sweet, because it loves sweet songs. Another possible derivation is from 'philos' and 'mene,' because in competing with another bird to produce the best song, the nightingale would rather run out of breath and expire than cease singing and give in to its opponent.

Though small in body, the nightingale has a great store of breath wherewith it produces a range of sounds no less remarkable for its modulated tones as for the multiplicity of its notes. One minute it sustains a long note with one continuous breath, and then it varies the tone like the inflections of a human singing voice. Again, it separates the notes with staccato effect, all the while maintaining a connected melody, so that the song on its outgoing breath is continued with matching force on inhalation. At varying times its song is full basso profundo; treble; prolonged in a trill; soprano; or reduced to a whisper—in essence, representing almost all of the tunes made by musical instruments. In my own observations of this bird I have remarked that it flies toward persons who are singing, provided they have a melodious voice; as long as these persons continue singing, the bird listens in silence;[83] but as soon as they stop, the nightingale takes up the song, as if responding in a roundelay chorus. Further-

83 Listening to music in silence is a traditional indication of Art Music in early literature.

more, these birds duplicate the same process in response to one another, provoking each other to song.[84]

[84] Magnus, *De Animalibus*, 315.

Finally, in view of the fact we know today, that all organs of the body vibrate to a musical pitch, we are drawn to this interesting observation by Albertus.

> The animosity between the wolf and sheep is so strong its influence extends to all of their anatomical parts; thus, musical strings made of sheep gut do not resonate in harmony with strings made of wolf gut.[85]

[85] Ibid., 158.

These philosophers and their work represent that extraordinary moment which saw the rediscovery of the ancient Greek philosophers and the birth of the modern universities. We have to be disappointed that this environment produced very little new philosophical thought on music, but no doubt that only reflects the strong reservations of the Church which are still reflected in these writers.

The exception is Roger Bacon, whom we regard as the most impressive thinker of this century. He alone views music as continuing to be a significant member of the Liberal Arts, indeed observing that music is fundamental to the understanding of both Grammar and Logic.

Bacon's most interesting contribution is his extended definition of music itself. He revives the ancient view that dance is not a separate art, but the visible form of Music and provides rare details regarding this perspective. Equally interesting is his definition of 'audible' music, which includes the extraordinary information that 'accent' comes from the Latin root, *accino*, meaning 'I sing!' Our only disappointment is that Bacon did not go into more detail on what he meant by 'mystical meanings' in reference to the use of musical instruments in the Old Testament.

Roger Bacon is also the only one of these philosophers who seemed to have intuitively grasped the basic nature of brain function and discussed it in terms which are usable by the modern reader. His famous observation, 'There are two modes of knowledge, reason and experience,' was not only correct, but gave for the first time significant recognition to a brain function other than Reason. His contemporaries, Duns Scotus and Grosseteste, were much higher regarded in their time, but on the subject of brain function they guessed wrong and took strange paths to oblivion.

20 AESTHETICS OF MUSIC IN THE WRITINGS OF THE CHURCH PHILOSOPHERS OF THE TWELFTH AND THIRTEENTH CENTURIES

During this period the Church faced its greatest crisis since the early years of persecution by the Romans. After centuries of placid continuation of the philosophical ideas of Augustine, during which the Liberal Arts were valued primarily for their aid in preparing the Christian for understanding the Scriptures, it suddenly had to face new currents of thought generated by the translation of the works of the Greek philosophers, Aristotle in particular.

With the availability of these new translations, beginning ca. 1150, it rapidly became apparent to many that these masterpieces of natural knowledge and philosophy, and Reason itself, were not compatible with the teachings of a Church based on Faith. The struggle to bring Aristotelian reason and logic into the framework of the Church began with a few brilliant men, such as Peter Abelard (1079–1144),[1] and was centered in the university life of Paris.

The Church was quickly divided between the new intellectuals and the followers of St. Francis, who continued to speak of Love and Faith as the road to eternity. The hierarchy was slow to see the importance of the new intellectual currents and those who wrote and spoke of the new ideas did so at great risk. Bernard of Clairvaux, 'St. Bernard,' (1090–1153) destroyed the career of Abelard because he was speaking of Reason and not Faith.

> Faith believes, it does not dispute. But this man [Abelard], apparently holding God suspect, will not believe anything until he has first examined it with his reason.[2]

The first sentence of this quotation summarizes Bernard's particular paranoia regarding the works of the ancient Greek philosophers. These works, it seemed to him, disturbed the quiet life of meditation and drew one out into the worldly confusion of the Socratic method of debate. The first danger signal, he warned his monks in a sermon, was intellectual curiosity itself.

---

1 A brilliant French scholastic philosopher and one of the most popular professors at the University of Paris. His tragic love affair with Heloise is one of the classic love stories. After being condemned by the Church, an action instigated by Bernard of Clairvaux, he ended his life under the protection of Peter the Venerable.

2 'Letter of Bernard of Clairvaux to Cardinal Haimeric,' in *The Letters of St. Bernard of Clairvaux*, trans. Bruno James (Chicago: Regnery, 1953), 328. Born to a family of French aristocracy, Bernard joined the monastic life in 1111 and even at an early age became influential in Church and secular politics.

The first step of pride, then, is curiosity, and you may recognize it by these marks. If you shall see a monk, whom you formerly trusted confidently, beginning to roam with his eyes, hold his head erect, prick up his ears, wherever he is standing, walking, sitting; you may know the changed inner man from the movements of the outer. For a wicked man *winketh with his eyes, speaketh with his feet, teacheth with his fingers*; and the strange movement of the body reveals a new disease in the soul, which has tired of introspection and which neglect of self makes curious toward others.[3]

3 *The Steps of Humility*, trans. George Burch (University of Notre Dame Press, 1963), 181.

A Church council in Paris, in 1210, forbade the reading of Aristotle's 'metaphysics and natural philosophy,' or the writing of any commentaries on these works. That the prohibition was repeated five years later tells us the first one had been largely ignored. Even by the end of the thirteenth century there were important writers, such as Ramón Lull (b. 1235, in Majorca), who were still frowning at this new emphasis on natural philosophy.

For through lust of knowledge do they fall into the greatest depths of impiety, insulting the name of God and with curses and incantations invoking evil spirits as good angels, investing them with the names of God and of good angels, and profaning holy things with figures and images and by writings. And through presumption all errors are implanted in the world.[4]

4 *The Book of the Lover and the Beloved*, 346, trans. Allison Peers (New York: Macmillan, 1923), 109.

It fell to Thomas Aquinas to devote his life's work and a hundred treatises to reconciling these two great forces. He did not quite achieve this, but, as Durant observes, his accomplishment was in some respects more remarkable.

He did not succeed in reconciling Aristotle and Christianity, but in the effort he won an epochal victory for reason. He had led reason as a captive into the citadel of faith; but in his triumph he had brought the Age of Faith to an end.[5]

5 Will Durant, *The Age of Faith* (New York: Simon and Schuster, 1950), 978.

ON THE PHYSIOLOGY OF AESTHETICS

The Churchmen of this period rarely discuss the Liberal Arts. One who does, John of Salisbury (first half, twelfth century),[6] points out that the term 'Liberal Arts' is based on the root of 'liberate' and while he does not explain the process, he gives their purpose as liberating us from 'cares incompatible with wisdom,' such as material necessities, so that we can apply ourselves to philosophy.[7]

Since he makes the interesting distinction that the Trivium[8] discloses 'the significance of all words,' while the Quadrivium[9] unveils 'the secrets of all nature,' he is left with the problem of poetry. It had traditionally been part of grammar, but Salisbury observes that some felt a strong association between poetry and Nature and therefore thought it should be a separate art. His own view was, 'either poetry will remain a part of grammar, or it will be dropped from the roll of liberal studies.'[10] The precedence he assigns to grammar was because he considered it the key to Reason.[11] Poetry, on the other hand, had a more complex relationship with Reason, due to its ancient association with Music. He illustrates this with an anecdote about Julius Caesar.

> For Grammar equips us both to receive and to impart knowledge. It modulates our accent, and regulates our very voice so that it is suited to all persons and matters. Poetry should be recited in one way; prose in another. The governing principle in pronunciation is at one time harmony, at another rhythm, at still another the sense. The law of harmony reigns in music. Caesar, while still a boy, with fine sarcasm remarked to a certain person,
>
> > If you're trying to read, you're singing, and if you're trying to sing, you're doing a miserable job.[12]

6 *The Metalogicon*, trans. Daniel McGarry (Berkeley: University of California Press, 1955), 36. Born of humble parents in southern England, John went to Paris in 1136, where he studied with Peter Abelard, Gilbert de la Porrée, William of Conches and others. With the aid of Bernard of Clairvaux he became Archbishop of Canterbury, where he became an intimate counselor of, and witnessed the murder of, Thomas Becket.

7 Ibid., 37.

8 Grammar, dialetic, and rhetoric.

9 Arithmetic, geometry, astronomy, and music.

10 *The Metalogicon*, 52.

11 In ibid., 39, he makes the interesting observation that the five elementary vowel-sounds are genetically common to all mankind.

12 Ibid., 61.

On Reason

It is no surprise that the Churchmen placed Reason above the senses. Salisbury did so[13] because of the following logic: The senses give birth to imagination, from these two come opinion, and from opinion derives 'scientific knowledge.'[14] The most interesting aspect of Salisbury's discussion of this topic is that he creates two plateaus *above* Reason. The first is intuitive understanding, which he says

13 Ibid., 228, 230.

14 Ibid., 222.

transcends Reason, as Reason transcends the senses. Intuitive understanding is a higher form of wisdom because it includes the perception of divine causes behind Reason.[15] Beyond this is 'original reason,' an error-free, divine form of truth behind all things.

15 Ibid., 230.

> In addition to reason in creatures, there is also that original reason which efficaciously comprehends all things, whether they be material or perceptible only by the intellect. Fully and accurately, that is without any error whatsoever this original reason determines the exact nature and precise power of everything. If I describe this original reason as the divine wisdom or power, and the firm foundation of all things, I am undoubtedly correct.[16]

16 Ibid., 250.

A particularly interesting contention by Salisbury has to do with the relationship of Reason and its medium of communication, speech. While it is obvious that Reason expresses itself through speech, Salisbury presents the hypothesis that there is a return street, that speech in some way teaches, or triggers, Reason. He praises this idea; it is too bad he did not explain it. Was he simply referring to one talking to one's self? This brings to mind the current theories of 'many minds,' in other words, when we talk to ourself is it possible that one of our minds is explaining something to, or trying to convince, another mind?

> Just as eloquence, unenlightened by reason, is rash and blind, so wisdom, without the power of expression, is feeble and maimed. Speechless wisdom may sometimes increase one's personal satisfaction, but it rarely and only slightly contributes to the welfare of human society. Reason, the mother, nurse, and guardian of knowledge, as well as of virtue, frequently conceives from speech, and by this same means bears more abundant and richer fruit. Reason would remain utterly barren, or at least would fail to yield a plenteous harvest, if the faculty of speech did not bring to light its feeble conceptions, and communicate the perceptions of the prudent exercise of the human mind. Indeed, it is this delightful and fruitful copulation of reason and speech which has given birth to so many outstanding cities, has made friends and allies of so many kingdoms, and has unified and knit together in bonds of love so many peoples.[17]

17 Ibid., 10ff.

It is interesting that, in another book, Salisbury feels compelled to give a little sales pitch for the importance of Reason. Obtaining

Reason is the really important thing in life, he says, and not things like the study of music and art!

> I never cease pondering nor can I marvel sufficiently, why, as the fact is, men do not cultivate their minds in the use of reason. And this reason, which is needful to all alike for their living, is not the reason which we mean when we speak of the rationale of painting or of playing upon a stringed instrument, which any good man is at liberty to despise without blameworthiness of mind, without shame, without trouble. I do not, like the Sibimeniae, know how to play on the flute, but I am not ashamed that I am not a flute player. I do not know, like Appelles, how to paint in colors, but I am not ashamed not to be a limner. And so in the case of the other arts, if I were to run through them all, you are at liberty without reproach to be ignorant of them.[18]

Truly objective speculation on the question of man's faculties had always been hindered somewhat among the Churchmen by the Church's adherence to the concept of a soul. Where, for example, is Reason? For Bernard of Clairvaux it was in the soul,[19] but for John of Salisbury it was found in the head. Mother Nature, he says, 'has made our head the seat of all sensation, in which citadel she has enthroned reason as queen.'[20]

The Church writer who was most verbose on the subject of the location of man's faculties was Hildegard von Bingen (1098–1179). She associated the senses with the head, understanding and insight with the soul, and the 'humors' with the liver.[21] Her famous book of visions contains a substantial proportion of visions which we have to characterize as 'weird science,' as for example a passage in which she describes how the various faculties work together.

> The soul pours its thoughts into the heart and collects them in the breast. Thence, these thoughts ascend to the head and into all the limbs of the body. They penetrate into the eyes as well; for the eyes are the windows through which the soul knows external nature.[22]

Related to this discussion is another curious vision in which she equates the head with the solar system.

> From the very top of our cranium to the outer edge of our forehead, seven points are found, separated from one another by equal intervals. This symbolizes the planets, which are also separated from one

18 'Policraticus,' trans. John Dickinson, in *The Statesman's Book of John of Salisbury* (New York: Russell & Russell, 1963), 272.

19 'On Conversion,' quoted in *Sermons on Conversion*, trans. Marie-Bernard Saïd (Kalamazoo: Cistercian Publications, 1981), 45.

20 *The Metalogicon*, 229.

21 *Book of Divine Works*, ed. Matthew Fox (Santa Fe: Bear & Company, 1987), 89, 93, and 68ff. Given to the Church by her parents in 1106, perhaps as a tithe, since she was the tenth child, Hildegard became one of the most influential writers in the twelfth-century Church, corresponding with the very highest secular and religious authorities.

22 'Vision Four: 103,' in ibid., 126.

another in the firmament by like intervals. The highest planet is indicated by the top of the cranium. In the most remote part of the forehead there is the moon, while the sun is found right in the midst of the space between the highest planet and the moon. On each side of this spot, the other planets—the two upper ones and the two lower ones—are seen; there is the same interval between them with respect to their distance from the sun and the other planets. For the features on our head are proportionately just as far apart from one another as the planets are from one another in the firmament.[23]

23 'Vision Four: 22,' in ibid., 97.

We know today that Reason is a function of the left hemisphere of the brain, which, in turn, is associated with the right hand. Because the right hemisphere is mute, the left hemisphere has proven in clinical studies to tend to pretend that the right hemisphere does not even exist. The significance of this for our topic, of course, is that the experience of music is found primarily in the right hemisphere. Thus there is in most people an unconscious preference for Reason over music, or left over right hemisphere. It also follows that we find in older literature the association of *good* with the right hand and *bad* with the left. These associations continue in the writings of the Churchmen of this period, as we can see in a particularly vivid example by John of Salisbury. In a chapter entitled, 'What is the Meaning of Inclining to the Right Hand or the Left, Which is Forbidden to the Prince,' he advises,

> He shall not incline to the right hand nor to the left. To incline to the right hand signifies to insist too enthusiastically on the virtues themselves. To incline to the right is to exceed the bounds of moderation in the works of virtue, the essence of which is moderation …
>
> To incline to the left means to slip or deviate from the way of virtue down the precipices of the vices.[24]

24 'Policraticus,' 43. Similar right-hand prejudice can be found in Bernard of Clairvaux, *Sermons on Conversion*, 162, 166, and 253.

On the Nature of the Senses

For Bonaventure (fl. thirteenth century), the senses exist for the soul to collect knowledge of the world and from this acquisition itself comes delight. It is clear by his remarks that he does not understand the relationship of the senses and the brain, finding the source of delight to be in the actual sense itself.

Man, a microcosm, has five senses that are like five doors through which everything he knows of the visible world enters his soul. Through the use of sight comes all starry and shining bodies as well as all colored ones. Through touch he contacts all solid earthly substances. Through the 'intermediate' senses he knows those things that exist between heaven and earth: he tastes liquids, hears sounds, and smells odors …

From the apprehension of a suitable object comes delight. The senses take delight in an object. Through the abstracted similitude beauty arises in seeing, sweetness in hearing or smelling, wholesomeness in taste and touch—we speak here by appropriation.[25]

Ramón Lull (1232–1315) finds the primary pleasure associated with the sense of hearing to be hearing the praise of God.

Hearing is the operation of the auditive faculty, which works by hearing so that through hearing the soul can take pleasure in remembering, understanding, and loving that hearing. And since God is praiseworthy, He therefore wants to be praised by man, and He wants people to find pleasure in hearing words of praise directed toward God.[26]

Hildegard von Bingen, in another one of her colorful analogies, describes the physical organization of the senses as follows,

Like the curvature of a revolving wheel, the top of the human head is the brain against which there leans a ladder with various stages of ascent—the eyes for seeing, the ears for hearing, the nose of smelling, the mouth for speaking. Through these sense organs we humans gaze out at all the creatures.[27]

In an elaboration of how the senses combine with other faculties, Bingen makes one of the more extraordinary observations to be found in early literature. When she says that knowledge 'divides itself on two sides' of the head, she appears to be one of the earliest writers to recognize the separate hemispheres of the brain, although she fails to tell us enough to know if she really understood what she implies.

The symmetry of the elements is related to the symmetry extending from the top of our head forward to the eyebrows, sideways to the ears, and backward to the beginning of the neck. In this way, three basic powers are present in the soul to the same degree: spiritualization [*expiratio*], knowledge [*scientia*], and sensation [*sensus*]. The soul fulfills its functions by means of these three powers. By spiritu-

[25] *The Mind's Journey to God*, trans. Lawrence Cunningham (Chicago: Franciscan Herald Press, 1979), 42ff.

[26] *Felix*, VIII, 863.

[27] *The Book of Divine Works*, Vision Four: 14.

alization, the soul undertakes whatever it can carry out, and this points to the anterior part of the head. By knowledge, the soul divides itself, so to speak, on two sides as far as the ears. And by sensation, the soul turns backward to a certain extent as far as the beginning of the neck. And these three powers ought to be symmetrical throughout, since the soul does not begin to achieve by spiritualization more than knowledge can grasp or sensation carry out. And thus these powers work in harmony since none of them exceeds another, just as our head, too, has its proper symmetry.[28]

28 Ibid., Vision Four: 17.

ON THE PSYCHOLOGY OF AESTHETICS

These serious Churchmen say very little about the usual human pleasures. Bernard of Clairvaux, for example, writes that happiness is the result of the 'contemplation of truths.'[29] Lull, holding to the same course, says man's greatest pleasure is to understand.[30]

29 Sermon 5, 'On the Four Kinds of Spirits,' in *The Works of Bernard of Clairvaux*, II, 25.

30 *Felix*, VIII, 855.

The sacred poet, Jacopone da Todi (1230–1306), has left a poem called 'The Five Senses.' In this work the various senses are arguing, each of them complaining that their sense has the most 'short-lived joy.' When it is Hearing's time to speak, we find a repetition of something which was a serious problem with music for earlier philosophers—the fact that it apparently immediately disappears and is gone.

> The first to speak is Hearing.
> 'The contest is over,' he announces,
> 'The sound I just heard is no more—
> It touched the ear and vanished.
> You can't deny that.'[31]

31 Jacopone da Todi, *The Lauds*, trans. Serge and Elizabeth Hughes (New York: Paulist Press, 1982), 76. Born to an aristocratic family, upon the death of his wife he became a ragged public penitent for ten years. During this time his poetry was written and he gained fame as a holy man.

The emotions are another subject which the Churchmen in general seemed uncomfortable to discuss at length. There is one interesting passage by John of Salisbury in which he hypothesizes that 'imagination is the offspring of sensation' and imagination, in turn, becomes the location of the emotions. He elects to discuss only one of the emotions in detail.

> Numbered among imagination's offspring is carnal lust, a poisonous pest, extremely opposed to the project of philosophizing. It is impossible to surrender oneself to the lusts of the flesh, and at the same time to dedicate oneself to philosophy.[32]

32 *The Metalogicon*, 218ff.

ON AESTHETICS

The only Churchman during this period who devotes an extended discussion to the definition of Beauty was Bonaventure. Following the teachings of Augustine, who spoke of the fundamental principle of numerical proportion in Beauty,[33] Bonaventure concludes,

> All things are beautiful and, in some sense, desirable yet neither beauty or desirability exist without proportion and proportion is rooted in number. It follows then that everything is in numerical harmony.[34]

Bonaventure also maintains that one is overwhelmed by the extremes in what the senses perceive and therefore delight is found in the mean.[35]

But perception and delight are not a sufficient definition of Beauty for Bonaventure. Like almost all early philosophers, Bonaventure could not accept significant meaning unless Reason were part of the equation. Of course, Reason is a natural companion for a definition of Beauty based on proportion and numbers, but Bonaventure also assigns to Reason the role of discrimination of Beauty.

> Beyond apprehension and delight there is judgment. Judgment does not only determine whether an object is black or white (this judgment pertains to an exterior sense) or harmful or helpful (this pertains to an interior sense) but judgment decides why an object delights. This judgment reaches into the very structure of the delight which the senses received from an object. Thus judgment asks why an object is beautiful, pleasing, and wholesome. The answer is harmonious proportion. This harmony is the same in large and small things, and is unaffected by size, change, or alteration. It is impervious to place, time and motion. It is immutable, unlimited, unending, and spiritual. Judgment, then, is an action through which the sensible species enters into the intellectual power of man after having been drawn from sense objects by a process of elimination and abstraction. Thus, the whole world can enter the human mind through the senses by means of the three operations just described (i.e., apprehension, delight, and judgment).[36]

The value of these operations, he says, is that when we see Beauty we see God, as if in a mirror.[37]

When Bonaventure lists one role of judgment being to decide if that which produces delight is harmful or helpful, there is an

---

33 See *Divine Providence and the Problem of Evil*, trans. Ludwig Schopp (New York: CIMA Publishing Co.), 309ff.

34 *The Mind's Journey to God*, 48.

35 Ibid., 44.

36 Ibid.

37 Ibid., 45.

implied utilitarian value in art. This subject is discussed further by Bernard of Cluny (fl. 1122–1156) relative to Beauty in poetry. He observes that the reason so many earlier writers chose poetry was that through the *melodiousness* of the words the listener would be inescapably caught up in the *virtue* of the words. In this process, again, there was a utilitarian purpose to poetry.

> Therefore, just as there is much of beauty in meter, so there is much usefulness in beauty, and either of these two depends on the other. That is very easily seen. For if the reader delights in the former, consequently he delights in the latter. And indeed one who considers the form of words with care often more carefully embraces the fruits of the things themselves. Hence it is that poets have written all, or almost all which they have written, in meter; they have published metrical writings, in song, so to speak, of course attending as much as possible to this, that what they were less able to render pleasing arranged in plain speech, they might render pleasing described in metrical speech.[38]

The most interesting discussion, among these Churchmen, of Art in general is found in John of Salisbury's *Metalogicon*. His entire discussion of the arts is inseparably tied to Nature, 'the best of all mothers,' and of course Reason.[39] His actual definition of Art goes beyond utilitarian to concentrate on efficiency.

> Art is a system that reason has devised in order to expedite, by its own short cut, our ability to do things within our natural capabilities.[40]

If this were a very modern writer we would presume he meant by 'within our natural capabilities' the right-hemisphere of the brain, the experiential side and the real us as opposed to the Rational left-hemisphere which consists entirely of second-hand knowledge, knowledge from other people. However, although he acknowledges there is such a thing as natural talent, for the most part Salisbury maintains that in order for Art to obtain the state characterized in his definition it must be studied. Learning begins with Nature and proceeds to Reason.

> Nature first evokes our natural capacity to perceive things, and then, as it were, deposits these perceptions in the secure treasure of our memory. Reason then examines, with its careful study, those things which have been perceived, and which are to be, or have been, com-

38 *Scorn for the World: Bernard of Cluny's* De Contemptu Mundi, trans. Ronald Pepin (East Lansing: Colleagues Press, 1991), 5ff. This Latin treatise by Cluny is written in poetry. Little is known of this monk who served under the abbacy of Peter the Venerable.

39 This discussion is found in bk. I, ch. 10 and following.

40 Quoted in *The Metalogicon*, 33.

mended to memory's custody. After its scrutiny of their nature, reason pronounces true and accurate judgment concerning each of these (unless, perchance, it errors in some regard).[41]

[41] Ibid., 34.

Regarding the second part of his definition, that one's accomplishment will be relative to one's natural capabilities, he, like Bonaventure, finds the most important virtue in the mean, and not in the extremes. He illustrates this by way of a charming story which he attributes to Bernard of Chartres.

> There are three kinds of natural capacities. The first flies, the second creeps, the third takes the intermediate course of walking. The flying one flits about, easily learning, but just as quickly forgetting, for it lacks stability. The creeping one is mired down to earth, and cannot rise, wherefore it can make no progress. But the one that goes to neither extreme and walks, both because he has his feet on the ground so he can firmly stand, and because he can climb, provides prospect of progress, and is admirably suited for philosophizing. For study enhances his effectiveness.[42]

[42] Ibid., 35.

In this process of study, and in the role of Nature and Reason, Cluny finds a hypothesis for the origin and development of art.

> Consider an example to illustrate the origin of an art. The first disputation developed by chance, and the practice of disputing grew with repetition. Reason then perceived the form of disputation, the art of this activity. This art, on being cultivated, conferred a corresponding faculty. The mother of the arts is nature, to despise whose progeny amounts to insulting their parent. Natural ability should accordingly be diligently cultivated. At the same time, study should be moderated by recreation, so that while one's natural ability waxes strong with the former, it may be refreshed by the latter.[43]

[43] Ibid., 35.

A very important contribution to the discussion of the relationship of Nature and the arts is contributed by John of Salisbury, who focuses on the communication of feelings. He is discussing poetry and presents two fragments of poems by Horace[44] in which the point is made that in poetry the voice is merely a surrogate for the emotions. This is also, of course, the entire point of music: music is not so important as what the music communicates. Since we know emotions are universal, we might say this is the most fundamental contribution of Nature to the arts.

[44] Horace's quote may be found in *De Arte Poetica liber*, ed. F. Vollmer (Leipzig, 1925), 108–111, 102, 103.

> Nature first adapts our soul to every
> Kind of fate: she delights us, arouses our wrath,
> Or overwhelms and tortures us with woe,
> After which she expresses these emotions
> Employing the tongue as their interpreter.

So true is this principle that a poet must never forsake the footsteps of nature. Rather, he should strain to cleave closely to nature in his bearing and gestures, as well as in his words:

> ... *If you expect me to weep, then first*
> *You yourself must mourn ...*

Likewise, if you want me to rejoice, you yourself must first be joyful.[45]

The views on Art by Bernard of Clairvaux are a return to the views of earlier Church writers, with an emphasis on the artist rather than on what he does. But they did not mean by this a recognition of the quality of the intuitive form of art within the artist, as we might today. They found it necessary to give credit to the artist, as a person, because God made the artist.

> We do not praise the pen or the brush when we judge a script or painting, nor do we attribute fame for eloquence to the lips and tongue of the orator. Listen for a moment to the Prophet: 'Does the axe claim more credit than the man who wields it, or the saw more strength than the man who handles it? It would be like the cudgel controlling the man who raises it, or the club moving what is not made of wood!'[46]

Finally, we must point out while these Churchmen left barely enough discussion dedicated to the arts to allow us a glimpse of their ideas, they were much more vividly outspoken in their views against mere amusement. John of Salisbury seems not only outspoken, but angry.

> Concerning actors and mimes, buffoons and harlots, panders and other like human monsters, which the prince ought rather to exterminate entirely than to foster, there needed no mention to be made in the law; which indeed not only excludes all such abominations from the court of the prince, but totally banishes them from among the people of God.[47]

---

45 Salisbury, *Metalogicon*, 51.

46 Sermon 13:6, 'On the Song of Songs,' in *The Works of Bernard of Clairvaux* (Spencer, MA: Cistercian Publications, 1971), II, 92ff.

47 'Policraticus,' IV, 4, in *The Statesman's Book of John of Salisbury*, 16.

Bernard of Clairvaux, in a letter to a canon, Oger, describes the theater as a place, 'where lust is excited by the effeminate and indecent contortions of the actors.'[48] In another place, Bernard points to a more comprehensible objection to entertainment, that money spent on amusement is money that could be spent on more pressing needs.

> The walls of the church are aglow, but the poor of the Church go hungry. The stones of the church are covered with gold, while its children are left naked. The food of the poor is taken to feed the eyes of the rich, and amusement is provided for the curious, while the needy have not even the necessities of life.[49]

ON AESTHETICS OF MUSIC

One of the questions the twelfth- and thirteenth-century Churchmen must have often discussed was the position they should take on the use of instrumental music in the church, and in particular toward the jongleur who performed this music. Although the Church had tried to ban instrumental music for a thousand years, it was never completely successful and now she must have sensed the tide was moving against her.

By the twelfth century there were new pressures undermining the older conservative views of the Church. First, with the great progress in secular music, the citizens were regularly hearing music which was more interesting than that heard in the church. We assume it would only be consistent with human nature that some of this new music was beginning to creep from outside to inside the church. We find evidence of this in a reform of the Antiphonary used by the Cistercians under the leadership of Bernard of Clairvaux. When he states his purpose for the revision was, 'the removal of the defiling impurity of errors, and by the rejection of the illicit liberties taken by unskilled hands,' we read this to mean it was his contemporaries who had been making changes in the music.[50] This seems confirmed by his warning to the monks not to oppose the rules of Church music[51] and in his firm order, 'we forbid that [the music] be changed in any respect by any person,'[52] which in itself suggests he feared changes would continue to be made.

48 *The Letters of St. Bernard of Clairvaux*, 135.

49 'An Apologia to Abbot William,' in *The Works of Bernard of Clairvaux*, I, 66.

50 *De Revisione Cantus Cistercienis*, trans. Francisco Guentner (American Institute of Musicology, 1974), 43. Bernard says that for the actual musical preparation he called upon, 'some of these very brethren who have been found to be better instructed and more skilled in the theory and practice of chant,' but we believe the accompanying prose was either his or written under his personal supervision.

51 Ibid.

52 Ibid., 42.

In an enlightening final statement, one which would have been characteristic of many Churchmen of the twelfth century, Bernard just could not understand why those 'illicit liberties' made in the ancient Gregorian Chant were so popular!

> ... not even two provinces sing the same Antiphonary. It must, therefore, seem remarkable just why they have had such ... widespread fame, since they are false rather than true, defective rather than sound.[53]

We cannot help but wonder what the 'illicit' music was like! Much of it must have been improvised, for Bernhard characterized it as being governed by 'chance,'[54] and not by Reason, as was his music. In any case, it must have been good, for he solemnly announces that he has replaced it all with 'sober and sensible music.'[55]

Another source of pressure on the Church was local folk traditions. In 1237 a group of the faithful in Eichstadt rebelled against an interdict by Bishop Friedrich III which forbad them to continue to bury their dead with the accompaniment of instruments.[56] Popular enthusiasm for dancing became at this time a particular problem for the Church. On the eve of important religious festivals in 1209, the Council of Avignon declared,

> There should not be, in the churches, any of this theatrical dancing, these immodest rejoicings, these meetings of singers with their worldly songs, which incite the souls of those who hear them to sin.[57]

Similarly, in 1212 the Council of Paris ruled,

> Gatherings of women for the purpose of dancing and singing shall not be granted permission to enter cemeteries or to tread on consecrated ground ... Nuns will not set themselves at the head of processions which sing and dance on the grounds of churches and their chapels ... for according to St. Gregory it is better to plough and dig on the Sabbath than to conduct these dances.[58]

A thirteenth-century interdiction by the Council of Bayeux is even stronger.

> Priests will forbid gatherings for dancing and singing in churches and cemeteries, on pain of excommunication.[59]

---

53 Ibid., 59.

54 Ibid.

55 Ibid., 45.

56 *The New Grove Dictionary of Music and Musicians*, ed. Stanley Sadie, 1980, VII, 810.

57 Quoted in Romain Goldron, *Minstrels and Masters* (H.S. Stuttman, 1968), 19.

58 Ibid.

59 Ibid.

Clearly attitudes were destined to change with the appearance of the organ, beginning in the tenth century. Even its acceptance was slow and by the twelfth century some still saw a basic distinction between the organ and other wind instruments.

> And of the organ alone the church has made use of in various kinds of singing ... other instruments being commonly rejected because of the abuses of the jongleurs.[60]

But the organ was only the surrogate for a real wind band, the sound being that of a wind band and its pipes being named for wind instruments. The real thing could not be far off.

The monks also needed entertainment and by the thirteenth century one begins to see frequent payment, or food and shelter, to jongleurs for performance in individual monasteries and priories, particularly in those of the Augustinian and Benedictine orders.[61] An attractive story says that in 1224 a Benedictine house in England received with joy two visitors assumed by their dress to be jongleurs. When it was discovered the two visitors were only visiting friars, they threw them out!

Gradually the Church itself begins to take advantage of the interest the instrumental musicians could bring to their festivities. Even the popes began to include instrumental music in their coronations during the thirteenth century. A report of the coronation of Gregory IX, in 1227, says, 'the crowds were taken by the sound of the trumpets.'[62] We begin to hear of church princes enjoying the prerogatives of their secular brothers, as in an example given by Ramón Lull.

> It happened one day that, while a certain Cardinal was dining, there came to his court a jongleur who was very well arrayed and adorned; he was a man of pleasing speech and personable, and he sang and played upon instruments very skillfully.[63]

And we even find in England wind instruments accompanied the singers in a Te Deum *inside* the church for the installation of a new abbot for St. Albans.[64]

Regarding the jongleur himself, by this period it was probably not so much a musical objection which the Church held as a hesitation to consider as a colleague the wandering, homeless instrumentalist. In the condemnation by some Churchmen, we learn some

---

60 Gilles de Zamore, 'Ars Musica,' in Martin Gerbert, *Scriptores ecclesiastici de musica sacra* (Saint Blaisen, 1784), II, 388.

61 E. K. Chambers, *The Mediaeval Stage* (Oxford: Clarendon Press, 1903), I, 56.

62 Alessandro Vessella, *La Banda*, 35.

63 Libre d'Evast e d'Aloma e de Banquerna, quoted in Christopher Page, *Voices and Instruments of the Middle Ages* (London: Dent, 1987), 181.

64 Richard Rastall, 'Some English Consort-Groupings of the late Middle Ages,' *Music & Letters* 55, no. 2 (April 1974): 193.

interesting details of these musicians and their activities. Lull, in a long anecdote, criticized a jongleur who, for a small fee, praises a knight.[65] It appears the jongleurs had a bad reputation for performing such services, for we also find this mentioned by John of Salisbury. He associates musicians in general ('Apollo') with 'empty praises like unto wind instruments' and says these players 'seldom or never are caught praising a man for that which is truly his own.'[66] In another place, Salisbury pretends surprise that musicians were accepted into the company of the Muses.

> Those who, after setting eyes on Apollo, merited not only to be classed as musicians, but even to be accepted into the company of the Muses.[67]

A twelfth-century biography of the Englishman, Hereward the Wake, tells of a jongleur singing not praises, but verses of an abusive nature about this noble. Unfortunately for the jongleur, Hereward enters the hall unexpectedly and hears this performance.

> Eventually unable to tolerate this any longer, Hereward leapt out and struck him through with a single blow of his sword, and then turned to attack the guests. Some were incapable of rising because they were drunk, and others unable to go to their help because they were unarmed. So he laid low fourteen of them ... and set their heads over the gate.[68]

Ramón Lull provided the most detailed description of the jongleur of this period in the following prayer.[69]

HOW ONE SHOULD BE WARY OF THE DOINGS OF JONGLEURS

The art of the jongleurs, Lord, began in praising and in glorifying you, and it was for that purpose that instruments were invented, and dances and songs and new melodies with which men rejoice in you.

But, as we may now see, Lord, in our time all the art of the jongleurs is changed, for those who apply themselves to playing upon instruments, to dancing and to composing neither sing, nor play their instruments, nor compose poems or songs save on the subject of lust and the vanity of this world.

Such jongleurs, Lord, as play upon instruments and sing of wantonness, praising in their singing such things as are not worthy of praise; such are damned, for they pervert the art of the jongleurs away from the purpose for which it was founded in the beginning.

65 Felix, Book VIII, in *Selected Works of Ramon Llull*, trans. Anthony Bonner (Princeton: Princeton University Press, 1985), II, 863.

66 'Policraticus,' in *The Statesman's Book of John of Salisbury*, 269–271.

67 *The Metalogicon*, 16.

68 Richard of Ely, 'The Life of Hereward the Wake,' in *Three Lives of the Last Englishmen*, trans. Michael Swanton (New York: Garland Publishing, 1984), 63.

69 Libre de Contemplació en Deu, in Ramon Llull, *Obres Essencials* (Barcelona: Editorial Selecta, 1957, 1960), quoted (substituting 'minstrel' for 'jongleur') in Page, *Voices and Instruments of the Middle Ages*, 181.

But those jongleurs, Lord, who rejoice and take delight with their instruments, dances and songs in your praise, love and goodness are blessed, for they preserve the art of the jongleurs as it was first established ...

If Mankind could only beware of, Lord, the evil which ensues from jongleurs and composers and how their songs and instruments are wretched and useless things, then these jongleurs and composers would not be so readily welcomed and accepted as they are.

Through the instruments that the jongleurs play and the new poems which they compose and sing, through the new dances that they devise and the things which they say, your goodness is forgotten, Lord ...

Might and virtue, holiness, greatness and blessedness and nobility may be known to be in you, Lord, for I greatly desire that you might see true jongleurs who praise those things which are to be praised and decry those things which are to be decried; and I further desire that no man should be able either to compose, sing, or play any instrument if he be not a servant and jongleur of true love and true worth, and a subject and lover of truth ...

Lord, True God, who became incarnate in Our Lady Saint Mary so that you might renew the race of Mankind! We see, Lord, that jongleurs dance, sing and sound instruments before men, so that they move them to joy and pleasure with their singing and dancing and with the instruments which they play ...

Since jongleurs, Lord, through the art and skill which they possess, can harmonize the music, dances and songs which they perform on their instruments with the music which they imagine in their hearts, how does this wonder come about that they do not know how to open their hearts to praise you?

The phrase used in the last sentence, 'the music which they imagine in their hearts,' demonstrates that Lull understood that the music came from within the player, which is significant because some earlier writers often associated music with the instrument itself. We find a similar phrase in Book IV of the *History* by Orderic Vitalis (1075–1143) where in speaking of three Church composers he says, 'They had music in their souls.'[70]

The principal distinction Lull was making was between the jongleur who composes 'on the subject of lust and the vanity of this world' and sings of 'wantonness' and his perception of how they should be performing on behalf of God. Bernard of Clairvaux was another who made an effort to distinguish between the nature of

---

70 *The Ecclesiastical History of Orderic Vitalis*, trans. Marjorie Chibnall (Oxford: Clarendon Press, 1969), II, 299.

spiritual music and that of the public. He, for example, gave an entire sermon on the 'Song of Songs' (Song of Solomon) in which he attempts to explain how the wedding music described in this book differs from the usual wedding music. This, he says, is music divinely inspired and can be understood only by those whose mind is disciplined by preserving study.

> For it is not a melody that resounds abroad but the very music of the heart, not a trilling on the lips but an inward pulsing of delight, a harmony not of voices but of wills. It is a tune you will not hear in the streets, these notes do not sound where crowds assemble.[71]

There must have been some who were still in favor of no instrumental music at all. Among them we are astonished to find Peter Abelard, who was not only a forward thinking monk in many ways, but had been a talented composer and singer.[72] Of all people, we find him maintaining the Church's ancient deception that the references to musical instruments in the Old Testament were merely metaphors and not descriptions of real performances. He suggests, for example, that the passage, 'Praise him with the timbrel and dance,'[73] is actually a metaphor in which the timbrel stands for 'the mortification of the flesh,' and the dance represents, 'that concord of charity.'[74] In another place Abelard makes a prejudicial comment about instrumental music, specifically the aulos, an instrument not used in church music, distinguishing it from music with a higher purpose. The aulos, he says, 'emits a sound for the delectation of the sense, not for the understanding of the mind.'[75]

Unfortunately, 'for the understanding of the mind,' refers not to musical understanding, but simply to the understanding of the *words* of the music. This had long been the central point of church music in the eyes of many Churchmen. Bernard makes this point quite clearly in one of his letters.

> If there is to be singing, the melody should be grave and not flippant or uncouth. It should be sweet but not frivolous; it should both enchant the ears and move the heart; it should lighten sad hearts and soften angry passions; and it should never obscure but enhance the sense of the words. Not a little spiritual profit is lost when minds are distracted from the sense of the words by the frivolity of the melody, when more is conveyed by the modulations of the voice than by the variations of the meaning.[76]

---

71 'On the Song of Songs,' trans. Kilian Walsh, in *The Works of Bernard of Clairvux* (Spencer, MA: Cistercian Publications, 1971), II, 4ff.

72 In a letter to Heloise, in *The Letters of Abelard and Heloise*, trans. C.K. Scott Moncrieff (New York: Knopf, 1933), 210, Abelard indicates no prejudice toward vocal music, saying of the woman in charge of music in a convent, 'it is most fitting that she be lettered, and especially that she be not ignorant of music.'

73 Psalms 149:1.

74 Letter to Heloise, in *The Letters of Abelard and Heloise*, 144.

75 Letter to Heloise, in ibid., 254.

76 Letter to Abbot Guy, quoted in *The Letters of St. Bernard of Clairvaux*, trans. James, 502. This is the most extended comment on Church music by Bernard. In this same letter he mentions that he had composed a Hymn, 'but I kept the sense clear at the expense of the meter.'

We must point out a rather humorous exception which Bernard makes to his testimonial on the importance of the words. By this date the books of the Old Testament known today as the Apocrypha, which although long accepted by the Church, were apparently beginning to be considered doubtful by Bernhard. In this case of unapproved Scripture, he says, the words put you to sleep!

> We found the text of the old Antiphonary very loosely put together and carelessly constructed; interspersed with numerous falsehoods and with the trifling ditties of the Apochrypha, it aroused in those reading it not only boredom but also contempt—and this to such an extent that novices, who had been educated under ecclesiastical discipline, grew inattentive and weary of both text and melody of the Antiphonary, and became quite sluggish and drowsy during the divine praises.[77]

77 *De Revisione Cantus Cistercienis*, 45.

In addition to the elements listed above which distract from the listener concentrating on the words, the very precision of the performance was probably thought important for this reason. Bernhard actually defines music in these terms, 'Music is the science of singing correctly.'[78] Vitalis, in his description of a monk, uses language which seems to make the same point relative to precision.

78 Ibid., 44.

> He was thoroughly versed in reading and singing, and after he grew up taught these freely to others with meticulous accuracy.[79]

79 *The Ecclesiastical History of Orderic Vitalis*, II, 127.

John of Salisbury, in giving advise to rulers, focuses on the precision of string players to create an analogy on government.

> For if a cithern player and other performers on stringed instruments can by diligence find a way to correct the fault of a string which is out of tune and bring it again into accord with the other strings, and so out of discord make the sweetest harmony, not by breaking the strings but by making them tense or slack in due proportions; with how much care should the prince moderate his acts, now with the strictness of justice, and now with the leniency of mercy, to the end that he may make his subjects all be of one mind.[80]

80 'Policraticus,' 39.

As in the above quotation, the word, 'sweet,' is often found in this literature as an apparent primary virtue of music. Vitalis mentions a monk named Guitmund, whom he calls 'highly skilled in composition,' who had produced 'some of the sweetest melodies in our troper.'[81] In another place he refers to a German abbot, Ainard, whom he describes as,

> well versed in the twin sciences of poetry and music, and a most skilled writer of melodious songs. This is plain to all from the ... many other sweet songs which he composed to the glory of his Creator.[82]

An interesting passage in a letter of Heloise to Abelard mentions his skill in both composition and singing. Here she remembers those songs, written to relieve the tedium of study, had a sweetness which achieved universality.

> Wherewith as with a game, refreshing the labor of philosophic exercise, thou has left many songs composed in amatory measure or rhythm, which for the suavity both of words and of tune being oft repeated, have kept thy name without ceasing on the lips of all; since even illiterates the sweetness of thy melodies did not allow to forget thee.[83]

Certainly in secular music this 'sweetness' must have referred in part to harmony, which was based on the third long before it was the case in church music. This, indeed, was Lull's definition of music.

> Music is the art devised to arrange many voices so they may be concordant in a single song.[84]

There are a few more descriptions of music by these Churchmen which should be mentioned. Bernard of Clairvaux, in the notes to his Antiphonary, makes three interesting observations which he unfortunately does not explain. Unlike everyone else, he says, his purpose is selecting music is to follow 'Nature, rather than [common] usage.'[85] He equates *authentic* with joyfulness and *plagal* with gravity.[86] Finally, 'neumas,' he says, were invented by the Greeks in order that their 'modes could be perceived at the same time by ear and mind.'[87]

We leave for last one of the most interesting Church persons of this period, and one who made some of the most enlightening observations on music, Hildegard of Bingen.

The purpose of music, says Hildegard, is to soften hard hearts.[88] In another, and more important, definition of the purpose of music, Hildegard concentrates on the listener, the critical element in aesthetics in music. Following the Aristotelian definition of aesthetics, she says that what the listener hears affects the inner person. Her

---

81 *The Ecclesiastical History*, II, 109.

82 Ibid., II, 353ff.

83 Letter of Heloise to Abelard, quoted in *The Letters of Abelard and Heloise*, trans. Moncrieff, 59.

84 'Ars Brevis,' X, 85, in *Selected Works of Ramon Llull*, trans. Bonner, I, 623. The editor adds this note: 'Possibly the *only* common medieval subject on which Lull wrote almost nothing was music.'

85 *De Revisione Cantus Cistercienis*, 59.

86 Ibid., 56.

87 Ibid., 57. On page 46ff he seems to argue against any creativity in the addition of the B-flat and on page 53 he suggests the correct limit of range in church music is a tenth—corresponding to the 10-string psaltery.

88 Quoted in *Hildegard of Bingen*, ed. Fiona Bowie and Oliver Davies (New York: Crossroad, 1993), 83.

frame of reference here is, of course, a religious one, which follows her mention of the numerous references to the performance of music in the Old Testament.

> In these words outer realities [performance] teach us about inner ones—namely how, in accordance with the material composition and quality of instruments, we can best transform and shape the performance of our inner being towards praises of the Creator.[89]

In another place she again speaks of music reaching the heart of the listener, here in using an analogy of the flute to represent what a good teacher does.

> But persons who carry out their tasks in life by teaching others according to the command of almighty God resound, so to speak, on flutes of sanctity. For by the voice of reason they chant justice right into the hearts of men and women ... The Word is heard by means of sound, and it is also disseminated so that it can be heard. Just as a flute can strengthen the human voice, the teacher's voice can be strengthened among other human beings through the fear and love of God.[90]

And in one more place she mentions the impact of music on the listener, noting, 'at times, when hearing some melody, a human being often sighs and moans.'[91]

In 1178, Hildegard, in allowing the burial of a nobleman who had been excommunicated and subsequently reconciled to the Church, came in conflict with the prelates of Mainz. As a result, they placed Hildegard and her sisters under an interdict, which among other things ordered her to cease singing the divine Service. Her letter of response includes a very interesting condensed history of Church music. She begins by citing the use of music in the Old Testament and then gives the following explanation for the invention of musical instruments,[92] which again focuses on the impact of music on the listener.

> They invented musical instruments of diverse kinds ... by which the songs could be expressed in multitudinous sounds, so that listeners, aroused and made adept outwardly, might be nurtured within by the forms and qualities of the instruments, as by the meaning of the words performed with them.[93]

---

89 Letter to the Mainz prelates, in ibid., 150.

90 'Vision Seven: 10,' in *The Book of Divine Works*, ed. Matthew Fox (Santa Fe: Bear & Company, 1987), 194.

91 *Hildegard of Bingen*, 151.

92 In the *Divine Works*, 'Vision Seven: 10,' Hildegard suggests a slight preference for string instruments, which she says have 'look up to God ... with the simplicity of a dove.' Players of wind instruments, on the other hand, 'serve humbly upon the Earth.' We wonder if this simply reflected how the instruments looked when held, the lyre or harp being held against the chest and pointing up and the aulos type wind instrument pointing down when played.

93 Ibid., 150.

Next, she says, men invented organum, 'so that they could sing in the delight of their soul.' Her following comment is very important and requires some introduction. We are familiar with the 'chironomist' seen in the tomb paintings of the ancient Egyptians, a figure who was clearly a kind of conductor although in his frozen postures we cannot see how he functioned. When new systems of musical notation begin to appear, after the Dark Ages, we see notation by neume symbols, with curves and swirls looking very much like lines tracing gestures. It is our hypothesis that these neume symbols are in fact a kind of 'picture' of what the chironomist did with his hands in the tomb paintings, that is, that there was an unbroken tradition. We are therefore struck by Hildegard's next comment, which seems to confirm this kind of hand-symbol conducting was still known in the twelfth century!

> ... and they adapted their singing to the bending of the finger-joints.[94]

Finally, the imagery of angels singing was a familiar one among early Church writers, due to their performance at the birth of Jesus. Hildegard mentions angel choirs frequently, sometimes 'immeasurably large choirs of angels,'[95] and has left us with a very poetic description of her vision of these singers.

> For most of the good angels look up to God. They acknowledge God with all the melodious sound of their hymns of praise, and laud in wonderful harmony the mysteries that have always been with God and are still with God today. The angels can never stop praising God because they are unencumbered by earthly bodies. They bear witness to the Godhead through the living resonance of their splendid voices, which are more numerous than the sands of the sea and which outnumber all the fruits that the Earth might ever produce. Their voices have a richer harmony than all the sounds living creatures have ever produced, and their voices are brighter than all the splendor of the sun, moon, and stars sparkling in the waters. More wonderful is this sound than the music of the spheres that arises from the blowing of the winds that sustain the four elements and are well adjusted to them.[96]

94 Ibid., 151.

95 'Vision One: 8,' in *Book of Divine Works*, 14.

96 'Vision Six: 4,' in ibid., 181ff.

21 SAINT THOMAS AQUINAS

With Thomas Aquinas (1224–1274) we come to the most prolific Church writer of the late Middle Ages. Born to a noble family, Aquinas spent five years at the University of Naples where he came under the influence of the recently rediscovered works of the ancient Greek philosophers. As a result, Aquinas' admiration for Aristotle is apparent on nearly every page of his many books (a number of them based directly on Aristotle) and in his emphasis on Reason. His purpose was to demonstrate that the uncompromising logic of Aristotle could be reconciled to a religion based on unquestioned faith. His 'intellectualism' was not well received by the followers of Francis, who sought God by Augustine's mystic road of love.[1] John Peckham, who followed Bonaventura in the chair of Philosophy in Paris criticized Aquinas for involving himself in the philosophy of a pagan.

From our perspective, his unrelenting dependence on Aristotle prevented him from developing original thought and when he does launch off on his own, it is so much centered in angels and in the soul as to be difficult in modern application.

ON THE PHYSIOLOGY OF AESTHETICS

'Man is a fusion of two natures, intellective and sensitive.'[2] This extraordinary statement by Aquinas, which is followed by the observation that the devil makes use of a 'double incitement to sin' in appealing to both the intellect and the senses, reads as if by one conversant with the modern understanding of the right and left hemispheres of the brain and their separation of rational and emotional–experiential brain functions. Aquinas found his proof that the intellect and the senses could not be of the same nature in two observations. First, in animals, who obviously have senses, but not intellect, and second in the observation that the objects of sense are corporeal, whereas intellectual concepts are not.[3]

1 Will Durant, *The Age of Faith* (New York: Simon and Schuster, 1950), 977.

2 *Summa Theologiae* (London: Blackfriars, 1971), XLIV, 187. For the 60 volumes of the *Summa Theologiae*, we will cite the volume and page number of this complete edition, rather than the traditional academic citation, which in this case would read, '2a2ae. 165, 2,' in order to facilitate the reader. See also, ibid., III, 15.

3 *Summa Contra Gentiles* (London: Burns Oates & Washbourne, 1923), LXVI.

As to how man uses these two basic faculties, Aquinas was nearly, but not quite, correct. Whereas we understand the hemispheres as being designed by nature to deal with dissimilar tasks, for Aquinas it was an understanding that one or the other faculty subdues the other.

> Man has a double nature, intellectual and sensual, and one may prevail over the other so that he becomes all of one piece. His sensitive part may be quite obedient to reason, as in the virtuous, or his reason may be quite absorbed in passion, as in those out of their mind. Sometimes the position lies inbetween; though clouded over by passion, the reason keeps some free play. And to that extent a person can either repel passion or at least keep it in check. It will depend on the disposition in which he finds himself, for this may vary according to the different parts of the soul, for a thing will strike him differently as a reasonable being and as a creature of feeling.[4]

Unfortunately, Aquinas' theories of human faculties become considerably more complicated, because he confuses 'soul' with functions which belong to the brain ('The specific nature of the human soul [is] intellectual'[5]). He says it is the *soul's* power of sight which is in the eye and whose hearing is in the ear, accomplished through something he calls, 'internal sense power.'[6] Moreover the soul's powers of intellect and will are not said to be anywhere, specifically, in the body![7]

Now the body plays no part in the activity of the intellect.[8]

We will set aside Aquinas' specific theories of the soul and attempt to extract those ideas which are more meaningful in a modern context.

On Reason

We have mentioned above Aquinas' statement, 'Man is a fusion of two natures, intellective and sensitive.' It is in the cooperation of these two 'natures,' specifically the intellective taking from the sensitive, that Aquinas finds his explanation for man's mental processes. In a paraphrase of Aristotle, Aquinas states that sensory perception is common to all men and that 'all human knowledge originates with this.'[9]

---

4 *Summa Theologiae*, XVII, 93. In *Summa Contra Gentiles*, LVIII, Aquinas says that in the intellective soul we are men; in the sensitive soul we are animals; and in the nutritive soul we are living. The nutritive is ruled by the sensitive; the sensitive is ruled by the intellectual.

5 *Summa Theologiae*, XI, 23, 49, 147; XX, 123.

6 Ibid., XV, 31.

7 Ibid., 87. See also *Commentary on Peri Hermeneias*, trans. Jean Oesterle (Milwaukee: Marquette University Press, 1962), 115 (19a12.14.) and *Commentary on de Anima*, quoted in *Selected Writings of St. Thomas Aquinas*, ed. M.C. D'Arcy (New York: Dutton, 1950), 68.

8 Ibid., XV, 153. See also *Summa Contra Gentiles*, LXIX ('since the intellect is not the act of any part of the body').

9 *Commentary on the Metaphysics of Aristotle*, trans. John Rowan (Chicago: Henry Regnery, 1961), I, 19 (I. L. 2: C 45). Additional discussion of the role of the senses supplying information to the intellect can be found in *Summa Theologiae*, III, 41; X, 11; XI, 17, 113, 137; XIII, 27; XV, 25, and *Summa Contra Gentiles*, III, and XCVI.

The actual process, in Aquinas' view, is that information from the senses leads to memories, which lead to our taking 'observation of things, whereby we arrive at the understanding of the universal principles of sciences and arts.'[10] In somewhat more elaborate explanations of this process, he says,

> The human intellect only turns to sense-objects through the medium of images. From these images he arrives at ideas of sense-objects, and while considering these ideas, judges of the realities and disposes of them. So in every operation in which our intellect abstracts from images, it needs also to abstract from the senses.[11]
>
> ...
>
> The first step is the consideration of things of sense; the second is the transition from sensible to intelligible things; the third is the evaluation of the things of sense through those of mind; the fourth is the consideration in their own right of intelligible things which have been reached through the sensible; the fifth is the contemplation of intelligible realities which cannot be reached through the things of sense but can be understood by reason; the sixth is the consideration of intelligible things which the intellect can neither discover nor exhaust; this is the sublime contemplation of divine truth wherein contemplation is finally perfected.[12]

The point of all this, and it should be no surprise coming from a Churchman, was to demonstrate why the intellect is a higher power than the senses.

> Since mind in man dominates and rules his other powers, so their natural urges should be subordinated to mind. Hence it is generally held that it is right for all human tendencies to be directed according to intelligence.[13]

Aquinas found his primary justification for the higher recognition of Reason in two basic concepts. The first was a belief that the senses are entirely independent, thus each singularly limited.

> But there is a difference between sense and intellect, because a sense is not able to know all things, but sight can know only colors; hearing, only sounds; and so for the rest; whereas the intellect is able to know all things without such limitations.[14]

10 *Summa Contra Gentiles*, LXXXIII.

11 *Summa Theologiae*, XLV, 109.

12 Ibid., XLVI, 29.

13 Ibid., XXVIII, 91; XXXII, 5; *Summa Contra Gentiles*, LXXIII; and *The 'Summa Theologica' of St. Thomas Aquinas* (London: Burns Oates & Washbourne, 1927), II, 79.

14 *On the Unity of the Intellect Against the Averroists*, trans. Beatrice Zedler (Milwaukee: Marquette University Press, 1968), 30.

In another place one can see that Aquinas assumed if one were handicapped in one of the senses it would follow that intellectual discernment would be impaired.[15]

15 Ibid., XII, 45.

The second justification given for the prominence of Reason was that while the senses dwelt only with individual matter, Reason dwelt with universals.[16]

16 *Summa Theologiae*, III, 15. See also: XVI, 55, XXXIV, 37, and XXXVI, 13.

> Whoever knows universals knows in some respect the things which are subordinate to universals, because he knows the universal in them. But all things are subordinate to those which are the most universal. Therefore the one who knows the most universal things, knows in a sense all things …
>
> But those things which are most universal are farthest removed from sensible things, because the senses have to do with singular things. Hence universals are the most difficult for men to know.[17]

17 *Commentary on the Metaphysics of Aristotle*.

In spite of this vote of confidence in Reason, it is interesting that when it came to presenting 'divine matters' to the masses, Aquinas believed this could *only* be done through the senses, rather than Reason. This, he said, was the purpose of the ceremonial aspect of religion.[18]

18 *Summa Theologiae*, XXIX, 41.

Engaging in a bit of 'weird science,' Aquinas cites the heavenly bodies as being another influence on intelligence.

> We must observe that although heavenly bodies cannot be the direct cause of our knowledge, they can cooperate indirectly towards it … Thus, even as physicians are able to judge of a man's intelligence from his bodily temperament, as a proximate disposition thereto, so too can an astrologer, from the heavenly movements, as being a remote cause of this disposition. In this sense we can approve of the saying of Ptolemy:
>
> > When Mercury is in one of Saturn's houses at the time of a man's birth, he bestows on him a quick intelligence of the inner nature of things.[19]

19 *Summa Contra Gentiles*, LXXXIV. In ibid., XV, 107, Aquinas returns to his praise of astrologers for their ability to 'foretell the truth in the majority of cases,' regarding whether a man will be carried away by his passions or not. Further endorsement of astrology can be found in *Commentary on Peri Hermeneias*, 115 (19a12.14.) and 'Letter to Reginald of Piperno,' quoted in *Theological Texts*, trans. Thomas Gilby (London: Oxford University Press, 1955), 243.

Regarding genetic, or innate, intelligence, Aquinas is somewhat ambivalent. In several places he describes a kind of template of knowledge being innate in man. In speaking of the creation of the world, for example, Aquinas says God created things not simply to be themselves, but to be the 'originals and sources of other things.'

> Therefore the first man was so established by God that he understood everything which it is natural for man to be instructed in. This means

all things that exist virtually in self-evident principles, namely whatever men can get to know naturally.²⁰

20 *Summa Theologiae*, XIII, 97ff, 103.

In two places, he seems to suggest that Nature has provided certain genetic forms of knowledge.

> Principles instilled in [human reason] by nature provide general rules and measures for what men should do.²¹
>
> ...
>
> But although our intellect is self-actuated in certain ways, still certain things are provided for it by nature, e.g. first principles, about which it has no choice.²²

21 Ibid., XXVIII, 27. In ibid., XI, 139, Aquinas gives examples of genetic knowledge in animals.

22 Ibid., IV, 125.

In a more specific example, he suggests that it is a kind of pre-existent template which allows us to know God, whom we find in a kind of 'picture,' a 'likeness' innately implanted in us.²³

Still another form of innate knowledge, which we might call the knowledge necessary to use knowledge—something like the program of a computer which exists before data is entered—he identifies with the soul.²⁴

On the other hand, in other places he seems to take quite a different view of any form of genetic or innate knowledge. In a discussion of the transmission of original sin, for example, Aquinas contends that while the guilt of the original sin is passed on genetically through semen, 'a rational soul is *not* transmitted with the semen by generation.'²⁵

23 Ibid., III, 33. This is followed by the observation that the reason we cannot think of 'many things at once is that to think of them we need many likenesses in the mind, and one mind cannot be formed by many likenesses at once.' Psychologists today believe we have, in fact, 'many minds.'

24 Ibid., XII, 33ff; XI, 69.

25 Ibid., XXVI, 11.

It also appeared to be a problem for Aquinas that he could not account for the great variety of men, if genetic information were common to *all* men. As an illustration, he points out that if a man is asked to think of a 'stone,' while every man will correctly think of a general, abstract concept, each individual man, at the same time, will think of an individual stone.

> So that if there were one intellect in all men the various sense-images in this man and that could not give rise to different acts of understanding attributable to this man and that respectively. We are left with the fact that it is absolutely impossible and incongruous to posit one single power of understanding among all men.²⁶

26 Ibid., XI, 55.

Aquinas is also ambivalent in his statements about Truth, as it is found in mental faculties. In one place he writes, 'truth in the strict sense is in intellect alone,'[27] yet in his commentary on Aristotle's *Metaphysics* he seems inclined to find Truth 'on the other side,' in the senses.

> Hence, according to these thinkers, whatever appears in the senses is necessarily true; and since we must add that all knowing is sensory, it follows that whatever appears in any way at all to anyone is true.[28]

A final complication in the operation of Reason is the role of the will, which he says is to the mind as emotional appetite is to the senses.[29] His primary concern was that without the control of Reason, the will had a natural tendency toward objects of the senses.[30]

ON THE NATURE OF THE SENSES

Aquinas placed the senses in a specific hierarchy, the highest of which being sight. Sight, he calls the most spiritual of the senses and with the widest range of objects.[31] Hearing and smell he places in a lower category because 'their objects undergo physical change.' Touch and taste are the lowest, for the reason that they actually come in contact with their objects.

Among the animals, he observes that man has the most developed sense of touch, but the poorest sense of smell. The latter he attributes to his theory that the large brain in man is necessary to cool the heat of the heart, and a large brain, 'owing to its moistness, is a hindrance to the sense of smell which requires dryness.'[32]

Aquinas contends that in general we prize the senses because they give us pleasure and because they are useful. In his opinion, sight gives the most pleasure with regard to knowledge, but for sensory pleasure touch is the most appreciated due to our desire for 'food, sex, and the like.'[33]

It is interesting that Aquinas includes the senses as one of the 'sensitive powers,' among which are also imagination and memory.[34] It seemed obvious to him that imagination was tied to the senses, for how could a blind man imagine color?[35] Memory he includes here as he felt it was evident that it was based on images.[36]

---

27 Ibid., IV, 97.

28 *Commentary on the Metaphysics of Aristotle*, 270 (IV. L. 12: C 672).

29 *Summa Theologiae*, V, 5.

30 *Summa Contra Gentiles*, X; *Summa Theologiae*, XV, 25 and XXXVI, 137.

31 *Summa Theologiae*, XI, 133. The last statement is not quite accurate. Our visual range is slightly less than one octave, from infrared to ultraviolet, whereas hearing covers some eight octaves from about 60 to 16,000 hertz.

32 Ibid., XIII, 27. In some additional 'weird science,' Aquinas says the senses are hindered during sleep 'by vapors or gases that are released during digestion, and proportionately to their amount.' [Ibid., XII, 47]

33 Ibid., XX, 21. It is odd that he associates the sense of touch, rather than taste, with food!

34 *Summa Contra Gentiles*, LXXIII. Intuition, however, is information secretly provided us by angels. [Ibid., XCII]

35 *Summa Theologiae*, XV, 29. In Ibid., XX, 103, Aquinas makes it clear that imagination is a mental process, even though associated with the 'sensitive powers.' Here he notes, 'Perception by imagination and reason is more profound than perception by the sense of touch.'

36 Ibid., XXXVI, 63.

ON THE PSYCHOLOGY OF AESTHETICS

On Pleasure and Pain

In his discussion of Pleasure, Aquinas again returns to his concept of the intellectual and sensitive natures of man and finds Pleasure on both sides. Pleasure on the affective side is associated with pleasure of the senses, accompanied by physiological reaction, whereas on the rational side it is pleasures of the intellect, characterized by 'a movement of the will.'[37]

For a number of reasons, Aquinas concludes that of the two, the pleasures of the intellect are far preferable to those of the senses.

> A person gets far more pleasure from knowing something by understanding it than by feeling it ... Intellectual knowledge is more highly prized: a man would rather lose his sight than his sanity ...
>
> Spiritual good is greater than physical good, and is in fact preferred to it. An indication of this is the fact that people will forgo even the greatest pleasures of the body rather than suffer loss of honor; and honor is a good appreciated only by the intellect.[38]

None the less, observed Aquinas, most people seek the physical pleasures of the senses and he warned that only Reason could serve as a check on these impulses. Spiritual pleasures, on the other hand, being 'seated in the mind' were 'sober' by their very nature.[39]

But can Pleasure have an independent value? Aquinas, being mostly worried about Pleasure interfering with Reason, did not advance strong arguments in this regard. He did believe that Pleasure arising from the use of Reason had the effect of exercising that faculty.[40] Otherwise, Pleasure was at best a relief, 'Pleasure is to the experiences of the soul what natural rest is to the body.'[41]

On the whole, this solemn Churchman saw little to recommend in Pleasure for its own sake. Some of his strongest arguments against the dangers of Pleasure are found in a treatise, 'On the Governance of Rulers,' written for the king of Cyprus. Here, he warns,

> Indulgence in superfluous pleasure leads from the path of virtue, for nothing conduces more easily to immoderate increase which upsets the mean of virtue, than pleasure. Pleasure is, by its very nature, greedy, and thus on a slight occasion one is precipitated into the seductions of shameful pleasures just as a little spark is sufficient to kindle dry wood.

37 Ibid., XX, 13.

38 Ibid., 17.

39 Ibid., 19.

40 Ibid., 27.
41 Ibid., 63.

Also, they who give themselves up to pleasures grow soft in spirit and become weak-minded when it is a question of tackling some difficult enterprise, enduring toil, and facing dangers …

Finally, men who have become dissolute through pleasures usually grow lazy and, neglecting necessary matters and all the pursuits that duty lays upon them, devote themselves wholly to the quest of pleasure, on which they squander all that others had so carefully amassed.[42]

42 *On Kingship to the King of Cyprus*, trans. Gerald Phelan (Toronto: The Pontifical Institute of Mediaeval Studies, 1949), 79.

Looking at Pleasure relative to the life of the Christian, Aquinas, in his *Summa Contra Gentiles*, considers happiness from the perspective of the end of man. In a chapter called, 'Does Happiness consist in an Act of the Will?,' he eliminates both Delight and Desire as sources of ultimate happiness.[43] This is followed by a series of chapters, the titles of which outline his case.

43 *Summa Contra Gentiles*, VI.

That Human Happiness does not Consist in Carnal Pleasures
That Happiness does not Consist in Honors
That Man's Happiness Consists not in Glory
That Man's Happiness does not Consist in Wealth
That Happiness Consists not in Worldly Power
That Happiness Consists not in Goods of the Body
That Human Happiness is not Seated in the Senses
That Man's Ultimate Happiness does not Consist in Acts of Moral Virtue
That Ultimate Happiness does not Consist in the Act of Prudence
That Happiness does not Consist in the Practice of Art

This extensive pessimism finally reaches the conclusion, 'Therefore it is not possible for man to be happy in this life.'[44] The sole hope he holds out is, 'Man's ultimate happiness is essentially to know God by the intellect.'[45]

44 Ibid., XLVIII.

45 Ibid., XXVI.

Regarding Pain as a separate topic, Aquinas writes of exterior and interior pain, the former involving touch and the latter involving the imagination or the result of an activity which is not in concert with Reason.[46] Interior pain, he says, is 'more profound than perception by the sense of touch,' the latter being something we know today is only an illusion.[47]

46 *Summa Theologiae*, XX, 67, 81. Even contemplation can turn to Pain, if one's contemplation of an unworthy object prevents one from contemplating something more worthy. [Ibid., 97]

47 Ibid., 103. Of course his thesis is fundamentally wrong, for we understand today that *all* pain is interior pain. The phenomenon known as 'phantom limb,' where pain is experienced in an arm which no longer exists, proves that we only think we feel pain in the body.

He makes some important observations about Pain, beginning with the fact that it too can distract Reason. It can thus distract one from learning or prevent one from 'giving his attention to things he already knows.'[48]

48 Ibid., 125.

Pain can, in some cases, indirectly provide Pleasure, as in the case of the theater,[49] a line of thought he perhaps founded on Aristotle's concept of catharsis. Also, he points out, 'weeping and sobbing naturally assuage sorrow.' Since he says there is always some pleasure in an activity appropriate to one's state at the moment, it follows that weeping can be a form of pleasure to the extent that it relieves sorrow.[50] Regarding this idea, he quotes Aristotle as observing that the greater the pain, the more sensitive we are to the pleasure which soothes it, a comment which has direct relevance to the repertoire of the troubadours.[51]

49 Ibid., 87.

50 Ibid., 139.

51 Ibid., XXI, 125.

On the Emotions

The overall understanding of the emotions by Aquinas is summarized in the following statement.

> All the emotions issue from certain initial ones, namely love and hatred, and finish in certain others, namely pleasure and sorrow. In like manner, all the operations that are the matter of moral virtue are related to one another, and even to the emotions.[52]

52 Ibid., XXIII, 183. See also, ibid., XIX, 49, 51, 57.

He then arranges, under these categories, all the remaining emotions as he recognized them.

> We are now in a position to arrange all of the emotions in the order of their actual occurrence. First come love and hatred; second, desire and aversion; third, hope and despair; fourth, fear and courage; fifth, anger; sixth and last, joy or sadness, which come after all the emotions. From what we have said it is clear that, within these pairs, love has precedence over hatred, desire over aversion, fear over courage, and joy over sadness.[53]

53 Ibid., XIX, 55.

Aquinas is contradictory in his statements on where exactly in man the emotions are located. In one place he indicates that the emotions were not located in the cognitive side of man, but instead in the soul.[54] While it was clear to him they were related to the senses, in another place he concludes they must also be related to the intellect, on the basis that the Scriptures also mention love and joy with respect to God and the angels.[55] In yet another place he suggests that emotions exist in the intellect without a corporeal organ, but in the senses with corporeal organs.[56]

54 Ibid., 11.

55 Ibid., 13.

56 *Summa Contra Gentiles*, LXXXIII

Having noticed that physiological changes were associated with strong emotions, he incorrectly concludes that the senses themselves also change, for example the eye seeing a bright color becomes that color itself. The physical changes for an emotion such as anger, he attributed to 'the overheating of the blood around the heart.'[57]

After having made these observations, incorrect as they are, it is odd that Aquinas does not generally associate emotions as properties of the person himself so much as with the object which produces the emotions.

> Every emotion involves a movement either towards or away from some object ...
> Accordingly, there are two possible criteria of contrast between two emotions; one, their having contrary objects, viz. sense-good and sense-evil; the other, their involving a movement towards and a movement away from the same object.[58]
>
> ...
>
> The nature of an emotion is determined by its object just as these other things are characterized by their forms. Whatever is the cause of a form is a cause of what is constituted by that form; similarly, what causes an object is a cause of an emotion. The cause of an object may be either an agent or a material disposition. Thus the object of delight is what appears to be agreeable, suitable, and at hand.[59]

Because Aquinas focused on the object, rather than the person, he also failed to realize that the emotions are universal, indeed as we know today, genetic. Interestingly enough, Aquinas acknowledged that Aristotle had maintained that the emotions are universal, then goes on to say this view was now controversial, supplies a contemporary false explanation and, finally, his own incorrect analysis of what Aristotle *really* meant!

> There are some who object to Aristotle's position that passions of the soul, which vocal sounds signify, are the same for all men. Their argument against it is as follows: different men have different opinions about things; therefore, passions of the soul do not seem to be the same among all men ...
> Aristotle's statement should be referred to the simple conceptions of the intellect—that are signified by the incomplex vocal sounds— which are the same among all men.[60]

---

57 *Summa Theologiae*, XIX, 13.
58 Ibid., 23.
59 Ibid., XXI, 55.
60 *Commentary on Peri Hermeneias*, 27ff.

Aquinas is also somewhat contradictory in his discussions of the emotions and their moral characteristics. In one place he speaks as if the emotions themselves have a moral quality.

> Those emotions are good which create a favorable attitude towards something truly good or an unfavorable one towards something really evil; and those emotions are evil which create an unfavorable attitude toward something truly good, or a favorable one towards something really evil.[61]

61 Ibid., XIX, 43.

In another place, he clearly says the emotions themselves have no moral quality.

> Emotions in themselves are not sins. We censure them only when they follow after something bad, just as we praise them when they follow after the good.[62]

62 Ibid., XXXV, 23.

Usually, however, he speaks of the control of Reason as being the agent which determines the moral quality of emotions. It is this alone, he says, which separates man from the animals.

> There are two ways of looking at the emotions: intrinsically, or as subject to the control of reason and will. Now intrinsically of course the emotions are simply movements of the non-rational; one cannot therefore ascribe to them moral, good or evil, which we have shown to involve the reason.
> But in so far as the emotions are subject to the control of reason and will, moral judgments do apply to them.[63]
>
> ...
>
> Emotion leads one towards sin in so far as it is uncontrolled by reason; but in so far as it is rationally controlled, it is part of the virtuous life.[64]

63 Ibid., XIX, 33.

64 Ibid., 37.

Having stressed the importance of the emotions being under the control of Reason, Aquinas cautions that strong emotions have the capacity for blinding Reason.

> There are degrees in being transformed by passion. It may go so far as to blind the reason completely, as happens when vehement rage of concupiscence makes a man beside himself or out of his mind; this may come also from some physical disorder. Passion, remember, goes with physiological change. In this condition men become like the beasts, driven of necessity by passion; they are without the motion of reason, and, consequently, of will.[65]

65 Ibid., XVII, 91.

Not understanding that emotions are actually in the brain, Aquinas attributes the occurrence of the emotions overcoming Reason to some condition of the body.

> Now emotional appetite is an organic power, and in this it differs from intellective appetite or will, which is not. Every power using a bodily organ depends not only on a psychological ability but also on a physiological disposition, thus the act of seeing is both from the sense-power and from the condition of the eye, which may be a help or an hindrance. Likewise the activity of sensitive appetite flows not only from an appetitive force but also from a bodily disposition …
>
> That a man lusts, try not to as he will, is due to a disposition of body which holds up the sensitive appetite from perfect compliance with the command of reason.[66]

Aquinas again engages in a bit of 'weird science,' in attributing an influence on the emotions by the planets.

> We have already noted that emotional feeling is an act of a bodily organ. Consequently there is nothing to prevent us holding that impressions from heavenly bodies render some people more prompt to anger than others, or to concupiscence, or to some such emotion. Indeed they are such by temperamental constitution. Most men follow their passions; only the wise resist. And therefore in the majority of cases astrological predications may well be verified.[67]
>
> …
>
> [The heavenly bodies] may make impressions on our own body, and when the body is affected movements of the passions arise; either because such impressions make us liable to certain passions; for instance the bilious are prone to anger; or because they produce in us a bodily disposition that occasions a particular choice, thus when we are ill, we choose to take medicine. Sometimes too, the heavenly bodies are a cause of human acts, when through an indisposition of the body a person goes out of his mind, and loses the use of reason.[68]

In another place, Aquinas speaks of the temperamental constitution of the individual man, here suggesting it is perhaps genetic in origin.

> If the nature of a given individual be considered, in terms of his unique temperament, again anger is more natural than desire. Anger is easily aroused as a result of a natural, temperamental inclination to irascibility, more easily than desire or any other emotion. An irascible disposition is characteristic of a choleric temperament and

[66] Ibid., 199ff.

[67] Ibid., 79.

[68] *Summa Contra Gentiles*, LXXXV.

choler is more quickly aroused than other humors; it is said to be like fire. Thus a person who by temperament has a naturally irascible disposition will become angry more readily than one who has a pleasure-loving disposition will have his desires aroused. For this reason, too, Aristotle holds that anger is more likely to be inherited from one's parents than desire.[69]

69 *Summa Theologiae*, XXI, 99.

Finally, Aquinas makes an interesting speculation that all understanding in the mind is accompanied by an emotion, a thought that reminds us that some modern psychologists believe that all distant memories exist only because they are associated with emotions.

> No impression is made on the body as a result of an apprehension, unless united to the apprehension there be some emotion, such as joy, fear, desire, or some other passion.[70]

70 *Summa Contra Gentiles*, CIII.

ON AESTHETICS

It should be no surprise that Aquinas' definition of Beauty is framed in a reference to God.

> Nothing exists which does not participate in beauty and goodness, since each thing is beautiful and good according to its proper form …
> Created beauty is nothing other than a likeness of the divine beauty participated in things …
> For beauty three things are required: a) integrity or perfection, b) right proportion or consonance, c) splendor of form.[71]

71 Quoted in James F. Anderson, *An Introduction to the Metaphysics of St. Thomas Aquinas* (Chicago: Henry Regnery, 1953), 88.

In his most extended definition of Beauty, Aquinas again stresses the importance of proportion, in addition to discussing the difference between Beauty and the Good.

> A good thing is also in fact a beautiful thing, for both epithets have the same basis in reality, namely, the possession of form; and this is *why the good is esteemed beautiful*. Good and beautiful are not however synonymous. For good (being *what all things desire*) has to do properly with desire and so involves the idea of end (since desire is a kind of movement towards something.) Beauty, on the other hand, has to do with knowledge, and we call a thing beautiful when it pleases the eye of the beholder. This is why beauty is a matter of right proportion, for the senses delight in rightly proportioned things as

similar to themselves, the sense-faculty being a sort of proportion itself like all other knowing faculties. Now since knowing proceeds by imaging, and images have to do with form, beauty properly involves the notion of form.[72]

In another place where Aquinas contrasts Beauty and the Good, he adds the very interesting comment that of all the senses, only sight and hearing also contribute to knowledge in their association with Beauty.

> Those senses are therefore chiefly associated with beauty which contribute most to our knowledge, viz. sight and hearing when ministering to reason; thus we speak of beautiful sights and beautiful sounds, but not of beautiful tastes and smells: we do not speak of beauty in reference to the other three senses.[73]

A final observation on Beauty is very Aristotelian in character, in that the emphasis is on the observer. Aquinas makes a significant point in associating the perception of Beauty with the inherent quality of the observer himself. It suggests we should not try to use Art to educate the person, but we should educate the person to appreciate Art.

> In human matters beauty goes with what is well-ordered according to intelligence; Cicero speaks of a consonance with man's nobility, wherein he differs from other animate beings.
>
> ...
>
> We have pointed out that a thing is called valuable in itself because of its beauty shaped by intelligence. To this shapeliness we respond because of what we are by our nature: each and everything delights in what matches it.[74]

Aquinas uses the word, 'Art,' to include craftsmen and builders of utilitarian objects, and most of his commentary on Art concerns these crafts. A typical example:

> Now all practical sciences, arts and powers are lovable only for the sake of something else, since their end is not knowledge but work.[75]

But one can find among these ideas some which are also germane to real artists. He discusses the general field of Art from the perspective of the artist, his craft and the art object.

[72] *Summa Theologiae*, II, 73. Aquinas discusses the roles of form and matter in ibid., 97.

[73] Ibid., XIX, 77.

[74] Ibid., XLIII, 39, 77.

[75] *Summa Contra Gentiles*, XXV.

His comments on the artist center on whether Art is in the artist or the finished art object. The original form of any art work is in the mind of the creator and Aquinas in one place seems to be thinking of this creative, intuitive form of the Art work.

> Now the craftsman by the knowledge of his art knows even those things which are not yet produced by his art: since the forms of his art pass from his knowledge into external matter so as to produce the works of his art: and consequently nothing prevents forms which have not yet materialized outwardly from being in the craftsman's knowledge.[76]

76 Ibid., LXVI.

More frequently, Aquinas takes a more 'rational' view of the form of Art in the artist's mind and speaks of a kind of mental storehouse of the techniques of the art.

> An idea in the mind of the maker, which is called the rule and pattern of art, exists before the production of external works of art ...[77]
>
> ...
>
> Forgetting refers only to knowing, and so by forgetting a person can entirely lose an art, and likewise a science, for these lie in the mind.[78]

77 *Summa Theologiae*, XXXVII, 7. See also *Commentary on the Metaphysics of Aristotle*, 12ff (I. L. 1: C 18), 534 (VII. L. 6: C 1408).

78 *Summa Theologiae*, XXXVI, 51.

He places great importance in this kind of knowledge, pointing out that 'men who have an art are wiser and more knowing than those who have [mere] experience.'[79] And it is in this same light that he several times stresses that the man who has the ideas is more important than the man who carries them out.[80]

For the artist, Aquinas believed the next step was more important, the actual engagement of this technique. In one place he describes the process in the artist as being exactly like that of the speaker.

> An artist first intends his work of art, next shapes it in his mind and fancy, and then in his material. Similarly, a speaker first conceives the meaning he intends to convey, afterwards finds a sign for it [language], and finally pronounces it.[81]

79 *Commentary on the Metaphysics of Aristotle*, 15 (I. L. 1: C 29).

80 Ibid., 14 (I. L. 1:C 26), 19 (I. L. 2: C 41); *Commentary on Aristotle's Physics*, trans. Richard Blackwell (New Haven: Yale University Press, 1963), 84 (194 a 12 - b 15); and *Summa Theologiae*, I, 23.

81 *Disputations*, IV de Veritate, 1, quoted in *Theological Texts*, 63.

In several places, Aquinas clearly suggests that Art is in this technique, this carrying out of the Art work, and not in the Art object itself, concluding, 'Art does not exist in the thing produced by art but in something else.'[82] The beginning of Art, then, was in the beginning of the production.

82 *Commentary on the Metaphysics of Aristotle*, 529 (VII. L. 6: C 1381). In *Summa Contra Gentiles*, LXXV, Aquinas explains why the nature of the technique of the teacher to be more comparable to the physician than the builder of a house.

> The beginning of its essence is the principles intrinsically making up the art; of its working, the point of actual application to the matter at hand. In this sense we might speak of the foundation as the beginning of the building-art, meaning that it is there that the builder begins to work.[83]

It also follows that anything wrong in a work of art is synonymous with something wrong in the art which produced it. The very fact that it was possible for there to be errors in Art was for Aquinas therefore proof that there was a recognized 'correct' technique.

> Of the things which are made by art for the sake of something, some are made according to art and are made correctly. There are other things, however, in which the artisan fails, not acting according to his art, and in these cases error occurs, even though the art is acting for the sake of something. For if art does not act for a determinate end, then there would be no error no matter how the art was performed. For the operation of the art would be equally related to all things. The very fact, then, that there happens to be error in art is a sign that art acts for the sake of something. The same thing also happens in natural things in which monsters are, as it were, the errors of nature acting for the sake of something insofar as the correct operation of nature is deficient.[84]

In this regard, Aquinas felt it necessary to make a distinction between an error in art, versus an error in the artist.

> Particular ends are subordinate to the common end. Now since, as we have noted, a sin or failure is a deviation from the way to an end, there can be two sorts of mistakes in the activity of art. One is by deviating from the particular end the artist himself proposes, and this is a mistake or failure proper to art, for example, if he intends a good work and makes a bad one, or intends a bad one and makes a good one. The other is by deviating from the common end of human living; in this respect an artist is said to fail if he intends to make a bad work and succeeds to such effect as to beguile another. For the first sort of mistake he is blamed as an artist; for the second he is blamed as a man.[85]

But he also recognized that a mistake in the technique is not the same thing as deviation from the norm due to genius.

---

83 *Summa Theologiae*, XXXIII, 65.

84 *Commentary on Aristotle's Physics*, 121 (199 a 34 – b 33); and *Summa Theologiae*, XXV, 11.

85 *Summa Theologiae*, XVIII, 111.

An artist who deliberately breaks the rules of his art is reckoned a better artist, as keeping a sound judgment of what they are, than one who involuntarily breaks them, from a fault, it would seem, of judgment.[86]

86 Ibid., XXXVI, 29.

For Aquinas, one characteristic of the fine artist was that the technique, important as it is, should not be apparent in the performance of the art. For illustration, he provides here a rare reference to a musician.

It is obvious that art does not deliberate. Nor does the artisan deliberate insofar as he has the art, but insofar as he falls short of the certitude of the art. Hence the most certain arts do not deliberate, as the writer does not deliberate how he should form letters. Moreover, those artisans who do deliberate, after they have discovered the certain principles of the art, do not deliberate in the execution. Thus one who plays the harp would seem most inexperienced if he should deliberate in playing any chord.[87]

87 *Commentary on Aristotle's Physics*, 123 (199 a 34 – b 33). An exception, apparently, is the case of the dancer,

For men who do not have the art of dancing can move about but not in the way in which those men do who have this art. [*Commentary on the Metaphysics of Aristotle*, 546 (VII. L. 8: C 1439)].

He mentions the harpist again in observing that it is by experience that the artist acquires his technique.

For it seems impossible that anyone should become a builder who has not first built something; or that anyone should become a harpist who has not first played the harp.[88]

88 *Commentary on the Metaphysics of Aristotle*, 684–685 (IX.L.7:C 1850).

We have quoted Aquinas' views on Art in the mind of the artist and then regarding Art as it is found in the artist's technique. What about the art object itself? Again, Aquinas is somewhat contradictory. In several places he clearly argues that the *real* definition of Art is in the art object.

The value of an art lies in the thing produced rather than in the artist, since art is right judgment about works to be made … Now art is concerned with the making of things … Art does not require of an artist that his activity be good, but that his work be good …[89]

89 *Summa Theologiae*, XXIII, 55.

…

Art is nothing other than right judgment about things to be made. Yet the good of these things depends, not upon the disposition of the maker's appetite, but on the worth of the very work done. An artist as such is not commendable for the will with which he makes a work, but for its quality.[90]

90 Ibid., 47. See also Disputations, de Caritate, 2, quoted in *Theological Texts*, 211, 'what is good, will be found in [the artist's] work of art.'

But, in the case of music, we know this is not true—the finished composition being only a representation of the more important, and more complete, intuitive idea of the composer. Aquinas, too, in one place writes that the finished product cannot be thought of as something higher than the producer.

> The form of the thing produced is not the purpose of the production except in so far as it is the likeness of the producer's own form, a likeness which it is set to communicate. Otherwise, since an end is higher than the steps to it, we would have the anomaly of the form of the thing produced being better than the producer.[91]

In any case, Aquinas was not eager to praise Art too highly. He clearly understood that the finished art object was something different from the artist's original concept,[92] and, in the end, viewed Art only as an external object.

> Not every human good is the subject of art, but only ... the production of external things.[93]

This being the case, he was quick to point out that Art has a lesser value than human values.

> Science and art are about particular goods, not the ultimate end of human life, as in the case with the moral virtues.[94]

This, in turn, leads one to ask, What *is* the purpose of Art? Since Aquinas has written, 'All worldly objects may be reduced to three types: honors, riches, and sensual pleasures,'[95] one might conclude that he regarded the purpose of Art as pleasure. However, in the only place he associates Pleasure with the word 'Art,' he speaks only of the 'art' of cooking and perfumery.[96] In general, 'Pleasure' was a concept which Aquinas seems to have associated either with a variety of lower character traits[97] or as a rather meaningless activity for the purpose of rest, 'that thereby we may afterwards become more fit for studious occupation.'[98]

There are some places where Aquinas appears to view the purpose of Art as merely utilitarian.

> The end of the practice of art is the thing produced by art: and such a thing cannot be the ultimate end of human life; since rather is it we who are the end of those products, for they are all made for man's use.[99]

---

91 Ibid., VIII, 23.

92 *Commentary on the Metaphysics of Aristotle*, 533 (VII. L. 6: C 1404). See also *Summa Theologiae*, IV, 129.

93 *Summa Theologiae*, XX, 69.

94 Ibid., XXXIV, 31.

95 Ibid., XXX, 59.

96 Ibid., XX, 69.

97 Ibid., XLIV, 205, 223.

98 *Summa Contra Gentiles*, XXV.

99 Ibid., XXXVI.

On the other hand, in other places Aquinas suggests a more modern view, that the purpose of Art to be simply itself—Art for Art's sake.

> The worth of things produced by art, however, does not consist in their being good for human appetite, but in the good of the products of art themselves.
>
> ...
>
> Art is necessary, not that the artist may lead a good life, but so that he may produce a good and lasting work of art.[100]

100 *Summa Theologiae*, XXIII, 51, 55.

The 'good' which Aquinas speaks of here is clearly a reference to a moral virtue, as he points out in another passage.

> In order that a man may make good use of the art he has, he needs a good will, which is perfected by moral virtue.[101]

101 Ibid., 49. See also ibid., XLII, 171.

One of the moral virtues in Art which Aquinas mentions by name is Certitude.

> A certitude surpassing that characteristic of the workings of art is ascribed to the moral virtues. This is not surprising when we consider that they are applied to their operations by reason somewhat after the fashion in which nature itself is moved.[102]

102 Ibid., XXXIII, 41.

This last quotation brings us to the final subject which Aquinas discusses relative to Art, the very traditional topic of the relationship of Art and Nature. On this subject Aquinas' priorities were very clear.

> Works of human art and reason should be shaped according to those of nature.[103]

103 Ibid., XXXVI, 93. See also *Commentary on Aristotle's Physics*, 83 (194 a 12 – b 15), 'Art imitates nature.'

The reason why Art should imitate Nature was, of course, because Nature was created by God.

> As the operation of art presupposes the operation of nature, so the operation of nature presupposes the creative operation of God: because art takes it matter from nature, and nature receives its matter from God through creation.[104]

104 *Summa Contra Gentiles*, LXV.

What Art takes from Nature are the principles which he calls in one place, the 'Universals.'[105] In another place, Aquinas addresses this process as follows,

105 *Summa Theologiae*, V, 57.

> Nature does not create things which are proper to art, but only sets out certain principles, and, in a way, offers a model to the artist. While as far as art is concerned, it can see the things which are to be found in nature, and make use of them to perform its own task, but cannot create such things itself. So it is clear that reason can only know the things of nature, while it can both know and make the things of art.[106]

106 Commentary on the Politics of Aristotle, I, Lecture 1.

ON AESTHETICS IN MUSIC

Aquinas rarely speaks of music and why this is so is a mystery. When writing lengthy treatises on subjects like the Emotions, or Pleasure, why does he never associate these topics with music? Likewise, in a treatise on prophesy and a complete book on the ceremonial aspects of the Jewish religion,[107] Aquinas never once mentions music. In this case, since music is closely associated with both prophesy and religious ceremony in the Old Testament, his omission seems deliberate.

107 Ibid., XXIX.

There are almost no direct references in the writings of Aquinas to music performances he actually heard and the indirect references offer a mixed view of his sophistication as a listener. In one place it would appear he appreciated fine players, for in a discussion of the soul he mentions the body might be 'lissome and agile … like an instrument in the hands of a skilled player.'[108] But in another place we would have to question his ear, for he says it is no great sin, 'when someone brags about his singing, when in fact he was out of tune.'[109]

108 *Compendium Theologiae*, 168, quoted in *Theological Texts*, 409.

109 Disputations, IX de Malo, 2, c. & ad 8, quoted in ibid., 137.

All in all, it seems apparent that Aquinas was not enthusiastic about music in general, but why? Was it the the competition for the attention of the faithful from the rapidly developing secular music of the civic domain? Was it a disgust for the Church music he heard while teaching in Paris—especially in the example of the callous deception of the Church perpetrated by the thirteenth-century Motet? One cannot say.

110 Ibid., XXXIX, 249ff.

In his most lengthy discussion of music,[110] a discussion of Church music, it is very clear that on the balance Aquinas found little to recommend in it. In this discussion he presents four rather negative perspectives on Church music.

1. Jerome does not condemn singing absolutely, but he corrects those who sing theatrically, or who sing not in order to arouse devotion but to show off or to provoke pleasure.
2. Arousing men to devotion through preaching and teaching is a more excellent way than through singing.[111]
3. Musical instruments usually move the soul to pleasure rather than create a good disposition to it.
4. The soul is distracted from the meaning of a song when it is sung merely to arouse pleasure.

[111] Aquinas wrote a few hymn texts which are extant and are given in *Selected Writings of St. Thomas Aquinas*. Perhaps he found his preaching more successful than his composing.

It is in this discussion as well that Aquinas makes his only reference to the rich tradition of music in the Old Testament. It is a comment anti-Semitic throughout.

> Old Testament [musical] instruments were used both because the people were more coarse and carnal, so that they needed to be aroused by such instruments as well as with promises of temporal wealth, and because these instruments presaged the future.

In fact, the only vote of confidence Aquinas can make for Church music in this discussion is that it might help the fainthearted!

> Vocal praise is necessary to arouse man's devotion for God, and whatever is useful for this purpose is fittingly used in divine praise. Clearly, the human soul is moved in various ways by different sounds of music, as Aristotle and Boethius recognized. Wisely, therefore, song has been used in praising God so that the minds of the fainthearted may be incited to devotion.

Aside from this discussion there is only one significant reference to Music used in the Service, but it is an interesting one. Here,[112] he not only clearly associates singing with the 'mystery' of the Mass, but mentions that there is one reference in the New Testament to Jesus singing![113] He elaborates on neither.

His views on Church music notwithstanding, Aquinas gives evidence of familiarity of the history of early Christian music. In one interesting passage he mentions that the earliest period, when services were held in secret, included only silent recitation, but that singing began 'at a time when the faith had come out in the open.'[114]

Other than on the subject of Church music, Aquinas continued the view held by the writers who commented on the Liberal Arts during earlier centuries that Music 'takes its principles from arithmetic.'[115]

[112] Ibid., LIX, 159.

[113] Matthew 26:30.

[114] *Summa Theologiae*, XXXI, 53.

[115] Ibid., I, 11. See also *Commentary on Aristotle's Physics*, 12 (184 b 15 – 185 a 19), 'Music is subalternated to arithmetic,' and 80 (193 b 22 – 194 a 11).

Aquinas rarely mentions hearing when discussing the senses, and never with respect to Music, but in the following passage one can see that he trusted the eye more than the ear. The exception which he offers here seems little more than a disguised warning to the Christian not to question the Church.

> All things being equal, seeing is more certain than hearing. But if one from whom something is heard far excels the sight of one who sees, then hearing is more certain than seeing. An example: a person with scant learning is far surer of something he hears from an expert than he is of any insight of his own. Thus anyone is far surer of what he hears from the infallible God than of what he sees with his own fallible reason.[116]

116 Ibid., XXXIX, 145ff.

In only one place does Aquinas hit upon the essence of aesthetics in music—the nature of the perception of the listener. In this passage he is talking about the emotions, and not about music, but the point is an important one.

> The intensity of a given passion varies, not only with the active power of the agent, but also with the passive capacity of the patient.[117]

117 Ibid., XIX, 15.

The modern reader interested in philosophy has to be disappointed in Aquinas. Through a large number of volumes, on a great variety of topics, he is too prone to assign explanations to angels or the soul, rather than to engage in original thinking.

Aquinas provides virtually no enlightenment on the subject of music, a topic he rarely mentions. That he could write an entire book on ceremonial aspects of the Jewish service and never once mention music, even though the Old Testament places so much emphasis on it, seems deliberate. But why?

Nowhere in Aquinas is there the slightest evidence that he was aware of the tremendous cultural explosion going on all around him in music and literature, of the rebirth of philosophy or the blossoming of commerce, trade, travel and politics.[118] His vision was firmly fixed on the past, while the Renaissance was beginning all around him! He must have seen it all, but for a man who loved Aristotle almost as much as he loved the Church, to acknowledge it was probably a price too high.

118 Durant, without giving a source, explains,

He became so absorbed in the religious and intellectual life that he hardly noticed what happened about him. In the refectory his plate could be removed and replaced without his being aware of it. [*The Age of Faith*, 963]

22 AESTHETICS OF MUSIC IN THE FRENCH ROMANCES AND CHANSONS DE GESTE OF THE TWELFTH AND THIRTEENTH CENTURIES

IT IS INTERESTING THAT IN THE POETRY of the troubadours and trouvères we rarely encounter either the jongleur or the military musician, while in the Chansons de geste and the Romances we mostly read of the latter to the exclusion of the former. The jongleur of this period was primarily a musician and the literature suggests that some were quite proficient.

> I am a jongleur of the viele
> I know the muse, and the fretele
> And the harp, and the chifonie,
> And the gigue and the armonie:
> And I know how to sing well
> A melody on the salteire and rote.[1]

But for nearly a millennium the jongleur had been a general entertainer with other skills as well. One passage in *The Romance of the Rose* is surely a testimonial to the broad talents some of these jongleurs possessed.[2]

> Then with uplifted voice he sweetly sings,
> Expressing all his happy-heartedness,
> In place of masses, pretty chansonettes
> Of lovers' secrets; and the instruments,
> Of which he many owned, he makes resound
> Till one had thought the gods were back on earth.
> More skilled are his hands upon the strings
> Than Theban Amphion's fingers ever were;
> Zithers and harps, lutes and guitars he played.
> He had constructed clever chiming clocks,
> The artful wheels of which ran ceaselessly—
> Organs which could be carried in one hand,

---

1 'Les Deux Bourdeurs Ribauds,' in E. Faral, ed., *Mimes Français du XIII siècle* (Paris: Edmond Champion, 1910), 101.

2 Another talented jongleur is mentioned in Geoffrey of Monmouth's *The History of the Kings of Britain*. He refers to a 'Beldgabred,' as one who, 'surpassed all the musicians of ancient times, both in harmony and in playing every kind of musical instrument, so that he was called the god of minstrels.' [trans. Lewis Thorpe, (Baltimore: Penguin Books, 1966), 105.]

> Which he himself not only blows and plays
> But sings to their accompaniment sweet
> Full-voiced motets in tenor or treble strains.
> Then each in turn he sounds, and plays with care
> Cymbals and pipes and fifes and tambourines,
> Timbrels and chalms and flutes and psalteries,
> Bagpipes and trumpets, Cornish pipes and viols.
> See how he capers, dances, clogs, and trips,
> Cuts pigeonwings the whole length of the hall …³

In this literature the jongleur is typically found in an entertainment or background role singing and accompanying himself on the harp or vielle.

> They get plenty of venison of deer and wild boar,
> And also cranes, wild geese, and peacocks seasoned with pepper;
> Wine and clary are gushing forth in abundance;
> The jongleurs are singing and playing the vielle and the rote.⁴

The jongleurs also seem to have taken over the role of epic poetry, singing tales of the past heroes and their exploits. In the Romances of Marie de France, the source for the narrative itself is usually attributed to a jongleur. Thus, the 'Lay of the Dolorous Knight' begins, 'Listen now to the song that once I heard a minstrel singing to his harp.'⁵ Another, the 'Lay of Gugemar,' which she recalled as, 'fair is that song and sweet the tune,' contains some interesting information about these singers. She describes these songs as being sung by the fireplace and she makes the aesthetic observation that 'the singer must be wary not to spoil good music with unseemly words.'⁶ Then she digresses to speak of criticism, observing that the best singers are the most criticized.

> But this is the way of the world, that when a man or woman sings more tunably than his fellows, those about the fire fall upon him, pell-mell, for reason of their envy. They rehearse diligently the faults of his song, and steal away his praise with evil words. I will brand these folk as they deserve. They, and such as they, are like mad dogs—cowardly and felon—who traitorously bring to death men better than themselves.

---

3   Guillaume de Lorris and Jean de Meun, *The Romance of the Rose*, trans. Harry Robbins (New York: Dutton, 1962), XCVII, 153ff. The work of de Meun begins with Chapter XX.

4   'Pilgrimage of Charlemagne to Jerusalem,' ca. 1115, in *The Journey of Charlemagne*, trans. Jean-Louis Picherit (Birmingham, AL: Summa, 1984), 36. A similar description is found in the 'Song of Rainoart,' lines 2249-2250.

5   Eugene Mason, trans., *French Mediaeval Romances from the Lays of Marie de France* (London: Dent, 1924), 24. Except in titles, we prefer 'song' to 'lay.'

6   Ibid., 3.

A jongleur who similarly sings epic tales, we find in *The Song of William*, one of the oldest of the Chansons de geste. This jongleur seems to have been valued as much for his sword as for his music.

> Howbeit, a jongleur hath William my lord;
> In all France no singer so good will ye find,
> Nor a hardier dealer of blows with the sword.
> All the songs of history hath he in mind:
> Of Clovis, first of the Frankish kings
> Who in God our Lord and Ruler believed,
> Of Flovent his son, the fighter, he sings,
> Who from him the rule of sweet France received,
> Of all the kings of warlike renown
> Clean to Pepin, the short but valiant, down;
> Of Charlemagne, Roland his nephew dear,
> Of Girart and of Oliver the peer:
> My lord's kinsmen these and his forbears.
> Right worthily my lord's love he shares.
> Since in him he'th a singer so prized by us
> And in combat a vassal victorious,
> He bringeth him back from the battle thus.[7]

[7] 'La Chancun de Guillelme,' in *The Song of William*, trans. Edward Stone (Seattle: University of Washington Press, 1951), CXXXII.

ON THE PHILOSOPHY OF AESTHETICS

Emerging from the Dark Ages, secular philosophy had yet to regain its reputation, as we can see in an observation in *The Romance of the Rose*.

> The times have come to such a pass that now
> Good men who give their lives to learning's quest,
> Becoming doctors of philosophy,
> And journeying to many a foreign land,
> Get into debt and suffer poverty,
> And almost naked beg their barefoot way
> In search of knowledge; yet they are not loved.
> Less than an apple princes prize them now.[8]

[8] *The Romance of the Rose*, LXXXVI, 107ff.

It follows that these French writers did not, as did the ancient Greeks, struggle to explain rational knowledge versus sensory perception, or ponder the relationship of the emotions to Reason. But these subjects are always the foundations of aesthetic philosophy, and when Marie de France prepares to sing a lay and promises to do so 'to the best of my art and knowledge,'[9] there is an echo of ancient debates.

[9] 'The Lay of Eliduc,' in *French Medieval Romances from the Lays of Marie de France*, 31.

A discussion on the rational and emotional natures of man is found in the famous *Romance of the Rose*, where we are treated to a battle of wits between the allegorical god, Reason, and a lover. The passage begins with the lady expressing her regret that she did not take the advice of Reason.

> Well warned by Reason, mad I must have been
> When I took not the advice she freely gave
> And did not quit Love's service right away.
> Reason was right to blame me when I lent
> Myself to Love, incurring grievous woes.[10]

[10] *The Romance of the Rose*, XX, 60ff.

In the following section, called 'Reason remonstrates with the Lover,' Reason describes Love,[11] in part,

[11] Ibid., XXI, 50ff.

> Love is a troubled peace, an amorous war—
> A treasonous loyalty, disloyal faith—
> A fear that's full of hope, a desperate trust—
> A madman's logic, reasoned foolishness—
> A healthy sickness and most languorous health—
> A sadness gay, a frolicsomeness sad—
> A bitter sweetness, a sweet-tasting gall—

Reason concludes by defining Love as an,

> Imaginary illness freely spread
> Between two persons of opposing sex,
> Originating from disordered sight,
> Producing great desire to hug and kiss
> And seek enjoyment in a mutual lust.[12]

[12] Ibid., XXI, 112ff.

All of which, the reader is delighted to find, had no effect. In this case, feeling conquered Reason.

> Thus Reason preached, but Love set all at naught;
> For though I heard the sermon word for word
> I took no stock in it, so drawn was I
> To Love, who still my every thought pursued.[13]

[13] Ibid., XXIII.

We find a closely related passage in the Romance, 'The Knight with the Lion,' by Chrétien de Troyes. Here we believe the author means to suggest that it is the experiential, the feeling side of us, which gives meaning to Reason.

> Give me your heart and your ears, for words are lost completely unless they are understood by the heart. There are people who hear but do not understand, although they praise what they hear. Now they are capable only of hearing because their heart does not understand. The words come like the blowing wind to their ears; they do not linger or stay there, but pass quickly unless the heart is alert and ready to receive them. When they are heard, the heart can receive and enclose them, and make them stay. The ears are the route and channel the voice takes to the heart, and the heart embraces, inside the body, the voice that enters through the ears. Whoever would hear me now must lend me his heart and his ears.[14]

One of the psychological subjects relative to aesthetics is the concept of pleasure and pain. The two authors of *The Romance of the Rose* use musical references to briefly touch on this aspect of man and his emotions. In the first part, Guillaume de Lorris presents an almost Epicurean separation of the emotions.

> For you should know, in truth, that one in woe
> Has no desire for caroling or dance.
> Nor can she school herself, who lives in grief,
> To merriment. Joy is woe's opposite.[15]

But is it pain which defines and enables us to comprehend joy? What if there were only joy? Would it become wearisome? Can this be what the author of the second part of the Romance means when he has the allegorical character, 'Genius,' preaching a sermon on the joys of heaven and realizing he has lost his listeners, remark,

> What's this I pipe to you? High time it is
> I put my flute away. The sweetest tune
> Oftimes annoys.[16]

This same Romance engages another centuries old aesthetic question, in a chapter entitled, 'How Art strives with Nature.' Here there is little real debate, the author coming down firmly on the side of Nature.

14 David Staines, *The Complete Romances of Chrétien de Troyes* (Bloomington: Indiana University Press, 1993), 259.

15 *The Romance of the Rose*, II, 138.

16 Ibid., XCIV, 290. This use of a shepherd's pipe as a metaphor for communication is found again in Geoffrey of Monmouth, *The History of the Kings of Britain*, vii, 2, 'I therefore pressed my rustic reed-pipe to my lips and, modulating on it in all humility, I translated into Latin this work written in a language which is unknown to you.'

> Of Nature Art implores, demands, and prays,
> Like wretched mendicant, of sorry skill
> And strength, who struggles to pursue her ways,
> That she will teach him how she manages
> To reproduce all creatures properly
> In her designs, by her creative power.
> He watches how she works, and, most intent
> To do as well, like ape he copies her.
> But Art's so naked and devoid of skill
> That he can never bring a thing to life
> Or make it seem that it is natural.
>
> ...
>
> The best that he can do is to reduce
> Each to its constitution primitive.
> He'll ne'er attain to Nature's subtlety
> Though he should strive to do so all his life.[17]

17 Ibid., LXXVIII, 15ff.

The purpose of the music described in the French Romances and Chansons de Geste seems to have been simple joy and delight. No more poetic description of this joy can be found than that in the famous *Romance of the Rose*, where the very name given the (female!) musician is 'Gladness.'

> This noble company of which I speak
> Had ordered for themselves a caroling.
> A dame named Gladness led them in the tune;
> Most pleasantly and sweetly rang her voice.
> No one could more becomingly or well
> Produce such notes; she was just made for song.
> She had a voice that was both clear and pure;
> About her there was nothing rude, for she
> Knew well the dance steps, and could keep good time
> The while she voiced her song. Ever the first
> Was she, by custom, to begin the tune;
> For music was the trade that she knew best
> Ever to practice most agreeably.[18]

18 Ibid., III, 142ff.

Even the performance of the narrative Chanson de geste was for the purpose of delight. The following lines from Marie de France are also interesting in their reference to separate sung and written versions of the same tale.

> With a glad heart and right good mind will I tell the Lay that men call Honeysuckle; and that the truth may be known of all it shall be told as many a minstrel has sung it to my ear, and as the scribe hath written it for our delight.[19]

Wace takes the point even further, noting that in the retelling by scribe and singer as an art work, the factual aspect of the tale has long been lost.

> I know not if you have heard tell the marvelous gestes and errant deeds related so often of King Arthur. They have been noised about this mighty realm for so great a space that the truth has turned to fable and an idle song. Such rhymes are neither sheer bare lies, nor gospel truths. They should not be considered either an idiot's tale, or given by inspiration. The minstrel has sung his balled, the storyteller told over his story so frequently, little by little he has decked and painted, till by reason of his embellishment the truth stands hid in the trappings of a tale. Thus to make a delectable tune to your ear, history goes masking as fable.[20]

There are two interesting references in this literature to the power of art. The first, in Layamon's 'Brut,' a reworking of the Wace tale, Merlin relates to King Arthur what he describes as an ancient truth.

> Yes, lord king, it was of yore said, that better is art, than evil strength; for with art men may hold what strength may not obtain.[21]

The second has its roots in one of the most familiar of Greek myths, that of Orpheus taming the wild beasts with music. This charming invention reappears in a thirteenth-century collection of fables known as *Gesta Romanorum*. Here an emperor, faced with a wild elephant in his forest, finds two beautiful virgins who are musicians and sends them naked into the forest to tame the elephant. Sure enough, their music causes the elephant to fall asleep, with his head on one of the girls lap (!), whereupon the other girl cuts it off![22]

Finally, relative to philosophy, we should note that while the music theorists of the thirteenth century denounced the ancient concept of the 'Music of the Spheres,' it still surfaces in the literature of that period. In the *Romance of the Rose*, for example, the character, 'Nature,' says of the spheres,

19 'The Lay of the Honeysuckle,' in *French Medieval Romances from the Lays of Marie de France*, 102.

20 Robert Wace, *Roman de Brut*, trans. Gwyn Jones (London: Dent, 1962), 56.

21 Ibid., 158.

22 *Gesta Romanorum*, trans. Charles Swan (London: C. and J. Rivington, 1824), II, 128.

Sweet harmonies they make,
Which are the source of all the melodies
And divers tunes that we in concord set
In all our sorts of song. There is no thing
That would not sing in unison with them.[23]

ART MUSIC

One of the characteristics which we believe is synonymous with art music is the attentive, contemplative, listener. One of the most extraordinary twelfth-century accounts of an art performance, in the *Roman de Horn*, includes such an audience, which 'marvels' at what they heard.

> Then he took the harp to tune it. God! whoever saw how well he handled it, touching the strings and making them vibrate, sometimes causing them to sing and at other times join in harmonies, he would have been reminded of the heavenly harmony. This man, of all those that there are, causes most wonder. When he has played his notes he makes the harp go up so that the strings give out completely different notes. All those present marvel that he could play thus. And when he has done all this he begins to play the aforesaid lai of Baltof, in a loud and clear voice, just as the Bretons are versed in such performances. Afterwards he made the strings of the instrument play exactly the same melody as he had just sung; he performed the whole song [lai] for he wished to omit nothing.[24]

In the case of art music performed at a banquet, such descriptions are usually accompanied by some reference to the tables being cleared first, to distinguish music to listen to rather than to eat to. Both of these features are found in the description of a performance in the Romance, 'The Lay of the Thorn,' by Marie de France.

> After supper, when the tables were removed, the King seated himself for his delight upon a carpet spread before the daïs, his son and many a courteous lord with him. The fair company gave ear to the Lay of Alys, sweetly sung by a minstrel from Ireland, to the music of his rote. When his story was ended, forthwith he commenced another, and related the Lay of Orpheus; none being so bold as to disturb the singer, or to let his mind wander from the song. Afterwards the knights spoke together amongst themselves.[25]

23 *Romance of the Rose*, LXXXI, 187.

24 An Anglo-Norman work, in French, quoted in Christopher Page, *Voices and Instruments of the Middle Ages* (London: Dent, 1987), 4.

25 *French Medieval Romances from the Lays of Marie de France*, 140ff.

Another Romance[26] by this writer describes a lay as 'sweet to hear, and the tune thereof lovely to bear in mind,' which perhaps suggests the expectation of a listener attentive enough to actually remember the melody.

A twelfth-century epic, *Hervis de Metz*, includes a performance of art music, again with the author carefully specifying that the performance was *after* the meal.

> Hervis says: 'Noble minstrel, you are welcome!'
> He had him brought to the banquet, and after the meal he
> began to play the fiddle at once and to sing *sons d'amours*
> in a beautiful and sweet way; Hervis, courteous and
> noble, listened to him.[27]

One of the tales in the *Gesta Romanorum* involves an impromptu performance after a banquet. First, a king requests his daughter to play.

> She commanded the instrument to be brought, and began to touch it with infinite sweetness. Applause followed the performance, 'There never was,' said the courtiers, 'a better or a sweeter song.'

A visiting knight, named Apollonius, then volunteers to perform.

> Apollonius retired for a few moments, and decorated his head; then re-entering the Triclinium, he took the instrument, and struck it so gracefully and delightfully that they unanimously agreed, it was the harmony not of Apollonius, but of Apollo.
> The guests positively asserted, that they never heard or saw anything better.[28]

We include as art music the love songs characteristic of the troubadours and trouvéres. Among the references to similar love songs in the *Romance of the Rose*, there is a description, although ostensibly of birds singing, which we believe reflects art music.

> Sweetly and pleasantly they sang of love
> And chanted sonnets courteously and well.
> In part songs joining, one sang high, one low.
> Their singing was beyond reproach; their notes
> With sweetness and contentment filled my heart.[29]

26 'The Lay of Graelent,' in ibid., 148.

27 Quoted in Page, *Voices and Instruments of the Middle Ages*, 31.

28 *Gesta Romanorum*, ibid., II, 251ff. Later in this same tale the daughter again 'sang to an instrument, with such a sweet and ravishing melody, that Apollonius was enchanted.'

29 *The Romance of the Rose*, III, 124. Other references to love songs are found in XI, 62 and L, 135.

The most remarkable reference to love songs in this Romance, however, is more in the spirit of the satirical songs of the Goliards. A character says sending love songs to a lady is not nearly so effective as being rich!

> Someone may ask if it is not worth while
> To make and send to charm and hold his love
> Fair verses, motets, ballads, chansonettes.
> Alas, one gains not much from such pursuit—
> He need not pain himself to poetize—
> Perhaps the poem's praised, but that is all.
> But ample purse, filled and weighed down with gold,
> Will make them run to him with open arms
> When ladies see him draw and open it;
> Their desperation has become so great
> That they pursue naught but full pocketbooks.
> Once, to be sure, 'twas different; times are getting worse.[30]

30 Ibid., XL, 106ff.

FUNCTIONAL MUSIC

There are two rather unusual references to functional music in this literature, the first relative to executions. A tale in the *Gesta Romanorum* speaks of an unnamed king's custom of announcing to a condemned man that he was going to be put to death forthwith by arranging a predawn serenade with songs and trumpets at his house.[31]

31 *Gesta Romanorum*, ibid., II, 213ff.

Another description of functional music, unusual for the early date, is of the civic watchman–musician. Most medieval accounts of this person refer only to rather simple musical signals. In the *Romance of the Rose*, however, we find a watchman performing a number of sophisticated instruments and even singing from the tower.

> Each evening he would mount the battlements
> And play his bagpipe, trumpet, horn, or shalms.
> At one time he would sing descants and lays
> And all the latest songs, to Cornish pipes;
> Another time, accompanied with a flute,
> Dispraising ladies, he would sing like this:
>   There is no maid who will not smile
>   When she hears tales of lechery.

The whores will paint, men to beguile;
For all are full of treachery.
If the fool's not talking all the while,
She's mistress of the ogling style.
There is no maid who will not smile
When she hears tales of lechery.³²

32 *The Romance of the Rose*, XIX, 63.

Descriptions of church music in this French literature are rare, one of the more interesting being found in Wace's *Roman de Brut*.

> Now within the church Mass was commenced with due pomp and observance. The noise of the organ filled the church, and the clerks sang tunably in the choir. Their voices swelled or failed, according as the chant mounted to the roof, or died away in supplication. The knights passed from one church to the other.³³

33 *Roman de Brut*, trans. Jones, 67.

The English text upon which this passage is based seems more complementary to the quality of the musical performance.

> Afterwards, when the procession was over, so much organ music was played in the two churches and the choirs sang so sweetly that, because of the high standard of the music offered, the knights who were there hardly knew which of the churches to enter first. They flocked in crowds, first to this one, then to the other, so that if the whole day had been spent in celebration they would not have been bored. Finally, high mass was celebrated in both churches.³⁴

34 Geoffrey of Monmouth, *The History of the Kings of Britain*, 228.

After the organ was accepted into the church, gradually the rest of the instruments, for which the organ was only a surrogate, began to appear. A charming reference to the use of string instruments in the service in the thirteenth century is found in the works of Gautier de Coinci (ca. 1218–1236).

> When the mouth is working hard the heart should so strive, and so press upon the strings of its viele, and so tune them up, that with the first word the bright sound ascends without delay to Paradise. Then their singing is pleasing to God. But there are many [church singers] who have such a viele that will go out of tune all the time unless it is tuned up with strong wine.³⁵

35 V. R. Koenig, ed., *Les Miracles de Nostre Dame par Gautier de Coinci* (Geneva: Librarie Droz, 1955–1970), IV, 184.

Finally, because the French literature of this period, even the Romances which tell of King Arthur, concentrates a great deal on knightly battle, one can find an unusually large number of references to the use in battle of various horns and trumpet-types. The famous poem, *The Song of Roland*, is especially rich in the description of this kind of music. We find here trumpets whose sound is sometimes described as 'blare,'[36] but sometimes as 'clear-voiced.'[37] This certainly seems to suggest two different instruments, one perhaps a more primitive horn-type and the other the metallic instrument from the East. But there is no reference to the Crusades anywhere in this poem, so it would seem too early for the Eastern instrument, and besides there are also mentioned horns, clarions ('brilliant'),[38] and, of course, Roland's famous ivory 'oliphant.' Trumpet and horn relatives all, but the individual descriptions are too brief to allow us an understanding of their true identities.

We are told the trumpets were placed before and after the troops,[39] no doubt in order to insure the various signals would be heard by all. The descriptions of massed trumpets provides a few more clues to the sound of these instruments. When a *thousand* trumpets played a signal, to add 'more splendor,' it was nevertheless described as a deafening noise.[40] When *seven thousand* play 'sound the charge, the din is great throughout the countryside.'[41] When *sixty thousand* play, it created a 'blare so loud, the mountains ring, the valleys echo back.'[42] Is sixty thousand trumpets an exaggeration? Not by much, if one accepts the calculation here of more than three hundred thousand troops[43] and one remembers that it was crucial to the battle plan that every soldier be in range of hearing the signals being played by primitive instruments. Layamon's Romance, 'Brut' also mentions sixty thousand trumpets playing together, causing the ground to tremble.[44] Let us admit some literary exaggeration, but at a time when the loudest sound one might have heard was a small church organ, the aural phenomenon of battle field trumpets must have been impressive.

The central figure of this poem, Roland, a nephew to Charlemagne, plays an ivory horn called an oliphant. The descriptions of Roland playing this instrument are among the most remarkable in the early literature of the trumpet, reading like a personification of one of those trumpet players, their faces flushed with emotion, painted on the Sistine ceiling by Michelangelo.

> Count Roland brought the horn up to his mouth:
> he sets it firmly, blows with all his might.

---

36 *The Song of Roland*, trans. Robert Harrison (New York: Mentor, 1970), line 2116.

37 Ibid., 2150, 3194, 3309, and 3523.

38 Ibid., 3138.

39 Ibid., 1832.

40 Ibid., 1005.
41 Ibid., 1454.

42 Ibid., 2111.

43 Ibid., 3019ff.

44 *Roman de Brut*, trans. Jones, 253.

In producing this mighty blast, which we are told could be heard more than seventy miles away,[45] his temple burst!

> Count Roland, racked with agony and pain
> and great chagrin, now sounds his ivory horn:
> bright blood leaps in a torrent from his mouth:
> the temple has been ruptured in his brain.
> The horn he holds emits a piercing blast:
> Charles hears it as he crosses through the pass …
>
> Count Roland's mouth is filling up with blood;
> the temple has been ruptured in his brain.
> In grief and pain he sounds the oliphant;
> Charles hears it, and his Frenchmen listen, too.
> The king says then, 'That horn is long of wind.'[46]

Drums are mentioned, without description, and more interesting, singing on the battle field. It is an understandable prejudice that the allies *sing* their battle cry, while the pagans *bellow* theirs.[47] We wish we had more information in the two references to the victors singing 'mocking' songs to the defeated.[48]

ENTERTAINMENT MUSIC

The most extensive account of entertainment music in this literature is found in Wace's *Roman de Brut*. Here, for a banquet of King Arthur, in addition to story-tellers, chess and dice games, the guests were treated to an extraordinary variety of entertainment.

> Now to the court had gathered many tumblers, harpers, and makers of music, for Arthur's feast. He who would hear songs sung to the music of the rote, or would solace himself with the newest refrain of the minstrel, might win to his wish. Here stood the viol player, chanting ballads and lays to their appointed tunes. Everywhere might be heard the voice of viols and harp and flutes. In every place rose the sound of lyre and drum and shepherd's pipe, bagpipe, psaltery, cymbals, monochord, and all manner of music. Here the tumbler tumbled on his carpet. There the mime and the dancing girl put forth their feats.[49]

45 *The Song of Roland*, 1756 ('30 leagues').

46 Ibid., 1761ff.

47 Ibid., 1793 and 1921.

48 Ibid., 1014 and 1517.

49 *Roman de Brut*, trans. Jones, 69. The reference to the monochord here suggests that the writer was naming every instrument he knew, whether he had ever heard it or not!

A similar festive gathering of musicians is found in the Romance, 'Erec and Enide,' by Chrétien de Troyes. In this case the musicians are visitors, attracted by a wedding hosted by King Arthur. The celebrations lasted fifteen days and the musicians were richly rewarded, even by today's standards!

> All the minstrels were pleased with their excellent wages that day. Whatever had been due them was paid, and many beautiful gifts were presented to them: clothes of spotted fur and ermine, of rabbit and of purple cloth, and of rich gray wool or silk. Each man received his desire, whether a horse or money, according to his skill.[50]

[50] Staines, *The Complete Romances of Chrétien de Troyes*, 27.

23 AESTHETICS OF MUSIC IN THE SONGS OF THE TROUBADOURS AND TROUVÈRES OF THE TWELFTH AND THIRTEENTH CENTURIES

The themes of the renewal of Spring, rural simplicity and love, of which the early Greek lyric poets sang were, and are, universal. The repertoire of lyric poetry became smaller as Rome subjugation began, and smaller still as the influence of the Church began to dominate education. The Dark Ages have left us with an incomplete history of poetry, but it does seem apparent that the spirit of lyric poetry never completely died out.

In France, those who carried on this tradition during the glorious final two centuries of the Middle Ages are called, Troubadours. The troubadours sang in a new language, but they composed and sang poetry on the same themes as the Greek lyric poets. If their love songs seem more vivid and personal than the myths and allegories of the Greeks, it is because they celebrate their own experience rather than an allegorical one.

With the East to West shift in political power, which began in the eleventh century, the south of France began to flourish. One might say that the patronage of these aristocratic families represents the real beginning of the Renaissance in the arts. It was here that the troubadours had their origin, one of the first being William of Aquitaine, Count of Poitiers (1071–1127). If one recalls that the young Dante actually knew the last of these lyric poets, and mentions them in his works, one can see the troubadours as a unique link between the old world and the new.

We are fortunate to possess some biographical information about many of these troubadours, material which dates from just after the period in which they lived. It is generally assumed by scholars that these short biographies are somewhat exaggerated and romantically colored, but they nevertheless provide a valuable general view of this activity. We can see, for example, that the troubadours came from all levels of society. Some were nobles, some were poor bourgeois and even orphans, some were monks, and some were, or became, jongleurs—wandering musicians who traveled in many lands.

These early biographies also frankly tell us that some of the troubadours (Guillaume IX, Pons de Capdueill and Peire Vidal, for example) were outstanding composers and singers, while others are described as 'bad singers' (Gaucelm Faidit and Aimeric de Peguilhan). Within the latter category, presumably, were some who composed, but employed a jongleur to sing their songs for them. Such a one was Peire Cardenal, the son of aristocratic parents, who,

> went through the courts of kings and noble barons, bringing a joglar with him who sang his sirventes.[1]

And neither did being a noble guarantee lofty language. Jaufré Rudel, prince of Blaia, was described as composing 'good verses, but with poor words, though the tunes were good.'[2]

The relatively brief period during which the troubadours, and their northern colleagues, the trouvéres, existed, was the end of the era of chivalry and most literature presents them clothed in the romance of courtly life. Some of them, indeed, had reputations as great lovers, such as Guillem de Montanhagol, a knight of Provence, who was called in an early biographical note, 'a good troubadour and a great lover.'[3] One finds here as well truly romantic tales of love, such as that of the troubadour Raimon Jordan who was inaccurately reported to have been killed in battle and returned to find his grieving wife had joined a convent.

On the other hand, one finds in these early biographies examples of behavior which depart dramatically from the traditional image of the troubadour. Marcabru, we are told, even 'spoke badly of women and of love.'[4] This troubadour, who had a reputation for 'malicious songs,' was eventually murdered by one who was the object of his music. Peire Vidal, another who was known for speaking badly of others, had his tongue cut out by a noble!

Some troubadours, including Ventadorn, Mareuil and Cabestanh, violated the court's trust by making love with their patron's wife, although perhaps this was a frequent occurrence where marriages were often made only for political purposes. In the case of Cabestanh, the offended noble, Raimon, murdered him, carried the troubadour's heart home,

> and he had it roasted with pepper and served to his wife. And when the lady had eaten the heart of Cabestanh, Raimon told her what it was. When she heard that, she fainted away. And when she came to

---

[1] Quoted in Paul Blackburn, *Proensa* (Berkeley: University of California Press, 1978), 242. A *sirventes* was a song on a subject other than love.

[2] Ibid., 67.

[3] Ibid., 238.

[4] Ibid., 32.

she said, 'My lord, you have given me such a good meal I shall never take another.' Hearing her speak thus, he came at her with his sword and would have split her head, but she ran to a balcony and threw herself down to her death.[5]

5 Ibid., 189.

From the perspective of aesthetics, some of the most revealing information about the troubadours is found in their own words, in their songs. In this regard, the most interesting song of all is one by Peire d'Alvernhe which describes the musical characteristics of twelve troubadours and himself. As this song is by far the most important eye-witness document we have of these lyric poets, we shall quote it in entirety.

> I shall sing about those troubadours
> who sing in many fashions, and all praise
> their own verses, even the most appalling;
> but they shall have to sing elsewhere,
> for a hundred competing shepherds I hear,
> and not one knows whether the melody's rising or falling.
>
> In this Peire Rogier is guilty,
> thus he shall be the first accused,
> for he carries tunes of love in public right now,
> and he would do better to carry
> a Psalter in church, or a candlestick
> with a great big burning candle.
>
> And the second: Giraut de Bornelh,
> who looks like a goatskin dried out in the sun,
> with that meager voice of his, and that whine,
> it is the song of an old lady bearing buckets of water;
> if he saw himself in a mirror,
> he would think himself less than an eglantine.
>
> And the third: Bernart de Ventadorn,
> a hand's breadth smaller than Bornelh;
> a fellow who worked for a wage was his father,
> he shot a laburnum handbow well,
> and his mother heated the oven
> and gathered the brushwood together.
>
> And the fourth, from Brive, the Limousin,
> a jongleur, and the most beggarly man
> between Benevento and here;
> and he looks like a sick
> pilgrim when he sings, the wretch,
> so that I nearly pity him myself.

En Guillem de Ribas is the fifth,
who is bad outside and in,
he recites all his verses with a raucous voice,
so his singing sounds like hell,
for a dog would sing as well,
and his eyes roll up like Christ in silver.

And the sixth, Grimoart Gausmar,
a knight who tries to pass for a jongleur,
and whoever agrees to let him could not do worse,
God damn whoever gives him clothing of motley and green,
for once his costume has been seen,
a hundred more will want to be jongleurs.

And Peire de Monzó makes seven,
since the Count of Toulouse sang him
a charming song, though he himself never sang;
and whoever stole it from him is to be respected,
except it was a pity he neglected
to amputate the little foot that hangs.

And the eighth, Bernart de Sayssac,
who never knew any other work
but going around begging little gifts;
and I have not thought him worth a piece of mud
since he begged En Bertran de Cardalhac
for an old cloak that stank of sweat.

And the ninth is En Raimbaut,
who thinks so highly of his poetry;
but I think nothing of his rhymes,
they have neither warmth nor cheer,
therefore I rank him with the bagpipers
who come up to you and beg for coins.

En Ebles de Sagna is the tenth,
who never had any luck in love,
though he sweetly sings his little air;
a vulgar puffed-up shyster
who, they say, for two cents
rents himself here, and sells himself there.

And the eleventh, Gonzalgo Roïtz,
who vaunts his skill in song
and thus presumes to call himself a knight;
no strong blow was ever struck
by him, he was never that well armed,
unless, of course, he got off in flight.

And twelfth is an old Lombard,
who calls his friends all cowards,
and he himself is terrified;
and yet the songs he writes are valiant,
with bastard phrases neither Occitan nor Italian,
and he is known to all as Cossezen, 'Just Right.'

Peire d'Alvernhe, now he has such a voice
he sings the high notes, and the low (and the in-between).
and before all people gives himself much praise;
and so he is the master of all who here convene;
if only he would make his words a little clearer,
for hardly a man can tell what they mean.

This verse was made to the noise of bagpipes
at Puivert, with much laughter and play.[6]

6 'Cantarai d'aquestz trobadors,' quoted in Frederick Goldin, *Lyrics of the Troubadours and Trouvères* (Garden City: Anchor Books, 1973), 171.

Peire d'Alvernhe (fl. 1150–1180), as he freely admits here, was known for his propensity toward self-praise. In another song he suggests he has many jealous detractors, but knows he is the best because of the money he makes, 'of which there's plenty.'

And no matter who seethes or grumbles about it, since my style
of poetry is so fine ... ; for I am the root and say that I'm the
first in perfect speech, defeating my stupid assailants who raise
against me the outcry that I'm of no use in it.

Therefore, though they are all of one herd, they lie most softly
between their teeth, and I feel assured of the best that is and
that was, confident in my song and supreme over the deceivers;
and I know what I'm saying, for otherwise the grain would
not come of which there's plenty, in season.[7]

7 'Sobre.l vieill trobar,' in Alan Press, *Anthology of Troubadour Lyric Poetry* (Austin: University of Texas Press, 1971), 93.

He adds that the careful listener will agree that his work is the best, even though it will always be subjected to criticism. The latter, he says, one must simply ignore.

Anyone for whom fine verse is pleasant to hear from me, I
advise to listen to this one which I'm now about to recite; for
once his heart is set on hearing well the notes and the words
he'll never say that he ever heard finer things said in verse, near or far.

It's certainly not to be mocked at if one hears it, rather should
it be most pleasing, even though the opinions of the overweening,
with their stupid, feeble, feckless sniggers, drag down that
which is on high; we see that good makes its own way forward,
while mockery stays galloping behind.

Hence it is well to ignore it, for never does mockery or spite desist.[8]

8 'Cui bon vers,' in ibid., 97.

No less confident than d'Alvernhe, was Bernart de Ventadorn (fl. 1150–1180) who began a song, 'It is no wonder that I sing better than any other singer.'[9] This singer, who personifies as much as any the traditional image we have today of the troubadour, has left a song which speaks of the place of love and music in the courtly life and reflects his alarm in seeing the beginning of the decline of chivalry.

> I am so saddened by what I see that I do not feel like singing. Men used to strive hard to win worth, honor, and praise, but now I do not see or hear anyone speak of love, and, as a result, reputation, nobility and joy become matters of indifference ...
>
> Man can only achieve worthiness in the love and service of ladies, for sport and song, and all that pertains to nobility, begin there. No man is worth anything without love, and therefore I would not want to rule the whole world if I could not have joy.[10]

Another autobiographical reference, in a song by the troubadour Raimbaut d'Orange (1150–1173), is typical of several which seem to use the ancient term for the wandering musician, 'jongleur,' as synonymous with 'troubadour.'

> Jongleur they call me, I go singing
> mad with love, in courtly ways.[11]

Whatever the distinction between jongleur and troubadour in the twelfth century, it does seem clear that the former was no longer the wandering beggar and general entertainer of the early Middle Ages. We believe, therefore, that the modern editor is incorrect who remarks of the trouvère, Colin Muset, 'He was a jongleur and therefore of no social significance.'[12] On the contrary, we believe his own words suggest he was an aristocrat (praised for 'big spending').

> The other day, it was in May, one morning,
> the little birds awakened me,
> I picked a little willow shoot
> and made a flageolet;
> but no man can play on this flageolet
> unless he is praised by everyone
> for spending big and making honest love,
> without lies and without tricks.[13]

---

9 'Non es meravelha,' in Stephen Nichols, *The Songs of Bernart de Ventadorn* (Chapel Hill: The University of North Carolina Press, 1965), 133.

10 'Ges de chantar,' in ibid., 98.

11 'Escotatz, mas no say,' in Goldin, *Lyrics of the Troubadours and Trouvères*, 181.

12 Ibid., 414.

13 'In mai, quant li rossignolet,' in ibid., 421.

Certainly the wandering musician of ill repute was still in existence, but he is always described differently from these troubadours. Consider, for example, Giraut de Borneil's (1165–1211) description of one of these.

> Cardaillac, they tell me that you are coming in search of a sirventes with which to earn yourself some money; but before the door-keeper lets you in I want you to thank me from a distance, for your breath is rather bad and you are apt to come too close. This is why a man is better off sending you a few pence rather than waiting for you to approach; for he suffers great torment if he does not turn away his face or cover his nose! ...
>
> Since men call you then the 'woolly minstrel' ...[14]

An entirely different kind of person was Arnaut Daniel (fl. 1180–1200). Born a noble, and praised by Dante as a craftsman of the modern tongue,[15] he nevertheless describes himself as a traveler, too poor to own a horse.

> I am Arnaut, who gathers the wind, and hunts the hare on oxback, and swims against the rising tide.[16]

And there were some troubadours, like Cerverí de Girona (fl. 1250–1280), who though attached to the royal court of Aragon, seems to have been, regardless of title, rather despondent over his place in the court.

> I go singing, thinking, fixing, rhyming, honing praising
> loving commands of affection without pleasure ...
>
> Praising, waiting, singing;
> my life is ignominious.[17]

Finally, the troubadour songs rarely mention other kinds of court music. References to string players are usually negative, as we can see in the example by a troubadour known as the Monk of Montaudon (fl. 1180–1215).

> And it irritates me, I swear by Saint Salvat,
> to hear a vile violinist in a good court.[18]

---

[14] 'Cardaillac, per un sirventes,' in Ruth Sharman, *The Cansos and Sirventes of the Troubadour Giraut de Borneil* (Cambridge: Cambridge University Press, 1989), 401.

[15] *Purgatorio*, XXVI, 115ff.

[16] Arnaut Daniel, 'En cest sonet,' in Press, *Anthology of Troubadour Lyric Poetry*, 185.

[17] Quoted in Anthony Bonner, *Songs of the Troubadours* (New York: Schocken Books, 1972), 217. The manuscript of this song is written with one syllable to a line.

[18] 'Fort m'enoia,' in Blackburn, *Proensa*, 179.

This, even though troubadours may have accompanied themselves with such instruments. A song by the trouvère Colin Muset, for example, includes the lines,

> I went to her in the little field
> with fiddle and bow
> and sang her my muset
> with great love …[19]

19 'Volex oïr la muse Muset,' in Goldin, *Lyrics of the Troubadours and Trouvères*, 417.

A song of Guilhem de Montanhagol (1233–1270) mentions military trumpet-types and the performance of melodies on bells, an instrument we see in iconography but rarely read about.[20]

20 'Bel m'es quan d'armatz,' in Press, *Anthology of Troubadour Lyric Poetry*, 263, 265.

ON THE INSPIRATION OF THE COMPOSER

A large number of troubadour songs begin with a reference to the inspiration of the seasons, especially Spring which is associated with the renewal of life. A typical example can be seen in Ventadorn.

> When the flower appears by the green leaves, and I find the season clear and quiet, and soft songs of the birds in the grove sweeten my heart and refresh me, then the birds sing in their fashion; and I, who have more joy in my heart, must also sing well, for every day's work is mirth and melody; I think of nothing else.[21]

Compared to Spring, the other seasons are rarely mentioned as inspiring these songs. In one instance, another song by Ventadorn, the Fall season seems to inspire the composer, even though he has apparently not composed in two years.

21 'Can par la flors josta,' in Nichols, *The Songs of Bernart de Ventadorn*, 161. Additional troubadour repertoire which attributes inspiration to Spring are: Marcabru, 'Al departir'; Cercamon, 'Ab lo temps'; Ventadorn, 'Bel m'es qu'eu chan' and 'Can l'erba fresch'; Daniel, 'Doutz brais e critz' (specifically the birds of Spring); de Montanhagol, 'Ar ab lo coinde'; de Borneil, 'Tostemps mi sol,' 'Can creis la fresca' and 'Era, quan vei Reverdezitz'; and from the trouvère repertoire: de Couci, 'Li nouviauz tanz'; and Brulé, 'Les oiseillons.'

> When, throughout the plain, I see the leaves fall from the trees, just before the cold spreads abroad and the gentle season disappears, I like my song to be heard; for I have abstained from singing for more than two years, and it is proper for me to make amends.[22]

22 'Lancan vei per mei,' in ibid., 115.

By far the greatest inspiration for the troubadour repertoire is, of course, the joy of love, for love is the general subject of almost every one of their songs. Raimbaut d'Orange provides a typical example in which he begins by saying its not the seasons that inspire him, but love.

I sing not for bird or flower, not for snow or for ice and not even for cold or for warmth, nor for the meadow's growing green again; and for no other pleasure do I sing, nor have I ever sung, but for my mistress for whom I long, because she is the most lovely in the world.[23]

In a song by Arnaut Daniel, the credit to love for the inspiration comes only at the very end, just before he sends the song off with a messenger.

'Be off, my song, and present yourself to her.' Were it not for her, Arnaut would not have put his mind to it.[24]

Some of the most poignant songs are inspired not by the joy of love, but by the grief and pain which often accompany love. A song of Borneil is one of many which mention this confluence of emotions.

I grieve inwardly while outwardly I sing, so that this would seem like churlish inconstancy in me if I were not so firmly bound by Love, which teaches me that a sincere lover achieves perfection in his discouragement and that I should pretend to be cheerful and joyful and should suffer patiently; for the most precious riches are to be gained from noble suffering and fear.[25]

Another song of Borneil begins much more pessimistically, it being inspired by pain without hope.

I lament and sigh and weep and sing, but my song brings me no pleasure; for, instead, the more I sing, the more sad I become and the more I weaken my heart and my reason. And I do not wonder that a man who is saddened by song—which usually drives away pain and sorrow—should fear to see his mind and his affairs gravely altered![26]

Another poet, the trouvére, Blondel de Nesle (second half, twelfth century), also sings without hope, but adds that he only continues to sing because, 'I die more pleasantly that way.'[27]

We see the other side of the coin in a similarly inspired song by a rare female troubadour, La Comtessa de Dia (fl. ca. 1160).

It will be mine to sing of that which I would not desire,
I am so aggrieved by the one to whom I am the friend,
for I love him more than anything that can be.
Pity does not help me toward him, nor courtliness,

23 'Non chant per auzel,' in Press Anthology of Troubadour Lyric Poetry, 113.

24 'Quan chai la fuelha,' in Press, ibid., 183. Other troubadour songs which specifically mention love as their inspiration are: Ventadorn, 'Era'm cosselhatz,' 21, 'Can vei la lauzeta,' 59, 'Lo tems vai,' 22, 'Ab joi mou,' 'Lonc tems a qu'eu,' and 'Tant ai mo cor'; de Borneil, 'Ben for'oimais'; and from the trouvère repertoire: Blondel de Nesle, 'l'amours dont sui espris' and Thibaut, 'Chançon ferai.'

25 'Chans em broil,' in Sharman, *The Cansos and Sirventes of the Troubadour Giraut de Borneil*, 147. Troubadour poems of similar inspiration are: Ventadorn, 'Per melhs cobrir'; Vidal, 'Per miehs sofrir'; Borneil, 'Mas, com m'ave,' 'Quar non ai' and 'De chantar, Ab deport'; and trouvére poems by Bethune, 'Si voirement'; Couci, 'L'an que rose,' 19; and Brulé, 'De bone amour,' 'Desconfortez, plains d'ire' and 'Ire d'amors.'

26 'Plaing e sospir,' in ibid., 411.

27 'Se savoient mon tourment,' in Goldin, *Lyrics of the Troubadours and Trouvères*, 367, line 8ff.

> nor my beauty, nor my good name, nor my wit;
> and so I am cheated and betrayed as much
> as I'd deserve to be if I were ugly.[28]

28 'A chantar m'er,' in ibid., 185.

If, through this contest between joy and pain, the outcome should be a happy ending, then, of course, there is a burst of new inspiration. Such a song was composed by de Nesle.

> I must sing, for I have won joy again
> that always fled from me and stayed far away;
> I have paid with pain and sadness many a day—
> now it is my time to be free of pain;
> for the beautiful lady whom I have loved so long,
> who used to war against me for her love,
> has lately come to terms with me.[29]

29 'Chanter m'estuet,' in ibid., 369.

But, on the other hand, if love is lost, then, as in this example by Ventadorn, there is no inspiration at all and the voice of the singer is stilled.

> I want all those who ask me to sing to know the truth, if I have occasion or leisure for it. Let him sing who wants to. I have not been able to do it since I lost my happiness through my dark destiny.[30]

30 'Tuih cil que'm,' in Nichols, *The Songs of Bernart de Ventadorn*, 174.

There must have been many occasions when the troubadours were forced by necessity to write for monetary purposes. One song by Borneil begins by admitting that he must, 'put great effort into composing a song that I owe for my lodging.'[31] The trouvére, Colin Muset (fl. 1230), complains rather bitterly over the failure of his noble patron to provide the wages he feels entitled to.

31 'En un Chantar,' in Sharman, *The Cansos and Sirventes of the Troubadour Giraut de Borneil*, 300.

> My Lord Count, I have fiddled
> for you in your court,
> and yet you have given me no gift
> nor delivered me my wages:
> that is ignoble!
> Faith I owe holy Mary,
> I won't follow you like this.
> There's poor provisions in my bag,
> there's nothing in my wallet.
>
> My Lord Count, command me
> to do what you want,

only, Lord, if it please you,
make me a nice gift,
out of courtesy.³²

No doubt a frequent source of inspiration, although it is rarely mentioned, was the delight which the composer himself received from his art. The trouvère, Thibaut of Champagne (1201–1253), mentions a shepherdess, 'singing for her own pleasure'³³ and Borneil sings,

for now a man calls it folly if I amuse myself and rejoice and sing rather than doing what other men do!³⁴

Another source of inspiration came from the demands of the court itself, as the trouvére, Gace Brulé (fl. c. 1180–1213) diplomatically refers to it.

Meadows and gardens, parks and groves are for me no reason to sing. I can have no more fitting reason than when my lady wishes to command me.³⁵

Successful composition in the court environment brought, of course, important recognition and esteem to the composer for his work. Borneil, observes that, 'fair renown, once acknowledged, lasts and never varies in hue.'³⁶ In another song, he advises a colleague,

Why compose poetry if you do not wish everyone to know your poem immediately? For song brings no other reward.³⁷

For this proud troubadour, however, the esteem which comes to the composer is directly related to two aesthetic principles: the quality of the song itself and its reception by the listener. It is a perspective which corresponds perfectly with the Aristotelian definition of asthetics.

Then it is right that I sing in order to make entreaty as well as on command. But now they will say that it would be far better if I strove to sing in the light style. And yet this is not true, for poetry deep with meaning, rich and rare, brings and bestows fine reputation, just as unbridled nonsense detracts from it. But I firmly believe that a song is not worth as much to begin with, as later when a man understands it.³⁸

---

32 'Sire Cuens,' in Goldin, *Lyrics of the Troubadours and Trouvères*, 427.

33 'L'autrier par la matinee,' in ibid., 475, line 4.

34 'De chantar,' in Sharman, *The Cansos and Sirventes of the Troubadour Giraut de Borneil*, 250.

35 'Ne me sont,' in Hendrik van der Werf, *The Chansons of the Troubadours and Trouvéres* (Utrecht: A. Oosthoek, 1972), 106.

36 'S'es chantars,' in Sharman, *The Cansos and Sirventes of the Troubadour Giraut de Borneil*, 427.

37 'Era'm platz,' in ibid., 396.

38 'La flors,' in ibid., 172.

We can see just how important the listener was to Borneil in another song where he explains that he has no desire to compose for himself alone, nor any desire to compose for the people around him if they do not appreciate the purpose of his music.

> I am not giving up singing and delight and laughter to the extent that I do not turn to them eagerly still; but with solace and pleasant company no longer in favor, I have no wish to squander my fine and excellent poetry on myself alone; but as soon as I begin my pleasing songs I grit my teeth instead and dare not sing them, for I see no one around me who takes delight in Joy and find no one to follow my example when I rejoice and make merry.[39]

In another place, Borneil adds an additional aesthetic qualification. If his song is to have its true aesthetic effect, the listener must also be a listener of quality.

> Churlish men of base lineage consider many of my fine songs as idle nonsense, though no excellent man of noble birth, if he succeeded in catching their meaning, ever excused himself from listening to them or belittled the pleasure they afforded. And is a man who takes no pleasure in joy and song not thoroughly despicable?[40]

A specific source of inspiration which was related to the court was the death of the noble. Songs of this nature are invariably sincere, as we see in this example by the troubadour, Sordel (ca. 1200–1270).

> I want to mourn for En Blacatz in this simple song
> with a sad and desolate heart, and I have cause,
> for in him I have given up my dear friend and lord,
> and in his death every dignifying quality is lost.[41]

The noble was also the patron and one troubadour, Aimeric de Péguilhan (fl. 1195–1230), writing on the death of his employer, in ca. 1220, wonders, 'What will happen to all the minstrels?'

> For whom will come paid warriors here from afar, and the fine minstrels who come to visit him and whom he honored and held dear more than any prince this side of the sea or the other, and many folk too, without art, without minstrelsy?[42]

Finally, some songs address their inspiration to God. Although Nature is often praised in the love songs, God is rarely mentioned

---

39 'Ges aissi del tot,' in ibid., 268.

40 'De chantar, Ab deport,' in ibid., 458. Similar references to the esteem which comes from the composer's work are found in Ventadorn, 'Tant ai mo cor'; Borneil, 'Alegrar mi volgr'en,' 'Quar non ai,' 'De chantar,' and 'Be m'era bels chantars'; and Adam de la Halle, 'Merveille est.'

41 'Planher vuelh en Blacatz,' in Goldin, *Lyrics of the Troubadours and Trouvères*, 313.

42 'Era par ben,' in Press, *Anthology of Troubadour Lyric Poetry.*, 233.

by name. Borneil, however, who often complains of a decay in aristocratic culture which he perceived in the thirteenth century, is one troubadour whose songs take a definite turn toward religion. We quote excerpts from two of his works because of their important reflections on the changing aesthetic environment.

> If it were not for [God] who tells me that I should sing and be cheerful, I could never be stirred by the gentle season when the grass grows, nor by meadow or bough or woodland or flower, or hardhearted lord or vain love. But I comply with his request, for since joy fails and fades, renown and knighthood are in decline, and since the great rulers have forsaken joy, nothing that the worst among them does has been praised by me. For I have resolved not to seek the favor of any rich and powerful man who is an evil ruler.
>
> The world was good in the days when joy was welcomed by everyone, and when that man was well liked in whom joy most abounded, and when reputation and noble rank went hand in hand. For now the most vicious are called virtuous and the man sunk in deepest melancholy is held to be the best, and the man who takes the most he can from other people will be envied the most …
>
> I have seen a time when a man valued songs and found pleasure in dance melodies and lays. Now that courtly pleasures and gracious deeds are forsaken, and true lovers, in all their concerns, have left the straight path for the crooked, I see that all sense of right has fled …[43]
>
> …
>
> To the honor of God I return to my song, from which I had taken my leave and departed, and not to the calls and cries of the birds, nor to the leaf on the bough do I return, nor do I find any joy in singing. On the contrary, I am angry and full of sorrow, for in many writings do I see and recognize that sin is strengthening its hold, so that trust and faith are failing and wickedness flourishes.
>
> And I wonder greatly when I think of how the world has fallen [spiritually] asleep …[44]

43 'Si per mon Sobre-Totz,' in Sharman, *The Cansos and Sirventes of the Troubadour Giraut de Borneil*, 477.

44 'A l'honor Dieu,' in ibid., 417.

ON THE PURPOSE AND PROCESS OF COMPOSITION

The principal purpose of the entire repertoire of troubadour songs was, of course, to sing of love. Indeed, Bertran de Born (b. ca. 1140) observes that it is a sign that a lady has become old, if she doesn't like singers.[45] We might also note here a song by Borneil which suggests that, in the case of the troubadour in love with a noble lady, the strong emotions of love which could be communicated in song, might not be permitted in words.

> … for in no other way dare I say how she fills me with joy and sad longing.[46]

In their songs the troubadours cite a number of other specific purposes for their music. Several times we hear the poet say the purpose of his music is simply to bring pleasure. A song of Borneil says, 'I am composing just to give pleasure,'[47] and in another he says the troubadour 'is guilty of great stupidity if he objects to the delight and pleasure' his songs give to others.[48]

This troubadour admits in several songs, however, that he found it difficult to sing of joy and pleasure if his audience was not in a conducive mood.

> For I never had to be pressed to sing as long as a fine song was appreciated, but since joy and wit receive such a poor welcome, I do not know how to be friendly and cheerful in the company of so many sad people, or how to throw myself eagerly into writing fine songs.[49]

Another song makes his difficulty in singing aesthetically clear: it is the absence of the listener which inhibits him.

> The skills with which I was used to sing and the real inclination to do so are still mine as they were in days gone by, but there is nothing that delights or diverts me or makes me happy, since I find no one to share this with me. Ah, God! What harm and damage ensues when courtly joys and noble tradition fade and die as they do![50]

Given such an environment he tells us he would sometimes bring himself to sing only for his own pleasure.

Marginal notes:

45 'Bel m'es, quan vei chamjar,' line 14, in Goldin, *Lyrics of the Troubadours and Trouvères*, 241.

46 'Gen M'aten,' in Sharman, *The Cansos and Sirventes of the Troubadour Giraut de Borneil*, 112.

47 'A penas sai comenssar,' in ibid., 197.

48 'De chantar,' in ibid., 458.

49 'En un Chantar,' in ibid., 300. A similar protest he makes in 'Be m'era bels chantars.'

50 'Los apleiz,' in ibid., 256.

> Whoever is in the habit of singing and knows whom to sing about and believes that his pleasing service, his conversation and song may advance his case, let him sing graciously if he likes his theme, now that leaves and blossom appear on the boughs and the springtime fills with its hues the orchards and meadows. For I see nothing in the world to equal joy and the pleasures of company, since warfare and battle, quarrel and strife are nothing but deception and illusion to men of true excellence.
>
> And I, who am grieved by all this, sing, without greetings and commissions, little songs of my own inspiration because this brings me a few moments of joy.[51]

And yet on other occasions he would simply give up and not sing.

> I delight in joy and song, in courtly company and courtesy, but there is no pleasure for me in being the only one in a hundred to sing and rejoice. For I see hardly anyone who would cheerfully encourage me in these enjoyments and for this reason I abandon them.[52]

One must suppose that these troubadours often had to discipline themselves to sing for the pleasure of the company when their own personal circumstances prevented them from feeling the emotions of their music. The trouvère, Le Châtelain de Couci (d. 1203), has left a song which gives evidence of being in such a position.

> Imploring mercy for the mad thing I have done,
> I shall sound the last note of my songs,
> for my loving heart has purposely betrayed
> and slain me, and I ought to hate it—
> it has made me suffer to give others pleasure.[53]

Another purpose familiar to music of all periods, is to give comfort. One troubadour sings to bring comfort to a court he finds suffering for the chill of winter.

> I thought I would refrain from singing until the sweet and gentle season. Now since no one rejoices, and I see virtue and generosity dying out, I cannot help but strive in this frost for a new song which will be a comfort to others.[54]

Sometimes the purpose of the song is to give comfort to the singer himself, rather than to others. A song of Audefroy le Bastard, for example, begins,

---

51 'Qui chantar sol,' in ibid., 237.

52 'Iois e chanz,' in ibid., 275.

53 'Merci clamans de mon,' in Goldin, *Lyrics of the Troubadours and Trouvères*, 359.

54 Ventadorn, 'Be'm cuidei de chantar,' in Nichols, *The Songs of Bernart de Ventadorn*, 76.

> True love has given me hope and a desire to sing in order to lighten the woes which I am forced to suffer by the lady who would certainly be able to reduce my pain; but I am much afraid she wants to punish me because of a vile slanderer.[55]

But there are times when even his music fails to bring the troubadour comfort, as in Ventadorn's plaint,

> I will no longer be a singer … for neither my singing, my voice, nor my melodies do me any good.[56]

Direct didactic purpose is rare in this repertoire, although in one song by Borneil we find,

> For with melodies will I instruct and entreat those indifferent people who, wanting resolve rather than money, linger here rather than go in the service of God.[57]

Peire d'Auvergne, while he does not refer to teaching as such, does suggest that his songs have been regarded as models.

> I have the experience … which in this art they have held up as model, without collusion, so that the true path be not cut off.[58]

Closely related, is the purpose to inspire the noble listener to take a specific action. Bertran de Born, for example, sings,

> Since the barons are vexed and offended by this peace which the two kings have made, I'll compose such a song that, when it is known of, each one of them will long to be at war.[59]

The troubadour Montanhagol sends a song with political purpose to a noble in another city.

> Sirventes, go swiftly to the worthy Count of Toulouse; remind him of what they have done to him, and let him beware of them from this time forth.[60]

For troubadours who were not themselves nobles, composing songs of this nature was no doubt risky. Born suggests that such purpose has brought him unwanted trouble before.

---

55 'Fine amours,' in Hendrik van der Werf, *The Chansons of the Troubadours and Trouvères*, 120.

56 'Lo tems vai e ven e vire,' in Nichols, *The Songs of Bernart de Ventadorn*, 131. He makes a similar complaint in 'Peirol, com a vetz.'

57 'Jois sia commensamens,' in Sharman, *The Cansos and Sirventes of the Troubadour Giraut de Borneil*, 423.

58 'Sobre'l vieill trobar,' in Press, *Anthology of Troubadour Lyric Poetry*, 91.

59 'Puois als baros,' in ibid., 163.

60 'Del tot vey remaner,' in ibid., 241.

I hold my wits under lock and key these days,
they've gotten me into such scrapes with both
Aimar and Richard.⁶¹

61 'Un sirventes cui motz,' in Blackburn, *Proensa*, 148.

Finally, there are some songs which tell us that the poet's purpose was not achieved. Pons de Capdueill (1196–1236) finds his song does not gain his intended's love and mourns,

I stand singing for myself alone,
a damn fool in heart and sense.⁶²

62 'Qui per nesci cuidar,' in ibid., 217.

Another troubadour, sends his song off to his beloved with hope, yet prepared that its purpose may fail.

Go song, toward the lovely Eleanor.
Near her even perfection betters itself.
And I send you there to improve yourself, hear?
And if she makes you a fine welcome
walk full of confidence and cheer.

But if she does not give the script a passing glance,
go burn yourself, and do not fear the heat.⁶³

63 Aimeric de Belenoi, 'Nulhs hom no pot cumplir,' in ibid., 233.

This body of repertoire also contains songs which provide hints of the compositional process. As we shall see below, a well-crafted song was an important goal to these poets and one song by Borneil clearly suggests a period of drafting.

I must set to work on a song with which I have only toyed till now, and make it good enough to rank with the best; for, with the time and the gentle season in my favor, I shall receive no honor or renown unless I compose it in such a way as to win more praise than any other.⁶⁴

64 'Ben coven,' in Sharman, *The Cansos and Sirventes of the Troubadour Giraut de Borneil*, 128.

In composing another song he mentions, 'my progress is slow,' but that he has everything in his heart necessary for 'value and esteem' in a song.⁶⁵

65 'Tostemps mi sol,' in ibid., 138.

Some songs speak of a strong level of concentration in the creative process. Ventadorn, for example, states,

Now I fear neither rain nor wind, so preoccupied am I with composing this song.⁶⁶

66 'Lonc tems,' in Nichols, *The Songs of Bernart de Ventadorn*, 119.

Borneil observes that all he needs to make an excellent song is 'a theme, an occasion, opportunity and a fitting moment for singing.'[67] These kinds of court parameters seemed to give flight to his creativity and if they were missing there was no focus to his work.

> I am composing a song ... and I have no idea on what theme or about whom or how or why, nor can I remember anything that I know.[68]

Borneil maintained that he could compose easy and light songs 'almost without thinking about it,' and that he had the skill to make even difficult songs appear 'to have been simple and pleasant to compose.'[69] In another song, however, he makes it clear that composition was beyond him if his concentration were lacking.

> I would, if I could, compose a slight, clear song such as might match the wit of my godson and give delight to everyone; but this is beyond me, for my thoughts are on something else.[70]

The trouvère Blondel de Nesle found his 'writer's block' not in a lack of concentration, but in maintaining originality.

> It would be best to stop singing altogether,
> for when one sings nowadays, one doesn't know what to say.
> There's not a word or verse one can think up any more,
> no matter how much one picks and chooses,
> that hasn't been said and said again.[71]

It is interesting that sometimes we find a troubadour worrying about his own ability in composition. Ventadorn, for example, notes, 'I always need to make my song better than it is, although it is good.'[72] Borneil seems to find that as an older man he cannot compose as easily in some styles.

> If my heart does not serve me aright and if I do not incline it by force towards a subtle little song, it will not now, I think, bend willingly to the yoke of such broken words as these. There was a time when I sang in this subtle fashion more often than I do now, for my inspiration was greater, so that scarcely anyone recognized how subtly and minutely soldered were my light and cunning words.[73]

There is also evidence that these poets sometimes resorted to borrowing the music of others. Marcabru (1129–1150) begins a song,

---

[67] 'Nuilla res,' in Sharman, *The Cansos and Sirventes of the Troubadour Giraut de Borneil*, 143.

[68] 'Un sonet fatz,' in ibid., 371. Ventadorn, in 'Lo Rossinhols' and 'Peirol, com avetz estat,' mentions having to force himself to compose when the inspiration was absent.

[69] 'Ben deu en bona,' in ibid., 291.

[70] 'Ajtal cansoneta,' in ibid., 193.

[71] 'Mout se feïst,' in Goldin, *Lyrics of the Troubadours and Trouvères*, 371. Raimbaut d'Orange, in 'Escotatz, mas no say,' satirizes poets who claim their works are original.

[72] 'Ja mos chantars,' in Nichols, *The Songs of Bernart de Ventadorn*, 102.

[73] 'Si'l cors no'm ministr'a dreig,' in Sharman, *The Cansos and Sirventes of the Troubadour Giraut de Borneil*, 213.

'Singing on borrowed tune I'll see if I can make a poem.'[74] A song of Borneil, however, confirms that this was not an accepted policy.

> The poem that was heard and sung abroad as the work of a good troubadour later turned into a falsehood when the song was recognized, for … one man claimed as his own the words which another had stolen.[75]

All in all, most of the troubadours and trouvères who are known to us today were probably proud of their ability in composition. William IX, Count of Poitiers, mentions in a song, 'the melody, which I myself am happy about, is fine and good.'[76] And speaking of himself, Marcabru sings,

> Following his distinct grasp, Marcabru
> knows how to weave subject and theme,
> to so accord the vers that no man can
> pluck from the line a word.[77]

Criticism, on the other hand, robs even the finest artist of his confidence, as Peirc d'Auvergne cries.

> Ah! Merit, how you are muted, deaf and squint, and Worthiness, how broken I see you and dragged to and fro! For whoever wants to so ill-treats you that a vile and wicked people, pulling and pushing and snapping, have confused and perverted you; and this robs you of sense and guidance.[78]

ON THE CHARACTERISTICS OF A GOOD SONG

The first requirement of a good song is obvious, 'For it is the theme that makes the song.'[79] Beyond this, it is clear that the best troubadours took great pride in the careful use of language itself. The troubadour Gavaudan (1195–1230) simply concludes, 'the song [vers] is good if it is well written.'[80] Arnaut Daniel gives more detail.

> And I then, whose heart is set on the most noble, should above all make a song finely wrought, so that there be in it no false word or rime unanswered.[81]

---

74 'Al son desvïat chantaire,' in Press, *Anthology of Troubadour Lyric Poetry*, 55.

75 'S'es chantars ben entendutz,' in Sharman, *The Cansos and Sirventes of the Troubadour Giraut de Borneil*, 428.

76 'Pus vezem de novel florir,' in Goldin, *Lyrics of the Troubadours and Trouvères*, 39.

77 'Aujatz de chan,' in Blackburn, *Proensa*, 33.

78 'Belh m'es qu'ieu,' in Press, *Anthology of Troubadour Lyric Poetry*, 95.

79 Borneil, 'De Bels Digz,' in Sharman, *The Cansos and Sirventes of the Troubadour Giraut de Borneil*, 432.

80 'Lo vers dech far,' in Blackburn, *Proensa*, 212.

81 'Doutz braise e critz,' in Press, *Anthology of Troubadour Lyric Poetry*, 177.

In another song,[82] he mentions fashioning words, 'I carve and plane them, so they'll be true and sure,' to a preexistent melody.

Beyond 'finely wrought,' one may assume there was a goal of eloquence and sophistication, appropriate to music associated with court life. One anonymous song begins, 'No country bumpkin made this song.'[83] The trouvère, Colin Muset, says in one song, that he 'made it handsome, fine, and elegant.'[84]

The most frequently mentioned characteristics of a good song all deal with meaning. First, a number of troubadours mention that an important feature of their music is Truth, that it come from the heart. A song of Ventadorn begins, 'There is no use in singing if the song does not spring from the heart.'[85] Some apparently did, however, for the trouvère Gace Brulé seems to want to set himself apart from his colleagues.

> Most have sung of Love
> as an exercise and insincerely;
> so Love should give me thanks
> because I never sang like a hypocrite.[86]

Borneil seems to offer an apology for language that may not be appropriate to the court, for he is only being true to his heart.

> My tongue cannot keep itself from saying what my heart entrusts to it, for the heart acts in the manner of an overlord, each day giving orders to the limbs. And, therefore, if such speech is not akin to courtliness, it seems to me that the tongue can, without question, excuse itself on its lord's authority, since the tongue is the faithful servant of the heart.[87]

Finally, a song which the famous trouvère, Richard Coeur de Lion (1157–1199), wrote while a prisoner in an Austrian castle, suggests that he found he could express through music, feelings which his circumstances did not permit in words.

> No prisoner will ever speak his mind
> fittingly unless he speaks in grief.
> But he can, for consolation, make a song.[88]

Next, a song must have meaning expressed in subtle language, due to the troubadour's position in court. Borneil observes that if

---

[82] 'En cest sonet.'

[83] 'Volez vos que,' in Goldin, *Lyrics of the Troubadours and Trouvères*, 409.

[84] 'Volez oïr la muse Muset,' in ibid., 417.

[85] 'Chantars no pot,' in Nichols, *The Songs of Bernart de Ventadorn*, 81.

[86] 'Li Pluseur,' in Goldin, *Lyrics of the Troubadours and Trouvères*, 385.

[87] 'No's pot sufrir,' in Sharman, *The Cansos and Sirventes of the Troubadour Giraut de Borneil*, 441.

[88] 'Ja nus hons pris,' in Goldin, *Lyrics of the Troubadours and Trouvères*, 377.

this, together with hard work, does not make a fine song, he doesn't know what does.

> If neither subtle meaning nor sheer effort help to improve the value of my light and easy song, raising it on high and refining it, I see no way in which it can be worth much.[89]

This poet admits that sometime he gets a little too subtle!

> The better to construct my song, I keep looking for words which are gentle on the rein, all loaded to the full with meanings foreign to them and yet wholly theirs, though not everyone knows what those meanings are.[90]

Several poets emphasize the importance of genuine emotions to the success of a song. Borneil saw this as an indispensable prerequisite.

> No song, it seems to me, can have value or merit if expectation or fear, anxiety or pleasure do not teach a man how to sing.[91]

Because most of this repertoire consists of love songs, it is the emotions of love which are found most frequently. Several songs, such as this one by Ventadorn, argue on behalf of love that the joy is always stronger than the pain.

> Love will be worth more than any other good, even if it causes you so much grief; for if it causes pain, it compensates later on. A man can seldom have any real good without pain, but the joy always surpasses the weeping.[92]

Several of these poets seemed to have had a kind of masochistic enjoyment of the pain of love. The trouvère Blondel de Nesle sang, 'Love is killing me with a martyrdom so pleasant,'[93] and the troubadour Aimeric de Péguilhan concludes,

> For the pleasures are more than the pangs of Love, the good than the bad, the solace than the anguish, the joys than the sorrows, and the gay moments than the grievous; the advantages than the harms are more, and the smiles more than the tears. I do not say by this at all that therein is no ill, but the illness one has of it is worth more than if one were cured; for he who loves nobly seeks not to be cured of Love's ill, so sweet it is to suffer.[94]

---

89 'Si soutils senz,' in Sharman, *The Cansos and Sirventes of the Troubadour Giraut de Borneil*, 296.

90 'Si'm sentis fizels amics,' in ibid., 185.

91 'Si soutils senz,' *The Cansos and Sirventes of the Troubadour Giraut de Borneil*.

92 'Amics Bernartz de Ventadorn,' in Nichols, *The Songs of Bernart de Ventadorn*, 46.

93 'Mout se feïst bon tenir de chanter,' in Goldin, *Lyrics of the Troubadours and Trouvères*, 371.

94 'Cel qui s'irais,' in Press, *Anthology of Troubadour Lyric Poetry*, 227.

But Raimbaut d'Orange was no masochist, he was afraid it might kill him to put his true feelings into his song.

> I would willingly make up a little song, simple to say, but of it I fear that I'll die; so I'll make it such that it conceals its sense.[95]

We may assume that, as in all eras, originality was a respected characteristic of a good song. Guilhem de Montanhagol voices a natural concern which probably many of these troubadours felt.

> The early troubadours have not said and composed so much on the subject of love, in the past when times were gay, that we may not still, after them, compose songs worthwhile, new, pleasant, and true; for one can say what may not have been said, and in no other way is a troubadour good or fine but in making his songs gay, new, and nobly fashioned, with new things to say with new art.
>
> But in song the first poets say so much inspired by love that to say anything new becomes difficult. Yet new it is when the experts say that which nowhere else has been said in song before, and new if someone says what he has never heard; and new when I say things which no one has said, for love has given me the knowledge and so instructs me that, had no one made poetry, I would a poet be.[96]

The central aesthetic focus for most of these poets was the listener: the song must be understood.[97] A song by Borneil explains, 'I have made an effort for you to understand the type of songs I am composing.'[98] For Ventadorn, this was the very definition of a good song.

> The verse is perfect and well-written and good if one understands it well.[99]

Whether the song was serious or just for fun, the highest form of this aesthetic was universality. A song by Peire Cardenal (1180–1278), who was worried about greed, begins,

> I want to recite my song to all peoples in common, and if they deign to hear it and understand it and can construe it, each will be able to distinguish good from evil.[100]

Finally, the repertoire of the troubadours mention prevalent styles from time to time, especially the virtues of the so-called simple style versus the complex style. Raimbaut d'Orange notes in one poem that 'he is liked more and more esteemed who [writes]

---

95 'Una chansoneta fera,' in ibid., 109.

96 'Non an tan dig li primier trobador,' in ibid., 265.

97 A few troubadours, such as Arnaut Daniel, were known for songs which were difficult to understand.

98 'Non puesc,' in Sharman, *The Cansos and Sirventes of the Troubadour Giraut de Borneil*, 220.

99 'Chantars no pot,' in Nichols, *The Songs of Bernart de Ventadorn*, 82.

100 'Mon chantar,' in Press, *Anthology of Troubadour Lyric Poetry*, 285.

plainly and simply."¹⁰¹ At the same time, he saw that the style had changed and that he, too, must learn this style.

101 'Ara'm platz,' in ibid., 117.

> Since the plain style is in such demand, it will be very hard for me if I don't excel in it; for it seems right that he who composes such words as were never before spoken in song should be able, if he so wishes, to say at another time those which are said and sung every day.¹⁰²

102 'Pos trobars plans,' in ibid., 119.

The troubadour Guiraut Riquier (1230–1292) seemed puzzled by the change in the style favored by the court and doubted whether he was suited to compose light songs.

> Never more will a man be in this world thanked for well composing fair words and pleasant melodies, nor for being eager for esteem, so much is the world come to its decline. For that which used to inspire merit, approval, and praise, I hear blamed as the utmost folly; and that which one used to criticize and blame, I see upheld, and hear it praised by all.¹⁰³
>
> ...
>
> I should abstain from singing,
> for the lightness of joy alone befits the song,
> and I am weighed down by thoughts
> on every side that make me grave,
> thinking back upon my heavy past,
> and my present, seeing how it is oppressed,
> pondering the future,
> I have cause for tears and deep unrest.
>
> My song would not have its savor for me,
> because it does not have that lightness;
> except that God has given me the skill
> such that singing I must retrace my foolishness,
> my sense, my rejoicing, my chagrin,
> the truth of my loss and gain,
> for otherwise there is no good to what I say.
> But I have come too late.
>
> For now no craft is less esteemed
> at court than the beautiful mastery
> of song, because they notice nothing
> there but their ridiculous manners
> and their shrieks of dishonor.
> The things the court would once applaud
> are all forgotten now,
> for the world exults in fraud.¹⁰⁴

103 'Ja mas non er hom,' in ibid., 315.

104 'Be'm degra de chantar tener,' in Goldin, *Lyrics of the Troubadours and Trouvères*, 325.

Another who had difficulty in adjusting to the new popular style was Borneil. He describes working an entire day just trying to get started. By a later poem he seems to have convinced himself, saying, in effect, 'Well, one should not be serious all the time!'

> I hardly know how to begin a 'vers' which I want to make light and easy, and so I have been thinking since yesterday how to compose it on a theme which would be easy for everyone to understand and easy to sing, since I am composing it just to give pleasure.
>
> I could certainly make it less explicit, but a song does not have perfect merit unless everyone can enjoy it. Whoever else this may annoy, I am glad when I hear hoarse and clear voices vying with one another to sing my song, and when I hear it being taken to the well.
>
> Few can reach my level, I think, if ever I wish to sing in the difficult style, and so I must indeed compose a light love song; and it seems to me that it requires as much wit to sustain a [single] theme as to weave together [rich and unusual] words.[105]
>
> ...
>
> But no man is courtly in my opinion if he always wants to be serious. I take great delight in splendid folly, retained in service or discharged according to the changes of time and place, for it makes wisdom manifest and heightens and clarifies it. And, truly, I, who am a singer myself, would put song aside rather than sing if Joy were a burden and courtliness affliction.[106]

The troubadour Sordello, on the other hand, is willing to write, for the sake of love, in whatever style his lover wants to hear.

> I'm happy to make with easy words a pleasant song, and with gay melody, for the best lady that a man can choose, to whom I devote and yield and render myself, neither desires nor is pleased by the elaborate style of singing; and since she is not pleased by it, I'll make from now on my song easy to sing and agreeable to hear, clear and simple to understand, for one who chooses it simple.[107]

---

105 'A penas sai comenssar,' in Sharman, *The Cansos and Sirventes of the Troubadour Giraut de Borneil*, 197. In 'Era'm platz, Guiraut de Borneill,' this poet creates a dialog on the pros and cons of the simple style.

106 'De chantar,' in ibid., 250.

107 'Bel m'es ab motz leugiers,' in Press, *Anthology of Troubadour Lyric Poetry*, 243.

ON PERFORMANCE

Taking for granted inspiration, intent and skill in composition, these composers, as now, understood that it was in performance that their song must succeed or fail. This is surely what Borneil had in mind when he made this observation regarding the audience's ability to make a determination of a song's value.

> If a song is properly understood and if it were to promise merit and renown, why is it unseemly for a troubadour to praise his own song, once it is known?—Because it is clear from the performance whether it deserves praise or blame.[108]

These troubadours tell us in their songs the characteristics of an ideal performance. 'Eloquently, surely, I take up a fine song,' says Borneil.[109] In another song, he begins,

> Whoever is in the habit of singing and knows whom to sing about and believes that his pleasing service, his conversation and song may advance his case, let him sing graciously.[110]

The vocal style the troubadours distinctly objected to, they called 'braying.' Guillaume IX commands, 'sing this nicely, do not bray it out.'[111] And Peire d'Auvergne defends his work with this wish,

> With noble joy the poem begins which rimes fair words together, and there's no fault in anything therein; but it pleases me not that such a one should learn it whom my song does not befit. I've no wish that some wretched singer, the sort who ruins any song, should turn my sweet melody into braying.[112]

It was no doubt such a singer that Raimbaut d'Orange feared when he sought a messenger to take his song to his beloved. He wished for a singer, 'who can sing nobly, with joy, for [my song] befits no base singer.'[113]

There are a few references to a fine singer who finds himself, due to the passions of love, singing in a style he himself does not respect. Raimbaut d'Orange surely hints at this when he complains to his lover, 'you make me sing in joyful rage.'[114] Marcabru is much more outspoken.

> But what summons me to be an enemy is
> that this bitch *likes* to hear me roar and cry.[115]

---

108 'S'es chantars ben entendutz,' in Sharman, *The Cansos and Sirventes of the Troubadour Giraut de Borneil*, 427.

109 'Gen M'aten,' in ibid., 112.

110 'Qui chantar sol,' in ibid., 237.

111 'Farai chansoneta nueva,' in Goldin, *Lyrics of the Troubadours and Trouvères*, 43.

112 'Ab fina joia comenssa,' in Press, *Anthology of Troubadour Lyric Poetry*, 89.

113 'Ar resplan la flors,' in ibid., 109.

114 'Escotatz, mas no say,' line 30, in Goldin, *Lyrics of the Troubadours and Trouvères*, 181.

115 'Aujatz de chan com,' in Blackburn, *Proensa*, 33.

An eloquent performance requires an appropriate atmosphere, which Borneil summarizes as follows.

> With love and gratitude, the occasion and the right moment, it is easy to sing well.[116]

These poets also give us hints which describe those atmospheres which are not conducive to fine performance. For Bertran de Born it is dinner music, 'repasts to the noise of viol and song.'[117] The Monk of Montaudon composed a song listing 'what annoys me most,' and includes having to wait for his performance.

> What gives me a rash is waiting too long
> at table, for the instruments to finish.[118]

Ventadorn reminds us that a proper psychological frame of mind is also necessary to a fine performance. He observes, 'Rarely will you see a singer sing well if things are going badly for him.'[119] He undoubtedly regarded this as a vicious circle—a singer needing to sing to be in a positive frame of mind—for in another song he complains,

> Everything has been unpleasant since I gave up singing, and the longer I remain mute, the more I contribute to my own undoing.[120]

---

116 'A ben chantar,' in Sharman, *The Cansos and Sirventes of the Troubadour Giraut de Borneil*, 123.

117 'Mon chan fenisc,' in Goldin, *Lyrics of the Troubadours and Trouvères*, 231.

118 'Fort m'enoia, so auzes dir,' in Blackburn, *Proensa*, 179.

119 'Pois preyatz me,' in Nichols, *The Songs of Bernart de Ventadorn*, 147.

120 'Estat ai com,' in ibid., 92.

24 AESTHETICS OF MUSIC IN ITALIAN LITERATURE OF THE TWELFTH AND THIRTEENTH CENTURIES

WE BEGIN BY REMINDING THE READER that there is an extant body of twelfth- and thirteenth-century poetry by Italian troubadours, smaller in size but otherwise comparable to the repertoire of the French troubadours and trouvères. Like their French contemporaries, they sang of Spring[1] and Love and often conclude with a reference to the messenger who will deliver, and sing, the song to the beloved. Two of these postscripts are especially interesting, one for the quaint hope the poet placed in his music.

> Song, you know it was from the books of Love
> I copied you, when I saw my lady;
> now let me put my trust in you.[2]

Another postscript confirms that this repertoire was associated with the higher, and not the lower, level of society.

> Song, I know that when I've sent you forth
> you will go about speaking to many ladies …
> And if you don't wish to travel in vain,
> don't stop where there are base people; contrive, if you can,
> to show yourself only to ladies or men of courteous mind,
> who will lead you quickly to your destination.[3]

No lover suffers like an Italian lover, and indeed the twelfth-century Italian author of *The Art of Courtly Love* actually defines Love as a form of suffering.

> Love is a certain inborn suffering derived from the sight of and excessive meditation upon the beauty of the opposite sex.[4]

It follows, therefore, that some of the most interesting of the Italian songs are those which sing of the pain of love. A song by Guittone d'Arezzo (ca. 1235–1294) is a typical example.

---

1 An excellent example is 'Fresca rosa novella,' by Guido Cavalcanti, in Frederick Goldin, *German and Italian Lyrics of the Middle Ages* (Garden City: Anchor Books, 1973), 313.

2 Cavalcanti, 'Io non pensava,' in ibid., 319.

3 Dante, 'Donne ch'avete intelletto d'armore,' in *Dante's Lyric Poetry*, trans. Kenelm Foster and Patrick Boyde (Oxford: Clarendon Press, 1967), 63.

4 Andreas Capellanus, *The Art of Courtly Love*, trans. John Parry (New York: Frederick Ungar, 1957), 3.

No sweetness in voice or melody
can ever rejoice my heart again—
I remember I am severed and am far
from the one I love, will love, have loved.

Nor for the sweetness in singing shall I ever raise my voice,
I shall sing henceforth only from pain:
I shall sound sweet songs like a once free bird
that is trapped in a cage and suffers much regret.[5]

> 5 'Dolcezza alcuna o di voce o di sono,' in Goldin, *German and Italian Lyrics of the Middle Ages*, 259.

We have associated all the troubadour songs with Art Music, in part because they carry the presumption of an attentive listener. Some lovely lines of Dante speak of himself as the listener.

If I am there to hear
my beautiful, my Fioretta singing,
I shall say my lady
wears my sighs upon her head.[6]

> 6 'Per una ghirlandetta,' in ibid., 367.

Finally, as a change in courtly taste brought an end to the era of the French troubadours towards the end of the thirteenth century, so in Italy a new style emerged, the more abstruse *dolce stil novo*. One of the old-fashioned lyric poets, Bonagiunta Orbicciani da Lucca (d. ca. 1296), addresses a poem of complaint to one of the proponents of the new style.

You who have changed the manner
of the once delightful songs of love,
transmuted it in form and essence
in order to surpass every other poet …

And you, you surpass everyone in complexity,
and there's not one man who can explain you,
so obscure are your discourses.

And it is considered a strange thing,
even though the sense comes from Bologna,
to drag a song out of learned sources.[7]

> 7 'To Guinizelli,' in ibid., 271. This poet's answer, 'a Bonagiunta da Lucca,' in ibid., 295ff, includes the following insult.
>
> God set degrees in nature and
> the world
> and made unequal wits
> and intellects;
> therefore, what the average man
> thinks he should not tell.

DANTE (1265–1321)

ON THE PHYSIOLOGY OF AESTHETICS

Dante once defined philosophy as, 'nothing other than a love of wisdom or of knowledge.'[8] The drive for the acquisition of knowledge he saw as innate, and its accomplishment the highest form of happiness. Paraphrasing Aristotle, he concludes,

> All men naturally desire to possess knowledge. This can, and should, be traced to the fact that every being has a drive inherent in its own nature directing it towards its own perfection. Since knowledge is the highest perfection of our soul, in which our supreme happiness is found, we are all by our very nature driven to the desire to attain this.[9]

This limited definition of happiness was not his alone. A poem by his contemporary, Guido Guinizelli (fl. 1250–1300), sings the same theme.

> Since nature
> and instruction
> are the origins of all knowledge,
> I inquire whence
> knowledge has its greater
> cause—from nurture or from nature.
> If one should say
> that knowledge
> rather comes from nature,
> he would speak in error,
> for no science
> would, without learning,
> ascent to great heights
> alone by its own desire.
>
> But by study
> knowledge increases,
> which gives perfect joy.
> Thus, in this view,
> it is the learned man
> who reaches perfect good, without deceit;
> wherefore it seems that learning
> and nature live
> together sharing one
> single hope, one desire.[10]

[8] *The Banquet*, trans. Christopher Ryan (Stanford University: Anma Libri, 1989), III, xi, 6.

[9] Ibid., I, i, 1.

[10] 'In quanto la natura,' in Goldin, *German and Italian Lyrics of the Middle Ages*, 291.

These are, unfortunately, rather narrow views of human faculties, for the rational attributes are only half of man's faculties. The other faculties, in particular the senses, Dante regarded as distinctly lower in priority. In fact, he makes the rather extraordinary statement that the senses 'exist for reason's sake alone.'[11] In one of his poems he even suggests that a sensation such as pain cannot be understood by mere experience, but must be understood by reason as well.[12]

All of this has rather dismal implications for any theory of the aesthetics of art, as the following confirms.

> Things are properly designated by the highest nobility possessed by their form, as man, for instance, is designated by reason and not by the senses or by anything less noble. So when it is said that man lives, this must be understood to mean that he uses his reason, which is the life specific to him and the activity of his most noble part. So anyone who sets reason aside and uses only his sensitive part lives not as a man but as a beast, a point made by the most excellent Boethius when he says: 'He lives as an ass.' I quite agree, for thought is the act proper to reason; animals do not think, because they lack that faculty—a description that fits not only the lower animals but those who have a human appearance but the spirit of a sheep or of some other vile beast.[13]

Dante uses this expression again in his *Divine Comedy*.

> You were not made to live like beasts, but for
> The pursuit of virtue and of knowledge.[14]

However, all this confidence in Reason notwithstanding, when it came to Love, Dante realized that there was an important part of man's experience which somehow stood apart from rational understanding.

> Love, who in my mind discourses
> fervently of my lady,
> often puts forth such things concerning her,
> the intellect loses its way with them …
> And surely I must first give up—
> if I wish to treat of what I hear of her—
> what my intellect does not understand;
> and a great part
> of what it understands, for I could not express it.

---

11 *The Banquet*, III, xv, 4.

12 'To Dante da Maiano,' in Foster and Boyde, *Dante's Lyric Poetry*, 11.

13 *The Banquet*, II, vii, 3.

14 *Inferno*, XXVI.

> Therefore, if my verses are not adequate
> that undertake the praise of her,
> let the infirm intellect be blamed,
> and our speech, which does not have the power
> to recount all that Love speaks forth.[15]

[15] 'Amor che ne la mente mi ragiona,' in Goldin, *German and Italian Lyrics of the Middle Ages*, 373.

A passage in the *Divine Comedy*, suggests that Dante observed that in music also the rational failed in the same way.

> Voices sang *'Beat pauperes spiritu,'*
> In such a way that words could not convey it.[16]

[16] *Purgatory*, XII.

Guido Cavalcanti (1259–1300) had the same experience regarding Love, observing,

> Something happens to me when I am in her presence,
> I cannot describe it to the intellect.[17]

[17] 'Veggio negli occhi,' in Goldin, *German and Italian Lyrics of the Middle Ages*, 323.

Cavalcanti, however, gives the correct answer to this apparent problem: the separate natures of the intellect and feeling (the separate hemispheres of the brain, actually).

> It is not a faculty of the soul, but derives
> from the soul, which is the form of man—
> not the rational soul, as I say, but that which feels.
> It deprives reason of well-being,
> for now desire does the work of reason.[18]

[18] 'Donna me prega,' in ibid., 327.

Only in the introduction to one of his sonnets does Dante admit to understanding this same separation of faculties.

> In this sonnet I make two parts of myself in accordance with the way in which my thoughts were divided. One I call *heart*, that is desire; the other *soul*, that is reason; and I relate what one says to the other.[19]

[19] *Vita Nuova*, trans. Mark Musa (Oxford: Oxford University Press, 1992), 76.

And, when Reason does speak to Desire, what does it say?

> Who is this one
> that comes with consolation for our mind
> and who, possessing such outrageous strength,
> will not allow another thought to stay?[20]

[20] Ibid., 77.

This must have been impressive, if confusing, to Dante—that feeling could so overpower Reason. In one poem he observes that Love overcomes the intellect like a ray of sunlight overcoming eyes that are weak.[21] He returns to this idea twice in the *Divine Comedy*, a reference at the beginning of *Paradise* again using his terms of desire and intellect.

[21] 'Amor che ne la mente mi ragiona,' lines 59–60, in Goldin, *German and Italian Lyrics of the Middle Ages*, 377.

> As it approaches its desire,
> Our intellect submerges so profoundly
> That our memory is unable to go back.[22]

[22] *Paradise*, I.

In the *Inferno*, he speaks of other emotions which have the same power over the intellect.

> Who could ever tell, even in straight prose,
> The full story of the blood and of the wounds
> That I now saw, often though it be told?
> Certainly every tongue would falter, for
> Neither our speech nor our intellect
> Is capable of encompassing so much.[23]

[23] *Inferno*, XXVIII.

These passages demonstrate that he was clearly aware that there is more to man than Reason.

On the Psychology of Aesthetics

Nearly all references to Pleasure and Pain by poets of this period are used in descriptions of the complexities of Love. Dante, in a poem sent to an unknown correspondent, contributes such an observation.

> For the suffering brought by Love is outweighed six times over by the sweetness of his joy.[24]

[24] Foster and Boyde, *Dante's Lyric Poetry*, 19.

The only other reference to Pleasure and Pain as abstract concepts by Dante is found in the *Inferno*. Here the narrator asks if the suffering he sees will be less or greater after the Day of Judgment. The brief, but interesting, answer is,

> 'Refer to your philosophy,' he said,
> 'Which claims that, the more perfect a thing is,
> The more perfect its sense of pain and pleasure.'[25]

[25] *Inferno*, VI.

Similarly, Dante rarely discusses the emotions as abstract entities. In one place, in the tradition of the ancient Greek philosophers, he lists the emotions of the soul. Here, as part of a discussion of a woman, the six emotions he catalogs are rather curious, especially as both Joy and Pain are missing.

> Since, then, there are six emotions proper to the human soul, namely, graciousness, zeal, pity, envy, love and shame.[26]

[26] *The Banquet*, III, viii, 10.

He continues by repeating the inaccurate observation of many early philosophers that these emotions are primarily exhibited in the eyes, rather than in the entire face. He adds the extraordinary information that for this reason the ancients often tore out their own eyes, in order not to betray their emotions.

Hardly any of the early philosophers seemed to have been aware that the basic emotions of man are in fact universal, due to their being genetic and not learned. This being the case, our attention was drawn to a discussion of the natural attraction of man to learning, in which Dante observed, 'the emotions pertaining to man's essence are common to all mankind.'[27]

[27] Ibid., III, xi, 7.

On Aesthetics

Dante, in his writings, did not elaborate on a personal philosophy of aesthetics in the arts. In a discussion of Tragedy we can see evidence of such a philosophy, although a precise definition is missing.

> The highest things are worthy of the highest, and because the style which we call tragic appears to be the highest style, those things which we have distinguished as being worthy of the highest song are to be sung in that style alone.[28]

[28] 'De Vulgari Eloquentia,' in *The Portable Dante*, ed. Paolo Milano (New York: Viking Press, 1969), 'The Tragic Style,' 637.

It is interesting that the one characteristic which Dante focuses on, relative to the 'highest style,' is the contribution of discipline and hard work. We may assume it is a reflection of his own experience as a writer, when he advises that native genius is not enough.

> But it is in the exercise of the needful caution and discernment that the real difficulty lies; for this can never be attained to without strenuous efforts of genius, constant practice in the art, and the habit of the sciences ... And therefore let those who, innocent of art and science,

and trusting to genius alone, rush forward to sing of the highest subjects in the highest style, confess their folly and cease from such presumption; and if in their natural sluggishness they are but geese, let them abstain from imitating the eagle soaring to the stars.[29]

29 Ibid., 638.

In a discussion comparing Latin with Italian, Dante provides his most precise definition of Beauty. It is a definition by one who sees from the perspective of Reason, focusing on the one element of art which is most susceptible of rational description: the orderly relationship of subordinate parts.

> Something is said to be beautiful when its parts are in proper accord with each other, because the harmony among them is a source of pleasure for us. So someone is considered beautiful when his bodily members are in proper accord with each other; we call a song beautiful when its sounds accord with each other in conformity with the dictates of art.[30]

30 *The Banquet*, I, v, 13.

The source for this appreciation of order, Dante finds in an innate facet of the faculty of Reason, comparable to the faculty which permits sense perception.

> Just as the sensitive part of the soul has eyes with which it can differentiate among things with respect to their external coloring, so the rational part has its eye with which it can differentiate among things with respect to their being ordered to some proper end; this is called the power of discrimination.[31]

31 Ibid., I, xi, 3.

But passages such as these are perhaps an unfair representation of Dante's philosophy of aesthetics, a topic on which he wrote very little to begin with. There are other places, for instance, where he indirectly betrays a much broader aesthetic sensitivity. For example, in one discussion of language, the inseparable associate of Reason, Dante reveals an ear unmatched by any early writer. It is almost as if he were describing music itself.

> Everyone should recognize that no writing fashioned into a harmonious unity by its musical form can be translated from its original language without all its sweetness and harmony being destroyed. That is why Homer has not been translated from Greek into Latin, unlike the other writings which the Greeks have bequeathed to us. That is why the verses of the Psalter lack music and harmony: they were translated from Hebrew to Greek, and from Greek to Latin, all their sweetness disappearing with that first translation.[32]

32 Ibid., I, vii, 15.

And in the *Purgatorio* there is a line which clearly demonstrates that Dante understood a distinction between Reason and Art. Here we meet an unidentified ghost whom we are told was the most talented writer of all, but who was never recognized by the masses and hence enjoyed no fame. The masses, Dante says, followed opinion, 'without first listening to reason or to art.'[33]

There is another place where Dante expresses a lack of faith in the ability of the masses to judge art. Here he observes that most men are so absorbed in their own craft, or the work of the moment, that they never develop a broader sense of discrimination. Thus he agrees with Boethius, whom he quotes as saying, 'popular esteem is worthless.'[34]

But if Dante finds the masses incapable of judging art, he does seem prepared to grant them the ability to judge on matters requiring Reason, quoting Aristotle as saying, 'What most people judge to be true cannot be wholly false.' He goes on to point out how the senses are obviously capable of reporting inaccurate information. Then, in a passage which makes for rather humorous reading today, he intends to demonstrate that Reason never errors—and in the process only proves how remarkably it can.

> Where the Philosopher says, then, 'What most people judge to be true cannot be wholly false,' he is not referring to the superficial judgment formed by the senses, but to the interior judgment made by reason. For judgment formed by the senses is, in most people, often quite false, especially with regard to things that are perceived by the several senses together, since in these cases what the senses report is very frequently mistaken. We know, for instance, that to most people the diameter of the sun appears to be one foot across, but this is quite false; human reason, making observations and discoveries with the various skills at its command, has shown that the diameter of the body of the sun is five-and-a-half times that of the earth. Where the earth is 6,500 miles in diameter, the diameter of the sun, which to judgments formed by the senses is one foot across, is in fact 35,750 miles across.[35]

When addressing aesthetics in music, Dante presents a very limited definition, again emphasizing the order and relationship of the constituent parts. Here, like the ancient Greek philosophers, he illustrates this point by drawing an analogy with grammar.

33 *Purgatorio*, XXVI.

34 *The Banquet*, I, xi, 7.

35 Ibid., IV, viii, 6. The actual diameter of the earth is 7,926 miles and that of the sun, 864,930 miles!

> Music is entirely a matter of relationships, as is evident in speech, in respect of poetry, and in songs, for the sweetness of the harmony created by any one of these works is in proportion to the beauty of the relationship within it; it is in this science that we principally find the beauty specific to relationship, for relationship is its principal concern.[36]

[36] Ibid., II, xiii, 23.

We gain an additional insight into what Dante means by this relationship in music when he uses music as an analogy for the effect of a mirror. Here, he says, when one looks into the mirror and sees a perfect likeness, 'the two accord the way a note does with its rhythm.'[37]

[37] *Paradiso*, XXVIII.

In the *Divine Comedy*, Dante frequently employs a chorus of spirits, which reminds us somewhat of the Chorus in Greek Tragedy. It is in these several choral appearances that we find some references by Dante to the purpose of music. A passage in the *Purgatorio* repeats the often cited purpose of music as being to provide delight, although here, interestingly enough, it is delight accompanied by sorrow.

> When, lo, a weeping and a singing could be heard,
> *Labia mea, domine*, of such a kind
> That it brought forth delight as well as sorrow.[38]

[38] *Purgatorio*, XXIII.

One of Dante's poems contains a similar thought. Here, surrounded by unhappiness, the purpose of the music is to keep pleasure alive.

> Now that the cold
> dispels the unworthy,
> and joy, song, love
> falter and grow weak,
> I have a will to sing
> to keep pleasure alive,
> though loss and injury,
> torment and trouble,
> come at me from every corner—
> for they withdraw before my force.[39]

[39] 'Ora che la freddore,' in Goldin, *German and Italian Lyrics of the Middle Ages*, 259.

Another purpose of music often mentioned in early literature is to soothe the emotions of the listener. Dante presents an unusually vivid reference to this power of music in the *Purgatorio*.

> I now heard voices, each one of which
> Seemed to be praying for pity and for peace
> To the Lamb of God, who lifts our sins from us.

> They all started with the *Agnus Dei*,
> And kept together in both word and measure,
> So that there seemed among them every concord.
> 'Those are spirits, master, that I hear?'
> I said; and he to me: 'You are correct;
> They go about untying knots of rage.'⁴⁰

40 *Purgatorio*, XVI.

In a similar passage, we can see the effect of this soothing quality.

> Singing *Ave Maria, gratia*
> *Plena*, now opened wide his wings before her.
> From every side the blessed court responded
> To the celestial melody, so that
> Every face looked more serene because of it.⁴¹

41 *Paradiso*, XXXII.

The most interesting and valuable comments relating to the aesthetics of music by Dante are those focused on the listener. First, he makes the observation that the listener can be moved by music even if he does not 'understand' music, by which he means, of course, the technical, conceptual aspects of music.

> And as the harp and viol, their many strings
> Tuned in accord, make sweet sonorities
> For him who does not understand the notes ...⁴²

42 Ibid., XIV.

He makes the same point, by way of analogy, in describing a winged image:

> It sang as it circled, and said: 'What my notes
> Are to you who do not comprehend them,
> Eternal judgment is to all you mortals.'⁴³

43 Ibid., XIX.

Dante seemed to be particularly impressed with the fact that music had the power to make the contemplative listener 'forget' everything else. Two descriptions of this phenomenon are mentioned in the *Purgatorio*.

> He thereupon began to sing, so sweetly
> That I hear the sweetness of it still inside me.
> My master and I, and all those people
> Standing there with him, seemed so delighted
> That nothing else appeared to touch our minds.
> We were all transfixed there, listening ...
>
> ...

From his mouth, and in such tender tones,
That it made me lose awareness of myself.[44]

44 *Purgatorio*, II and VIII.

Dante, lacking our modern understanding of the rather exclusive functions of left and right brain hemispheres, turns to the soul for an inventive explanation of how the power of music seems to so focus the attention of the listener.

Music draws to itself the various spirits in a person (which may be said to consist mainly of vapors of the heart) to the extent that they almost cease to carry out any of their functions: to such a degree does the soul form a single entity when it hears music, that the power in all the spirits rushes, as it were, to the sensitive spirit, which receives the sound.[45]

45 *The Banquet*, II, xiii, 24.

Although he does not specifically mention music, a passage in the *Purgatorio* seems to be referring to the same process.

When through a feeling of delight or pain,
Experienced by some faculty of ours,
The soul gathers round that single sense,
It seems inattentive to all others.
This goes counter to that error which believes
That one soul burns within us on another;
So that when something is heard or seen
That strongly holds the soul's attention, time
Passes by and man is unaware of it.
For the power of listening is one thing,
And another that which commands the whole soul.[46]

46 *Purgatorio*, IV.

Finally, Dante makes a reference to another characteristic of the separate functions of the hemispheres of our brains, a problem which would become familiar to centuries of composers. When we are contemplative listeners of music with words, it is possible to be so focused in the right hemisphere that it is often difficult to pay attention to the words, which are understood in the left hemisphere. It was to solve this problem that the recitative and aria evolved, to essentially allow us to listen first with one hemisphere and then the other. Dante had observed this problem with regard to listening to church music.

I turned attentively to the first tones
And believed I heard *Te Deum laudamus*
In a voice that blended with sweet music.
What I heard gave me the same impression
That people are accustomed to receive
When singing is accompanied by organ:
Now the words are understood, now they are not.[47]

[47] *Purgatorio*, IX.

In summary, our chief interest in this period is, of course, Dante, the greatest of his contemporaries. We are disappointed to find in Dante so apparently narrow a view of human nature, professing a faith solely in the rational side of man. Only when it came to Love, did Dante seem to admit there is an important faculty which lies outside Reason, indeed which Reason could not explain.

Only a few additional hints of his philosophy of aesthetics in music can be found, namely that the purpose of music is for delight and to soothe the listener. It is in his description of the listener, that we discover Dante actually was a much more acute observer of musical performance. He noticed first, that the power of music was felt even in the listener who had no 'knowledge' of music itself. More important, he observed that the attentive listener was so absorbed by music that his other senses seemed not to operate, that he appeared 'transfixed' and experienced a loss of awareness of self. We can only regret that this great writer did not choose to ponder these phenomena further and to hypothesize on the aesthetic principles which produced them.

25 AESTHETICS OF MUSIC IN THE MINNESINGER SONGS AND GERMAN ROMANCES OF THE TWELFTH AND THIRTEENTH CENTURIES

LIKE THE BETTER KNOWN TROUBADOURS AND TROUVÉRES of France, the German minnesingers (*love singers*) performed in an aristocratic environment and were themselves representatives of all levels of society, some aristocrats and some representatives of the broad class of traveling entertainers known as jongleurs.

The best known of the minnesingers was Walther von der Vogelweide (ca. 1170–1230). He apparently traveled widely ('from Mur to Seine … from Po to Trave'[1]) seeking permanent employment and one song tells us he resented always being the guest and wished that he could be the noble host.

> Guest and lodging ofttimes make one sore ashamed.
> Ah, might I but receive a guest, and take
> As host the bows that he would have to make!
> 'Stay here tonight! Tomorrow's fare!'—
> What life is this, the jongleur's?[2]

Another song, composed upon his securing employment in a court, reflects on his less fortunate days and provides a description of what must have been the fate of many of his wandering colleagues.

> I've got my fief, everybody, I've got my fief!
> Now when it's cold I don't have to fear for my toes,
> I will beg a little less at stingy masters' doors—
> I have fresh air in the summer, in winter my fire roars,
> and the noble king, the sweet king, is the one I have to thank.
> My neighbors find me a much more presentable man—
> they don't look at me as though I were a scarecrow any more.
> I hated being poor, and I was poor too long—
> my mouth was so full of reproaches, my breath stank.
> Now the king has sweetened my breath—and my song.[3]

1 'Wealth more than Honor,' in W. Alison Phillips, trans., *Selected Poems of Walter von der Vogelweide* (London: Smith, Elder, & Co., 1896), 85.

2 'Host and Guest,' in ibid., 77.

3 'Dankspruch,' in Frederick Goldin, *German and Italian Lyrics of the Middle Ages* (Garden City: Anchor Books, 1973), 109.

A song composed at the end of his life[4] reveals that he had been a minnesinger for forty years. Earlier, he says, he sang with joy, but now he gets nothing from it and continues only in the hope for his listener's good wishes.

One minnesinger of the thirteenth century, Tannhäuser, had been a noble, but upon losing his fortune lived a life similar to that described by Vogelweide.

> The way things used to be with me the best of men would say
> that I was welcome everywhere; my kin were kind before.
> But now who once was glad to see me turns and looks away,
> and since I've lost my property none greet me anymore.
> I have to step aside for him (so altered is my state)
> who rightly yielded once to me, but now I have to wait.
> Who once along with me were guests have houses now, I know,
> but my condition is the same as twenty years ago.
> For I'm a guest and never host, my life's an errant one,
> and those who think it isn't hard should live as I have done.[5]

Among his former possessions was a villa in Vienna,[6] and perhaps the loss of his fortune may have been related to his complaint in one song that Vienna has too many lawyers![7] This same song describes what he has seen in his travels, which seem to have included most of Europe, North Africa, and Jerusalem.

Another song complains that he too is no longer welcome at court and in so doing he mentions the main themes of which all minnesingers sang: Love, Nature, Spring, Summer dances with music, and religion.

> I ought to be at court, you know, so they could hear me sing.
> The trouble is that no one gives me pretty melodies.
> If I had some, then I would tell of every courtly thing:
> of lovely ladies I'd sing well—and better far—with ease.
> I'd sing about the meadow and the foliage and of May;
> I'd sing about the summertime, of dance and roundelay.
> I'd sing of chilling snow and rain, and what the winds have done;
> I'd sing about the father, mother, and their infant son.
> Who will redeem my pledge? Alas, how sad that I have none.[8]

Of these themes, it is the singing of love songs with which these poets are most associated, as their very name signifies. Vogelweide

---

4 'Ir reinen wîp, ir werden man,' in ibid., 131.

5 'Hie vor do stvnt min ding also,' in J. W. Thomas, trans., *Tannhäuser: Poet and Legend* (Chapel Hill: University of North Carolina Press, 1974), 161.

6 'Ze wiene hat ich eine hof,' in ibid., 173.

7 'Der kvnig von marroch,' line 59, in ibid., 133.

8 'Das ich ze herren niht,' line 10ff, in ibid., 171.

has left a song which is an elegy for a minnesinger known as Reinmar (ca. 1150–1210), whom he felt exemplified this duty most nobly.

> Alas, that wisdom, and youth,
> and the beauty of man, and his craft
> cannot be handed down when the body dies away.
> A man who has lived can mourn for this,
> who is awake to human hurt.
> Reinmar, what great art dies with you.
> You've the right to rejoice till the end of days
> that you never lost the taste, not once,
> for singing noble women's praise.
> They ought to thank your tongue forever.
> If you had sung but the one theme—if that were all—
> 'Joy to you, Woman, how pure a name,' with that alone you would have striven
> so for their praise's sake, let every woman pray for mercy on your soul.[9]

The late twelfth-century *Nibelungenlied* has a character, Folker, who is described as a 'noble minstrel,' and was sufficiently wealthy that he traveled with thirty of his own knights and squires.[10] This same work includes an account of a tourney hosted by Siegmund which describes a number of visiting minstrels who played all day without rest and were rewarded so freely with gold, clothes, and horses that one would have thought the nobles hadn't another day to live.[11] A similar reference to traveling minstrels being richly rewarded is found in Wolfram von Eschenbach's (ca. 1170–1220) *Parzival*.[12]

The literature of this period never describes the details of where in the noble residence the art songs were sung. One passing reference to dinner music, in *Parzival*, does mention, 'At the foot of his table sat his minstrels.'[13] In the case of art music, we may assume that a performance at such a banquet was given 'after the tables were cleared,' a common description indicating music to be listened to, rather than to eat by. Indeed, such a phrase is used in the account of an outdoor banquet in the anonymous thirteenth-century Romance, 'Laurin.'

> After they had eaten and drunk and the tables had been cleared, the princes sat there and listened to the singing and recitation that was performed before them. This was followed by music from so many stringed instruments that the entire mountain resounded.[14]

---

9 'Owê, daz wîsheit unde jugent,' in Goldin, *German and Italian Lyrics of the Middle Ages*, 129.

10 'Twenty-fourth Adventure.'

11 'Second Adventure.'

12 Book II, 101.

13 Wolfram von Eschenbach, *Parzival*, trans. Helen Mustard and Charles Passage (New York: Vintage Books, 1961), bk. I, p. 20.

14 'Laurin,' trans., J. W. Thomas, in *The Best Novellas of Medieval Germany* (Columbia, SC: Camden House, 1984), 72.

ART MUSIC

The majority of minnesinger art songs are songs sung for aristocratic ladies, songs which Vogelweide says, brought 'the glow of rose and lily to their cheeks.'[15] The minnesinger, Ulrich von Liechtenstein (1198–1276), tells us that these songs in praise of ladies were as familiar to court life as clothes themselves.

> There is so much honor in the praise I sing,
> it passes well in court
> and belongs there, without shame,
> more than the raiment of a king.[16]

Gottfried von Strassburg (fl. 1200–1210) provides a touching description of the role these minnesingers (here 'Nightingales') played in aristocratic life. Of particular interest in this passage is the reference to aesthetics, in the reaction of the listeners to these songs.

> 'Nightingales' there are many, but I shall not speak of them, since they do not belong to this company. Thus I shall say no more of them than what I must always say—they are adepts at their task and sing their sweet summer songs most excellently. Their voices are clear and pleasing, they raise our spirits and gladden our hearts within us. The world would be full of apathy and live as if on sufferance but for this sweet bird-song, which time and again brings back to any who has loved, things both pleasant and good, and varied emotions that soothe a noble heart. When this sweet bird-song begins to tell us of its joy it awakens intimate feelings that give rise to tender thoughts.[17]

Sometimes we are told that the minnesinger has been hired to sing on behalf of some lover.[18] More often, as in the case of the troubadour and trouvére repertoire, these songs are personal, reflecting the love of the minnesinger for a noble lady. A song by Vogelweide begins,

> Never before had I such hope of bliss!
> And hence it comes that I perforce must sing.
> Hail to the maid who shall requite me this!
> To her pure worth it is my song I bring.[19]

In a time when aristocratic marriages were made of political purpose and not love, this was allowed the minnesinger. On the

---

15 'Rome's Lord,' in Phillips, *Selected Poems of Walter von der Vogelweide*, 78.

16 'Wizzet, frouwe wol getân,' in Goldin, *German and Italian Lyrics of the Middle Ages*, 185.

17 Gottfried von Strassburg, *Tristan*, trans. Arthus Hatto (Harmondsworth: Penguin Books, 1960), 106ff. In this same passage he speaks of a rare lady minnesinger, who specializes in the songs of Vogelweide, while accompanying herself on a small organ.

18 'Iarlang blozet sich der walt,' line 13, in *Tannhäuser*, 151.

19 Phillips, *Selected Poems of Walter von der Vogelweide*, 48.

other hand, one song by Vogelweide mentions that he was criticized for singing songs of praise 'of one not nobly born.'[20]

These love songs were often sent by messenger who sang them on behalf of the composer. Ulrich von Liechtenstein, in his *In Service of Ladies*, tells of one extraordinary case in which a minnesinger chops off his finger and sends it with the song, as a demonstration of commitment.[21] We often read of the messenger, but almost never of how the song is received by the lady. Liechtenstein gives us a rare view of the other end of this process, in this case a rejection of the minnesinger's love.

> I was a faithful messenger
> and told her that you loved her best,
> more than yourself and all the rest.
>
> I said much more; before I closed
> I [sang] the song which you composed.
> Then spoke your charming lady fair,
> 'It really is a pretty tune,
> but one he might as well have kept;
> his service I cannot accept
> and want to hear no more of this.
> The topic we shall now dismiss.'[22]

Songs which bemoan the disappointment of lost love nearly always result in the poet contemplating the futility of further singing, as in this example by Neidhart von Reuental (fl. 1210–1237).

> The lady has my heart so in her power
> I must waste my days without joy.
> All that I have sung for so long now—it does no good,
> I could just as well be silent from now on.[23]

Vogelweide, finding himself in the same position, has left a song in which he tells us he stopped singing, but was enticed into resuming. He supports his self-esteem with the notion that if he stops singing her praises her status in the court will be adversely affected.

> To be long silent was my thought:
> now I shall sing once again as before.
> Gentle people brought me back to it:
> they have the right to command me.
> I shall sing and make up words,
> and do what they desire; then they must lament my grief.

[20] 'God be with thee, dearest maid,' in ibid., 22.

[21] Ulrich von Liechtenstein, *In Service of Ladies*, trans. J. W. Thomas (Chapel Hill: The University of North Carolina Press, 1969), lines 440ff. One of the minnesinger songs from this work was used by Mendelssohn in his op. 19.

[22] Ibid., 73ff.

[23] 'Sumer, dîner süezen,' in Goldin, *German and Italian Lyrics of the Middle Ages*, 165.

> Listen to this wonder, how I fared
> for all my hard work:
> a certain woman will not look at me—
> and it was I that brought her up to that esteem
> which makes her so high-minded now.
> She does not know: when I leave off singing,
> her praise will die away.
>
> Lord what curses she'd endure,
> were I to stop my song!
> All those who praise her now, I know
> they'll rebuke her then—against my will.[24]

[24] 'Lange swîgen des hât ich gedâht,' in Goldin, *German and Italian Lyrics of the Middle Ages*, 117.

A song by Ulrich von Liechtenstein is quite different. Here the minnesinger is bemoaning the fact that he has been dismissed from a lady's service. He regrets he was never properly paid for his services to her, but nothing can make him give up his art of singing.

> Oh to lose and to regret
> that which I cannot forget
> evermore!
> Joy and all my better days—
> gone with melancholy lays.
> Wounded sore,
> I must bear
> life given o'er to grieving care:
> death is less than such distress
>
> There my service was to be
> with such constant loyalty
> through the years.
> Still no pay will she accord
> and no prospect of reward ...
>
> Many years, I see with pain,
> I have squandered all in vain
> for someone
> who can never fully pay
> me for just a single day ...
>
> But I could not neglect my art
> nor leave off singing women's praise.[25]

[25] 'Twenty-first Dance Tune,' in Liechtenstein, *In Service of Ladies*.

Of course, songs in praise of the noble himself were another common theme. Tannhäuser sings,

> I'll sing the prince's fame
> that all will know his name.
> His greeting and his laughter
> can bring me joy thereafter.[26]

The minnesinger repertoire contains few hints regarding their compositional process. We find one comment by Vogelweide referring to his composition as 'toil,'[27] and Ulrich von Liechtenstein has a minnesinger tell a messenger, who was taking a song to a lady, that he had worked a long time on the song and 'with all my skill.'[28]

We can assume the better minnesingers were proud of their art, as seems apparent in a song by Vogelweide.

> But, lady, understand one thing:
> no other man can sing your praise so well.[29]

The versatility which some of these singers must have had can be seen in the representation of a minstrel, in *Tristan*, who knows a variety of forms[30] and accompanies himself as he sings in several languages.

> He played so beautifully and went with his music in so masterly a fashion that the [listener] was amazed. And at the appropriate places, sweetly and rapturously, the accomplished youth would wing his song to meet it. He sang the notes of his song so beautifully in Breton, Welsh, Latin, and French that you could not tell which was sweeter or deserving of more praise, his harping or his singing.[31]

Finally, during the thirteenth century there are complaints by the minnesingers of a decline in aristocratic support and interest in their art. Tannhäuser protests that, 'he who would restore good manners is not honored as before.'[32] Vogelweide composed an entire song on the subject of this decline in courtly manners.

> Alas, courtly singing,
> that uncouth strains
> should supplant you at the court.
> God bring dishonor on them soon.
> Alas that your dignity should be laid low.
> All your friends are sad.
> It must be; let it be:
> Lady Vulgarity, you have won.

---

26 'Ich mvs clagen,' lines 144ff., in *Tannhäuser*, 147.

27 'I sang her praise,' in Phillips, *Selected Poems of Walter von der Vogelweide*, 47.

28 Liechtenstein, *In Service of Ladies*, lines 110ff.

29 'Saget mir ieman,' in Goldin, *German and Italian Lyrics of the Middle Ages*, 117.

30 Strassburg, *Tristan*, 71.

31 Ibid., 90.

32 'Dank habe der meie,' in trans. Thomas, *Tannhäuser: Poet and Legend*, 175.

Should any man restore our courteous
and gentle joy,
Oh how well we'd praise him
every time we spoke of what he did.
That would be the soul of courtliness,
I shall always hope for it,
it would suit lords and ladies well.
Oh sorrow no one does it.

Those who drown out the good singing --
there's many more of them
than those who want to hear it.
But I still follow the old teaching:
I shall not set my music to the mill,
for the stone goes round so raucously
and the wheel has such awful melodies.
Notice who would harp there.

Those who make their shameful noise
make me laugh with anger,
they're so pleased
with such gross things.
They're like frogs in a pond
who like their own croaking so much,
the nightingale loses heart,
though it gladly would sing more.

If anyone commanded vulgarity be silent,
drove it away from the castles
so that it oppressed these happy few no more --
what joys we'd sing about.
If it were barred from the great courts
that would all be as I wish.
I'd have it lodge with peasants;
that's where it came from.[33]

---

[33] 'Owê, hovelîchez singen,' in Golden, *German and Italian Lyrics of the Middle Ages*, 127.

AESTHETICS IN MINNESINGER ART SONGS

One of the important psychological foundations of aesthetics, the concept of pleasure and pain, had been little discussed during the Middle Ages, but surfaces again in the repertoire of the minnesingers, troubadours and trouvères in connection with the inseparable emotions of pleasure and pain associated with love. Hartmann von Aue (ca. 1160–1210), in his 'Poor Henry,' states this in the strongest of terms:

> We see our laughter oft enough
> Drowned out in tears! This life is fixed
> So that the sweetest sweet is mixed
> With the bitterest gall.[34]

Vogelweide, who mentions this same idea in several songs, suggests that it is this pain, 'love's sweet distress,' which provides the emotional perspective for one to sing of joy.

> These raise a man in worthiness.
> He also who love's sweet distress
> Knows, for their sakes, to bear aright,
> May sing indeed of heart's delight.[35]

It seems apparent from objections which two minnesingers raise to criticism, that an important aesthetic expectation was Truth, that they sing from the heart. Vogelweide answers that although he is in pain, it is the memory of the joy of love that allows him to continue.

> Many there are that mock my pain,
> And ever say that 'tis not truly from the heart I sing;
> These but spend their breath in vain,
> Since they can never yet have known love's joy and suffering;
> And so it is they judge me wrong:
> Whoever knows
> All that from true love flows,
> Would not misunderstand my song.[36]

Heinrich von Morungen (d. 1222) answers the same criticism with his own version of the maxim, 'If you laugh, the world laughs with you; if you cry, you cry alone.'

---

34 'Der Arme Heinrich,' in Clair Bell, trans., *Peasant Life in Old German Epics* (New York: Octagon Books, 1965), lines 106ff.

35 'Summer returned,' in Phillips, *Selected Poems of Walter von der Vogelweide*, 31. Another reference to pleasure mixed with pain can be found in 'In honor of my lady-love,' ibid., 54.

36 Ibid., 43.

Many a one of them says, 'Aha! look at him singing!
If he [really] suffered, he wouldn't do that.'
A man like that cannot know what drives me to sing.
But now, as in former days, I shall raise my voice.
When I stood mute in sorrow, I was worth nothing to her.
That is the anguish that oppresses me:
Sorrow is despised where men rejoice.[37]

The most important presentation of aesthetic ideas among the minnesingers is found in *Tristan* by Gottfried von Strassburg. First, in his Prologue, he sets forth ten philosophical precepts which he apparently intends to exemplify in his story to follow. Three of these are important statements of aesthetics:

Praise and esteem bring art on where art deserves commendation. When art is adorned with praise it blossoms in profusion.

However well art and criticism seem to live together, if envy comes to lodge with them it stifles both art and criticism.

O Excellence! how narrow are thy paths, how arduous thy ways! Happy the man who can climb thy paths and tread thy ways![38]

Strassburg makes two additional observations which touch on aesthetics in a general context. First, he has Tristan say that the goal of his poetry is Universality, 'I make my words agreeable to all ears.'[39] Second, in describing a lady, Floraete, Strassburg makes a statement which sounds very much like a contemporary reference to the separate natures of the left and right hemispheres of the brain: 'Her words and her feelings were in perfect harmony.'[40]

Tristan is a very gifted minstrel, and it strikes one immediately that the extraordinary descriptions of this musician and his performances are too vivid to have been invented. That is, Strassburg must have known musicians and performances similar to those which he describes. To begin with, perhaps we may have, in Tristan, a view of the training of the most gifted performers. We are told that, in addition to languages and extensive reading of books, he studied all the string instruments for seven years, practicing all day long, beginning at age seven.[41]

From the perspective of aesthetics, by far the most interesting and valuable contribution of Strassburg is his focus on the listener. As we have discussed extensively in volume one, our contention is

37 'Leitlîche blicke und grôzliche riuwe,' in Goldin, *German and Italian Lyrics of the Middle Ages*, 45.

38 Strassburg, *Tristan*, 41.

39 Ibid., 108.

40 Ibid., 113.

41 Ibid., 69, 91. He played harp, fiddle, organistrum, rote, lyre and sambuca.

that it is only in the listener that aesthetics is capable of meaningful discussion. It was here, in the listener, that Aristotle focused his definition of aesthetics when he founded this separate branch of philosophy.[42] In the following descriptions of Tristan's listeners, notice not only their emotional reaction to the music, but the lengths to which Strassburg goes to establish them as *intently* listening. These performances are not mere 'background music.'

Tristan is given a small hunting horn which he blew so splendidly and so entrancingly, that all who rode with him could,

scarcely wait to join him for *sheer joy.*

They enter the castle and fill the castle with music, this 'skillful' and 'strange' hunting music.

The king and his household, never having heard such music, were *shocked to the very marrow.*[43]

After supper, Tristan hears a harpist playing, 'correctly and with sad passion.' Tristan then takes the harp and plays 'preludes and phrases, fine, sweet, and haunting.' Then he tunes, 'adjusting pegs and strings, some up, some down, until they were to his liking.' He begins to play again, haunting, sweetly and melodious.

The [listeners] '*all came running up, one calling another.*'

Now Tristan begins to play 'excellent sweet music in the Breton style.'

Many a man sitting or standing there forgot his very name. Hearts and ears began to play the fool and desert their rightful paths ... Nor was there sparing of eyes: a host of them were bent on him, following his hands.[44]

Tristan arrives at the shore of Ireland in a boat. Those listeners on the shore heard 'sweet strains of a harp' playing softly,

to their hearts' delight.

Tristan was singing so 'enchantingly' and 'most marvelous' that the listeners,

were rooted to the spot as long as he harped and sang.[45]

42 *Poetics.*

43 Strassburg, *Tristan*, 84.

44 Ibid., 89ff.

45 Ibid., 141.

Here Strassburg interrupts his story to make one of the most important statements on aesthetics in music of the Middle Ages. His definition is relative to Truth in performance, the honest intent of the performer to communicate genuine feelings.

> But the pleasure they had from him was short-lived, since the sounds that he made for them with hands or lips did not come from the depths—his heart was not in his music. For it is of the nature of music that one cannot play for any length of time unless one is in the mood. Although it is a very common thing, what one plays superficially in a heartless and soulless way cannot really claim to be music.[46]

46 Ibid.

Strassburg returns to the performance he was discussing above.

The listeners on the shore relate hearing Tristan to others, saying, 'God himself would love to hear it in His heavenly choirs.' Others come to the shore to listen, Tristan plays,

> and he *moved them all to pity*.[47]

47 Ibid., 143.

Now Tristan plays before Isolde for the first time. 'He was playing better than he had ever played before, for he played to them not as a lifeless man, [but] with animation, in the best of spirits ... In a brief [period],

> he *won the favor of them all*.'[48]

48 Ibid., 145.

Isolde now becomes a student of Tristan and, in spite of her accomplishments, made much improvement. She is called to perform before her father and his guests, who found 'no Lady ever struck strings more sweetly.' In response to her performance,

> *many hearts grew full of longing; because of her, all manner of thoughts and ideas presented themselves. No end of things came to mind.*[49]

49 Ibid., 148.

Next, she sang openly and secretly, in through ears and eyes,

> to where many a heart was stirred.

The song which she sang openly in this and other places was her own sweet singing and soft sounding of strings that echoed for all to hear through the kingdom of the ears deep down into the heart. But her secret song ... stole with its rapturous music hidden and unseen through the windows of the eyes into many noble hearts and,

> soothed on the magic which took thoughts prisoner suddenly, and, taking them, fettered them with desire!

Later, Tristan plays his harp for Isolde, striking 'a song of such surpassing sweetness' that it stole into Isolde's heart,

> and pervaded her whole consciousness to the point where she left her weeping and was lost in thoughts of her lover.[50]

50 Ibid., 217.

The impact on the listener here is Aristotelian aesthetics, pure and simple. At the same time it is clear that Strassburg could not have written such descriptions had he not been familiar with serious artists performing art music, and not casual entertainment music, before attentive listeners.

FUNCTIONAL MUSIC

The minnesinger songs include some interesting examples of music used for signal giving purposes, such as the 'blast on a horn' to call Siegfried's hunters back to camp in the *Nibelungenlied*.[51]

51 'Sixteenth Adventure.'

We know that by the Baroque Period it was a common practice for a noble to have his personal trumpets precede him, announcing him, as an aural symbol equivalent to the use of the coat of arms as a visual symbol. Ulrich von Liechtenstein provides an early example of this practice, which is interesting because the trumpets play not just a 'blast,' but an actual melody for this purpose.

> My buglers played a melody,
> a pretty tune in a treble key,
> and thus they told all people near
> that I was shortly to appear.[52]

52 *In Service of Ladies*, lines 580ff.

Given the nature of these 'love singers,' it is no surprise that the watchman–musician on the tower, who plays during the night as a surrogate clock, is frequently mentioned in this repertoire. It was a custom to play a special melodic signal, called the *Aubade*, just before dawn, to warn lovers to run back to their own houses before first light. One example of several by Wolfram von Eschenbach goes,

At daybreak you have always sung
the dirge of secret love,
the bitterness following on the sweet.
No matter what you urged upon them
when the morning star was rising,
those who received love and woman's favor
in such a way
that they had to part,
Watchman, be quiet,
sing of that no more![53]

[53] 'Der helnden minne ir klage,' in *Wolfram von Eschenbach, Titurel and the Songs*, trans. Marion Gibbs and Sidney Johnson (New York: Garland Publishing, 1988), 83.

The use of music for battle is also a familiar theme, as well as for the music of the tourney, which was in part a form of practice for battle.

Then the trumpets were blown lustily, and the noise of drums and flutes was so loud that Worms, the wide town, rang therewith.[54]

[54] Niebelungenlied, 'Thirteenth Adventure.'

The Romance, *Erec*, by Hartmann von Aue, reveals that in the case of personal combat between knights, the winner had the right to play a horn signal announcing to all his victory.

'Sir, you should now get up and go blow the horn joyfully, for it is there if anyone should defeat me so that he can immediately announce this to the people by blowing three times. It has hung there unblown much too long for me, for as long as this has been my home.' Now he took it from the post and asked Erec to blow it. He immediately put it to his mouth. The horn resounded loudly, for it was long and large.[55]

[55] Hartmann von Aue, *Erec*, trans. Thomas Keller (New York: Garland, 1987), 133.

Wolfram von Eschenbach's epic poem, *Willehalm*, a Romance of chivalry dealing with the campaigns against the Saracens, includes some extraordinary descriptions of actual battle music. In one place he describes the 'heathen's' use of the modern-type metal trumpet (800 of them!), which we know the Western armies brought back from the crusades.

Eight hundred trumpets the king ordered to blow 'Advance at the gallop!' It is still a known fact that trumpets were invented in his country; they were brought from Thusi.[56]

[56] Wolfram von Eschenbach, *Willehalm*, trans. Charles Passage (New York: Ungar, 1977), 202.

[57] Ibid., 231.

In another place he mentions the roll of a thousand drums![57]

In *Parzival*, it is the sound, rather than the numbers, of these same heathen musicians, which is meant to impress us.

> He rode up with six banners, in front of which fighting began in early dawn. Trumpeters sounded ringing blasts, like thunder rousing fear and dread, and drummers beat a lively accompaniment to the noise of the trumpets.[58]

58 *Parzival*, 203.

Finally there are some interesting references to the use of music in the processions by which nobles traveled, including string players playing on horseback! Ulrich von Liechtenstein gives the entire order of such a procession, including knights, cooks and men carrying banners, etc. When he comes to the musicians, we read,

> A flutist was the next to come
> who beat with skill upon a drum.
> Four squires were riding after him
> in uniforms of modish trim
> and each had brought three spears along,
> well-made and large, which with thong
> were bound together. One could praise
> these bearers for their courtly ways.
>
> Two maidens rode behind the squires
> and every bit of their attires
> was gleaming white from head to toe.
> The both looked very pretty so.
> A fiddler rode behind each maid;
> my heart was happy when they played,
> and when the two would fiddle high
> a marching tune most pleased was I.[59]

59 *In Service of Ladies*, lines 485ffr. The first musician mentioned here is the 'one-man band' known as the pipe and tabor player.

Wolfram von Eschenbach provides the details of a similar procession.

> After these rode trumpeters, who are still required today, and a drummer kept hitting his drum and swinging it high in the air. The master would not have thought much of the lot if flute players had not been riding along with the rest, and three good fiddlers.[60]

60 *Parzival*, 12.

ENTERTAINMENT MUSIC

Gottfried von Strassburg describes what many days in palace life must have been like in the thirteenth century: during the day hunting and 'at night here at home we shall sustain ourselves with courtly pursuits, such as harping, fiddling, and singing.'[61] On special occasions, such as the visit of a noble from a distant country, there must have been a much broader range of entertainment. We have a glimpse of an elaborate outdoor entertainment in the anonymous Romance, *Laurin*.

[61] *Tristan*, 92.

> The noble guests saw many beautiful things and were treated very well. They were seated on golden benches that sparkled with precious stones, and the best of wine and mead was poured for them. There was much entertainment of different kinds for them to watch. On one side there was singing; on the other men were jumping and engaged in tests of strength; then came the spear throwing and stone throwing, with several events going on at the same time; riders charged into each other right in front of them, and many spears were broken in jousts; they heard a large number of skillful musicians: fiddlers, harpers, and pipers.
>
> Later two short fiddlers, delightful dwarfs in rich and elegant clothing, came before the princes. The fiddles they carried were of red gold, glittered with jewels, and were worth more than a country. Their strings made sweet music. The princes enjoyed the fiddling, and time passed quickly …
>
> Afterwards two fine singers and narrators appeared and sang many courtly tales to amuse and charm the guests … Anyone who was well-versed in song would have forgotten all his sorrow.[62]

[62] J. W. Thomas, *The Best Novellas of Medieval Germany*, 71ff.

Gottfried von Strassburg makes a clear aesthetic division in entertainment between musicians and entertainers such as magicians and story tellers. This last type of entertainer offers nothing to delight the heart, they are, he says, like a tree without leaves.

> Inventors of wild tales, hired hunters after stories, who cheat with chains and dupe dull minds, who turn rubbish into gold for children and from magic boxes pour pearls of dust!—these give us shade with a bare staff, not with the green leaves and twigs and boughs of May. Their shade never soothes a stranger's eyes. To speak the truth, no pleasurable emotion comes from it, there is nothing in it to delight the heart. Their poetry is not such that a noble heart can laugh with it.[63]

[63] *Tristan*, 105.

There are also a number of interesting references to banquet music in the minnesinger repertoire. In *Parzival* we read of some of the squires playing fiddle after dinner. But apparently their level of performance was not satisfactory, 'their mastery did not go beyond playing old-fashioned dances,' so a call goes out for any visiting minstrels who may be in court.[64]

Accounts of court festivities often mention that these visiting minstrels were well paid. The anonymous Romance, *Duke Ernst*, describes a wedding banquet for the emperor and the lavish gifts he gave his knights and ladies in attendance. The visiting musicians were included in this largess.

> The host of wandering minstrels there also received plenty of gifts, so they too were joyous.[65]

Hartmann von Aue tells of a similar wedding festivity in which he assures us there were no fewer than three thousand visiting musicians!

> A dance began as soon as the meal was finished and lasted until nightfall. Sadness vanished. If they had been unhappy, their joy was now as great. They went to the ladies who received them warmly. There the entertainment was good. In addition they were delighted by sweet string music and other pastimes—storytelling and singing, and lively dancing. All types of skills were presented, and each by a master in his field. There were easily three thousand or more of the very best minstrels in the world there, who were called masters. Never was there greater splendor neither before nor since than at this celebration.[66]

In the *Nibelungenlied* we read of a minstrel who was not so fortunate. Playing for a banquet, he was caught in a scene of slaughter.

> He saw a minstrel sitting at Etzel's table, and sprang at him in wrath, and lopped off his right hand on his viol: 'Take that for the message thou broughtest to the Burgundians.'
> 'Woe is me for my hand!' cried Werbel. 'Sir Hagen of Trony, what have I done to thee? I rode with true heart to thy master's land. How shall I make my music now?'
> Little recked Hagen if he never fiddled more.[67]

Associations of music and dance are common in all literature, but in the minnesinger repertoire one often finds dance with singing.

[64] Book XIII, 639.

[65] Duke Ernst, trans. J. W. Thomas and Carolyn Dussere, in *Medieval Tales* (New York: Continuum, 1983), 27.

[66] *Erec*, lines 2142ff.

[67] 'Thirty-Third Adventure.'

Among several such references in *Tannhäuser*, we find this recommendation to youth:

> Come, young folks, taste it, life is sweet!
> And since God gave us voice and feet,
> we'll seize this chance to sing and dance.[68]

[68] 'Uns kvmt ein wunneklichu zit,' in *Tannhäuser*, 103.

Many of these songs with dance are seasonal and outdoors, such as for May-day. But there is also some indication that they were performed during any festivity. Such a dance occurs after jousting, for example, in Wernher der Gartenaere's Romance, *Meier Helmbrecht*.

> When they had finished with the lance
> They trod the measures of a dance
> Accompanied by dashing song.
> To no one did the time seem long.[69]

[69] *Peasant Life in Old German Epics*, trans. Claire Bell (New York: Octagon Books, 1965), 62.

In summary we wish to emphasize that it is in Strassburg's story of Tristan that we find an extraordinary demonstration of Aristotle's premise of aesthetics: that the definition lies in the effect of the music on the listener. These passages constitute, at the same time, the most vivid evidence of a high level of art music in the thirteenth century. Just look at his descriptions of the reaction of the listeners: some are 'shocked to the very marrow,' some are 'rooted to the spot,' some actually forget their names, their hearts and eyes become irrational ('play the fool') and the thoughts of some are 'taken prisoner' by the music!

We think it is not reasonable to suppose that such powerful art music and listeners of such concentration could be imagined by Strassburg had he not observed similar performances. We regard it as equally unlikely that performances of art music of this sophistication could suddenly appear, without tradition, at the beginning of the thirteenth century. Although the literature of the Dark Ages describes little art music, there must have been an unbroken chain of tradition from the period of Ancient Greece.

26 AESTHETICS OF MUSIC IN THE POETRY OF THE GOLIARDS OF THE TWELFTH AND THIRTEENTH CENTURIES

Standing apart from the aristocratic poetry of the Minnesingers, troubadours and trouvères is a smaller body of work reflecting the lower side of society and a group of people we call, collectively, the goliards.[1] While the former poetry was sung in the new indigenous languages of German and French, the latter is in Latin, the language of both cleric and student.

A number of these goliard poets were disaffected clerics, the result of a period of questioning caused not only by the bitter struggles between emperor and pope, but by important new heresies, in particular the Albigensian heresy. It follows that an interesting common thread in the goliard poetry is a return to references of pagan gods.

One of these former Churchmen, a cleric turned harpist singing in taverns, was the poet, Walter of Châtillon,[2] one of only two goliards we know by name.

> In the tavern let me die,
> That's my resolution,
> Bring me wine for lips so dry
> At life's dissolution.
> Joyfully the angel's choir
> Then will sing my glory:
> 'Sit deus propicius
> Huic potatori.'[3]

One scholar refers to these wandering clerics as the 'ecclesiastical equivalent of jongleurs,'[4] and indeed the song of one of them suggests the same impoverished existence.

> I, a cleric on the loose,
> Given to tribulation,
> Am for toil and travail born,
> Poverty's my ration.

[1] From *Golias*, a variant of Goliath, or perhaps *gula* (gullet). By the thirteenth century the term had become one of reproach.

[2] First known as 'Gualtherus ab Insulis,' Walther was born in Lille, became canon in Reims. While part of the chancery of Henry II, of England, he was present when Thomas à Becket was murdered. He enjoyed a great reputation as head of the cathedral school of Châtillon. The other, Hugh of Orléans, spent his life as a genuine vagabond, always broke and generally being evicted from some house because of his sharp tongue.

[3] 'The Vagabond's Confession,' in *Vagabond Verse*, trans. Edwin H. Zeydel (Detroit: Wayne State University Press, 1966), 63, 'May God be well-disposed to this old drunk.'

[4] George Whicher, *The Goliard Poets* (George Whicher, 1949), 4.

For the arts and literature
I possess a yearning,
Still, my indigence compels
Me to cease from learning.

All my clothing that I wear,
Frail it is and torn;
Oftentimes I suffer cold
Since of warmth I'm shorn …

Take St. Martin's attitude,
Never mean or shoddy,
Give the pilgrim-scholar clothes,
Cover up his body.[5]

Some of these disaffected poets were students, as is evident in the song which begins, 'Cast aside dull books and thought; Sweet is folly, sweet is play.'[6] They dropped out, or traveled from school to school, and we associate with them especially the Latin repertoire of German songs known as the 'Carmina Burana.' One of these, in fact, is composed by a person who identifies himself as a student from Paris, and one skilled in singing,

with other men
who are skilled in singing
various songs and in giving
their joys to spring.[7]

In another song, a German student also mentions Paris and his desire to study philosophy there.

Dear my fatherland, to you,
Sweet Swabian Swabia, adieu,
Beloved France to which I roam,
All hail! Philosophy's your home!
Take the foreign student up
To your bosom, please,
And when the time's ripe, send him back
Well trained like Socrates![8]

Some goliards, like the anonymous poet known as the Archpoet of Cologne, drifted in and out of the court environment, probably never adjusting to the demands of that life-style.

---

5 'Exul ego clericus,' in Zeydel, *Vagabond Verse*, 73.

6 'Quittamus studia,' from the Carmina Burana literature, quoted in John Symonds, *Wine Women and Song; Mediaeval Latin Students' Songs* (New York: Cooper Square Publishers, 1966), 99.

7 'Si de More,' in E. D. Blodgett, trans., *The Love Songs of the Carmina Burana* (New York: Garland Publishing, Inc., 1987), 221. Codex latinus 4660, in the Bavarian State Library, this manuscript came from the monastery of the Benediktbeuren, south of München, where it had been kept in a secret cabinet of 'forbidden' books. The manuscript contains 131 love songs, 55 moral, satirical or historical songs, 35 vagabond songs and 6 religious plays.

8 'Hospita in Gallia,' in Zeydel, *Vagabond Verse*, 77.

Public life, there's no mistake,
Certain poets find irking;
Courts they willingly forsake,
In seclusion lurking;
There they study, drudge, and wake,
No endeavor shirking,
Hoping one great poem to make
Ere they cease from working.

Starveling rhymesters, when they thirst
Water is their potion!
City din they count accurst
And the crowd's commotion.
Foundlings by the Muses nursed,
Fame's their only notion:
Fame they sometimes win, but first
Die of their devotion.[9]

Like their more noble cousins, the Minnesingers and troubadours, the goliards sing of the seasons,[10] especially Spring, and of love. Whereas the former sang of aristocratic ladies and the most noble forms of love, the goliard sings of peasant girls[11] and makes love the subject for satire. In one example, the poet suddenly finds himself disagreeing with what he had been singing.

Stop, this song displeases me
That I've recited,
My opinion contradicts
What I've indited.

For punishment, he recommends that the young lady lock him up in her bedroom![12]

While the troubadour hoped to win his lady through the quality of his song, Hugh of Orléans says, no, the women are mainly interested in food, not music!

Dinner they love far more than music, whatever the type.
When the aroma approaches their nose, they will relish tripe
Or a plateful of rubbish, but music, it has no appeal.[13]

In only one goliard song, from the Carmina Burana collection, do we find the genuine expression of pain felt by an unhappy lover.

9 'Estuans intrinsecus,' known as 'The Confession of Golias,' in Whicher, *The Goliard Poets*, 111.

10 One of the Carmina Burana songs, 'Quocumque More Motu Volvuntur Tempora,' begins,

Whichever way the seasons turn in their movement,
Accordingly I beat my trusty, well-tempered drums.

11 Only one goliard song, 'Nahtegel, sing einen Don mit Sinne,' from the Carmina Burana collection, refers to an aristocratic lady.

12 'Volo virum vivere,' in Zeydel, *Vagabond Verse*, 139.

13 'Quid luges, lirice,' in ibid., 237.

> Grief, lament, sadness, anxiety
> have encumbered my quaking limbs all at once.
>
> For grief, as if it spoke in verse,
> my song abates: nothing remains but lament.
>
> To an awful fate my lyre is bound;
> despised, it mourns.[14]

[14] 'Captus Amore Gravi.'

In our favorite goliard song a poet–musician tells us that wine brings feelings of love, and love feelings of music, but he would give up both wine and love before music.

> Bacchus wakes within my breast
> Love and love's desire,
> Venus comes and stirs the blessed
> Rage of Phoebus's fire;
> Deathless honor is our due
> From the laureled sire:
> Woe should I turn traitor to
> Wine and love and lyre!
>
> Should a tyrant rise and say,
> 'Give up wine!' I'd do it;
> 'Love no girls!' I would obey,
> Though my heart should rue it.
> 'Dash thy lyre!' suppose he saith,
> Naught should bring me to it;
> 'Yield thy lyre or die!' my breath,
> Dying, should thrill through it![15]

[15] Quoted in Symonds, *Wine Women and Song*, 162.

[16] 'Bacchic Frenzy,' in ibid., 173.

A number of surviving goliard songs like the above attribute the inspiration of their music and poetry to wine. One poet says he drinks not for thirst, but for better thinking ability.[16] Another is somewhat more specific, contending that the quality of his poetry is dependent on the quality of the wine!

> Special gifts for every man
> Nature will produce,
> I, when I compose my verse,
> Vintage wine must use,
> All the best the cellar's casks
> Hold of these libations.
> Such a wine calls forth from me
> Copious conversations.

> My verse has the quality
> Of the wine I sip,
> I can not do much until
> Food has passed my lip,
> What I write when starved and parched
> Is of the lowest class,
> When I'm tight, with verse I make
> Ovid I surpass.
>
> As a poet n'er can I
> Be appreciated
> Till my stomach has been well
> Filled with food and sated,
> When god Bacchus gains my brain's
> Lofty citadel
> Phoebus rushes in to voice
> Many a miracle.[17]

The wandering Archpoet of Cologne frankly tells us he writes from a different form of inspiration.

> And poems more sweet than tongue can tell
> I'll write you—if you pay me well.[18]

The goliard literature reveals little regarding aesthetic purpose in music. Hugh of Orléans speaks of the ability of music to relieve grief, here the grief brought by Fate.

> Let us endure what cannot be changed, let's bear it serenely!
> Only the lyre assuages the grief that smarts ever keenly.[19]

One of the most famous of the Carmina Burana songs, 'The Wheel of Fortune,' seems to have the same meaning.

> Don't delay,
> Strike the lyre with grave intent;
> How our fate
> Fells what's great!
> Come ye, join in my lament.[20]

Another of the Carmina Burana songs not only gives the purpose of music to soothe, but to actually *change* the state of the listener.

[17] In 'Estuans intrinsecus,' in Zeydel, *Vagabond Verse*, 67.

[18] In 'Fama tuba dante sonum,' in Whicher, *The Goliard Poets*, 123.

[19] In 'Quid luges, lirice,' in Zeydel, *Vagabond Verse*, 237.

[20] 'O Fortuna,' in ibid., 47.

So the power
of lyre-strings soothes the breast
and change
the heart that wavers
from the plights of love.[21]

21 'Dum Diane Vitrea,' in Blodgett, *The Love Songs of the Carmina Burana*, 22.

This repertoire of tavern songs, Church satire, and political protest never addresses the importance to man of engaging in emotional communication through music. Only in the most indirect reference do we find some hint that this universal facet of music was understood, such as in the song quoted above in which the compulsion to compose is described as the 'blessed rage of Phoebus's fire.'

27 AESTHETICS IN THE MUSIC TREATISES OF THE TWELFTH AND THIRTEENTH CENTURIES

FOLLOWING THE PROGRESS made in the eleventh century toward a more comprehensive notational system, the theorists of the twelfth and thirteenth centuries concentrated on making further definitions in notation, especially with regard to rhythm. The values and aesthetics of music are now rarely mentioned. We should like to think they were now taken for granted, but it is more likely that the enthusiasm of the theorists was elsewhere. Johannes de Grocheo mentions this emphasis on the practical, or as we would say today, the conceptional, and adds a curious and tantalizing suggestion that some of the most interesting thought of the period may be lost.

> At the present time it happens that many people seek the practical side of this art, but few pay attention to its speculative character. And, for this reason, many speculative thinkers make a secret of their calculations and their discoveries, not wishing to reveal them to others, although any man ought to publish the truth about them for the praise and revelation of derived truth.[1]

The accuracy of Grocheo's observation can be seen in the fact that several treatises, such as Johannes de Garlandia's *De Mensurabili Musica*, the anonymous *Ad Organum Faciendum* and *Item de Organo* and the manuscript by a writer known as Anonymous IV contain not a word regarding the subjective aspects of music, aesthetics or its values.

In view of the limited scope of our purpose, we shall discuss only these topics relative to the following treatises.

[1] Johannes de Grocheo, *De Musica*, trans. Albert Seay (Colorado Springs: Colorado College Music Press, 1967), 2. By 'speculation,' Grocheo means the subjective, as the reader will find below, and not the use of this word by earlier theorists to mean music theory.

ANONYMOUS
DE MUSICA MENSURATA (CA. 1279)

In two places in this treatise, the author explains why he has presented his text in poetry, rather than prose. The chief reason he cites, that one remembers better if the material is in poetry, is one which had been given by ancient writers.

> Since every treatise should be one and the same to everyone, we have given it composed in verse, because we speak briefly and openly in verse, for in verse sophistical reasonings are laid to rest. And also things composed in verse are received more easily in the store-house of memory than things composed in prose, and since they are impressed easily on the memory they are more quickly recalled. Also verses arouse the minds of the listeners more favorably than prose.[2]

This writer offers without elaboration several definitions of music taken from earlier writers, chiefly Boethius and Isidore. Neither is he interested in commenting on the virtues of music.

> We leave the burden of expounding upon the discovery or praise of music to the philosophers who deal with the subject, lest the verbosity of the explanation burden or disturb the ears of our listeners.[3]

His definition of the notational sign he calls 'the representation of a sound,'[4] and gives no hint that he understands it as a symbol for anything more subjective, such as feeling. On the other hand, he does have some clear aesthetic beliefs about tonal sound itself.

> It is clear that a composite sounding note in this art is more worthy and more noble than a single one.[5]
>
> ...
>
> Discord ... is a vice that should be avoided.[6]

It is also evident that in this writer's concept of aesthetic values, melody is the most important element of the art. First, regarding notational symbols, he observes, 'the body is more important in notes themselves than are the tails,'[7] by which we understand him to suggest melody is more important than rhythm.

With regard to harmony, this anonymous writer quotes Isidore as saying the purpose of harmony is to inspire and instruct the sing-

---

2 The Anonymous of St. Emmeram, *De Musica Mensurata*, trans. Jeremy Judkin (Bloomington: Indiana University Press, 1990), 75.

3 Ibid., 67.

4 Ibid., 87.

5 Ibid.

6 Ibid., 149.

7 Ibid., 101.

ers of melody. In his own comment which immediately follows, he objects to such 'interesting' developments, such as hocket, which detract from melody.

> You should pay attention therefore, my beloved, you who desire to drain the thirst-quenching waters of so much sweetness and sound, so that you may take up those things which follow with the alert ear of desire, and put them peacefully in the book-case of your heart, lest something that is understood by few and honorably reserved should be widely promulgated and now become worthless.[8]

[8] Ibid., 225.

Finally, we should point out that this author, rather inadvertently finds himself on the subject of Reason versus the senses. At first he seems to want to acknowledge that it is the senses which are most germane to the nature of music itself, but then he remembers his Boethius and backtracks to defend Reason.

> That which is grasped with the senses is perceived to be grasped without labor, but that which is grasped with the intellect is grasped with difficulty and with the judgment of reason; and so the one which pertains to the senses is more desirable, and the other should be avoided. Only the intellect is based on the thing itself and is not without reason. And this reason indeed dominates in the particular sense and also in everything, for a work without reason is empty and hollow.[9]

[9] Ibid., 135.

JOHANNES DE GARLANDIA
DE MENSURABILI MUSICA (CA. 1279)

As mentioned above, the portion of this work by Garlandia does not touch on our subject. However, in an additional chapter in the hand of Jerome of Moravia there is a single aesthetic thought which is significant. He observes,

> Repetition ... makes unknown sound known, through which recognition the sense of hearing is pleased.[10]

He further implies that it is for this reason that repetition frequently appears in popular music.

It is significant that he speaks here of the pleasure of the 'sense of hearing,' rather than Reason. More important, he addresses, for

[10] Johannes de Garlandia, *De Mensurabili Musica*, trans. Stanley Birnbaum (Colorado Springs: Colorado College Music Press, 1978), 54. The idea he addresses here is not the same as that pondered by Aristotle in his famous question, 'Why do we prefer music we already know?' (*Problemata*).

the first time in this meaning, we believe, a unique property of the right hemisphere of the brain, and one not found in the left hemisphere at all. It is only in the right hemisphere, where we experience music, that we find pleasure in the da capo, recapitulation, rondos, seeing an old town we haven't seen in years, seeing the face of an old friend, and so on. It is the gradual recognition and appreciation of this phenomenon which leads to the architectural forms of the eighteenth century.

JOHANNES DE GROCHEO
DE MUSICA (CA. 1300)

This treatise by Grocheo stands apart from all similar works of the late Middle Ages. While he also presents the usual highly technical descriptions of music, he also seems aware that there is something more to music. It is important, and refreshing, to know that someone was thinking along these lines at this time.

Grocheo begins his treatise, not with the usual definition of music, but rather with a defense of why music is important.

> An understanding of music is necessary to those who wish to have a complete understanding of bodies moving and moved. It treats principally of sound, which is perceivable by our own senses and which is the object of our apprehending abilities. It is also good in a practical sense, for it corrects and improves the customs of men if used in the proper way. In this also it stands above the other arts, for it is more immediately and completely constructed for the praise and glory of the Creator.[11]

11 Grocheo, *De Musica*, 1.

Now Grocheo seeks to define the basic nature of music. His own definition here is extraordinary: that music is a principal means of the intellect explaining itself. It can certainly be said, that music is the most immediate means of communication of the right hemisphere of the brain, which is otherwise mute. He could not have understood this in these terms, of course, but he was clearly deducing the real process of musical communication. His statement is a great advance in understanding from some of his immediate predecessors who, for example, thought of flute music as music made by a flute, and not by the man playing the flute.

Also significant here, is the importance given to performance, that is to say, *live* music. When he says, yes, numbers may define the form of music, but it is of the nature of music to be performed, he has left Boethius far behind.

> Certain people, considering its form and material, describe music by saying that it is a science of number related to sound. Others, looking at its performance, say that it is an art devoted to singing. We, however, intend to take it in both ways, just as it is made known as a tool and ought to be made known as an art. Just as natural warmth is a first tool through which the soul exercises its functions, so as an art [music] is a principal tool or rule through which the practical intellect explains and exposes its functions. We may say, therefore, that music is an art or science concerning numbered sound taken harmonically, designed for singing easily. I say also a *science*, insofar as it treats of the knowledge of principles, an *art*, insofar as it rules the practical intellect in performing, concerning *harmonic sound*, since it is this basic material around which it is performed. By *number* its form is defined. But by *singing* performance is touched upon, to which it is properly *designated*.[12]

12 Ibid., 9.

Turning now to the classification of music, Grocheo mentions the three genre of Boethius: Music of the Spheres, Human Music, and Instrumental Music. Although music theorists had accepted this classification without comment for half a millennium, Grocheo now blasts Boethius into oblivion. He courageously attacks the faulty logic, the pseudo-science, the beliefs of the Church and, let us say, the nonsense which Boethius had put forth.

> Those who make this kind of division either invent their opinion or they wish to obey the Pythagoreans or others more than the truth, or they are ignorant of nature and logic. First of all, they say universally that music is a science concerning numbered sound. Nevertheless, celestial bodies in movement do not make a sound, although our ancestors believed this, nor do they divide their rotation as does Aristotle, whose idea and hypothesis in his book concerning the theory of the planets should be proposed. Nor is sound properly to be found in the human constitution. Who has heard a constitution sounding?[13] The third type which is called *musica instrumentalis* is distributed in three parts, that is, in the diatonic, chromatic and enharmonic, according to which they say the three concords of the monochord come. They call that diatonic which proceeds by tone, tone and semitone, according to the manner which most melodies

13 Physicists of the late twentieth century! Every organ of the body produces a pitch.

use; chromatic which proceeds by diesis, diesis and three semitones. And they say the planets use such a song. They also call that enharmonic which proceeds by diesis, diesis and ditone. They say this is the sweetest, since angels use it. We do not understand this division, since they distinguish here only *musica instrumentalis*, leaving out the other categories.[14] Nor is it pertinent for a musicians to treat of the song of angels, unless he has been at the same time a theologian and a prophet; no one can have any experience of such song except by divine inspiration. When they say the planets sing, they seem to be ignorant of what is a sound.[15]

14 Grocheo means that angels were traditionally associated with singing, not playing instruments. In the Baroque, we might point out, they are pictured as instrumentalists.

15 Ibid., 10.

Grocheo proposes to bring music down from the spheres and instead will use the practical classifications practiced by 'the men in Paris,' for it is there that the principles of all liberal arts are 'sought out diligently.' Therefore, to replace the three classifications of Boethius, Grocheo presents three new ones:

1. Civic or simple music, which they call vulgar [*vulgus*: of the masses] music
2. Composed or regular music by rule, which they call measured music
3. Ecclesiastic music, designed for praising the Creator, made from the first two and to which these two are best adapted.[16]

16 Ibid., 11.

It is for his subsequent elaboration of specific forms of secular and sacred music that Grocheo's treatise is best known, and indeed it is a discussion of secular forms which will not be equaled until the *Syntagma Musica* of Praetorius in 1619. For us, however, it is even more significant that after so many centuries someone returns to a serious consideration of the influence of music on character. For each form he discusses, he defines the specific purpose it has with regard to influencing the state of the listener. The diversity of these purposes carries the aesthetic definition of Aristotle, and the notion of the Greek *ethos*, to a level of precision advanced by no earlier philosopher.

He begins with vocal Civic, or popular, music and the *cantus gestual*, the epic song of former great leaders and their deeds.

> This kind of song ought to be provided for old men, working citizens and for average people when they rest from their accustomed labor, so that, having heard the miseries and calamities of others, they might more easily bear up under their own, and so that their own

tasks be more gladly approached. Thus, this kind of song is a support for the whole state.[17]

17 Ibid., 15.

Next he discusses the *coronate cantus*, a song of quality, accompanied on instruments 'by masters and students,' which deals with 'delightful and serious material, as about friendship and charity.'

> This is normally composed by kings and nobles and performed before the kings and princes of the earth so that it may move their souls to audacity and bravery, to magnanimity and liberality, which lead all things to a good order.[18]

18 Ibid., 16.

The *versiculate* is similar to the *coronate cantus*, but not of such high quality, and is appropriate for the young, 'lest they fall completely into idleness.'[19]

19 Ibid.

He now turns his attention to three types of songs associated with young men and women. Of the round, or *rotundellus*, he notes only that it is slow, and performed by young people in festivals. The *stantipes*, is characterized by 'diversity' in both text and melody.

> This kind of song causes the souls of young men and girls to concentrate because of its difficulty and turns them from improper thinking.[20]

20 Ibid., 17.

Similarly, the *ductia* is a rapid, light song, sung in chorus.

> This influences the hearts of girls and young men and keeps them from vanity and is said to have force against that passion which is called love or Eros.[21]

21 Ibid.

Grocheo begins his discussion of instrumental music by giving aesthetic preference to the string family, because they are capable of 'a subtler and better difference of sound.'[22] Of these, he prefers the vielle as the principal melodic instrument most suitable to all kinds of music.

22 Ibid., 19. He mentions the psalter, cithara, lyre, Saracen guitar, and vielle.

> As some instruments by their sound may move the souls of men more than others, for example, the drum and trumpet in war games and tournaments, on the vielle, however, all musical forms are understood more thoroughly.[23]

23 Ibid., 19.

The instrumental *ductia* is accompanied by percussion instruments, which 'measure' it and the movement of the performer,

> and excite the soul of man to moving ornately according to that art they call dancing, and they measure its movement in ductiae and in choral dance.[24]

The instrumental *stantipes* is not accompanied by percussion and is characterized by 'a complicated succession of concords.' The latter,

> makes the soul of the performer and also the soul of the listener pay close attention and frequently turns aside the souls of the wealthy from depraved thinking.[25]

It was for these instrumental forms, which lack the syllables of the text to identify the groupings of the notes intended by the composer, that Grocheo says the custom of using ligatures was adopted.[26] This is a very important musical insight, for twentieth-century texts have taken the position that the ligatures were nothing but a form of shorthand for the scribes. In Praetorius, however, in 1716, there is the suggestion that these ligatures have a sole similar to the modern slurs—indeed Praetorius mentions that the slur marks are beginning to replace the ligatures. So, one wonders if the concept of phrasing had a form of notation much earlier than is generally accepted today.

Now Grocheo turns to church music, beginning with the famous thirteenth-century *motet*.

> This kind of song ought not to be propagated among the vulgar, since they do not understand its subtlety nor do they delight in its hearing, but it should be performed for the learned and those who seek after the subtleties of the arts.[27]

Organum is ecclesiastical music, sung for the praise of God. Music in the same style which is sung at 'parties and feasts given by the learned and the rich,' is called *conductus*. Commonly, he says, both are called *organum*.

Hocket is 'a cut-up song,' composed in two or more voices, 'pleasing to the hot-tempered and to young men because of its mobility and speed.'[28]

The *Hymn* is 'an ornate song, having many verses,' sung for the faithful, that 'it may excite their hearts and souls to devotion,' before the readings and psalms. It is sung again afterward to 'reawake them and reinvigorate them' for the reading of the evangelical psalms.[29]

---

24 Ibid.

25 Ibid., 20.

26 Ibid., 24.

27 Ibid., 25.

28 Ibid., 26.

29 Ibid., 35.

Finally, Grocheo discusses the intended influence on the listener of the various parts of the Mass. The *Kyrie Eleyson* is intended to 'move the hearts of those hearing it to devout praying and to listening devoutly to the Oration.' He adds to this description a curious footnote.

> It is performed in the Greek language, either because the Latins seem to have gotten the foundations of all the arts from the Greeks, or because Greek words are more weighty than others or more exact in designation, or because of some mystery which we do not wish to express at the present time.[30]

30 Ibid., 38.

And, as the reader may know, the Kyrie remains today the only part of the Catholic Mass which is in Greek.

The *Responsory* and *Alleluia* are sung 'in the manner of *stantipes* or *coronate cantus*, so that they may impose devotion and humility in the hearts of their audience.' But the *Sequence* is sung,

> in the manner of *ductia*, so that it may make them joyful and lead them to receive correctly the words of the New Testament.[31]

31 Ibid., 40.

The *Preface*, he calls a simple song intended to make the faithful devout and prepared for the *Sanctus*. The latter he calls 'a sign of the earthly and militant Church,' and is sung 'ornately and slowly, to move Christians to fervent charity and delight in God.'[32]

32 Ibid., 41.

The *Agnus Dei*, Grocheo suggests, is to create in the listener a feeling of 'peace and concord.'[33]

33 Ibid.

EPILOGUE

The great stigma of the Middle Ages is that a few centuries which are accurately represented by the label, 'Dark Ages,' have made this name a synonym for the entire period. While it is true that much of this period is characterized by a decline in traditional literature and the taking over of education by a Church with very narrow interests, the 'Dark Ages' were, nevertheless, *never* completely dark. For example, the references to musical performance, especially art music, suggest that the main streams of musical culture in Western Europe were never completely interrupted. We must resist allowing the presence of a lesser volume of extent literature which describes music to cause us to think that it follows that there was a lack of art music. Neither should traditional labels blind us to larger perspectives, as for example in failing to see that the ancient Greek lyric poetry and the poetry of the troubadours were anything other than two points on a continuous line.[1]

The greatest need, in our view, is for someone to write a history of medieval music in Western Europe which presents Church music for what it really was—a small, single branch in a wide musical current. The traditional focus on Church music has prevented many students from forming a perspective of the broader, and older, traditions of man and his music. One wonders, as a consequence, what connections may have been missed. Is it possible, to cite only one example, that those early medieval neumes, with their curves and swirls, are in fact a kind of pictorial notation for the gestures of the chironomist who stands frozen in his postures in the Egyptian tomb paintings?

If the practice of Art Music never died out during the Middle Ages, is it appropriate to call what follows the *Renaissance*? What, with regard to the aesthetics of music, does that term mean? The answers to these questions we hope to address in a following book.

---

1 An example of an important scholar who missed this connection is Hugo Leichtentritt, *Music, History, and Ideas* (Cambridge: Harvard University Press, 1958), 60, who, in speaking of the music of the troubadours, writes,

> The high perfection of lyric style in this literature cannot, of course, have sprung into existence suddenly; the troubadours must have had a long chain of predecessors, of whom nothing is recorded as yet in the annals of history.

BIBLIOGRAPHY

'Beowulf.' Translated by Francis Gummere, in *Epic and Saga*, vol. 49, *The Harvard Classics*. New York: Collier, 1909–1910.
'Joinville's Chronicle of the Crusade of St. Lewis,' in *Memoirs of the Crusades*. Translated by Frank Marzials. London: J. M. Dent, 1926.
'La Chronique de Rains.' Translated by Edward Stone, in *Three Old French Chronicles of the Crusades*. Seattle: University of Washington Press, 1939.
'Song of Atli,' in 'Songs from the Elder Edda,' in *Epic and Saga*, vol. 49, *The Harvard Classics*. New York: Collier, 1909–1910.
'The Destruction of Da Derga's Hostel.' Translated by Whitley Stokes, in *Epic and Saga*, vol. 49, *The Harvard Classics*. New York: Collier, 1909–1910.
'The Lament of Oddrun,' in 'Songs from the Elder Edda,' in *Epic and Saga*, vol. 49, *The Harvard Classics*. New York: Collier, 1909–1910.
'The Lay of Hamdir,' in 'Songs from the Elder Edda,' in *Epic and Saga*, vol. 49, *The Harvard Classics*. New York: Collier, 1909–1910.
'The Story of the Volsungs and Niblungs.' Translated by Eirikr Magnusson and William Morris, in *Epic and Saga*, vol. 49, *The Harvard Classics*. New York: Collier, 1909–1910.
Adomnan. *Life of Columba*. Translated by Alan Anderson and Marjorie Anderson. London: Nelson, 1961.
Aelius Donatus, 'On Comedy and Tragedy.' Translated by Barrett H. Clark, in *European Theories of the Drama*. New York: Crown, 1959.
Albertus Magnus. *De Animalibus*. Translated by James Scanlan. Binghamton, NY: Medieval & Renaissance Texts, 1987.
Alcuin. *Rhetoric*. Translated by Wilbur Howell. New York: Russell & Russell, 1965.
———. *The Bishops, Kings, and Saint of York*. Edited by Peter Godman. Oxford: Clarendon Press, 1982.
Ambrose, Saint. 'Death as a Good.' Translated by Michael P. McHugh, in *Seven Exegetical Works*. Washington, DC: The Catholic University of America, 1985.
———. 'Jacob and the Happy Life.' Translated by Michael P. McHugh, in *Seven Exegetical Works*. Washington, DC: The Catholic University of America, 1985.
———. 'Six Days of Creation: Five.' Translated by John J. Savage, in *Hexameron, Paradise, and Cain and Abel*. New York: Fathers of the Church, 1961.
———. 'Six Days of Creation: Four.' Translated by John J. Savage, in *Hexameron, Paradise, and Cain and Abel*. New York: Fathers of the Church, 1961.
———. 'Six Days of Creation: One.' Translated by John J. Savage, in *Hexameron, Paradise, and Cain and Abel*. New York: Fathers of the Church, 1961.
———. 'Six Days of Creation: Six.' Translated by John J. Savage, in *Hexameron, Paradise, and Cain and Abel*. New York: Fathers of the Church, 1961.
———. 'Six Days of Creation: Two.' Translated by John J. Savage, in *Hexameron, Paradise, and Cain and Abel*. New York: Fathers of the Church, 1961.
———. 'The Prayer of Job and David.' Translated by Michael P. McHugh, in *Seven Exegetical Works*. Washington, DC: The Catholic University of America, 1985.

Ammianus Marcellinus. *Constantius et Gallus*. Translated by John C. Rolfe. London: Heinemann, 1935.

Anderson, James F. *An Introduction to the Metaphysics of St. Thomas Aquinas*. Chicago: Henry Regnery, 1953.

Anderson, Warren D. *Ethos and Education in Greek Music*. Cambridge: Harvard University Press, 1966.

Anonymous of St. Emmeram. *De Musica Mensurata*. Translated by Jeremy Judkin. Bloomington: Indiana Universtiy Press, 1990.

Anonymous. *Of Symphonies*. Quoted in Oliver Strunk, *Source Readings in Music History*. New York: Norton, 1950.

Acquinas, Saint Thomas. *On Kingship to the King of Cyprus*. Translated by Gerald Phelan. Toronto: The Pontifical Institute of Mediaeval Studies, 1949.

———. *Theological Texts*. Translated by Thomas Gilby. London: Oxford University Press, 1955.

———. *Commentary on Aristotle's Physics*. Translated by Richard Blackwell. New Haven: Yale University Press, 1963.

———. *Commentary on Peri Hermeneias*. Translated by Jean Oesterle. Milwaukee: Marquette University Press, 1962.

———. *Commentary on the Metaphysics of Aristotle*. Translated by John Rowan. Chicago: Henry Regnery, 1961.

———. *On the Unity of the Intellect Against the Averroists*. Translated by Beatrice Zedler. Milwaukee: Marquette University Press, 1968.

———. *Summa Contra Gentiles*. London: Burns Oates & Washbourne, 1923.

———. *Summa Theologiae*. London: Blackfriars, 1971.

Augustine, Saint. 'Letter to Jerome.' Translated by Sister Wilfrid Parsons, in *Letters of Saint Augustine*. New York: Fathers of the Church, 1955.

———. 'Letter to Nebridius.' Translated by Sister Wilfrid Parsons, in *Letters of Saint Augustine*. New York: Fathers of the Church, 1951.

———. 'On Music.' Translated by Robert Taliaferro, in *Writings of Saint Augustine*. New York: Fathers of the Church, 1947.

———. 'Sermon 243.' Translated by Sister Mary Muldowney, in *Sermons on the Liturgical Seasons*. New York: Fathers of the Church, 1959.

———. 'Sermon 247.' Translated by Sister Mary Muldowney, in *Sermons on the Liturgical Seasons*. New York: Fathers of the Church, 1959.

———. 'Sermon 248.' Translated by Sister Mary Muldowney, in *Sermons on the Liturgical Seasons*. New York: Fathers of the Church, 1959.

———. *Against Julian*. Translated by Matthew A. Schumacher. New York: Fathers of the Church, 1957.

———. *Answer to Skeptics*. Translated by Ludwig Schopp. New York: CIMA Publishing Co., 1948.

———. *Divine Providence and the Problem of Evil*. Translated by Ludwig Schopp. New York: CIMA Publishing Co., 1948.

———. *Eighty-Three Different Questions*. Translated by David L. Mosher. Washington, DC: The Catholic University of America Press, 1981.

———. *On Genesis*. Translated by Roland Teske. Washington, DC: The Catholic University of America Press, 1990.

———. *The City of God*. Translated by Gerald G. Walsh. New York: Fathers of the Church, 1954.

———. *The Confessions*. Translated by Edward B. Pusey. New York: Collier, 1909.

———. *The Free Choice of the Will*. Translated by Robert P. Russell. Washington, DC: The Catholic University of America Press, 1968.
———. *The Immortality of the Soul*. Translated by Ludwig Schopp. New York: CIMA, 1947.
———. *The Magnitude of the Soul*. Translated by Ludwig Schopp. New York: CIMA, 1947.
———. *The Retractions*. Translated by Sister Mary Bogan. Washington, DC: The Catholic University of America, 1968.
———. *The Teacher*. Translated by Robert Russell. Washington, DC: The Catholic University of America Press, 1968.
Aurelian of Réome. *The Discipline of Music*. Translated by Joseph Ponte. Colorado Springs: Colorado College Music Press, 1968.
Ausonius. Translated by Hugh G. Evelyn White. London: Heinemann, 1961.
Basil, Saint. 'Homily 10.' Translated by Sister Agnew Way, in *Exegetic Homilies*. Washington, DC: The Catholic University of America Press, 1981.
———. 'Homily 14.' Translated by Sister Agnew Way, in *Exegetic Homilies*. Washington, DC: The Catholic University of America Press, 1981.
———. 'Homily 21.' Translated by Sister Agnew Way, in *Exegetic Homilies*. Washington, DC: The Catholic University of America Press, 1981.
———. 'Homily on the First Psalm,' in Oliver Strunk, *Source Readings in Music History*. New York: Norton, 1950.
———. 'Letter Concerning the Perfection of the Monastic Life.' Translated by Sister Agnes Way, in *Letters of Saint Basil*. New York: Fathers of the Church, 1951.
———. 'Letter to Glycerius.' Translated by Sister Agnes Way, in *Letters of Saint Basil*. New York: Fathers of the Church, 1951.
———. 'Letter to Gregory of Nazianzus.' Translated by Sister Agnes Way, in *Letters of Saint Basil*. New York: Fathers of the Church, 1951.
———. 'Letter to his Pupil, Chilo.' Translated by Sister Agnes Way, in *Letters of Saint Basil*. New York: Fathers of the Church, 1951.
———. 'Letter to the Governor of Neo-Caesarea.' Translated by Sister Agnes Way, in *Letters of Saint Basil*. New York: Fathers of the Church, 1951.
———. 'The Long Rules.' Translated by Sister Monica Wagner, in *Saint Basil Ascetical Works*. New York: Fathers of the Church, Inc., 1950.
———. 'The Long Rules.' Translated by Sister Monica Wagner, in *Ascetical Works*. New York: Fathers of the Church, 1950.
Bernard of Clairvaux, Saint. 'On Conversion,' in *Sermons on Conversion*. Translated by Marie-Bernard Saïd. Kalamazoo: Cistercian Publications, 1981.
———. *De Revisione Cantus Cistercienis*. Translated by Francisco Guentner. Middleton, WI: American Institute of Musicology (CSM-24).
———. *The Book of the Lover and the Beloved*. Translated by Allison Peers. New York: Macmillian, 1923.
———. *The Steps of Humility*. Translated by George Burch. Notre Dame, IN: University of Notre Dame Press, 1963.
———. *The Works of Bernard of Clairvaux*. Spencer, MA: Cistercian Publications, 1971.
Bernard of Cluny. *Scorn for the World: Bernard of Cluny's* De Contemptu Mundi. Translated by Ronald E. Pepin. East Lansing: Colleagues Press, 1991.

Bernhard, M. Bernard. *Notice sur la Confrérie des Joueurs d'Instruments d'Alsace*. Paris: Bureau de l'Annuiare de la noblesse, 1844.
Blackburn, Paul. *Proensa*. Berkeley: University of California Press, 1978.
Boethius. *Consolatione Philosophiae*. Translated by Samuel Fox. London: George Bell, 1895.
———. *Fundamentals of Music*. Translated by Calvin Bower. New Haven: Yale University Press, 1989.
Bonanni, Filippo. *Gabinetto armonico*. Roma: Nella stamperìa di G. Placho, 1723.
Bonaventure. *The Mind's Journey to God*. Translated by Lawrence Cunningham. Chicago: Franciscan Herald Press, 1979.
Bonfadini, R, 'Le origini del Comune di Milano,' in *Albori della Vita Italiana*. Milano: Treves, 1897.
Bonner, Anthony. *Songs of the Troubadours*. New York: Schocken Books, 1972.
Callimachus. Translated by C. A. Trypanis. Cambridge: Harvard University Press, 1975.
Capellanus, Andreas. *The Art of Courtly Love*. Translated by John Parry. New York: Frederick Ungar, 1957.
Carpenter, Nan Cooke. *Music in the Medieval and Renaissance Universities*. Norman: University of Oklahoma Press, 1958.
Cassiodorus. 'Letter to Agapitus, Praefectus Urbis.' Translated by Thomas Hodgkin, in *Variae*. London: Frowde, 1886.
———. 'Letter to Boethius.' Translated by Thomas Hodgkin, in *The Letters of Cassiodorus*. London: Frowde, 1886.
———. 'Letter to Maximus, Illustris, Consul.' Translated by Thomas Hodgkin, in *Variae*. London: Frowde, 1886.
———. 'Letter to the Illustrious Consularis.' Translated by Thomas Hodgkin, in *Variae*. London: Frowde, 1886.
———. 'Letter to the King of the Vandals.' Translated by Thomas Hodgkin, in *Variae*. London: Frowde, 1886.
———. 'Letter to the Patrician Symmachus.' Translated by Thomas Hodgkin, in *Variae*. London: Frowde, 1886.
———. 'On Dialectic.' Translated by Leslie Jones, in *An Introduction to Divine and Human Readings*. New York: Octagon Books, 1966.
———. *Divine Letters*. Translated by Leslie W. Jones. New York: Octagon Books, 1966.
Cavalcanti, Guido. *Vita Nuova*. Translated by Mark Musa. Oxford: Oxford University Press, 1992.
Chambers, E. K. *The Mediaeval Stage*. Oxford: Clarendon Press, 1903.
Chrysostom, Saint John. 'Exposition of Psalm XLI,' in Oliver Strunk, *Source Readings in Music History*. New York: Norton, 1950.
———. *Baptismal Instructions*. Translated by Paul W. Harkins. Westminster, MD: The Newman Press, 1963.
———. *Commentary on Saint John, Homilies 1–47*. Translated by Sister Thomas Aquinas Goggin. New York: Fathers of the Church, 1957.
———. *Commentary on Saint John*. Translated by Sister Thomas Aquinas Goggin. New York: Fathers of the Church, 1960.
———. *Discourses Against Judaizing Christians*. Translated by Paul W. Harkins. Washington, DC: The Catholic University of America, 1988.
———. *Homilies on Genesis 46–67*. Translated by Robert C. Hill. Washington, DC: The Catholic University of America Press, 1992.
Clark, Kenneth. *Civilisation*. New York: Harper & Row, 1969.

Clement of Alexandria. 'The Miscellanies.' Translated by Alexander Roberts, in *Ante-Nicene Christian Library*. Edinburgh: T. & T. Clark, 1869.
———. *Exhortation to the Greeks*. Translated by G. W. Butterworth. Cambridge: Harvard University Press, 1939.
———. *The Instructor*. Translated by William Wilson. Edinburgh: T. & T. Clark, 1884.
———. *The Miscellanies*. Translated by Alexander Roberts. Edinburgh: T. & T. Clark, 1869.
Commodianus. 'In Favor of Christian Discipline,' in *The Writings of Tertullianus*. Edinburgh: T. & T. Clark, 1895.
Corio, Bernardino. *L'Historia di Milano volgamente scritta*. Padoa, 1646.
Cyprian, Saint. *On the Dress of Virgins*. Translated by Sister Angela E. Keenan. New York: Fathers of the Church, Inc., 1958.
Dante. *The Banquet*. Translated by Christopher Ryan. Palo Alto: Stanford University [Anma Libri], 1989.
Dante's Lyric Poetry. Translated by Kenelm Foster and Patrick Boyde. Oxford: Clarendon Press, 1967.
Davis, H. W. C. *Medieval England*. Oxford: Clarendon Press, 1928.
Der mittelenglische Versroman über Richard Löwenherz. Edited by Karl Brunner. Vienna and Leipzig: W. Braunmüller, 1913.
Devizes, Richard, 'The Crusade of Richard Coeur de Lion,' in *Chronicles of the Crusades*. London: G. Bell and Sons, 1914
Dudden, F. H. *Gregory the Great*. London: Longmans, Green & Co., 1905.
Duncan, Edmondstoune. *The Story of Minstrelsy*. Detroit: Singing Tree Press, 1968.
Durant, Will. *Caesar and Christ*. New York: Simon and Schuster, 1944.
———. *The Age of Faith*. New York: Simon and Schuster, 1950.
Ehmann, Wilhelm. *Tibilustrium*. Kassel: Bärenreiter-Verlag, 1950.
Einhard and Notker the Stammerer. *Two Lives of Charlemagne*. Translated by Lewis Thorpe. Harmondsworth: Penguin Books, 1981.
Farmer, Henry G. *The Rise and Development of Military Music*. London: William Reeves, 1912.
———. 'Crusading Martial Music,' *Music & Letters* 30, no. 3 (July 1949): 243–249.
———. *Al-Farabi's Writings on Music*. New York: Hinrichsen, 1934.
Fortunatus. *The Miscellanea*. Translated by Geoffrey Cook. Rhinebeck, NY: Open Studio, 1981.
French Mediaeval Romances from the Lays of Marie de France. Translated by Eugene Mason. London: Dent, 1924.
Galen. *On the Natural Faculties*. Translated by Arthur John Brock. Cambridge: Harvard University Press, 1979.
———. *On the Passions and Errors of the Soul*. Translated by Paul W. Harkins. Columbus: Ohio State University Press, 1963.
Gentry, Francis G. *German Medieval Tales*. New York: Continuum, 1983.
Geoffrey de Vinsauf, 'Itinerary of Richard I to the Holy Land,' in *Chronicles of the Crusades*. London: G. Bell and Sons, 1914.
Geoffrey of Monmouth. *The History of the Kings of Brittan*. Translated by Lewis Thorpe. Baltimore: Penguin Books, 1966.
Gerbert, Martin. *Scriptores ecclesiastici de musica sacra*. St. Blaisen, 1784.
Gesta Romanorum. Translated by Charles Swan. London: C. and J. Rivington, 1824.

Gibbon, Edward. *The History of the Decline and Fall of the Roman Empire*. Boston: Phillips, Samson & Co., 1850; reprinted Philadelphia: Coates, n.d.

Goldin, Frederick. *German and Italian Lyrics of the Middle Ages*. Garden City: Anchor Books, 1973.

———. *Lyrics of the Troubadours and Trouvères*. Garden City: Anchor Books, 1973.

Goldron, Romain. *Minstrels and Masters*. [n.p], 1968.

Gottfried von Strassburg. *Tristan*. Translated by Arthus Hatto. Harmondsworth: Penguin Books, 1960.

Gregory of Nazianzus, Saint. *Concerning Himself and the Bishops*. Translated by Denis Meehan. Washington, DC: The Catholic University of America Press, 1987.

———. *Concerning his own Affairs*. Translated by Denis Meehan. Washington, DC: The Catholic University of America Press, 1987.

———. *Concerning his own Life*. Transcribed by Denis Meehan. Washington, DC: The Catholic University of America Press, 1987.

Gregory of Tours, 'The Suffering and Miracles of the Martyr St. Julian.' Translated by Raymond Van Dam, in *Saints and their Miracles in late Antique Gaul*. Princeton: Princeton University Press, 1993.

———. *The History of the Franks*. Translated by Lewis Thorpe. Harmondsworth: Penguin Books, 1974.

Gregory the Great. *Dialogue Four*. Translated by Odo Zimmerman. New York: Fathers of the Church, 1959.

———. *Dialogue Three*, 28. Translated by Odo Zimmerman. New York: Fathers of the Church, 1959.

———. *Pastoral Care*. Translated by Henry Davis. New York: Newman Press, 1978.

Grove, George. *The New Grove Dictionary of Music and Musicians*. Edited by Stanley Sadie. London: Macmillan, 1980.

Guillaume de Lorris and Jean de Meun. *The Romance of the Rose*. Translated by Harry Robbins. New York: Dutton, 1962.

Hartmann von Aue. *Erec*. Translated by Thomas Keller. New York: Garland, 1987.

Hildegard of Bingen. Edited by Fiona Bowie and Oliver Davies. New York: Crossroad, 1993.

Hildegard von Bingen. *Book of Divine Works*. Edited by Matthew Fox. Santa Fe: Bear & Company, 1987.

Hillgarth, Jocelyn N. *The Spanish Kingdoms*. Oxford: Clarendon Press, 1976

Hucbald, Guido, and John on Music. Translated by Warren Babb. New Haven: Yale University Press, 1978.

Inge, W. R. *Philosophy of Plotinus*. London: Longmans, Green, 1929.

Isidore of Seville, 'Etymologiarum.' Translated by W. M. Linsay, in Oliver Strunk, *Source Readings in Music History*. New York: Norton, 1950.

Jacopone da Todi. *The Lauds*. Translated by Serge and Elizabeth Hughes. New York: Paulist Press, 1982.

Jerome, Saint. 'Letter to Damasus.' Translated by Charles C. Mierow, in *The Letters of St. Jerome*. Westminster, MD: The Newman Press, 1963.

Joannes Scotus Eriugena. *Periphyseon on the Division of Nature*. Translated by Myra Uhlfelder. Indianapolis: Bobbs-Merrill, 1976.

Johannes de Garlandia. *De Mensurabili Musica*. Translated by Stanley Birnbaum. Colorado Springs: Colorado College Music Press, 1978.

Johannes de Grocheo. *De Musica*. Translated by Albert Seay. Colorado Springs: Colorado College Music Press, 1967.

John Duns Scotus, 'Concerning Human Knowldege.' Translated by Allan Wolter, in *Philosophical Writings of John Duns Scotus*. Indianapolis: Bobbs-Merrill, 1962.

John Duns Scotus. *God and Creatures*. Translated by Felix Alluntis and Allan Wolter. Princeton: Princeton University Press, 1975.

John Duns Scotus. *Will and Morality*. Translated by Allan Wolter. Washington, DC: The Catholic University of America Press, 1986.
John of Salisbury, 'Policraticus,' in *The Statesman's Book of John of Salisbury*. Translated by John Dickinson. New York: Russell & Russell, 1963.
John of Salisbury. *The Metalogicon*. Translated by Daniel McGarry. Berkeley: University of California Press, 1955.
Julian, 'Misopogon.' Translated by Wilmer Wright, in *The Works of the Emperor Julian*. London: Heinemann, 1913.
Julian, 'Panegyric in Honor of Constantius.' Translated by Wilmer Wright, in *The Works of the Emperor Julian*. London: Heinemann, 1913.
Julian, 'Panegyric in Honor of Eusebia.' Translated by Wilmer Wright, in *The Works of the Emperor Julian*. London: Heinemann, 1913.
Julian, 'The Heroic Deeds of Constantius.' Translated by Wilmer Wright, in *The Works of the Emperor Julian*. London: Heinemann, 1913.
Julian, 'To the Cynic Heracleios.' Translated by Wilmer Wright, in *The Works of the Emperor Julian*. London: Heinemann, 1913.
Julian, 'To the Uneducated Cynics.' Translated by Wilmer Wright, in *The Works of the Emperor Julian*. London: Heinemann, 1913.
Justin, Martyr, 'Discourse to the Greeks.' Translated by Thomas B. Fall, in *Saint Justin Martyr*. New York: Christian Heritage, 1948.
Justin, Martyr, 'the First Apology.' Translated by Thomas B. Fall, in *Saint Justin Martyr*. New York: Christian Heritage, 1948.
Justin, Martyr, 'The Monarchy or The Rule of God.' Translated by Thomas B. Fall, in *Saint Justin Martyr*. New York: Christian Heritage, 1948.
Kantorowicz, Ernst. *Frederick the Second*. Translated by Emily O. Lorimer. New York: Frederick Ungar, 1957.
Lactantius, 'Epitome of the Divine Institutes.' Translated by William Fletcher, in *The Works of Lactantius*. Edinburgh: T. & T. Clark, 1871.
Lactantius, 'On the Workmanship of God.' Translated by William Fletcher, in *The Works of Lactantius*. Edinburgh: T. & T. Clark, 1871.
Lactantius, 'The Divine Institutes.' Translated by William Fletcher in *The Works of Lactantius*. Edinburgh: T. & T. Clark, 1886.
Leichtentritt, Hugo. *Music History and Ideas*. Cambridge: Harvard University Press, 1958.
Les Miracles de Nostre Dame par Gautier de Coinci. Edited by V. R. Koenig. Geneva: Librarie Droz, 1970.
Lindberg, David. *Roger Bacon's Philosophy of Nature*. Oxford: Clarendon, 1983.
Llull, Ramon. *Obres Essencials*. Barcelona: Editorial Selecta, 1957.
Longinus. *On the Sublime*. Translated by W. Rhys Roberts. Cambridge: University Press, 1935.
Longus. *Daphnis & Chloe*. Translated by Paul Turner. London: Penguin Books, 1956.
Marcus Minucius Felix. *Octavius*. Translated by G. W. Clarke. New York: Newman Press, 1974.
Martianus Capella and the Seven Liberal Arts. Translated by William Harris Stahl and Richard Johnson. New York: Columbia University Press, 1977.
Masson, Georgina. *Frederick II of Hohenstaufen*. New York: Octagon Books, 1973.
McEvoy, James. *The Philosophy of Robert Grosseteste*. Oxford: Clarendon, 1982.
McKinney, Howard D. and W. R. Anderson. *Music in History*. New York: American Book Co., 1940.

McKinnon, James W. 'Musical Instruments in Medieval Psalm Commentaries and Psalters.' *Journal of the American Musicological Society* 21, no. 1 (Spring 1968): 3–20.

Michael Psellus. *Chronographia*. Translated by E. R. A. Sewter. Baltimore: Penguin Books, 1966.

Mimes Franais du XIII siècle. Edited by Edmond Feral. Paris: Edmond Champion, 1910.

Mizwa, Stephen. *Nicholas Copernicus*. New York: Kessinger Publications, 1943.

Musaeus. *Hero and Leander*. Translated by Cedric Whitman. Cambridge: Harvard University Press, 1975.

Nichols, Stephen. *The Songs of Bernart de Ventadorn*. Chapel Hill: The University of North Carolina Press, 1965.

Novatian, 'The Spectacles.' Translated by Russell J. DeSimone, in *Fathers of the Church*. Washington, DC: The Catholic University of America Press, 1947.

Odo of Cluny. *Enchiridion musices*. Quoted in Oliver Strunk, in *Source Readings in Music History*. New York: Norton, 1950.

Origen. 'Against Celsus.' Translated by Frederick Crombie, in *The Writings of Origen*. Edinburgh: T. & T. Clark, 1871.

———. 'De Principiis.' Translated by Frederick Crombie, in *The Writings of Origen*. Edinburgh: T. & T. Clark, 1871.

———. 'Word as Flesh,' in Hans Urs von Balthasar, *Spirit and Fire*. Translated by Robert J. Daly. Washington, DC: The Catholic University of America Press, 1984.

Otto of Freising. *The Deeds of Frederick Barbarossa*. Translated by Charles Mierow. New York: Columbia University Press, 1953.

Page, Christopher. *Voices and Instruments of the Middle Ages*. London: Dent, 1987.

Paris, Matthew. *English History*. Translated by J. A. Giles. London: Bohn, 1852.

Peasant Life in Old German Epics. Translated by Clair Bell. New York: Octagon Books, 1965.

Peter Damian. *On the Joyes & Glory of Paradise*. Translated by Stephen Hurlbut. Washington, DC: St. Albans Press, 1928.

Press, Alan. *Anthology of Troubadour Lyric Poetry*. Austin: University of Texas Press, 1971.

Procopius. *The Secret History*. Harmondsworth: Penguin Books, 1981.

Pseudo-Dionysius Areopagite. *The Divine Names and Mystical Theology*. Translated by John Jones. Milwaukee: Marquette University Press, 1980.

———. *The Ecclesiastical Hierarchy*. Translated by Thomas Campbell. Washington, DC: University Press of America, 1981.

Rabanus Maurus. *The Life of Saint Mary Magdalene and of her Sister Saint Martha*. Translated by David Mycoff. Kalamazoo: Cistercian Publications, 1989.

Rashdall, Hastings. *The Universities of Europe in the Middle Ages*. Oxford: Clarenden Press, 1936.

Rastall, Richard, 'Some English Consort-Groupings of the late Middle Ages.' *Music & Letters* 55, no. 2 (April 1974): 179–202.

Saint Ambrose. *See* Ambrose, Saint.

Saint Augustine. *See* Augustine, Saint.

Saint Basil. *See* Basil, Saint.

Saint Bernard of Clairvaux. *See* Bernard of Clairvaux, Saint.

Saint Cyprian. *See* Cyprian, Saint.

Saint Gregory of Nazianzus. *See* Gregory of Nazianzus, Saint.

Saint John Chrysostom. *See* Chrysostom, Saint John.

Saint Jerome. *See* Jerome, Saint.

Saint Thomas Aquinas. *See* Aquinas, Saint Thomas.

Saldoni y Remendo, Baltasar. *Diccionario biografio-bibliografico de Efemérides de musicos españos*. Madrid: Imp. Á cargo de A. Perez Dubeull, 1880.

Salvian. *On the Government of God*. Translated by Eva Sanford. New York: Columbia University Press, 1930.

Secular Latin Poems of the Middle Ages. Translated by Edwin H. Zeydel. Detroit: Wayne State University Press, 1966.

Selected Poems of Walter von der Vogelweide. Translated by W. Alison Phillips. London: Smith, Elder & Co., 1896.

Selected Writings of St. Thomas Aquinas. Edited by M. C. D'Arcy. New York: Dutton, 1950..

Sextus Empiricus. *Against the Logicians*. Translated by R. G. Bury. London: Heinemann, 1935.

———. *Against the Professors*. Translated by R. G. Bury. Cambridge: Harvard University Press, 1949.

———. *Outlines of Pyrrhonism*. Translated by R. G. Bury. London: Heinemann, 1933.

Sharman, Ruth. *The Cassos and Sirventes of the Troubadour Giraut de Borneil*. Cambridge: Cambridge University Press, 1989.

Sidonius Poems and Letters. Translated by W. B. Anderson. Cambridge: Harvard University Press, 1965.

Southern, R. W. *Robert Grosseteste*. Oxford: Clarendon Press, 1992.

Staines, David. *The Complete Romances of Chrétien de Troyes*. Bloomington: Indiana University Press, 1993.

Steele, Robert. *Medieval Lore of Bartholomew Anglicus*. London: Stock, 1893.

Stow, John. *The Survey of London*. London: George Purslowe, 1618.

Symonds, John. *Wine Women and Song: Mediaeval Latin Students' Songs*. New York: Cooper Square Publishers, 1966.

Tannhäuser: Poet and Legend. Translated by J. W. Thomas. Chapel Hill: The University of North Carolina Press, 1974.

Tertullian, 'De Anima.' Translated by Alexander Roberts, in *Ante-Nicene Christian Library*. Edinburgh: T. & T. Clark, 1884.

———. 'On Prescription Against Heretics.' Translated by Alexander Roberts, in *Ante-Nicene Christian Library*. Edinburgh: T. & T. Clark, 1884.

———. 'Spectacles.' Translated by Rudolph Arbesmann, in *Disciplinary, Moral and Ascetical Works*. New York: Fathers of the Church, 1959.

———. *On the Soul*. Translated by Edwin A. Quain. New York: Fathers of the Church, Inc., 1950.

———. *The Testimony of the Soul*. Translated by Rudolph Arbesmann. New York: Fathers of the Church, Inc., 1950.

Tertullianus. *De Anima*. Translated by Alexander Roberts and James Donalson. Edinburgh: T. & T. Clark, 1884.

The Chronicle of Richard of Devizes. Edited by John T. Appleby. London: Nelson, 1963.

The Ecclesiastical History of Orderic Vitalis. Translated by Marjorie Chibnall. Oxford: Clarendon Press, 1969.

The Exter Book. Translated by Sir. Israel Gollancz and William Soutar Mackie. London: Oxford University Press, 1958.

The Greek Anthology. Translated by W. R. Paton. Cambridge: Harvard University Press, 1939.

The Holy Bible. [Revised Standard Version]. New York: Thomas Nelson & Sons, 1952.

The Journey of Charlemagne. Translated by Jean-Louis Picherit. Birmingham, AL: Summa, 1984.

The Letters of Abelard and Heloise. Translated by C. K. Scott Moncrieff. New York: Knopf, 1933.

The Letters of Gerbert. Translated by Harriet Lattin. New York: Columbia University Press, 1961.
The Letters of Peter Damian. Translated by Owen Blum. Washington, DC: The Catholic University of America Press, 1990.
The Letters of Sidonius. Translated by O. M. Dalton. Oxford: Clarendon Press, 1915.
The Letters of St. Bernard of Clairvaux. Translated by Bruno James. Chicago: Regnery, 1953.
The Love Songs of the Çarmina Burana. Translated by E. D. Blodgett. New York: Garland Publishing, Inc., 1987.
The Opus Majus of Roger Bacon. Translated by Robert Burke. New York: Russell & Russell, 1962.
The Plays of Hrotswitha of Gandersheim. Translated by Larissa Bonfante. New York: New York University Press, 1979.
The Poems of St. Paulinus of Nola. Translated by P. G. Walsh. New York: Newman Press, 1975.
The Portable Dante. Edited by Paolo Milano. New York: Viking Press, 1969.
The Scriptoires Historiae Augustae. Translated by David Magie. London: Heinemann, 1924.
The Song of Roland. Translated by Robert Harrison. New York: Mentor, 1970.
The Song of William. Translated by Edward Stone. Seattle: University of Washington Press, 1951.
The Venerable Bede, 'Life of St. Cuthbert.' Translated by Bertram Colgrave, in *Two Lives of Saint Cuthbert*. New York: Greenwood Press, 1969.
The Venerable Bede. *Ecclesiastical History of England*. Translated by J. A. Giles. London: Bohn, 1849.
Theophilus, 'Schedule diversarum atrium.' Edward Dillon, *Glass*. New York: G. P. Putnam, 1907.
Theophilus. *The Various Arts*. Translated by C. R. Dodwell. London: Nelson, 1961.
Thomas, J. W. *The Best Novellas of Medieval Germany*. Columbia, SC: Camden House, 1984.
Thorndike, Lynn. *History of Magic and Experimental Science*. New York: Macmillan, 1929.
Ulrich von Liechtenstein. *In Service of Ladies*. Translated by J. W. Thomas. Chapel Hill: The University of North Carolina Press, 1969.
Vagabond Verse. Translated by Edwin H. Zeydel. Detroit: Wayne State University Press, 1966.
Veit, Gottfried. *Die Blasmusik*. Bozen: Verband Sudtiroler Musikkapellen, 1972.
Vessella, Alessandro. *La Banda*. Milano: Istituto editoriale nazionale, 1935.
Victorinus, Bishop of Petau. *The Writings of Tertullianus*. Edinburgh: T. & T. Clark, 1895.
Vitalis, Ordericus. *The Ecclesiastical History of England*. Translated by Thomas Forester. London: Henry G. Bohn, 1854.
Vitalis, Ordericus. *The Ecclesiastical History of England*. Translated by Marjorie Chibnall. Oxford: Clarendon Press, 1878.
Wace, Robert. *Roman de Brut*. Translated by Gwyn Jones. London: Dent, 1962.
Waesberghe, Joseph Smits van. *Musikerziehung, Lehre und Theorie der Musik in Mittelalter*. Leipzig: VEB Deutscher Verlag für Musik, 1969.
Werf, Hendrik van der. *The Chansons of the Troubadours and Trouvères*. Utrecht: A. Oosthoek, 1972.
Whicher, George. *The Goliard Poets*. [George Whicher], 1949.
Wilkinson, L. P. 'Philodemus in Ethos in Music.' *Classical Quarterly* 32 (1938).
William of Malmesbury. *Three Lives of the Last Englishmen*. Translated by Michael Swanton. New York: Garland Publishing, 1984.
Wolfram von Eschenbach. *Parzival*. Translated by Helen Mustard and Charles Passage. New York: Vingate Books, 1961.
Wolfram von Eschenbach. *Willehalm*. Translated by Charles Passage. New York: Ungar, 1977.

Wolfram von Eschenbch, Titurel and the Songs. Translated by Marion Gibbs and Sidney Johnson. New York: Garland Publishing, 1988.

Zeydel, Edwin H. *Vagabond Verse*. Detroit: Wayne State University Press, 1966.

Zippel, Giuseppe. *I Suonatori della Signoria di Firenze*. Trento, 1892.

INDEX

A

Abelard, Peter, 1079–1144, Church writer, 311, 328, 330
Adelinda, 1086 English jongleur, 237
Adomnan, 7th century Church writer, 210ff
Aeschylus, 525–456 BC, Greek playwright, 12
Agathias Scholasticus, 530–594, Greek poet, 197ff
Aimeric de Peguilhan, fl. 1195–1230, troubadour, 370, 380, 389
Ainard, 12th century German abbot, 330
Alcman, 7th century BC lyric poet, 39
Alcuin, 740–804, English scholar and poet, 180, 184ff, 188
Al-Farabi, 10th century music theorist, 265ff
Alpharabius (Al-Farabi), 872–951, 293
Ambrose, a jongleur to Richard I, 282ff
Anacharsis the Scythian, 6th century BC, 21
Anonymous, 'Beowulf,' 206
Anonymous, 'De Musica Mensurata' (ca. 1279), 434
Anonymous, 'Scholia enchiriadis,' (ca. 900 AD), 254ff
Anonymous, 2nd century, 'The Shepherd of Herman,' 45
Antipater of Thessalonica, Greek poet, 1st century, 39
Apollo (Phoebus), mythical god of music and medicine, 4, 39, 99, 101 [Truth], 198, 326, 430ff

Aquinas, Saint Thomas, 1224–1274, Church writer, 312, 333ff
Archias, 1st century poet, 44
Archilochus, 680–645 BC, Greek poet, 20
Archimedes, 213
Archpoet of Cologne, 12th century Golliard, 276, 428, 431
Aribert, Archbishop of Milan, 11th century, 238
Arion, mythical Greek singer, 308
Aristotle, 384–322 BC, Greek philosopher, 12, 16, 72, 154, 213, 216, 249, 271, 290, 296, 303, 311ff, 333, 338, 341ff, 345, 349, 353, 403
Aristoxenus, fl. 355 BC, philosopher, student of Aristotle, 68, 114, 200
Arthur, mythical king of England, 361, 365, 367ff
Asclepiades, 3rd century BC philosopher, 27, 96 [music therapy]
Athanasius, Bishop of Alexandria, 367 AD, 82, fn. 8 [Creation of the NT]
Attila the Hun, 94 [funeral]
Audefroy le Bastard, troubadour, 383
Aurelian of Réome, 9th century music theorist, 248ff
Aurelian, Roman Emperor, 3rd century, 8
Ausonius, 4th century poet, 93, 99ff

B

Bacchylides, ancient Greek lyric poet, 17

Bacon, Roger, b. ca. 1214, English scholar, 291ff, 297, 300, 302ff, 305, 310
Baldwin, king of Jerusalem, 11th century, 281
Bartholomew Anglicus, 13th century philosopher, 302, 306
Bede (Venerable Bede), 672–735, monk and historian, 177, 196, 211ff
Beldgabred, medieval minstrel of fame, 355, fn. 2.
Belisarius, 500–565, Byzantine general, 195
Berdic, 1086 English jongleur, 237
Bernard of Chartres, fl. 1115–1124, 321
Bernard of Cluny, fl. 1122–1156, Church writer, 320ff
Bernart de Sayssac, troubadour, 372
Bernart de Ventadorn, fl. 1150–1180, troubadour, 370ff, 374, 376, 384ff, 388ff, 394
Bertran de Born, b. ca. 1140, troubadour, 382, 384
Blondel de Nesle, 12th century, trouvère, 275, 377ff, 386, 389
Boethius, 480–525, mathematician, philosopher, 183ff, 188ff, 213ff, 224, 247ff, 261, 353, 403, 434, 437ff
Bonagiunta Orbicciani da Lucca, d. 1296, Italian poet, 396
Bonaventure, 13th century Church writer, 316ff, 319ff
Brive, the Limousin, jongleur, 371

Brulé, Gace, fl. ca. 1180–1213, trouvère, 379, 388

C

Cabestanh, troubadour, 370
Caedmon, d. 670, Anglo-Saxon monk, poet, 196
Callimachus, 3rd century poet, 6, 8
Capella, Martianus, 5th century poet, 95, 104ff, 109ff, 112ff
Cardenal, Peire, 1180–1278, troubadour, 370, 390
Carinus, 3rd century Roman emperor, 8
Carus, 3rd century Roman emperor, 8
Cassiodorus, 485–585, Roman statesman and philosopher, 175ff, 187ff, 189ff, 193ff, 213, 219ff, 224, 248
Cerveri de Girona, fl. 1250–1280, troubadour, court of Aragon, 375
Charlemagne, 742–814, 180ff, 188, 235, 252, 357, 366
Charon, mythical ferryman of Hell, 4
Châtelain de Couci, d. 1203, trouvère, 383
Chilperic, King of Neustria, 539–584, 210
Chosroes, 6th century, king of Persia, 196
Chrétien de Troyes, 12th century writer, 359ff, 368
Cicero, 106–43 BC, Roman philosopher, 139
Clement of Alexandria, 2nd century Church philosopher, 6
Clement of Alexandria, Christian father, 150–215 AD, 46ff, 53ff, 59ff, 66, 70, 73, 75, 77ff
Clovis, Christian king of the Franks, 482–611, 189
Clytosthenes, 2nd century musician, 40
Commodianus, 3rd century Christian poet, 50
Comtessa de Dia, fl, ca. 1160, troubadour, 377
Conrad II, 11th century Franconian king, 238
Constantine IX, 1042–1055, 231
Constantine, 306–337 AD, Roman emperor, 88, 107
Cossezen, troubadour, 372
Cybele, mythical god of Nature, 6, 138ff
Cyrus, 1st century poet, 43

D

Daniel, Arnaut, fl. 1180–1200, troubadour, 375, 377, 387
Dante, 1265–1321, Latin poet, 369, 3974ff
Democritus, 460–370 BC, Greek philosopher, 24
Demophilus, first century poet, 5
Demosthenes, 384–322 BC, Greek orator, 19
Desiderius, Bishop of Vienne, 6th century, 176
Diogenes, 230–150 BC, Stoic philosopher, 32ff
Dionysius, ancient Greek philosopher, 27
Dioscorides, 2nd century poet, 6
Donatus, Aelius, 4th century professor of rhetoric, 92
Dryden, John, 1631–1700, English poet, 11

E

Ealhhild, British queen, 8th century, 202
Ebles de Sagna, troubadour, 372
Elagabalus, 219–222 AD, Roman emperor, 3

En Rambaut, traubodour, 372
Euclid, 4th century BC mathematician, 213
Eudes, English bishop, 11th century, 239
Eunomus, ancient Greek lyre player, 4
Euripides, 480–406 BC, Greek playwright, 17ff, 52
Eutychides, first century Greek lyric poet, 3
Evrardus of Venator, 12th century court brass player, 281

F

Faidit, Gaucelm, troubadour, 370
Fortunatus, d. 7th century, Greek poet, 200
Frederick I, 1122–1190, emperor, Holy Roman Empire, 278
Frederick II, 1194–1250, emperor, Holy Roman Empire, 274, 277ff, 280, 285ff
Friedrich III, Bishop of Chur, 324
Fulcher of Chartres, d. 1130, historian, 281

G

Galen, 2nd century writer on medicine, 9, 22, 26ff, 28
Gausmar, Grimoart, troubadour, 372
Gautier de Coinci, 1218–1236, writer, 365
Gavaudan, 1195–1230, troubadour, 387
Gelimer, King of the Vandals, 530–534, 193
Geoffrey of Monmouth, 12th century writer, 355, fn, 2
Gibbon, Edward, 1737–1794, English historian, 6, 8, 87ff, 179, 195ff, 201, 229, 237ff
Giraut de Borneil, 1165–1211, troubadour, 371, 375, 377ff, 379ff, 384ff, 388ff, 3392ff

INDEX 459

Gottfried von Strassburg, fl. 1200–1210, Geman poet, 412ff, 418ff, 424
Gregory IX, 13th century pope, 325
Gregory of Tours, Bishop of Tours, 538–594, historian, 178, 209ff
Gregory the Great, 540–604, pope, 176, 189ff, 194, 198, 210, 286, 324
Guido Cavalcanti, 1259–1300, Italian poet, 399
Guido de Arezzo, 990–1050, music teacher, 236, 257ff, 262
Guido Guinizelli, fl. 1250–1300, Italian poet, 397
Guilhem de Montanhagol, 1233–1270, troubadour, 370, 376, 384, 390
Guillaume de Lorris, 'Romance of the Rose,' 355ff
Guillaume IX, Count of Poitiers, troubadour, 370, 387, 393
Guillem de Ribas, troubadour, 372
Guiraut Riquier, 1230–1292, troubadour, 391
Guittone d'Arezzo, ca. 1235–1294, Italian poet, 395
Guthere, King of the Burgundians, 5th century, 202

H

Hartmann von Aue, ca. 1160–1210, German poet, 417ff, 422, 425
Healfdene, early 6th century Danish king, 206
Hegelochus, first century poet, 5
Heinrich von Morungen, d. 1222, Minnesinger, 417ff
Henri d'Andeli, 13th century trouvère and writer, 289
Henry I of England, 274

Henry III of England, 1207–1272, 273, 278, 286
Heracleitus, 540–475 BC, Greek philosopher, 24
Hereward the Wake, English noble and writer, 12th century, 279, 326
Herodotus, 484–425 BC, Greek historian, 20
Herophilus, 335–280 BC, Greek physician, 96 [music therapy]
Hildegard von Bingen, 1098–1179, nun, philosopher, 315ff, 330ff
Hippocrates, 460–370 BC, physician, 198
Homer, ancient Greek poet, 17, 20, 40, 74, 200
Honestus, 1st century poet, 4
Horace, 321
Hrotswitha, 10th century nun, writer, 233
Hucbald, 9th century music theorist, 253
Hudo, Duke of Burgandy, 12th century, 284
Hugh of Orléans, 12th century Golliard, 429, 431

I

Innocent III, pope, 13th century, 285
Innocent IV, 12th century pope, 272
Ion, 5th – 4th centuries BC, rhapsodist, 17
Isidore of Sevile, 560–636, philosopher, 213, 221ff, 248, 251, 434

J

Jacopone da Todi, 1230–1306, sacred poet, 318
Jaufré Rudel, Prince of Blaia, troubadour, 370
Jerome of Moravic, 13th century music theorist, 435

Jesus, 353 [singing]
Joannes Scotus Eriugena, 9th century Irish philosopher, 230ff
Johannes de Garlandia, ca. 1279, music theorist, 433, 435ff
Johannes de Grecheo, ca. 1300, music theorist, 433, 436ff
John Duns Scotus, 13th century English philosopher, 299, 301ff, 303
John of Salisbury, 12th century Church philosopher, 313ff, 316, 318, 320ff, 322, 326
John, 12th century music theorist, 261ff
Joinville, 13th century historian, 285ff
Jordan, Raimon, troubadour, 370
Julian, 361–363 AD, Roman emperor, 88, 90, 91 92ff, 107ff, 110ff, 112ff
Julius Caesar, Roman emperor, 313
Justin Martyr, 2nd century Church father, 47, 73ff
Justinian, , 6th century emperor, 179

L

Lactantius, 250–325 professor of rhetoric, 43, 51ff, 57, 59, 61, 67ff, 70ff, 72ff, 75
Lampidius, Gallic poet, 5th century, 89
Leo V, 9th century Byzantine emperor, 238
Leontius Scholasticus, 1st century poet, 40
Libanius, b. 314, professor at Athens, 107
Longinus, 1st century philosopher, 11ff
Longus, 2nd century poet, 7, 40

Louis I of France, 814–840, 239
Louis VII of France, 281
Louis IX, 13th century king of France, 285
Lucilius, 1st century poet, 7, 9
Lull, Ramón, 1232-1315, 274, 312, 317, 325ff, 330

M

Macedonius, 500-560, Greek poet, 198ff
Magnus, Albertus, b. 1193, German philosopher, 301ff 307ff
Mahler, Gustav, 263
Mallulf, Bishop of Senlis, 6th century, 210
Marcabru, 1129-1150 troubadour, 386, 370, 393
Marcellinus, Ammianus, 4th century Roman historian, 90ff, 94ff, 97 [military music]
Mareuil, troubadour, 370
Marie de France, 12th century writer, 356ff, 362ff
Menander, 342-291, Greek playwright, 83, 200
Michael VII, Byzantine emperor, 1071-1078, 231ff
Minucius Felix, 2nd – 3rd century, Roman philosopher, 47ff, 64, 73
Miriam, sister to Moses, 295
Monk of Montaudon, fl. 1180-1215, troubadour, 375, 394
Musaeus, 5th century poet, 100
Muset, Colin, fl. ca. 1230, trouvère, 374ff, 376, 378, 388

N

Neidhart von Reuental, fl. 1210-1237 German poet, 413
Nestor of Nicaea, ancient Greek poet, 5
Novatian, 3rd century Church philosopher, 48ff, 56ff, 79
Numerian, 3rd century Roman emperor, 8

O

Odo of Cluny, 878-942, Abbot of Cluny, music teacher, 236, 256
Origen, 184-254, Alexandrian scholar, 52ff, 61ff, 66, 74ff
Orpheus, mythical god of music, 40, 106, 186, 200, 243, 307, 361ff
Ovid, Latin poet, 200, 308

P

Palladas, 5th century poet, 102
Paris, Matthew, 13th century historian, 272, 276, 280, 296, 290
Paulinus, Bishop of Nola, 354-431 AD, 90ff, 95, 104
Paulus Silentiarius, d. 150, Byzantine poet, 197ff
Peckham, John, professor at Paris, 333
Pedro III, 1276-1285, of Aragon, 274
Peire d'Auvergne, fl. 1150-1180, troubadour, 371ff, 373, 384, 387, 393
Peire de Monzó, troubadour, 372
Peter Damian, 11th century Church writer, 229, 232, 237
Peter the Deacon of Pisa, 6th century, 180
Philetaerus, 343-263 BC, Greek politician, military leader, 83
Philippus, 2nd century poet, 7
Philodemus of Gadara, 1st century epicurean philosopher, 29ff
Pindar, ancient Greek lyric poet, 17
Plato, 1st century lyre player, 40
Plato, 427-347 BC, Greek philosopher, 20, 139, 213, 218ff
Pons de Capdueill, 1196-1236, troubadour, 370, 385
Pope, Alexander, 1688-1744, English poet, 11
Praetorius, 17th century German composer, conductor, 438, 440
Procopius, 500-565, Byzantine historian, 193ff
Protagoras of Abdera, 5th century BC, 22
Psellus, 1017-1078, Byzantine monk and philosopher, 231ff, 237, 239
Pseudo-Dionysius Areopagite, 5th – 6th century, Church philosopher, 184ff, 209
Ptolemy, 213, 336
Pythagoras, 570-495 BC, philosopher, 35ff 60, 114, 213, 248, 336 437

R

Rabanus Maurus, 9th century writer, 233
Rahere, d. 1144, a jongleur of Henry I of England, 274
Raimbaut d'Orange, 1150-1173, troubadour, 374ff, 376, 390, 393
Reginald of Châtillon, 12th century, 282
Reinmar, ca. 1150-1210, German Minnesinger, 411
Richard I, 1157-1199, of England, 275, 277, 287ff, 388
Richard, Earl of England, fl. 1243, 278, 280
Robert Grosseteste, d. 1253, philosopher, 290ff, 296ff, 303ff, 306
Rogier, Peire, troubadour, 371
Roïtz, Gonzalgo, troubadour, 372

Roland, nephew to Charlemagne, 357, 366ff
Roscius, 126–62 BC, roman actor, 152

S

Saladin, 12th century Sultan, 282, 285
Salvian, 5th century Church father, 116ff, 120ff
Seneca, 4 BC – 65 AD, Roman philosopher, 302
Severinus, Bishop of Cologne, 4th century, 211
Severus Alexander, 222–235 AD, Roman Emperor, 3
Sextus Empiricus, 2nd century philosopher, 21ff, 35ff
Sidonius, Gallic poet, 5th century, 89, 91, 96ff, 102
Sigemund, Norse mythical hero, 207, 245
Simylus, first century poet, 5
Sylvester II, 10th century pope, 229
Socrates, 469–399 BC, 35ff, 52, 60, 428
Sophocles, 496–406 BC, Greek playwright, 17, 52
Sordel (Sordello), ca. 1200–1270, troubadour, 380, 392
Speusippus of Athens, 408–338 BC, 24
St. Ambrose, 4th century Church father at Milan, 121ff, 125ff 127ff, 129
St. Augustine, 354–430, Church philosopher, 135ff, 167 [on conducting], 301, 311
St. Basil, 4th century Church father, 45, 107, 115ff, 119, 123ff, 125ff, 130, 132
St. Bernard of Clairvaux, 1090–1153, 248, 281, 311ff, 315, 318, 322ff, 327ff, 330
St. Columba of Ireland, 521–597, 210ff
St. Cuthbert, 634–687, Anglo-Saxon monk, 211
St. Cyprian, 3rd century Church father, 46
St. Francis of Assai, 311
St. Gregory Nazianzus, 4th century Church father, 116ff, 123ff, 131
St. Jerome, 337–420, Church father, 122, 132ff, 353
St. John Chrysostom, 342–407, Church father, 95, 107, 115ff, 117ff, 121ff, 124ff, 127ff, 129ff, 134
St. Paul, 262
St. Paulinus of Nola, 131
Stesichorus, 640–555 BC Greek poet, 20

T

Taillefer, jongleur of William the conqueror, 237
Telephanes, 1st century aulos player, 40
Terentianus, fl. 110–136 AD, Roman writer, 191
Tertullian, 2nd century Church philosopher, 4, 46ff, 48ff, 58ff, 62ff, 69ff, 72
Theodora of Constantinople, 11th century Byzantine empress, 237
Theodore of Cyrus, d. 460, Church philosopher, 130
Theodoric, king of the Goths, 454–526 AD, 97
Theodorus, 465–396 BC, teacher, 197
Theophilus, 12th century priest, philosopher in Germany, 271, 296
Theophilus, Archbishop of Alexandria, d. 412, 177
Theophrastus, 371–287 BC, Greek teacher, 96 [music therapy], 114
Theopompus, 378–320 BC, Greek historian, 16
Thibaut of Champagne, 1201–1253, trouvère, 379
Tullius Sabinus, 1st century Greek poet, 39
Tullius, King of Rome, reigned 578–535 BC, 184
Tymnus, 2nd century poet, 7

U

Ulrich von Liechtenstein, 1198–1276, German Minnesinger, 412ff, 421ff
Urban II, 11th century pope, 281

V

Valentinian, 364–375 AD, Roman emperor, 90
Varro, Marcus, 116–27 BC, Roman scholar, 140
Vidal, Peire, troubadour, 370
Virgil, 70–19 BC, roman poet, 122, 177, 200
Vitalis, Orderic, 1075–1143, English chronicler, 327, 329ff
Vogelweide, Walther von der, ca. 1170–1230, German poet, 409ff

W

Wace, Robert, 12th century English writer, 361ff, 365ff
Walter of Châtillon, 12 century Golliard, 427
Wernher der Gartenaere, 13th century, Minnesinger, 426
Widsith, 8th century British poet, 202
William of Aquitaine, Count of Poitiers, 1071–1127, 369
William the Conqueror, 11th century, 237
Wolfram von Eschenbach, ca. 1170–1220, German poet, 411, 422ff

X

Xenocrates, 396–314 BC, Greek philosopher, 96 [music therapy]

ABOUT THE AUTHOR

Dr. David Whitwell is a graduate ('with distinction') of the University of Michigan and the Catholic University of America, Washington DC (PhD, Musicology, Distinguished Alumni Award, 2000) and has studied conducting with Eugene Ormandy and at the Akademie fur Musik, Vienna. Prior to coming to Northridge, Dr. Whitwell participated in concerts throughout the United States and Asia as Associate First Horn in the USAF Band and Orchestra in Washington DC, and in recitals throughout South America in cooperation with the United States State Department.

At the California State University, Northridge, which is in Los Angeles, Dr. Whitwell developed the CSUN Wind Ensemble into an ensemble of international reputation, with international tours to Europe in 1981 and 1989 and to Japan in 1984. The CSUN Wind Ensemble has made professional studio recordings for BBC (London), the Koln Westdeutscher Rundfunk (Germany), NOS National Radio (The Netherlands), Zurich Radio (Switzerland), the Television Broadcasting System (Japan) as well as for the United States State Department for broadcast on its 'Voice of America' program. The CSUN Wind Ensemble's recording with the Mirecourt Trio in 1982 was named the 'Record of the Year' by The Village Voice. Composers who have guest conducted Whitwell's ensembles include Aaron Copland, Ernest Krenek, Alan Hovhaness, Morton Gould, Karel Husa, Frank Erickson and Vaclav Nelhybel.

Dr. Whitwell has been a guest professor in 100 different universities and conservatories throughout the United States and in 23 foreign countries (most recently in China, in an elite school housed in the Forbidden City). Guest conducting experiences have included the Philadelphia Orchestra, Seattle Symphony Orchestra, the Czech Radio Orchestras of Brno and Bratislava, The National Youth Orchestra of Israel, as well as resident wind ensembles in Russia, Israel, Austria, Switzerland, Germany, England, Wales, The Netherlands, Portugal, Peru, Korea, Japan, Taiwan, Canada and the United States.

He is a past president of the College Band Directors National Association, a member of the Prasidium of the International Society for the Promotion of Band Music, and was a member of the founding board of directors of the World Association for Symphonic Bands and Ensembles (WASBE). In 1964 he was made an honorary life member of Kappa Kappa Psi, a national professional music fraternity. In September, 2001, he was a delegate to the UNESCO Conference on Global Music in Tokyo. He has been knighted by sovereign organizations in France, Portugal and Scotland and has been awarded the gold medal of Kerkrade, The Netherlands, and the silver medal of Wangen, Germany, the highest honor given wind conductors in the United States, the medal of the Academy of Wind and Percussion Arts (National Band Association) and the highest honor given wind conductors in Austria, the gold medal of the Austrian Band Association. He is a member of the Hall of Fame of the California Music Educators Association.

Dr. Whitwell's publications include more than 127 articles on wind literature including publications in Music and Letters (London), the London Musical Times, the Mozart-Jahrbuch (Salzburg), and 39 books, among which is his 13-volume *History and Literature of the Wind Band and Wind Ensemble* and an 8-volume series on *Aesthetics in Music*. In addition to numerous modern editions of early wind band music his original compositions include 5 symphonies.

David Whitwell was named as one of six men who have determined the course of American bands during the second half of the 20th century, in the definitive history, *The Twentieth Century American Wind Band* (Meredith Music).

A doctoral dissertation by German Gonzales (2007, Arizona State University) is dedicated to the life and conducting career of David Whitwell through the year 1977. David Whitwell is one of nine men described by Paula A. Crider in *The Conductor's Legacy* (Chicago: GIA, 2010) as 'the legendary conductors' of the 20th century.

> 'I can't imagine the 2nd half of the 20th century—without David Whitwell and what he has given to all of the rest of us.' Frederick Fennell (1993)

www.ingramcontent.com/pod-product-compliance
Lightning Source LLC
Chambersburg PA
CBHW080721300426
44114CB00019B/2449